Language and Cognitive Development in Second Language Learning

Language and Cognitive Development in Second Language Learning

Educational Implications for Children and Adults

Edited by Virginia Gonzalez
Texas A & M University

Allyn and Bacon
Boston   London   Toronto   Sydney   Tokyo   Singapore

Senior Editor: Virginia Lanigan
Editorial Assistant: Bridget Keane
Marketing Managers: Brad Perkins and Ellen Dolberg
Cover Administrator: Brian Gogolin
Composition Buyer: Linda Cox
Manufacturing Buyer: Suzanne Lareau
Production Coordinator: Deborah Brown
Editorial-Production Service: Anne Rebecca Starr

Copyright © 1999 by Allyn and Bacon
A Viacom Company
160 Gould Street
Needham Heights, Massachusetts 02194

Internet: www.abacon.com
America Online: Keyword: college online

All rights reserved. No part of the material protected by this copyright notice may be reproduced or utilized in any form or by any means, electronic or mechanical, including photocopying, recording, or any information storage or retrieval system, without written permission of the copyright owner.

QUEST is copyrighted by Virginia Gonzalez.

Library of Congress Cataloging-In-Publication Data

Language and cognitive development in second language learning:
    educational implications for children and adults/edited by
    Virginia Gonzalez.
        p.   cm.
    Includes bibliographical references and index.
    ISBN 0–205–26170–1

    1. Second language acquisition. 2. Bilingualism. 3. Cognition.
4. Language and culture. 5. Language and languages—Ability testing. I. Gonzalez, Virginia.
P118.2.L36   1998
404′.2′019—dc21   98–12792
                                              CIP

Printed in the United States of America
10 9 8 7 6 5 4 3 2 1   03 02 01 00 99 98

To my beloved firstborn baby boy,
Christian Emmanuel,
who is becoming bilingual;
for all the inspiration that his birth
brought to my life while
I was writing this book.

Contents

PREFACE   xiii

SECTION I   **Philosophical and Theoretical Models**   1

CHAPTER 1   A Folkloric and Historical Views of Giftedness in Language-Minority Children   1
Virginia Gonzalez and Ellen Riojas-Clark

   A Brief Overview of Folkloric and Historic Giftedness   2
   A Folkloric View of Giftedness in Language-Minority Children   4
      A Definition of Folklore *and Its Functions*   4
      Verbal and Nonverbal Representations of Folklore   4
      Linguistic and Cultural Ways of Representing Giftedness   6
   Historical View of Giftedness   8
      Traditional Standardized IQ and Achievement Tests   8
      Alternative Approaches   11
   Educational Implications   14
   References   15

CHAPTER 2   An Integrative Analysis of the Cognitive Development of Bilingual and Bicultural Children and Adults   19
Virginia Gonzalez and Diane L. Schallert

   Issues in the Study of Cognitive and Language Development in Bilinguals   20
      The Effects of Bilingualism on Cognitive Performance   20
      Representation of Knowledge in Bilinguals   22
      The Mapping Process of Conceptual and Semantic Development   26

The Proposed Triple-Interactional Model of Cognitive, Linguistic, and Cultural Variables   33
The Influence of Cognitive, Linguistic, and Cultural Factors on the Conceptual and Semantic Development of Bilinguals   38
The Direction of the Mapping Process Between Conceptual and Semantic Development   38
The Interaction of Verbal and Nonverbal Representational Systems   40
Methodological Differences in Classification Tasks   41
Problems with Operational Definitions of Representational and Mapping Processes   42
Representational Systems as Structures Versus Category Formation as a Process   43
The Influence of Sociocultural Factors on Conceptual and Semantic Development   45

Conclusions   46
References   48

SECTION II   Cognitive and Language Development in Bilingual Children and Adults   56

CHAPTER 3   Construction of a Phonological Development Test for Monolingual Spanish Preschoolers Learning English as a Second Language   56
Virginia Gonzalez

Review of the Literature   58
  Jakobson's Model of Distinctive Features   58
  The Natural Phonology Theory   60

Hypotheses   62

Method   63
  Design   63
  Subjects   63
  Content Sample   63
  Instruments   63
  Pilot Test   64
  Procedure   64

Results and Discussion   65
  Item Analysis   66
  Criterion-Related Validity   68
  Reliability   70
  Test of Hypotheses   70
  Implications for Diagnosis   72
  Phonemes in English and Spanish   73

Other Administrations of the Phonological Development Test   75
Diagnostic Categories   76
Conclusions   77
References   78

CHAPTER 4   Models for the Relationship Among Language, Relative Degree of Bilingualism, Phonological Strategies, and Reading Readiness in Bilingual Spanish/English Children   80
Virginia Gonzalez

The Assessment of Cognitive and Language Development in Bilingual Children   81
   Need for Alternative Assessments   *81*
   Need to Differentiate Between Assessment and Diagnosis   *83*
   Need to Assess Bilingual Children in Their First and Second Languages   *85*
   Phonological Development in Bilingual Children   *86*
   Phonological Development and Reading Readiness in Bilingual Children   *87*

Method   89
   Research Questions   *89*
   Symmetric Models   *91*
   Asymmetric Models   *91*
   Research Design   *92*
   The Models Explored   *92*
   Operational Definitions of Variables   *93*
   Subjects   *93*
   Procedure   *94*

Results and Discussion   94
   Symmetric Model   *94*
   Asymmetric Model   *97*

Conclusions   99
References   100

CHAPTER 5   Why Is It *Una Persona* and Not *Un Persona*? Influence of Linguistic and Cultural Variables on Conceptual Learning in Second Language Situations   104
Virginia Gonzalez, Diane L. Schallert, Sonia de Rivera, Martha Flores, and Lorri M. Perrodin

Concept Construction and Strategy Use in Second Language Learning   108

    Language Learning Processes and Forms of Knowledge 108
    Developmental Phases in Language Learning 109
    Language Learning Strategies 110
  Methodological Problems 111
    The Exploratory-Interpretative Paradigm 111
    Methods of Data Analysis 111
  The Proposed Multidimensional Model 112
  Method 115
    Design 115
    Research Questions 115
    Subjects 116
    Instructional Method 118
    Tasks 121
    Data Analysis 122
  Results and Discussion 127
    Definition Task 128
    Role-Playying Task 134
    Emerging Theses, Themes, and Topics 139
  Conclusions 150
  References 151
  APPENDIX 5A: Semantic Categories for Gender 153

CHAPTER 6 Conceptualizations of *Ser* and *Estar* by College Students Learning Spanish as a Second Language and Adult Spanish Native Speakers 156
Virginia Gonzalez and Sonia de Rivera

  Literature Review 157
    Semantic Categories in Ser *and* Estar 157
    Developmental Stages for Acquiring Ser *and* Estar 159
    Learning Ser *and* Estar *as a Concept Formation Process* 163
    Second Language Learning Methodologies 164
  Method 166
    Design 166
    Research Questions 166
    Subjects 167
    Stimuli 168
    Procedure 169
    Data Analysis Design 170
  Results and Discussion 174
  Conclusions 185

References   186

APPENDIX 6A: Sentence Pairs Using *Ser* and *Estar*   188

SECTION III   Alternative Assessment of Language-Minority Children   190

CHAPTER 7   Alternative Assessment Models of Language-Minority Children: Is There a Match with Teachers' Attitudes and Instruction?   190
Maria Felix-Holt and Virginia Gonzalez

Study Overview   190

Statement of the Problem   191

Theoretical Framework   193

Literature Review   193
  Gardner's Socioeducational Model   193
  Modified Version of Gardner's Model   194
  Factors Affecting Second Language Learning   196

Method   198
  Research Design   198
  Subjects   198
  Instruments   200
  Procedure   202
  Methodology of Data Analysis and Explanation   203

Results and Discussion   203
  First Research Question   204
  Second Research Question   206
  Third Research Question   209

Conclusions   212

References   213

APPENDIX 7A: Teachers' Interview Questions   216

APPENDIX 7B: Categories for Coding Teachers' Responses to Interview Questions   217

APPENDIX 7C: Summaries of Findings for Different Subjects   221

CHAPTER 8   Standardized and Alternative Assessments: Diagnosis Accuracy in Minority Children Referred for Special Education Assessment   227
M. Dynah Oviedo and Virginia Gonzalez

Study Overview   227

Statement of the Problem   228

Assessment Model   229

Literature Review   229
   Demographic Overview of Minority Children in Special Education   230
   Validity Issues in the Assessment and Diagnosis of Minority Children   232
   Evaluators' Influence on Assessment   234
   Teachers' Influence on Assessment   235

Method   236
   Research Design   236
   Subjects   237
   Instruments   237
   Procedure   240
   Research Coding Design   241
   Data Analysis and Design   242

Case Studies for Research Question 1   243
   First Case Study: Alejandra   243
   Second Case Study: Ricardo   250
   Third Case Study: Lily   253
   Fourth Case Study: Antonio   256
   Research Question 1 Conclusion   259

Case Studies for Research Question 2   261
   Patterns of Nonverbal, Verbal, and Achievement Performance   261
   Research Question 2 Conclusion   263

Conclusions   264
References   265

CHAPTER 9   **Influence of Evaluators' Beliefs and Personal Backgrounds on Their Diagnostic and Placement Decisions**   269
Virginia Gonzalez, Patricia Bauerle, Wendy Black, and Maria Felix-Holt

Literature Review   270
   Effect of Evaluators' Personalities   270
   Interaction of Evaluators' Personalities and Their Diagnostic and Placement Decisions   275

Research Questions   275

Method   276
   Research Design   276
   Subjects   277
   Instruments   278
   Vignette Case Study   280
   Procedure   281
   Data Analysis Design   282

Results   282
   First Thesis: Evaluators' Beliefs About Cognitive and Language Development and Measures   282

Second Thesis: Evaluators' Cultural-Linguistic Backgrounds   285
Third Thesis: Relationship of Evaluators' Personal Backgrounds, Beliefs, and Assessment Behaviors   286
Fourth Thesis: Effect of Evaluators' Beliefs on Diagnostic and Placement Decisions   288

Discussion   288

Conclusions   292

References   293

APPENDIX 9A: Interview Questions   295

APPENDIX 9B: Categories for Analyzing the Evaluators' Responses to the Interview   296

SECTION IV Conclusions   298

CHAPTER 10   The Impact of Paradigmatic Shifts on Second Language Research: Patterns and Conclusions   298
Virginia Gonzalez

INDEX   303

Preface

THIS BOOK PRESENTS STATE-OF-THE-ART EMPIRICAL RESEARCH STUDIES that use contemporary cognitive psychology theory as a framework for investigating polemical and philosophical traditional and modern issues in bilingual education and second language learning. Studies that apply cognitive psychology to the investigation of bilingual issues are scarce in the literature. Indeed, few researchers exist at the national and international level who have a psychological background and are producing research studies applied to bilingual issues. Thus, this application of cognitive psychology theory and methodology to the study of bilinguals contributes significantly to the literature, advances psychological knowledge, and suggests sound practical implications for bilingual education and second language learning.

PHILOSOPHY OF THIS BOOK

This book contains both qualitative and statistical research studies on second language learning. The heuristic research studies that are exploring new frontiers of knowledge and opening new questions need qualitative designs that allow for an in-depth analysis of fewer subjects with a broader number of variables. Once these studies have been conducted successfully, they can be combined meaningfully with statistical designs that include a larger number of subjects and fewer variables that have been identified as significant. My belief is that the most powerful combination of research designs includes both qualitative and quantitative analyses of data, so that multiple variables can be analyzed qualitatively and statistical results generalized to other samples.

Although results from heuristic qualitative studies have limitations when generalized to independent samples, they make the important contribution of opening new frontiers of knowledge. Thus, most of the qualitative studies in this book represent state-of-the-art research in second language learning, involving the application of cognitive psychology theory and methodology. This new era of research that originated in the early 1980s has resulted in new applications to assessment and instruction, also represented in the studies included here. New instructional and qualitative assessment approaches, such as conceptual learning and instruction, and alternative or qualitative evaluation approaches, have been derived from this new generation of second language research.

A contemporary cognitive psychology approach applied to second language learning situations helps us to understand the internal representational and thinking processes involved in this learning within and between individuals. One of the major characteristics of contemporary research in cognitive psychology is the study of the effect of external factors, such as culture and language, on cognitive processes, such as second language learning. Thus, second language learning is considered a creative, dynamic, individual, and complex multidimensional process that is influenced by multiple internal and external variables derived not only from cognitive dimensions, but also from affective-motivational and cultural-social dimensions. The research studies presented in this book emphasize this sociocultural dimension.

Within this contemporary approach, developmental variables are also considered as influencing the process of second language learning. When comparing children and adults, both differences and commonalities can be found. Thus, a cognitive psychology approach emphasizes continuity in the instructional and assessment process of second language learners. Therefore, the focus of those studying both children and adults should always be on stimulating and measuring their thinking processes when using a first or second representational system. Both children and adults should be able to think directly in their first and second languages so that new knowledge can be created to represent the unique cultural and social dimensions of each language system. In this book, the dual cultural and social components of cognitive processes involved in first and second language learning are studied through innovative cognitive approaches applied to the analysis of data.

The "ethnic researcher" approach is emphasized in this book. With this approach, the assessors of culturally and linguistically diverse second language learners must value their idiosyncratic characteristics and celebrate their differences. Assessment procedures need to represent the culture and language of the minority child so that the genuine verbal and nonverbal cognitive developmental levels of the child can be measured. Some of the studies included in this book indicate that, due to developmental variables in young bilingual children, their nonverbal cognitive level is always higher than the verbal one. In addition, these studies suggest that content variables influence the nonverbal and verbal levels achieved by young children. For instance, some content variables include whether the assessment is conducted in the child's first or second language and which kind of cultural dimensions are represented in the measurement. These variables also affect adult second language learners; college students, for example, also go through stages for thinking with the new linguistic and cultural representations to which they have been exposed.

PREFACE   xvii

THEMES ACROSS CHAPTERS

The major theme emphasized in this book deals with the cognitive dimensions of second language learning within a sociocultural and socioeducational environment. That is, in both children and adults, the process of learning two languages takes place within a particular ethnic and cultural system that influences the construction of these individuals' symbolic representations. Becoming bilingual involves a transformation of thinking processes, resulting in a bicultural individual who is able to think with two representational systems or languages. Learning how to speak a language includes the understanding of not only its phonological, grammatical, and syntactic structures, but also its semantic system, which represents meaning in a particular cultural and social reality.

A second theme highlighted across chapters in this book refers to the need to develop measures for bilingual children that take into account the interface of cognition, culture, and language. These measures need to be constructed within a strong psychological framework that includes developmental factors. Instruments that are used for monolingual children cannot be applied unthinkingly to bilingual children, since the underlying constructs that need to be measured are dramatically different. The differences in the cognitive and linguistic development between monolingual and bilingual children can be summarized by the following statement: One monolingual plus one monolingual does not equal a bilingual. In other words, the influence of two languages and cultures on cognition is a geometric process, not an additive one. The nature of the internal mental representations of bilingual children results from the influence of two social and cultural systems that interact reciprocally, generating a third, different dimension.

A third theme is the need to represent in constructs measured not only in the mainstream view, but also the minority view. The traditional mainstream view focuses solely on the influence of internal factors on second language learning. In contrast, the minority view highlights the influence of external sociocultural factors (e.g., socioeconomic status, schooling, stimulation, parental educational level) on second language learning. For example, Chapter 1 highlights the construct of giftedness as represented very differently by teachers (who have been influenced by the mainstream school culture definitions) and minority mothers. A key factor in increasing construct validity is that the researcher(s) take into account the perceptions of minority informants in the assessment process. Giftedness, like any other cognitive factor, cannot be measured in isolation from the influence of cultural and social factors. On the contrary, it is an abstraction created within the context of a specific sociocultural reality, resulting in a construct that reflects the perceptions, attitudes, beliefs, and value systems shared by individuals living in that particular reality.

A fourth theme, emphasized in Section III, deals with the multidimensional process of assessing cognitive and language development in bilingual children. This multidimensionality can be captured only by using multiple measures and informants in the assessment process. Through a problem-solving approach, we can try to alleviate the subjectivity inherent in the interpretation of students' performance in assessment measures. By collecting across contexts, direct measures of observed behaviors, and indirect measures of perceptions of behaviors by informants, evaluators can reconstruct the dynamic and multidimensional aspects of cognitive and linguistic processes. In fitting together the pieces of these measures, evaluators find similarities and contradictions that point out the complexity of processes with multiple dimensions (such as the influence of bilingual and bicultural environments on cognition).

A fifth related theme, highlighted primarily in Section III, is the need to expand construct validity, or to include interpretations and uses of measures by evaluators. The modern conceptualization of construct validity includes the existence of evidence based on data for demonstrating the application of the measure for a social or educational use within a particular sociocultural context or population. Evaluators should be knowledgeable users who ethically and wisely apply the measures for the sociocultural contexts and populations for which those measures have been validated. Diagnosis is an interpretation of the sociocultural meaning of the behaviors represented in the performance of individuals, which are mapped or theoretically related to the constructs measured. This means that no score has meaning per se; rather, the evaluator interprets and makes inferences about test scores.

The assessment process does not occur in isolation from the person who does the assessment. The evaluator is the major source of subjectivity and bias, due primarily to the influence of his or her own cultural and linguistic background, knowledge level of the constructs to be measured, and attitudes. Thus, the focus of the study of assessment problems in language-minority children shifts from the instruments themselves to the users of the instruments. Evaluators need to be aware of the effect of subjectivity on constructs measured and acknowledge it, especially when there is a problem with the validity of measures of cognition and language of language-minority children.

The sixth and last related theme, also emphasized in Section III, is the need for evaluators of language-minority children to become advocates for the children. Because the instruments for measuring complex constructs such as cognitive and language development may not be psychometrically sound, the subjectivity of the evaluators is a factor in evaluation. Thus, evaluators need to be aware of the implications of their diagnoses in the daily lives of bilingual children. Inaccurately placing a language-minority child can have devastating implications on the child's cognitive and language development; misplacing a bilingual child in real need of special education services is also a serious problem. Thus, evaluators have a major responsibility: They need to be very aware of and sensitive to the possible effects of misdiagnosing bilingual children. The most important educational implication of this book is to recommend the establishment of guidelines for educators, derived from empirical research, that will lead to high-quality instructional and assessment services in second language and bilingual educational settings.

OVERVIEW OF THE BOOK

The nine chapters that follow have been divided into three sections, plus the overall conclusions for the book in Chapter 10. Section I comprises two chapters that provide context for understanding the data-based chapters in Sections II and III. These chapters provide the philosophical and theoretical models for the integration of social, cultural, educational, linguistic, and cognitive factors when conceptualizing and measuring development in bilinguals. They help readers to understand the complexity of cognitive and language development in bilinguals, as well as the even more complex endeavor of assessing these processes.

Chapter 1 presents the major theme of this book: the multidimensional interaction of cognitive, sociocultural, and linguistic processes. It then provides a broad context in which to understand the themes of this book as reflected in the data-based chapters. It presents a real-life case and a philosophical framework for conceptualizing and measuring complex cognitive and linguistic constructs, such as giftedness, in bilingual children. This chapter highlights another theme of the book: the need to represent in constructs measured by the minority view. Chapter 1 represents my collaborative intragenerational projects with a colleague, Dr. Ellen Riojas-Clark, associate professor of the Division of Bilingual/Bicultural Studies at the University of Texas at San Antonio.

Chapter 2 provides a theoretical framework for the book; it includes a critical integration of contemporary literature on how culture and language influence the representation of knowledge in bilingual and bicultural individuals. This chapter establishes a multidisciplinary and multidimensional view of the influence of cognition, language, and culture on conceptual and semantic development in bilingual children. Thus, it highlights the major theme of this book: the sociocultural and socioeducational context for cognitive and language development in bilinguals. In particular, Chapter 2 creates an interface between two separate modules of literature—cognitive psychology and bilingual education—which converge in the study of bilingual children's conceptual and semantic development. Chapter 2 is an intergenerational work from when I was a doctoral student of educational psychology at the University of Texas at Austin, with my former mentor, Professor Diane Schallert.

Section II, comprising Chapters 3 through 6, presents empirical studies on cognitive development and second language learning processes in children and adults. The chapters set out an integrated framework that provides a unique bilingual perspective on educational psychology research. Thus, they present an interface between bilingual/bicultural studies, and cognitive and language development. The research work explored provides empirical support for the study of bilingual issues that have been raised in the literature at the philosophical and polemical levels.

The first chapter of the second section, Chapter 3, presents a psychometric study with the objective of constructing a phonological test for Spanish monolingual preschoolers learning English as a second language. This chapter integrates two themes: the need to construct assessments based on strong models and the need to take into account the minority view of the interaction between cognition, culture, and language. Chapter 4 presents a statistical study to develop a model that explains the relationship among relative degree of bilingualism, phonological strategies, and reading readiness in bilingual Hispanic children. The chapter highlights the theme of including a multidimensional view of the assessment of cognition and language in bilingual children. This chapter also clearly demonstrates the second theme of the book: the need to account for the interface between cognition, culture, and language when assessing bilingual children. Chapters 3 and 4 reflect my independent work at the University of Arizona.

Chapters 5 and 6 highlight the major theme of the book: the influence of culture and language on the construction of semantic representations in bilingual learners. These chapters refer to cognitive and linguistic processes for linguistic gender and the semantic structure of the verb "to be" in Spanish (*ser* and *estar*) for adults learning Spanish as a foreign language. In Chapter 5 college students learning Spanish participated in "thinking-aloud" interviews to study their cognitive and metacognitive strategies related to explicit (consciously learned) or implicit (subconscious and automatic) levels of knowledge of linguistic gender in Spanish. The students were taking an intensive undergraduate Spanish course that I was teaching using a conceptual approach to second language learning. Chapter 5 represents an intergenerational mentorship relationship between me; my former mentor at the University of Texas at Austin, Dr. Diane Schallert; and my mentees at the University of Arizona, graduate students Martha Flores and Sonia de Rivera, and undergraduate student Lorri Perrodin.

Chapter 6, the final chapter of Section II, presents a qualitative comparative study of conceptualizations of the verb "to be" in Spanish (*ser* and *estar*) by English-speaking college students and adult native Spanish speakers. This chapter is the product of an intergenerational mentorship relationship between me and a graduate student at the University of Arizona, Sonia de Rivera.

Section III, comprising Chapters 7 through 9, clusters empirical studies on the alternative assessment of language-minority children. Chapter 7 presents a qualitative approach to the study of the link between assessment and teachers' attitudes and instruction. It examines case studies of alternative assessments used for identifying giftedness in language-minority children. The chapter presents a follow-up study of Hispanic first graders who were placed in gifted bilingual classrooms. These placement recommendations were given by independent evaluators using alternative assessments. The study's objective was to investigate, using alternative assessments, the teachers' perceptions and attitudes toward the placements recommended by independent evaluators, and the quality of instruction provided for the children by teachers. Chapter 7 represents intergenerational collaborative work between Maria Felix-Holt and me.

Chapter 8, another qualitative case study, compares standardized and alternative assessments used for the diagnoses of minority children. This chapter examines case studies of elementary school children who were placed in special education classes following recommendations resulting from standardized testing done by school district evaluators. The objective of the study was to investigate the accuracy of these special education placements by assessing and diagnosing the minority students again, this time with alternative assessments. Thus, this chapter deals with the problematic issue of differentially diagnosing normal second language learning from genuine disabling conditions in young minority children. Chapter 8 was developed by Dynah Oviedo in collaborative intergenerational work with me. Both Chapters 7 and 8 were derived from a broader research project that I had initiated. Maria Felix-Holt and Dynah Oviedo developed their master's theses from this project.

Chapter 9 closes this section with an empirical qualitative study of the influence of evaluators' biases—their personal, cultural, and linguistic backgrounds, knowledge levels of constructs measured, and attitudes—on their diagnostic decisions for young language-minority children. This focus on the evaluators' biases, rather than on the tests themselves, is a major trend of the mid- and late 1990s. Interesting patterns resulted from using an alternative assessment model designed for language-minority children. This chapter reports the results of a collaborative intergenerational study conducted with graduate students Patricia Bauerle, Wendy Black, and Maria Felix-Holt.

Chapters 7 through 9 highlight the major theme of the book, the sociocultural context for assessment, and provide a socioeducational framework to view evaluation. Within this sociocultural-socioeducational perspective, materials and tests need to be analyzed as they are used subjectively by evaluators. This third cluster of studies provides a holistic view to the assessment of language-minority children since the cultural and linguistic backgrounds, perspectives, knowledge level, and attitudes of informants and evaluators are also included.

In addition, the three studies clustered in this third section also present the third and fourth themes of the book: the need to represent the minority perspective in multiple measures of cognition and language in bilinguals. These chapters also illustrate the fifth and sixth themes: the need to include in the construct validity of measures of language of bilinguals and the responsibility of evaluators to assume an advocacy role in order to protect the children being assessed.

Finally, Chapter 10 presents patterns and conclusions related to the change in paradigms reflected in the major advances in second language research that have occurred during the last 20 years. The six themes that permeate the preceding chapters are related to these patterns and conclusions as they reflect current research trends and paradigmatic shifts in the area of second language learning.

The research studies included in this book illustrate advances in the field of second language learning as it has been influenced by cognitive psychology theory and methodology. The philosophy underlying this book endorses conceptual learning and alternative assessment approaches derived from an "ethnic researcher" approach that values cultural and linguistic differences present across individuals. The major theme emerging throughout the chapters of this book has to do with the sociocultural dimension of the cognitive processes involved in second language learning in children and adults.

THE TALE BEHIND THIS BOOK

It is with great joy that I give closure to this book project on second language learning research, an area of my independent and collaborative research work during the first five years of my academic career. This book contains collaborative research work of three generations of scholars: my previous doctoral studies mentor, my colleagues and myself, and my mentees. First, it includes research studies that I started as a doctoral student of educational psychology at the University of Texas at Austin, under the mentorship of Dr. Diane Schallert. Second, research studies that I conducted independently as a young scholar during my early years as an assistant professor at the University of Arizona are included. Third, within this book you will find research work that I conducted in collaboration with students whom I was mentoring at the University of Arizona. Finally, a representative study of the many collaborative research projects that I have conducted with colleagues during my early professional career is also included.

Six of my mentees were graduate students at the University of Arizona: (1) Patricia Bauerle, then an educational specialist student of school psychology, now an evaluator of ethnic and linguistic minority children in a school in Rio Rico, Arizona; (2) Wendy Black, a doctoral student in the Language, Reading, and Culture Department; (3) Maria Felix-Holt, then a master's student of educational psychology, now an evaluator and counselor at La Frontera, a center for low-income minority students serving the Tucson community; (4) Martha Flores, a doctoral student of school psychology and an evaluator of ethnic and linguistic minority children for the Tucson Independent School District; (5) Dynah Oviedo, then a master's student at the Department of Educational Psychology, now a research specialist at the Tucson Unified School District, and (6) Sonia de Rivera, then a master's student of bilingual education, now a bilingual special education teacher at the Amphitheater Unified School District in Tucson. In addition, Lorri Perrodin, one of my mentees, was an honor undergraduate student at the University of Arizona, and has become an elementary bilingual special education school teacher and teacher supervisor. Five of these seven students have started their professional careers serving ethnic minority students.

This book shows the continuity needed in mentoring new scholars, like a neverending chain of academic and personal relationships across generations of established scholars and scholars-to-be. An empathic and friendly mentoring relationship needs to be created between research experts and students in order to provide a nurturing environment in which role models guide students through the adventures of doing research. It is through this process of mentoring that students become independent scholars and professionals.

One chapter in this book represents collaboration with supportive colleagues who share a commitment to scholarly work. It is through a dynamic interchange of ideas and expert knowledge that scholars renew themselves within a collaborative collegial relationship, with the objective of opening new adventures in research. Working with Ellen Riojas-Clark from the Division of Bilingual and Bicultural Studies at the University of Texas at San Antonio brought about lively scholarly dialogue and new ways of thinking. This kind of collegial relationship is also extremely important in the chain of scholarly activities. Thus, not only intergenerational relationships are needed, but networks of the intragenerational kind are also vital for us to continue growing as scholars. Being a scholar brings satisfaction to our lives not only because of the created products of research studies that lead to new theoretical and applied knowledge, but also because of the joy derived from the many personal friendships and the meaningful relationships that we are able to establish in our collaborative endeavors. My greatest joy comes from being able to help college students accomplish their academic and personal goals, being able to assist them to graduate and become independent scholars and professionals, who in their turn help others to achieve their dreams. My former relationship with my mentor, Diane Schallert, has become a collegial relationship of friendship since I graduated in 1991, a story that has re-created itself between my former mentees and myself.

Acknowledgments

I thank all the chapter authors who have made this book possible. Without their dedication and motivation, this project could not have been accomplished. My appreciation extends beyond the actual research studies in which we collaborated to the meaningful personal and professional relationships that were created in this process of learning together.

I am grateful to Dr. Miri Fleming, director of the Exceptional Bilingual Education Department at Tucson Unified School District, for her invaluable help in obtaining permission to conduct the studies in which we needed the participation of children and the consent of their parents. I also appreciate the willingness of parents to allow their children to be part of our research studies. I am grateful to the college undergraduate students studying Spanish both at the University of Texas at Austin and the University of Arizona who volunteered to participate as subjects in our projects.

The financial support received for the research studies presented in Chapters 5, 6, and 9 came from the University of Arizona, Office of the Vice President for Research, in conjunction with the University of Arizona Foundation and the College of Education.

My deepest appreciation goes to the three academic reviewers, Rita Brusca-Vega of Northeastern Illinois University, Robert D. Milk of the University of Texas at San Antonio, and John W. Oller, Jr., of the University of Southern Louisiana, who invested valuable time and effort to suggest many editorial changes to improve this book.

V. G.

List of Contributors

Patricia Bauerle
Bilingual evaluator
Rio Rico School District
Rio Rico, AZ

Wendy Black
Doctoral student
Language, Reading, and Culture Department
The University of Arizona
Tucson, AZ

Maria Felix-Holt
Minority children evaluator and family
  counselor
La Frontera
Tucson, AZ

Martha Flores
Doctoral student
School Psychology program
The University of Arizona, and
  Bilingual evaluator
Tucson Unified School District
Tucson, AZ

Virginia Gonzalez, Editor
Associate Professor
Department of Educational Curriculum and
  Instruction
Bilingual/ESL program
Texas A & M University
College Station, TX

M. Dynah Oviedo
Research specialist
Tucson Unified School District
Tucson, AZ

Lorri M. Perrodin
Bilingual special elementary teacher
Tucson Unified School District, and
  Teacher supervisor
The University of Arizona
Tucson, AZ

Ellen Riojas-Clark
Associate Professor
Division of Bilingual/Bicultural Studies
The University of Texas at San Antonio
San Antonio, TX

Sonia de Rivera
Bilingual special education elementary
  teacher
Amphitheater School District
Tucson, AZ

Diane L. Schallert
Professor
Department of Educational Psychology
The University of Texas at Austin
Austin, TX

CHAPTER

1

Folkloric and Historical Views of Giftedness in Language-Minority Children

VIRGINIA GONZALEZ AND ELLEN RIOJAS-CLARK

THIS CHAPTER PROVIDES A PHILOSOPHICAL FRAMEWORK AS A CONTEXT FOR understanding the major theme of this book: the cognitive dimensions of second language learning within a sociocultural and socioeducational environment (see the preface). It also highlights another theme of the book: the need to represent not only the mainstream view, but also the minority view of the constructs measured. It portrays these themes in relation to the cultural conceptualizations of abstract constructs such as giftedness in minority children who are bilingual. This chapter argues that because the perceptions of teachers and parents of gifted minority children are influenced by different sociocultural contexts, their conceptualizations of abstract constructs, specifically giftedness, differ.

This chapter contrasts folkloric and historical definitions of giftedness and their implications in identifying gifted language-minority children, with special attention to Hispanic bilingual children. The first section presents a critical discussion of the folkloric, or cultural, views of giftedness in language-minority children: definitions of folklore and its functions, verbal and nonverbal representations of folklore, and linguistic and cultural ways of representing giftedness. The second section critically discusses the historical view of giftedness that encompasses both traditional and more contemporary models of identifying gifted children: cut-off scores in standardized IQ and achievement tests and alternative approaches using divergent and developmental multidimensional models. The third section discusses some educational implications of the use of alternative developmental assessments for identifying gifted language-minority children. This last section puts special emphasis on the role of educators as mediators for merging the folkloric and historical views of giftedness.

A Brief Overview of Folkloric and Historic Giftedness

This quotation from a Hispanic mother who was asked to describe the cognitive and linguistic abilities of her kindergarten son portrays an example of a folkloric definition of giftedness: *"Mi hijo es bien educado, es servicial, es sano, es simpático, tiene paciencia, es respetuoso, es un niño ejemplar."* If, as bilingual speakers of English and Spanish, we translate this description, we would not be able to represent the cultural meanings of all of these Spanish words with succinct English labels and concepts. Cultural or folkloric meanings can be fully captured only by bilingual readers who show metalinguistic awareness. That is, bilinguals are able to think about language because they construct different cultural representations for the connotative or folkloric meanings of the two languages learned. In fact, it is the dual representation of meanings using both Spanish and English that shows cultural and linguistic giftedness.

This quotation exemplifies what we propose to be a folkloric definition of the child's giftedness. This Spanish-speaking mother described her son using cultural understandings of what giftedness means within a Hispanic home environment. From a Hispanic sociocultural perspective, giftedness is much more than just being intelligent (as understood from a mainstream perspective centered on cognitive abilities). Within the Hispanic culture, it is more important to be *bien educado* (literally translated as "well educated"), a term that has the sociocultural and affective/moral connotation of being "well raised" or "well mannered." A folkloric definition of giftedness uses descriptions that reflect cultural factors—that is, cultural representations expressed through connotative meanings of words that reflect the actual cultural identities of the speakers.

In contrast, the bilingual Hispanic teacher of the same child describes him as "smart, creative, adventurous, with good reasoning skills, interested in learning, with an expanded vocabulary, task committed, eager to learn, mature for his age, and with the ability to do very detailed drawings." We consider this description to be a historical definition of the child's giftedness—that is, it was given by an educator (a minority or majority teacher, evaluator, or administrator) who represents the mainstream school culture. Even if teachers are from the same minority culture as their students, their formal professional training has shaped and formed their conceptualizations of giftedness using a historical, and not a folkloric, perspective. We propose that a historical perspective of giftedness involves documentation, data-driven models and theories centered on cognitive and linguistic processes, factual information presented as evidence, and mainstream cultural values and philosophies endorsed when interpreting factual information.

This example illustrates the objective of this chapter: contrasting folkloric and historical definitions of giftedness and examining the implications of the unequal definitions in identifying gifted language-minority children, especially bilingual Hispanic children. We propose that folklore can become history if educators use alternative developmental assessments that represent cultural and linguistic dimensions of giftedness in language-minority children.

We also propose that we can make history out of folklore by taking into account evaluators' subjectivity in new conceptualizations of the validity assessment. According to Messick (1995) and Moss (1992), validity is not simply what traditional definitions based on psychometrics have described as "what the test pertains to measure." Instead, contemporary definitions of validity, such as that of Messick, consider it a unified concept centered around construct validity, which includes the social and ethical implications of the uses and interpretations of test scores. Messick proposed that new psychometric definitions of construct validity should encompass the subjectivity present in evaluators who are going through a process of rhetoric interpretations and inferences for making diagnostic and placement decisions based on test scores. Then, following Messick, validity is not only a scientific procedure that ensures objectivity in measurement; it is also a subjective process of value judgment. Thus, according to Messick, new validity conceptualizations must take into account educational, ethical, moral, and socioeconomic intended and unintended consequences of tests' use and interpretations for minority and majority students. (For further discussion of the modern conceptualization of validity applied to the assessment of intelligence in minority and majority children, see Gonzalez, 1996.)

In addition, the participation of minority parents in conjunction with multidisciplinary educators in the nomination, screening, and identification of gifted language-minority children can enlighten the process of making history out of folklore. Educators can use alternative developmental measures that show a psychometrically sound theoretical basis and empirical evidence to represent the folkloric as well as the historical dimensions of cultural and linguistic giftedness. Minority parents and educators who are drawn into the assessment process can become advocates of a folkloric minority culture perspective and at the same time represent the academic school culture from a historical or mainstream perspective. (For a study of the role of the background of evaluators on the assessment of minority children, see Chapter 7.) Moreover, involving teachers directly in the assessment process, and not giving the responsibility of identifying giftedness solely to evaluators, can help us link assessment with instruction. (For the role of teachers on the identification of giftedness, see Chapter 9.) Within the alternative developmental assessment model, teachers can also act as evaluators in order to apply cultural and linguistic components of giftedness directly to teaching academic content. Regarding the need for teachers to act as advocates in their double role as instructors and evaluators, Cummins's (1984) empowerment model speaks to the participation of teachers as cultural and linguistic advocates in assessment. He proposed that teachers can serve as mediators between the mainstream school culture (which holds a historical view of giftedness) and the minority home culture (which holds a folkloric view of giftedness) for communicating successfully with minority parents.

In sum, teachers are social agents within the negotiation process of developing an interface of the folkloric and historical views of giftedness.

A Folkloric View of Giftedness in Language-Minority Children

A Definition of Folklore and Its Functions

A common definition for *folklore* is based on the oral tradition transmitted by a group of people who share a common ethnic identity. According to Dundes (1965), "a member of a group may not know all members, but he will probably know the common core of traditions belonging to the group, traditions which help the group have a sense of group identity" (p. 2). Therefore, every group has a *folkloric* way of transmitting, in an oral or kinesthetic manner, its culture in the form of ideas, concepts, beliefs, customs, values, rites, metaphors, symbolic connotative meanings, and traditions. The dynamics of diverse ethnic and linguistic societies are based on interactions between different ways of seeing, thinking, and expressing—verbally and nonverbally—cultural meanings. Diverse groups can bring their own contributions, modes of adaptation, and inventions of new ways to the larger society.

Folklore has different functions in society. Dundes (1965) says that "it can express concepts within a particular cultural context and environmental setting, it can validate culture by justifying its beliefs, it can serve an educational purpose" (p. 294), and "insures conformity to the accepted cultural norms and continuity from generation to generation" (p. 297).

Verbal and Nonverbal Representations of Folklore

Cultural experience, or folklore, can sometimes be expressed by a linguistic representation. As cognition involves the formation of concepts, and these concepts involve verbal classification systems, clusters, and networks; language and cognition are clearly related. That is, the linguistic concepts that lead to verbal representations and classifications can be explicitly communicated by the speaker of a language in a conscious manner. For instance, Casson (1981) referred to verbal representations in this way:

> Constructs for identifying and classifying plants, kinsmen, diseases, and events, for example, are generally encoded in words, and principles for diagnosing illnesses, for postmarital residence, for descent group membership, and for arithmetical calculation and logical reasoning are often overtly verbalizable. (p. 20)

In addition, native speakers of a language do not always show explicit knowledge of the grammatical and syntactic aspects of the linguistic structures and markers of a language. Most native speakers automatically use the correct forms of linguistic structures and markers for communicating successfully within a sociocultural community and following folkloric aspects of meaning. However, most native speakers will not be able to explain why they chose to use specific grammatical and syntactic rules. In other words, most native speakers have only an implicit knowledge of the connotative meanings or folkloric aspects of their language that is subconscious (see Chapters 5 and 6, and also Gonzalez & Felix-Holt, 1995, for further discussion of this issue).

As stated by Casson (1981):

> Although the phonemes of a person's language and the syntactic rules for forming certain types of sentences are for the most part out of the individual's conscious awareness, the individual, nonetheless, has knowledge of these categories and principles and utilizes them in speaking. (p. 20)

However, there are some nonverbal concepts that cannot be expressed explicitly through language. These nonverbal concepts are also part of the folkloric culture because they refer to symbolic connotations that cannot be expressed using linguistic structures. These nonverbal cultural concepts are implicitly communicated because they are subconscious to the speaker.

As stated by Casson (1981):

> In fact, many constructs and principles are not only covert and unverbalizable but are unconscious in the sense that they are out of the individual's awareness, even though they guide his or her behavior.... Parallel examples of unconscious cultural schemata are the covert categories that occur in classification systems, the tacit procedures and strategies that are employed in certain kinds of decision-making and problem solving. (pp. 20–21)

That is, cultural concepts that are communicated nonverbally can also influence the behaviors and cognitive processes of native speakers in a subconscious manner. In fact, fluent speakers of a language need more than just a linguistic knowledge of verbal concept formation at an implicit or explicit level; they must also have cultural knowledge of social conventions and connotative meanings present in nonverbal symbolic behaviors (see Chapters 5 and 6, and also Gonzalez & Felix-Holt, 1995, for a study of this topic).

In sum, folkloric or cultural representations may take verbal or *linguistic*, or nonverbal or *cultural*, forms that explicitly or implicitly communicate the symbolic sociocultural conventions of the ethnic group of which the speaker is a member. That is, both verbal and nonverbal folkloric representations influence, consciously or subconsciously, the behaviors and cognitive-affective processes of the members of a particular ethnic group. Then, folkloric nonverbal and verbal representations used by ethnic group members communicate unique symbolic interpretations of the world. Thus, members of different ethnic groups and speakers of different languages will interpret the folkloric meaning of *giftedness* differently.

Linguistic and Cultural Ways of Representing Giftedness

Studies about folkloric definitions of giftedness conducted with language-minority students are still scarce (Renzulli, 1991), even though authors began to understand the cultural dimensions of the giftedness construct more than twenty-five years ago (e.g., Bernal, 1974; Ramirez, 1972; Renzulli, 1978). In one of these early studies, Bernal found that characteristics attributed by parents to gifted Mexican-American children were of a behavioral rather than a cognitive nature. In a more contemporary study, Marquez (1992) showed an interest in understanding the folkloric definitions of giftedness present in parents' descriptions of their gifted children. Marquez developed a profile of gifted Hispanic children as described by their parents that included the following characteristics: curious, motivated, creative, observant, inquisitive, able to find multiple uses for objects and to solve problems, and interested in trying new things and in reading. Another contemporary survey study, conducted by Scott, Perou, Urbano, Hogan, and Gold (1992), showed that when comparing parents' descriptions of African-American, Hispanic, and white children, some similarities (e.g., talked early, learns quickly, has good memory, and is above peers) as well as some differences were present (such as, Hispanic gifted children, but not the others, were described by their parents as communicative and expressive, loving books, observant, and excelling in academic skills).

Ethnic groups have their own folkloric ways to describe constructs such as giftedness. For instance, Stern and Cicala (1991) referred to the creativity present in folkloric/ethnic ways of communicating, which take a dynamic social form. This dynamic interaction implies that both group and individuals' understandings of social meanings or constructs such as giftedness are influenced by being an ethnic group member. Stern and Cicala stated, "Choosing an ethnic expression, applying it to diverse situations, and transmitting it through time and space are based on decision making and community interplay that require a great deal of creativity and inspiration" (p. xii). Regarding the term *dynamic social interaction*, they stated, "Ethnic folklore may be viewed as representing both the broader historical conditions that influence ethnicity as well as the manner in which ethnicity shapes peoples' quests for meaning" (p. xii). They also discuss creative ways in which folklore is adapted to different historical conceptualizations of the same cultural constructs, such as giftedness, stating, "Strategies of ethnic adaptation influence how ethnic symbols are applied to concrete situations and how they are modified to changing contexts and times" (p. xiii).

Applying Stern and Cicala's (1991) explanation to the educational setting, different ethnic groups offer their own creative flexibility in cultural expressions that expand traditional definitions of giftedness. The labels or words used to describe the cultural components of giftedness vary depending on the group's linguistic and cultural representations, and even vary in subgroups within a society. Thus, the mainstream school culture views giftedness as an intellectual process that can be measured, while Hispanic individuals view giftedness as an expression of sociocultural, affective, emotional, and moral talents. Terms such as *sano* (translated literally as "healthy") and *bien educado* (translated literally as "well educated") are used within the Hispanic community with the additional cultural meanings of "morally healthy" and "honest" or "mature," which can be interpreted as sound behaviors that are culturally valued and considered signs of giftedness in a child. Thus, within the Hispanic community, *bien educado* has a folkloric meaning of "well raised" or "well mannered." Hispanic mothers use the phrase *es un niño bien educado* (literally translated as "is a well-educated child") for describing a child who knows or has learned to behave not just appropriately, but in an outstanding manner in varying social situations within the Hispanic community.

Moreover, the term *bien educado* is contrasted to the term *malcriado* (literally translated as "ill bred"). These terms are used to cross-analyze behaviors by Hispanic parents and to instill and develop in their children consciousness that their behaviors are inappropriate and will reflect badly on the family. Thus, gifted children are the ones who can analyze a situation, determine the appropriate behavior, and perform in an exemplary manner that will reflect well on themselves and on their families. In addition, the term *simpático*, used by Hispanic mothers to describe their gifted children, does not just mean "charming" but is used to describe someone who has "*gracia*." That is, it describes someone who fits his or her charm, behavior, personality, and language to the situational needs of the social interaction. In other words, the child's way of seeing, thinking, and speaking is creatively adjusted to connect to someone else's frame of reference. Without a doubt, this folkloric definition of giftedness is in conflict with the school's historical definition, a limited cognitive and linguistic trait measured with standardized IQ and achievement tests.

In sum, folkloric verbal and nonverbal representations of constructs reflect explicit or implicit sociocultural meanings internalized by ethnic group members. When Hispanic mothers are asked to describe the cognitive and linguistic abilities of their gifted children, they use social, affective, emotional, and moral domains of psychological behaviors. These descriptions reflect how members of the Hispanic ethnic group have internalized, perhaps unconsciously, cultural meanings and values. Hispanic mothers may use folkloric terms of the Spanish language pretty much in an automatic, implicit manner. That is, they may not be aware of their grammatical and syntactic knowledge, and of the folkloric symbolic connotations their choice of terms communicate. However, it is clear that folkloric definitions of giftedness communicate verbal and nonverbal representations that differ dramatically from mainstream historical ways of conceptualizing giftedness within the school's mainstream culture. Thus, educators who understand folkloric definitions of giftedness expressed by ethnic minority and majority groups may have broader views when identifying gifted language-minority children.

Historical View of Giftedness

Traditional and contemporary models for identifying giftedness in language-minority children include cut-off scores on standardized IQ and achievement tests and alternative models (divergent and multidimensional developmental models). In this section, we offer some explanations as to why traditional identification models, such as standardized IQ and achievement tests, are not applicable to language-minority children. Then we review some alternative models that have recently been recommended. We argue that multidimensional cultural and linguistic definitions of giftedness need to be taken into consideration when identifying gifted language-minority children. We need to use multiple informants and nominations, not only from teachers representing historical definitions of giftedness, but also from minority parents representing cultural and linguistic folkloric views of giftedness. We support Messick's (1995) view that accurate ways of assessing giftedness in language-minority children should include multidimensional developmental measurements with construct validity as they are based on sound theories and multiple empirical evidence.

Traditional Standardized IQ and Achievement Tests

The meaning of the word *gifted* still reflects a rather dated view since criteria for identifying gifted children continue to include cut-off scores on IQ and achievement tests. These traditional criteria relate back to Terman's framework put forth in the 1920s. In his longitudinal study of gifted subjects, Terman (1926) presented a rather narrow definition of giftedness, referring to those people in "the top one percent in general intellectual ability, as measured by the Stanford-Binet Intelligence Scale or a comparable instrument" (p. 237). He thought that the best individual standardized instrument for identifying giftedness was the Stanford-Binet Intelligence Scale, developed in the 1920s. The surprising fact is that in the 1990s, we are still using these IQ traditional instruments and criteria for identifying giftedness among school children. In fact, the Stanford-Binet is a highly verbal test; therefore, a high score on it is an indication that a person possesses good reading skills and has internalized much of the mainstream culture (Byran & Byran, 1979). (See Gonzalez, 1996, for further discussion of the assessment of intelligence in minority and majority children.)

Many other difficulties plague the study of the relationship between bilingualism and intelligence. Measurement of bilingual language proficiency has been a special problem, not only because discrete-point tests involve many areas in which cognitive and linguistic processes interact (e.g., phonology, lexicon, speaking, reading, writing), but also because bilingualism has been defined differently within and between disciplines. Moreover, the measurement of English-language proficiency in bilingual children independent of cognitive development has become a differential diagnosis problem. Additionally, we feel that *diagnosis* is not the same as *assessment*. Whereas diagnosis involves reaching a conclusion on the presence or absence of an intrinsic or an extrinsic cause for the learning problem in the bilingual child based on multiple sources and areas of information, assessment simply deals with test taking and test scoring by an examiner. Moreover, the process of diagnosis aims to establish a link between assessment, placement, and instruction. In order to reach an accurate differential diagnosis regarding normal second language learning, genuine disabling conditions and disabilities, and giftedness, evaluators need to be knowledgeable and aware of their own biases. They must have a broad knowledge of the constructs measured, such as cognitive and language development, for the specific cultural and linguistic backgrounds of the population served. In addition, they need to become aware of their own attitudes, ideologies, values, attributions, and in general their identities and personality factors, all of which affect their diagnostic and placement decisions for bilingual children. (See Chapters 7, 8, and 9 in this book; see also Gonzalez & Felix-Holt, 1995.)

For the accurate identification of gifted language-minority children, educators should aim instead at measuring the potential for learning that results from the interaction between internal (e.g., genetic endowment, temperament, maturation, birth weight, and so forth) and external (e.g., socioeconomic status, stimulation, parental attitudes, peer and adult role models, cultural environment, and so forth) developmental factors (see Gonzalez & Yawkey, 1993). There is a major methodological flaw in the traditional argument that intelligence tests measure primarily innate factors, when in fact they represent in their items cultural definitions of intelligence and giftedness. For instance, Getzels and Jackson (1963) and Gowan (1971) showed that traditional IQ tests should not be used even for identifying gifted majority students (and less so for minority students). These tests measure convergent thinking, which will not tap the divergent thinking skills and creativity of gifted children. Divergent thinkers will not accept one answer or conclusion, or limit their responses to rote learning and providing lists of factual information as required by traditional IQ tests. Many linguistically and culturally gifted minority children do not surface with such traditional means of identification.

Studies during the 1970s and later reported an association between bilingualism and divergent thinking. Landry (1974) and Cummins (1977) found that learning a second language in elementary school might increase divergent thinking. Balkan (1970), Cummins (1975), and Cummins and Gulutsan (1974) also found that bilingual children performed significantly better on tests of cognitive flexibility, such as the Embedded Figures Test. Barik and Swain (1976) showed a greater cognitive growth among third-grade gifted bilingual Canadian students than among their monolingual counterparts. Carringer (1974) reported that 24 Spanish-English balanced bilinguals performed at a significantly higher level than their monolingual Spanish counterparts on several measures of divergent thinking, such as metalinguistic awareness.

Note that different authors have defined and discussed metalinguistic awareness. For instance, Cummins (1978) defined it as the ability to understand the arbitrary nature of word-referent relationships and to use sophisticated reasoning strategies. Diaz (1985) defined metalinguistic awareness as the ability to analyze and objectify language that resulted from bilingualism. Bialystock (1986) thought that early word concept development and level of bilingualism and biliteracy influenced metalinguistic awareness, a composite of two skills: analysis of linguistic knowledge and control of attention for linguistic processing. Finally, Snow (1992) believed that early bilingualism could influence positively metalinguistic awareness.

The methodological flaws present in standardized IQ tests when used with language-minority, low socioeconomic status (SES) children have been clear since the 1970s. Peal and Lambert's landmark study on bilingualism and cognition (1962) was the first to show the presence of confounding variables. Their research on French-English bilingual children in Montreal showed that bilingual children had a more flexible cognitive structure when control for confounding variables was taken (e.g., SES and first and second language proficiency). This pioneering study became the inspiration and motivation for more modern second language researchers to demonstrate the cognitive advantages of becoming bilingual.

Mercer (1973) showed that African-American and Mexican-American children who scored high on IQ tests came from homes that had the same SES and parental educational levels as the mainstream children in the normed group. As stated by Mercer, "Results of such IQ tests affect to a great degree persons from a different cultural background and those from lower SES" (p. 3). These IQ tests mirror the standard values and experiences of the white mainstream middle class. Since the definition of giftedness has been reduced traditionally to a specific cut-off score on IQ standardized tests, in order for children to be identified as gifted, they would need to share the same demographic characteristics of the normed group. For instance, the cut-off score for being identified as gifted for the Stanford-Binet Intelligence Scale is 132 and for the Wechsler Intelligence Scale is 130. Anyone achieving scores above 130 is considered as having a superior intelligence (Seagoe, 1975). As more and more minority families achieve middle-class status, larger numbers of higher IQ minority children who resemble the normed group will surface. But the culturally and linguistically different children from low SES will still suffer, unless schools use identification criteria that are not bound to the mainstream middle-class linguistic and cultural definitions of giftedness.

Moreover, Mercer (1973) showed that more than four times as many Mexican-Americans and twice as many African-Americans were enrolled in educable mentally retarded (EMR) classes, a disproportionate number for the minority groups. When IQ scores were interpreted with the knowledge that sociocultural factors bias them, Mercer showed that the racial imbalance in EMR classes disappeared. She argued that approximately 15 percent of the children in her study who were enrolled in EMR classes were mislabeled and misplaced in an environment not conducive to learning, and consequently suffered from lower self-esteem. Regarding the overrepresentation of minorities in special education categories, Samuda (1991) stated, "Available empirical evidence indicates that mental capacity and learning potential are equally distributed across all races, ethnic groups, and social classes" (p. 181).

In many studies conducted during the 1980s and 1990s with majority and minority children, compelling evidence emerged pointing to the significant effect of SES on cognitive development, specifically during early childhood (between birth and 8 years of age). For instance, the parental level of education has been demonstrated to explain significant variance in the IQ test scores of young children (Kaufman & Kaufman, 1983), which leads to major differences in diagnostic categories of up to three standard deviations. In addition, Trueba (1991) showed that language-minority children who were mislabeled and misplaced suffered from emotional distress that resulted from lack of success in their learning experiences within the mainstream school culture. He explained that emotional distress is a much more acute form of depression than just the low self-esteem and low self-concept that unsuccessful learning attempts bring to language-minority children. Rather, children suffering from emotional distress become withdrawn, show lack of motivation to communicate with the environment, and show symptoms of clinical depression.

In summary, several landmark studies conducted during the 1970s, 1980s, and 1990s showed overwhelming evidence that bilingualism stimulates high-level thinking skills and strategies (e.g., metalinguistic awareness) when external factors such as SES and parental educational levels are controlled for. Therefore, cut-off scores in IQ or achievement standardized tests should not be used for identifying gifted language-minority children because they do not represent cultural and linguistic definitions of giftedness.

Alternative Approaches

Two modern alternative identification approaches of giftedness are the divergent and the developmental multidimensional models, both using creative problem-solving abilities. According to Getzels and Jackson (1963), tests of divergent thinking may involve finding geometric forms hidden in a larger geometric pattern (e.g., Embedded Figures Test, Wilkin, 1971), writing different endings to a story, or giving different and original uses for items that are usually thought of as having only one use. Torrance and Torrance (1973) defined creative thinking as a natural human process in which a person (1) becomes aware of a problem, a difficulty, or a gap in information for which there is no learned response; (2) searches for possible solutions from past experiences (including those of others); (3) formulates hypotheses about possible solutions; (4) evaluates, tests, modifies, and retests these possible solutions; and (5) communicates the result to others successfully.

A second model that can be used as a basis for the identification of gifted language-minority students is based on the following set of creative characteristics derived by Torrance and Torrance (1973) from a series of research studies: (1) high nonverbal fluency and originality; (2) high creative productivity in small groups; (3) adeptness in visual art activities; (4) high creativity in movement, dance, and other physical activities; and (5) an ability to be highly motivated by games, music, sports, humor, concrete objects, and language rich in image. Moreover, Torrance and Torrance (1973) and Bernal (1974) have listed humor as one of the typical characteristics of gifted children, indicating their use of transformational abilities or metalinguistic awareness. Guilford (1972) also referred to the creative gifted children who show their flair for flexibility in the use and understanding of humor. As described before, *metalinguistic awareness* refers to thinking about language, or the ability to become conscious of underlying folkloric meanings of language. Then, metalinguistic awareness or transformation is the basis for the understanding of a semantic "metaphor" present in humor. Gowan (1971) stated that "creativity is behavioral and can be seen and measured in action" (p. 156), a description that reinforces the argument that gifted children have a facility for verbal creativity such as humor.

A third model used for identifying giftedness is derived from Piagetian developmental theory that has been used successfully since the 1970s for assessing giftedness in language-minority children. For instance, De Avila and Havassy (1974) constructed a Piagetian developmental measure called the Cartoon Conservation Scales (CCS). This measure uses schematic drawings showing the Piagetian operation, or developmental construct, of conservation of substance, liquid, and number. Children are introduced to problem-solving situations using drawings and verbal explorations, and are asked to respond verbally or nonverbally by pointing to drawings. De Avila and Havassy found that this test showed (1) a developmentally appropriate performance for Mexican-Americans that was within the limits of expected levels for their chronological ages, (2) no gender or ethnic differences, and (3) no differences between Spanish and English administrations. Due to its psychometric characteristics, this cognitive measure can be used for the identification of gifted language-minority children. Clark (1981) used the CCS to identify gifted minority students and found a definite correlation between giftedness and proficient bilingualism.

More recently, Pascual-Leone and Ijaz (1991) also recommended neo-Piagetian tasks as good measures of capacities in language-minority children because they may lack first and second language proficiency but have good experiential and conceptual abilities. These authors also proposed that developmental theory provides the possibility of empirically verifying and correcting tasks as a function of variables such as age, different characteristics in children (e.g., bilingual versus monolingual, low versus high SES, and different first and second language proficiency levels). For validating developmental tasks, there is a need "to verify whether the theoretical task analyses of types of tasks serve to predict the tasks' relative developmental difficulty as well as the individual differences that might be found in it" (Pascual-Leone & Ijaz, 1991, pp. 160–161). In addition, these authors also stated that developmental tasks can be standardized more easily than traditional knowledge-based tests (such as IQ and achievement tests) because the theory on which they are based can be used to select the " 'ideal population' against which the tasks should be standardized" (p. 161). Gonzalez (1991, 1994, 1995) developed an alternative assessment called QUEST (Qualitative Use of Spanish and English Tasks) to measure cognitive and linguistic abilities in bilingual Hispanic children. QUEST presents five verbal and nonverbal classification problem-solving tasks (see Chapters 7, 8, and 9).

As recommended by different authors since the 1970s, multiple criteria and alternative assessment approaches must be used to identify gifted language-minority children. For instance, to facilitate test scores of Mexican-American students, Bernal (1974) used language screening, examiner-examinee matching, rapport building, small group testing, coaching on mechanics of test taking, and practice on items similar to the ones on the test. Moreover, several authors (e.g., Bernal, 1974; De Avila & Havassy, 1974; Mercer, 1973; Sato, 1974) have recommended that educators involved in the identification of gifted language-minority children should understand the environmental and sociological factors affecting the development of those children. Since the 1970s it has been argued that language-minority children should not be penalized by the social values that are reflected in the usual standardized IQ and achievement tests.

During the 1990s, Santos de Barona and Barona (1991) recommended the use of preassessment techniques such as: (1) medical histories, including developmental and sociocultural factors, (2) degree of acculturation of the family and assessment of its needs and strengths, and (3) analysis of the child's adjustment with the external school and family environments. They also recommended diagnostic placements for understanding instructional methodologies and materials that best meet the child's individual needs, and to measure progress over time while applying different experimental methods. Lewis (1991) recommended the use of an interdisciplinary team for assessing the potential for learning and focusing on the strengths of the language-minority child. Lewis acknowledged that qualitative assessments can measure how cognitive processes function in problem-solving verbal and nonverbal tasks (such as the verbal and nonverbal classification tasks used in QUEST [Gonzalez, 1991, 1994, 1995]). For instance, he recommended dynamic assessment, in which clinical observations of the learning process are used to diagnose potential for learning. Dynamic assessment links assessment with instruction and incorporates a developmental and cultural view as it is related to Vygotskyan definitions of intelligence development (i.e., potential for learning within a stimulating cultural environment providing social role models). Pascual-Leone and Ijaz (1991) also recommended dynamic assessment because it can be adjusted to the abilities and skills of the individual by adapting instructions and tasks, and by modeling tasks and interpreting responses. Also following a multidimensional view, Damico (cited in Hamayan, 1994) recommended a bilevel analysis paradigm in which both descriptive and explanatory analyses are made by evaluators. In this second level, evaluators can become advocates for finding possible extrinsic factors affecting the child's performance before using any internal factors as explanations. Relatedly, Hamayan (1994) recommended an ecological assessment approach that encompasses a holistic analysis of the external sociocultural factors and allows evaluators to take a learner-centered perspective.

Thus, since the 1970s, experts have focused on the use of multidimensional alternative assessments. They recommend the use of developmental tasks that measure potential for learning, link assessment with instruction, and examine the interaction of external and internal factors in learning and intelligence development. By using alternative assessments, general and special educators can better tap into and uncover the folkloric and linguistic dimensions of giftedness in the language-minority children assessed.

EDUCATIONAL IMPLICATIONS

General and special educators, including evaluators and administrators, must serve as advocates for establishing a link between the historical views of giftedness and the minority folkloric views. These educators can be leaders in integrating success in the mainstream school culture with respect and value given to the minority cultural identity of children. As they examine new paradigms for the identification of gifted children who are culturally and linguistically different from those in the mainstream school culture, they must challenge traditional assessment methods that reflect only the mainstream school culture perspective. For example, Gonzalez (1993) proposed that the most important tool for assessment is the personality of evaluators. In addition, educators' historical view of giftedness must be enhanced by the folkloric definitions of giftedness in our minority communities. Gonzalez and Felix-Holt (1995) presented a case study illustrating the cultural subjectivity present in diagnostic and placement decisions of evaluators. Gonzalez and Felix-Holt (1995) concluded that evaluators' knowledge levels of cognitive and linguistic development of language-minority children, beliefs and schools of thought endorsed, and views about traditional and alternative assessment influence the assessment process. (See Chapter 9 for a qualitative study of the influence of evaluators' backgrounds on the identification of gifted minority children.)

To prevent minority gifted children from suffering disastrous results such as maladjustment and lack of productivity in the school and social systems, early identification of giftedness is vital. Most language-minority children referred by minority and majority teachers show high linguistic and cognitive skills, are male, and have extroverted personalities (see Gonzalez, Bauerle, & Felix-Holt, 1996). In order to identify gifted language-minority children more accurately and with less bias, general and special educators need to become more sensitive to different cultural lifestyles. They should also familiarize themselves with philosophies and practices to deal with the high potential of gifted language-minority children (Samuda, 1991). Teachers need to act as advocates by nominating language-minority students for giftedness, based on both the folkloric, or cultural, and the historic definitions of giftedness. Most teachers, even those with a bilingual and bicultural background, have a mainstream school culture view of giftedness. (See Chapter 7 for a qualitative study of minority teachers' attitudes toward giftedness in minority children.)

Thus, evaluators need to become advocates and assume moral responsibility for representing the best interests of language-minority children (Samuda, 1991). Damico and Hamayan (1991) have recognized the dilemma in which evaluators are placed when assessing language-minority children, due to accountability issues related to the use of invalid and unreliable standardized tests. These authors argue that evaluators function as gatekeepers when they state, "A true advocate has the influence and ability to work within the system for positive results" (Damico & Hamayan, 1991, p. 308). They advise evaluators to be patient and to present compelling evidence that alternative assessments can accurately represent the abilities of language-minority children and will lead to valid diagnoses and placements. They assert that "evaluators need to abandon the attitude of learned helplessness and become agents of change" (Damico & Hamayan, 1991, p. 314). For change to occur in the area of the identification of giftedness, advocates for culturally and linguistically different children need to incorporate a folkloric and historic alternative approach to assessment that is valid and morally conscious.

REFERENCES

BALKAN, L. (1970). *Les effects du bilingualisme francais-anglais sur les aptitudes intellectualles.* Bruxelles: Aimay.
BARIK, H., & SWAIN, M. (1976). A longitudinal study of bilingual and cognitive development. *International Journal of Psychology, 11,* 252–263.
BERNAL, E. M., JR. (1974). *Analysis of giftedness in Mexican-American children and design of a prototype identification instrument.* Austin, TX: Southwest Educational Laboratory.

BIALYSTOCK, E. (1986). Factors in the growth of linguistic awareness. *Child Development, 57,* 498–510.
BYRAN, J. H., & BYRAN, T. H. (1979). *Exceptional children.* Sherman Oaks, CA: Alfred.
CARRINGER, D. C. (1974). Creative thinking abilities of Mexican youth: The relationship of bilingualism. *Journal of Cross-Cultural Psychology, 5,* 492–504.
CASSON, R. W. (1981). *Language, culture, and cognition: Anthropological perspective* (pp. 20–21). New York: Macmillan.
CLARK, E. R. (1981). *The determination of giftedness in lower socioeconomic third grade Mexican-American students.* Unpublished doctoral dissertation, University of Texas at Austin.
CUMMINS, J. (1975). The influence of bilingualism on cognitive growth: A synthesis of research findings and explanatory hypotheses. *Working Papers on Bilingualism, 9,* 123–134. Ontario, Canada: Ontario Institute for Studies of Education.
CUMMINS, J. (1977). Cognitive factors associated with the attainment of intermediate levels of bilingual skills. *Modern Language Journal, 61,* 3–12.
CUMMINS, J. (1978). Bilingualism and the development of metalinguistic awareness. *Journal of Cross-Cultural Psychology, 9,* 131–149.
CUMMINS, J. (1984). The construct of alarming disabilities. In J. Cummins (Ed.), *Bilingualism and special education: Issues in assessment and pedagogy* (pp. 80–92). Clevedon, England: Multilingual Matters.
CUMMINS, J. P., & GULUTSAN, M. (1974). Some effects of bilingualism on cognitive functioning. In S. Carey (Ed.), *Bilingualism, biculturalism, and education* (pp. 237–288). Proceedings from the conference at College Universitaire Saint Jean, University of Alberta.
DAMICO, J. S., & HAMAYAN. E. V. (1991). Implementing assessment in the real world. In E. V. Hamayan & J. S. Damico (Eds.), *Limiting bias in the assessment of bilingual students* (pp. 302–316). Austin, TX: Pro-Ed.
DE AVILA, E. A., & HAVASSY, B. (1974). *Intelligence and Mexican-American children: A field study comparing neo-Piagetian and traditional capacity and achievement measures.* Austin, TX: Dissemination Center for Bilingual Education.
DIAZ, R. M. (1985). Bilingual cognitive development: Addressing three gaps in current research. *Child Development, 56,* 1376–1388.
DUNDES, A. (1965). *The study of folklore.* Englewood Cliffs, NJ: Prentice Hall.
GETZELS, J. W., & JACKSON, P. W. (1963). *The gifted student: The study of giftedness— A multidimensional approach.* Chicago: University of Chicago Press.
GONZALEZ, V. (1991). *A model of cognitive, cultural, and linguistic variables affecting bilingual Spanish/English children's development of concepts and language.* Unpublished doctoral dissertation, University of Texas at Austin. (ERIC Document Reproduction Service No. ED 345 562)
GONZALEZ, V. (1993).The assessment of language-minority students: An awakening experience. *NABE NEWS, 17*(2), 9–10, 26.
GONZALEZ, V. (1994). A model of cognitive, cultural, and linguistic variables affecting bilingual Spanish/English children's development of concepts and language. *Hispanic Journal of Behavioral Sciences, 16*(4), 396–421.
GONZALEZ, V. (1995). *Cognition, culture, and language in bilingual children: Conceptual and semantic development.* Bethesda, MD: Austin & Windfield.
GONZALEZ, V. (1996). Do you believe in intelligence? Sociocultural dimensions of intelligence assessment in majority and minority students. *Educational Horizons, 75*(1), 45–52.

GONZALEZ, V., BAUERLE, P., & FELIX-HOLT, M. (1996). Theoretical and practical implications of assessing cognitive and language development in bilingual children with qualitative methods. *Bilingual Research Journal, 20*(1), 93–131.

GONZALEZ, V., & FELIX-HOLT, M. (1995). Influence of evaluators' prior academic knowledge on the diagnosis of cognitive and language development in bilingual Hispanic kindergartners. *New York State Association for Bilingual Education (NYSABE) Journal, 10*(1), 34–45.

GONZALEZ, V., & YAWKEY, T. D. (1993). The assessment of culturally and linguistically diverse students: Celebrating change. *Educational Horizons, 72*(1), 41–49.

GOWAN, J. C. (1971). Relation between creativity and giftedness. *Gifted Child Quarterly, 15*, 239–243.

GUILFORD, L. P. (1972). Intellect and the gifted. *Gifted Child Quarterly, 16*, 175–184.

HAMAYAN, E. V. (1994). Moving to a more ecological view of assessment. *NABE NEWS, 18*(1), 29–30.

KAUFMAN, A. S., & KAUFMAN, N. L. (1983). *Kaufman Assessment Battery for Children.* Circle Pines, MN: American Guidance Service.

LANDRY, R. G. (1974). A comparison of second-language learners and monolinguals on divergent thinking tasks at the elementary school level. *Modern Language Journal 58*, 10–15.

LEWIS, J. (1991). Innovative approaches in assessment. In R. J. Samuda & S. L. Kong (Eds.), *Assessment and placement of minority students* (pp. 123–142). Toronto, Ontario, Canada: Hogrefe.

MARQUEZ, J. A. (1992). Incorporating community perceptions in the identification of gifted and talented Hispanic students. *Journal of Educational Issues of Language Minority Students, 10*, 117–127.

MERCER, J. (1973). *Labelling the mentally retarded.* Los Angeles: University of California Press.

MESSICK, S. (1995). Validity of psychological assessment: Validation from persons' responses and performances as scientific inquiry into score meaning. *American Psychologist, 50*(9), 741–749.

MOSS, P. A. (1992). Shifting conceptions of validity in education measurement: Implications for performance assessment. *Review of Educational Research, 62*(3), 229–258.

PASCUAL-LEONE, J., & IJAZ, H. (1991). Mental capacity testing as a form of intellectual-developmental assessment. In R. J. Samuda & S. L. Kong (Eds.), *Assessment and placement of minority students* (pp. 143–171). Toronto, Canada: Hogrefe.

PEAL, E., & LAMBERT, A. (1962). *Representational processes in early language acquisition.* Boston: Rowley.

RAMIREZ, M. (1972). Value conflicts experienced by Mexican-American students. *El Grito 25*, 28–37.

RENZULLI, J. S. (1978). What makes giftedness? Reexamining a definition. In W. B. Barbe & J. S. Renzulli (Eds.), *Psychology and education of the gifted* (pp. 55–65). New York: Irvington Publishers.

RENZULLI, J. S. (1991). The national research center on the gifted and talented: The dream, the design, and the destination. *Gifted Child Quarterly, 35*(2), 73–80.

SAMUDA, R. J. (1991). Student assessment and placement in Ontario schools. In R. J. Samuda & S. L. Kong (Eds.), *Assessment and placement of minority students* (pp. 109–122). Toronto, Canada: Hogrefe.

SANTOS DE BARONA, M., & BARONA, A. (1991). The assessment of culturally and linguistically different preschoolers. *Early Childhood Research Quarterly, 6*(3), 363–376.

Sato, S. (1974, May). The culturally different gifted child: The drawing of this day. *Exceptional Children, 572–577.*
Scott, M. S., Perou, R., Urbano, R., Hogan, A., & Gold, S. (1992). The identification of giftedness: A comparison of white, hispanic, and black families. *Gifted Child Quarterly, 36*(3), 131–139.
Seagoe, M. V. (1975). *Terman and the gifted.* Los Altos, CA: William Kaufman.
Snow, C. E. (1992). Perspectives on second-language development: Implications for bilingual education. *Educational Researcher, 21*(2), 16–19.
Stern, S., & Cicala, J. A. (1991). *Creative ethnicity: Symbols and strategies of contemporary ethnic life.* Salt Lake City: Utah State University Press.
Terman, L. M. (1926). *Genetic studies of genius: Mental and physical traits of a thousand gifted children.* Stanford, CA: Stanford University Press.
Torrance, E. (1973, Spring). Non-test indicators of creative talent among disadvantaged children. *Gifted Child Quarterly,* 243–249.
Torrance, E., & Torrance, J. P. (1973). *Is creativity teachable?* Bloomington, IN: Delta Kappa Educational Foundation.
Trueba, H. T. (1991). Learning needs of minority children: Contributions of ethnography to educational research. In L. M. Malavé & G. Duquette (Eds.), *Language, culture, and cognition* (pp. 137–158). Clevedon, England: Multilingual Matters.
Wilkin, D. A. (1972). *Linguistics in language teaching.* London: Edward Arnold.

CHAPTER
2

An Integrative Analysis of the Cognitive Development of Bilingual and Bicultural Children and Adults

VIRGINIA GONZALEZ AND DIANE L. SCHALLERT

THIS CHAPTER PROVIDES A THEORETICAL FRAMEWORK AS A CONTEXT FOR the two clusters of data-based studies presented in this book. The chapter establishes a multidisciplinary and multidimensional view of the influence of cognition, language, and culture on conceptual and semantic development in bilingual children and adults. It highlights the major theme of this book: the sociocultural and socioeducational context for cognitive and language development in bilinguals. One of its goals is to contribute to the fields of cognitive psychology and bilingual education by presenting a careful analysis of these two separate modules of literature and how they converge in the study of bilingual children's conceptual and semantic development. Thus, this chapter presents an integrative view of the literature on the relationship of cognition, language, and culture by considering three related, and increasingly broader, questions:

1. Does developing one or two languages enhance or interfere with cognitive development?
2. Do bilinguals represent knowledge verbally or nonverbally?
3. What is the direction of the mapping process between conceptual and semantic development?

The first is an applied question from cognitive psychology and a theoretical question from the field of bilingual education that approaches the influence of language and culture on cognition at a product level. The second is a theoretical question from cognitive psychology that studies knowledge and memory at a structural level. The third is also a theoretical question from cognitive psychology, which focuses on the interaction of language, culture, and the acquisition of concepts at a semantic processes level. Thus, this chapter seeks to build a bridge between the theoretical and applied research questions stated within cognitive psychology and bilingual education.

We seek to contribute to the fields of cognitive psychology and bilingual education by proposing a triple-interactional model addressing the influence of cognitive, linguistic, and cultural factors on bilingual children's conceptual and semantic development. This model proposes a multidimensional view that encompasses the apparent differences of the interdisciplinary models and theoretical problems reviewed in this chapter. Our goal is to try to integrate these separate modules of literature by pointing out commonalities and possible theoretical or methodological factors that generate contradictory findings across these apparently disconnected disciplines. We will present some strengths and weaknesses that emerge from these different interdisciplinary modules of literature. In our integration, we believe that these three questions view the influence of cognition, language, and culture on cognitive and language development at three different but complementary levels: performance, structural, and semantic processes. Thus, cognitive and language development is studied from a multidisciplinary and multidimensional perspective.

The first section of this chapter is a critical review of the literature in which we discuss three major issues in the study of cognitive and language development in bilingual children and adults: (1) the effects of bilingualism on cognitive performance, (2) knowledge representation in bilinguals, and (3) the direction of the mapping process between conceptual and semantic development.

The second section of this chapter presents the triple-interactional model of the influence of cognitive, linguistic, and cultural variables on concept and semantic development in bilinguals. The third section discusses the influence of cognitive, linguistic, and cultural factors on bilinguals' conceptual and semantic development. Finally, conclusions are derived from the integration of the literature review.

ISSUES IN THE STUDY OF COGNITIVE AND LANGUAGE DEVELOPMENT IN BILINGUALS

The Effects of Bilingualism on Cognitive Performance

What are the effects of becoming bilingual on cognitive performance? Bilingualism and intelligence were first studied together in the 1920s (e.g., Saer, 1923; Yoshioka, 1929), and since then contradictory positions regarding the advantages or disadvantages of bilingualism on cognitive performance have been defended. Lower IQ scores among bilinguals tested in English in comparison to monolinguals were explained as a deficit in the areas of intelligence and language development, as it was concluded that bilinguals suffered in these areas due to having learned two languages.

Major reviews of studies conducted through the early 1960s on the relationship between bilingualism and intelligence (e.g., Barke, 1933; Carlson & Henderson, 1950; Darcy, 1953; Haugen, 1961; Jones, 1960; Peal & Lambert, 1962) concluded that most previous studies that indicated a superiority of monolingual children over bilingual children had major methodological flaws, such as linguistically and culturally biased English intelligence tests and a lack of control of external variables (i.e., socioeconomic status and bilingual language proficiency).

Some early authors (e.g., Vygotsky [written in the 1930s, but not published until 1962], 1962a, 1962b; Leopold, 1939) proposed and defended the advantages of being bilingual for cognitive development. Leopold's (1939) abstract thinking hypothesis suggested that the bilingual child probably has an early ability to separate the word as a symbol from its referent. Vygotsky (1962a, 1962b) suggested that because bilingual children could express the same thought in different languages, they could gain awareness of linguistic operations. Later, Peal and Lambert (1962) conducted a landmark research study in which they matched monolingual French and balanced bilingual French/English 10-year-olds on socioeconomic status, sex, age, and school system. In contrast to previous research on bilingualism and intelligence, they discovered that bilingual children showed superior performance on verbal and nonverbal standardized intelligence tests and a more heterogeneous pattern of intelligence, whereas monolingual children possessed a unitary structure of intelligence. They attributed the enhanced cognitive flexibility and creativity of bilinguals to their ability to form concepts separating the label from its symbolic meaning. Studies based on traditional cognitive developmental theories (e.g., Bruner, 1964; Piaget, 1965) have also indicated that the early word-object separation is important for cognitive development.

More recently, this cognitive ability to separate nonverbal conceptual meanings from corresponding words in different languages has been called *metalinguistic awareness*. Since Peal and Lambert (1962), a variety of studies (e.g., Ben-Zeev, 1977; Cummins, 1978a, 1978b, 1989; Feldman & Shen, 1971; Ianco-Worrall, 1972; Lambert, 1977; Lambert & Tucker, 1972; Landry, 1974; Torrance, Gowan, & Aliohi, 1970) have reported that when bilinguals are compared to monolinguals, they show advantages of cognitive flexibility, creativity, concept formation, and metalinguistic abilities. It is not possible to show a cause-and-effect relation between bilingualism and intelligence; that is, one cannot state whether the more intelligent child became a balanced bilingual, or whether bilingualism stimulated cognitive development. Cummins (1978b) and Skutnabb-Kangas and Toukomaa (1976) suggested that there may be language proficiency threshold levels that bilingual children must attain in order to avoid cognitive deficits (lower-level threshold) and to show advantages in cognitive development (higher-level threshold). Thus, those authors posit that the proficiency levels in both languages mediate the effects of bilingualism on cognition.

Cummins (1979a) pointed out that recent studies supporting the advantage hypothesis are better controlled methodologically than earlier studies. However, we propose that even recent studies are not free of such methodological flaws as the lack of: (1) control for background differences between bilinguals and monolinguals; (2) agreement on the operationalization of the construct of language proficiency in bilinguals; (3) valid and reliable assessment instruments that measure language proficiency in language-minority children, which leads to their overrepresentation in special education (Ortiz & Maldonado-Colon, 1986; Ortiz & Yates, 1983); (4) awareness of the correlation between cognitive and linguistic processes in standardized measures of language development, academic achievement, and verbal and nonverbal intelligence (e.g., see Alexander, Schallert, & Hare, 1991; Anderson & Pearson, 1984; Gonzalez, 1991; Oller, 1991); and (5) awareness of the conceptual difference between assessment and diagnosis.

Although recent studies are not methodologically flawless, the weight of the evidence suggests that additive bilingualism in early childhood can accelerate cognitive growth if the child has relatively high proficiency levels in both languages. Additive bilingualism refers to the parallel development of proficiency in first and second language since early childhood. Different authors have suggested that enhanced intellectual development from bilingualism fails to materialize in minority children in the United States because of socioeconomic or educational conditions (Bowen, 1977; Cummins 1979a, 1979b; Fishman, 1977; Tucker, 1977). In the United States, language-minority children are gradually replacing their first language by a more prestigious second language—that is, substractive bilingualism—and many bilinguals may be characterized by low levels of language proficiency in both languages.

In conclusion, the study of bilingualism and bicognitivism currently seems to be motivated by three major interests: (1) to demonstrate that being bilingual is an advantage, (2) to develop models that include sociocultural and socioemotional factors, and (3) to give recommendations about better assessment and educational practices for bilingual education. Although much of the research is still in progress or has yet to be conducted, the weight of the evidence supports the positive influence of bilingualism on cognitive development.

Representation of Knowledge in Bilinguals

A second issue in the study of cognitive and language development in bilinguals has to do with the different models of the symbolic nonverbal and verbal representational systems. Paivio (1991) identified three periods in the study of mental representation in bilinguals since the 1950s that emphasized (1) the language learning history of bilinguals emphasized by the compound-coordinate distinction, (2) memory storage systems in bilinguals, and (3) general theories of cognition that also include bilingual processing (a more recent trend in research).

The first period includes several theories that attempted to explain symbolic representation in bilinguals. Among the most important is the mediation theory of semantics (Lambert, Havelka, & Crosby, 1958), which has two hypotheses:

1. The *concept mediation hypothesis*, which suggests that words are stored in one representational system for both languages, where concepts are nonverbal symbols independent of language (compound bilingualism), and both languages were learned before 6 years of age within the same context.
2. The *word mediation hypothesis*, which suggests that words are stored in two representational systems, where there are two concepts—one for each language (coordinate bilingualism)—and the second language was learned after 6 years of age within a different context than the first language.

Inconsistent results have been obtained for these two hypotheses. Therefore, an alternative hypothesis, the *dual-code model* (Paivio, 1983; Paivio & Desrochers, 1980; Paivio & Lambert, 1981) was proposed. The dual-code model hypothesis suggested that overlap between imagery and the two linguistic systems is intermediate, with direct connections between languages involving only certain types of concepts. Other authors have also attempted to explain symbolic representation in bilinguals. For instance, Clark (1977) and Kolers and Brison (1984) have suggested that concrete semantic equivalents (i.e., translations and synonyms) between first and second languages should be stronger than for abstract or affective semantic equivalents and should converge in common imaginal representations.

Several other variants of the dual-code model have been proposed, focusing on only the verbal representational systems in both languages. One model, proposed by Kirsner, Smith, Lockhart, King, and Jain (1984), suggested that, within a language, bilinguals possess stronger links for direct translations and semantically related concepts. Another variant of this model proposed in the same study stated that bilinguals possess fewer, rather than weaker, cross-language linkages for highly typical exemplars in categories. A third variant of the model, proposed by Potter, So, Von Eckardt, and Feldman (1984), holds that lexical items are connected both within and between languages via a conceptual system that is language independent. This third variant is consistent with more of the data on cross-language priming effects than any of the other previous variants. Finally, Anderson (1985) suggested that bilinguals construct a new linking verbal schema that references the same domain in the first and the second language representational system. That is, an individual with domain-specific knowledge in two languages may begin to develop metalinguistic awareness, allowing him or her to see the different ways in which concepts can be expressed in the first and second languages.

Other variations of the dual-code model focus on the interconnection between the verbal and the nonverbal representational systems in both languages. Findings from a number of studies with bilinguals (e.g., Bates & McWhinney, 1981; D'Anglejan & Tucker, 1973; Fathman, 1975; Hakuta, 1975, 1976; Harley, 1982; Kang, 1982; Kellerman, 1978, 1979, 1983; Schachter, 1974) have shown that native language conceptual structure may influence and transfer to conceptual patterns and semantic, pragmatic, and perceptual strategies in the second language without becoming readily apparent in linguistic use. However, Gonzalez (1991, 1994, 1995) suggested that when linguistic structures, abstract concepts, and symbolic meanings are different across languages, the second language learner will need to construct new semantic concepts using an accommodation process. For instance, native-English-speaking college students who are studying Spanish as a second language will have difficulty learning the linguistic gender of nouns, the semantic meanings of the verb "to be" in Spanish (*ser* and *estar* forms), verb conjugations, and direct and indirect object pronouns in the target language. (See Chapters 5 and 6 on research studies on English-speaking college students' learning linguistic gender, and *ser* and *estar* in Spanish.)

More recently, Clark and Paivio (1991) have suggested that the assumptions of dual-code theory have to do with both basic mental *structures* and *processes*. Mental structures are associative networks of verbal and imaginal representations, and mental processes deal with the development and activation of those structures, including the effects of context and the spread of activation among representations. The verbal system of the mental representations contains visual, auditory, articulatory, and other modality-specific verbal codes, such as words in different languages. These wordlike codes are arbitrary symbols that denote concrete objects and events, as well as abstract ideas. That is, semantically equivalent words (e.g., "book," *libro* in Spanish and Italian, and *livre* in French) and their corresponding objects are encoded by distinct verbal and imaginal representations that do not converge on a single abstract code. Verbal codes retain their discrete identities even when connected in hierarchical and associative networks because they are processed sequentially. Nonverbal representations are perceptually similar to the events that they denote, and they are processed simultaneously. The dual-code theory also assumes that idiosyncratic and context-dependent connections between verbal and nonverbal representations exist and lead to a complex associative network called referential connections (e.g., connections from images to words or names to pictures). Thus, Clark and Paivio (1991) attempted to compare sequential and simultaneous processes and structures of knowledge representations, as parallel and independent verbal and imaginal representations.

A number of other studies have also pointed out the distinction between mental structures and processes in representational systems. According to Anderson (1978) and Lindsay (1988), the issue of representational format cannot be answered independent of the processes used in accessing those representations. Karmiloff-Smith (1985) pointed to the distinction between operations that create representations (structures) and operations that operate over representations (processes). On the other hand, researchers have called attention to the influence of sociocultural factors on the representational systems. Genesee (1989) suggested that bilingual children develop differentiated language systems and use them in ways sensitive to sociocultural contexts.

Although many studies have been conducted in the area of symbolic representation in bilinguals, we do not know whether bilingual individuals store knowledge in one or two systems. However, the current belief posits an interdependence or interaction between the nonverbal and the two verbal representational systems in bilinguals. Researchers are now realizing that the problem is more complex than they had initially thought when conceptualizing the problem of knowledge representation; they were originally primarily concerned with the representational structure in memory. One possible problem is that the different retrieval demands of the tasks and stimuli used in the studies may have influenced the format of the representational systems accessed in memory. Thus, different results were obtained that led to opposite conclusions.

Durgunoglu and Roediger (1987) suggested that the following specific factors play a role in determining the degree of interdependence or interaction between the nonverbal and the two verbal representational systems in bilinguals: (1) episodic versus semantic memory tasks (see Potter et al., 1984; Snodgrass, 1984); (2) concrete versus abstract materials (see Paivio, 1971; Paivio & Desrochers, 1980); and (3) data-driven versus conceptually driven processing (see Jacoby & Dallas, 1981; Madler, 1980); that is, tasks that require sequential memory versus tasks that call for concept formation and involve transformation of representations and meaning construction.

In addition, all the studies presented by Durgunoglu and Roediger (1987) used an experimental design, with laboratory control of conditions of tasks and stimuli that do not resemble the more qualitative natural conditions in which bilinguals represent and process knowledge. We propose later in this chapter a more natural problem-solving approach for studying the representation and processing of knowledge in bilinguals.

In summary, researchers studying knowledge representation have proposed various contradictory hypotheses and factors as causes for the different results and conclusions obtained in empirical studies. We clearly need a multidimensional perspective that integrates these different approaches in order to clarify how bilinguals represent and process knowledge in two linguistic and cultural systems.

The Mapping Process of Conceptual and Semantic Development

A third issue in the study of cognitive and language development in bilinguals has to do with the process of constructing nonverbal meanings and mapping them into verbal conceptual categories. This semantic process encompasses two traditional research problems: (1) the relationship of cognition, language, and culture and (2) the process of forming semantic categories.

The debate on the relationship between cognition and language in modern terms dates back to the mid-1950s. Five positions emerged that can be roughly characterized in the following statements:

1. Cognition is dependent on language (Whorf, 1956).
2. Language and cognition are independent of each other (Chomsky, 1957).
3. Language is dependent on prior cognitive development (in both a "strong" [Bloom, 1973; Macnamara, 1972; Sinclair-de-Zwart, 1969; Slobin, 1973; Piaget, 1970] and a "weak" hypothesis [Bowerman, 1976, 1977, 1985, 1988; Cromer, 1974, 1988; Furth, 1966; Karmiloff-Smith, 1985, Rice, 1980]).
4. Language and cognition share a common source and develop along parallel lines (Bates & MacWhinney, 1981).
5. Language and cognitive development interact with each other (Blanc, 1974; Gopnik & Mettzoff, 1984; Schlesinger, 1974, 1977; Wells, 1974).

The strong and weak cognition hypotheses will be reviewed in relation to conceptual and semantic development. The process of semantic category formation involves a close relationship between nonverbal and verbal conceptual categories, which can be measured through classification. Two general approaches to the explanation of semantic category formation are reviewed:

1. The traditional model, with two submodels:
   a. Strong cognition hypothesis (Anglin, 1975; Brown, 1958,1965; Bruner & Olver, 1963; Flavell, 1970; Furth, 1966; Inhelder & Piaget, 1964; Piaget, 1965, 1967; Sinclair-de-Zwart, 1969)
   b. Weak cognition hypotheses: semantic features hypothesis (Clark, 1977), semantic functional hypothesis (Nelson, 1974, 1977, 1983, 1987, 1988), and the semantic prototype hypothesis (Ijaz, 1978; Rosch & Mervis, 1975; Rosch, Mervis, Gray, Johnson, & Bayes-Braem, 1976)
2. The modern models, with two submodels:
   a. The constraint approach (Callanan, 1990; Gelman & Taylor, 1984; Macnamara, 1972; Markman, 1981; Markman & Hutchinson, 1984; Shipley, 1989; Waxman, 1990; Waxman & Gelman, 1986)
   b. The sociocultural content knowledge approach (Anderson, 1985; Matsuyama, 1983; Miller & Stigler, 1987; Palermo, 1983)

Traditional Model. *Strong Cognition Hypothesis.* Within the strong cognition hypothesis, language development is considered to be dependent on prior cognitive development. Piaget (1970) links the universality of expressed meanings, across children and across languages, to universally acquired cognitive concepts that have an origin deeper than and genetically prior to language. He held that nonverbal concepts are prerequisite for constructing internal objects of thought and that language is only part of the semiotic function (representational or symbolic). Thus, an elementary logic already exists in the motor-based concepts of infants that are yet neither verbal nor symbolic. Piaget stated that the preoperational child internalizes concepts in representational images. In contrast, the operational child uses logic for transforming representational images into operations and reversible groupings. According to Piaget, the semiotic function partially includes the figurative aspects of knowledge (i.e., perception, imitation, drawing, and pictorial representation in mental imagery) and language. However, language has a different status within the semiotic function; it is only partly figurative as it is a representational activity of mapping nonverbal concepts already constructed into linguistic devices. Thus, language is also semantic, because it attempts to transform reality in the process of mapping nonverbal into verbal representations.

One of the earliest researchers to attempt to test the strong cognitive hypothesis was Sinclair-de-Zwart (1969), who studied two groups of 5- to 7-year-old children: one preoperational group unable to attain the conservation concept, and the other an operational group able to attain the conservation concept. These two groups of children gave different verbal answers to class inclusion problems (e.g., the concepts of categories such as flowers and subcategories such as roses). Language differences between groups were attributed by Sinclair-de-Zwart to cognitive sources. The results of this study showed a relationship between linguistic and operational levels, but the direction of influence was not clear then, nor is it now. As part of the study, Sinclair-de-Zwart taught a group of younger subjects to use the verbal forms used by the older children. The operational level improved only in 10 percent of the children. She concluded that language does not seem to be the motor of operational evolution; rather, it is an instrument in the service of intelligence. For Sinclair-de-Zwart, "language" means "speech"; that is, language is the use of the linguistic system as a symbolic code for communication with grammatic and syntactic rules. Sinclair (personal communication with Gonzalez, May 1990) still held this view of the relationship between cognition and language (used with the connotation of "speech") during the early 1990s. For her, language remained solely a symbolic expression of deeper abstract conceptual operations. Nor did she accept that the relationship between cognition and language could be stated or studied. As an example, she mentioned that the class inclusion problem cannot be explained because of the influence of linguistic biases over the abstract classification systems. Semantics, she pointed out, is an area about which researchers should be cautious because of the interference of language on the study of cognition. However, Sinclair-de-Zwart's study was the first evidence for the weak cognition hypothesis that generated variations of the traditional model and new models for exploring the cause-and-effect relation between cognition and language (i.e., mapping nonverbal on verbal concepts).

Following Sinclair-de-Zwart, other authors (e.g., Macnamara, 1972; Slobin, 1973) proposed that children first learn meanings and later map meaning into language. Bloom (1973) proposed that object permanence is a prerequisite for stable word meanings. Bruner and Olver (1963) and Inhelder and Piaget (1964) presented similar evidence based primarily on grouping experiments. These authors used as instructions, "Put things together that go together," to show that younger children classify objects in terms of thematic groupings (i.e., nontaxonomic criteria), in contrast to adults who classify taxonomically (i.e., showing class inclusion and forming categories and subcategories). According to Inhelder and Piaget, young children failed to solve classification problems because they were unable to differentiate the intention (abstract and conceptual class properties) from the extension of a class (the concrete material from the real-world experiences such as properties or parts).

Traditional open-ended methods for assessing the formation of semantic categories have been criticized in three general areas:

1. The nonverbal stimuli used, which have typically been concrete objects classifiable only in terms of taxonomic levels and were related to sociocultural rather than to natural semantic categories.
2. The verbal questions used, which were ambiguous and unnatural.
3. Failure to consider the influence of the children's language proficiency level on their verbal explanations of their nonverbal classifications.

In relation to the last criticism, Piaget (1965) asserted that knowledge of "language" per se plays only a minor role in the mastery of hierarchical classifications. Sinclair-de-Zwart (1969) attributed most difficulties in the children's verbal answers in tasks of classification of semantic categories to cognitive sources. However, Sinclair-de-Zwart (1969) considered "language" to be only a symbolic code for communication. Actually, what the Genevan group considered "language" is in more modern terms "speech"—the concrete use of a denotative system independent of the more abstract conceptual and deeper connotative meaning of terms.

Weak Cognition Hypothesis. A reconsideration of the relationship of cognition, language, and culture in processing terms (from the perspective of the weak cognition hypothesis) leads to a reconsideration of the effect of language development on cognition. Cromer (1974, 1988) and Rice (1980) suggested that cognition accounts for meanings, but not for the way those meanings are mapped into linguistic representations. Cromer (1974) showed that children who had already acquired a linguistic way of encoding a particular meaning subsequently learned other, more complex linguistic devices for expressing the same meaning independent of changes in cognition. Other authors (e.g., Oller, 1997, personal communication) believe that a change in linguistic form also brings a difference in meaning in "some subtle way," and so also a change in cognitive processing and representational systems.

Karmiloff-Smith (1985) suggested that language may be the privileged area in which the following cognitive reorganizational processes are activated: (1) conceptualization or constructing possible denotata, (2) semantization or connecting language and the mental world, and (3) mapping or relating form and meaning. Bowerman (1976, 1977, 1985, 1988) posited that both semantic linguistic structure and children's nonlinguistic predispositions for categorizing contribute to the language learner's organization of meaning. She proposed that languages select and combine certain categorical oppositions from among all possible ways the human cognition can categorize experiences. Bowerman considered this selection a system of semantic organization that often differs markedly across languages. An example of such a difference across languages is that, unlike English speakers, Spanish speakers do have to worry about the influence of the *ser–estar* continuum, whereas for the English language, the single verb "to be" suffices (see Chapter 6 in this book). Working out how the semantic linguistic structure and children's nonlinguistic categorizations interact remains a complex problem confronting researchers today.

Semantic Features and Semantic Functional Hypotheses. A weak cognition hypothesis arose that took into account the influence of sociocultural factors. It accepted that cognition accounts for linguistic meanings, but at the same time the sociocultural environment influences the construction of nonverbal meanings and their mapping into words. According to Oller (1995, 1996), in the mid- and late 1800s, before the onset of modern cognitive psychology, Charles S. Peirce dealt with the relationship of language use, abstract representations, and true narrative representations (that is, the relationship of the three kinds of linguistic schemata: formal, abstract, and content). True narrative representations deal with the daily life experiences within a specific sociocultural environment, called by Peirce content schemata (in Oller, 1995). With the onset of cognitive psychology during the 1960s, it was Furth (1966) who first took into account the sociocultural environment as an intervening variable in the relation between nonverbal and verbal cognition. Moreover, within the cognitive psychology framework, Brown (1973), Clark (1973, 1977), and Nelson (1974, 1977) argued that it is the child's a priori conceptual knowledge that determines the first meanings for words and that the sociocultural environment is important to cognitive and language development. Clark (1973) presented a semantic feature hypothesis on how children use their first words for expressing perceptual similarities among objects that they have already constructed nonverbally. Nelson (1974) challenged Clark's ideas, proposing a complex model of functional core concepts based on thematic relations (event structures and scripts).

Clark (1973) and Nelson (1974) differed in their positions of how children map meanings into words (perceptual attributes versus function) and the developmental patterns that they present when learning a language. In spite of the differences, the two positions also hold two assumptions in common:

1. Children invent their own categories.
2. Nonlinguistic and semantic concepts are defined by common attributes.

Nelson (1983) also pointed out the limitations of Piagetian theory in not considering language as a sociocultural representation. She proposed that the dynamic sociocultural-linguistic environment supports the acquisition of more complex cultural and semantic knowledge, and that language is an abstract symbolic tool for transforming such knowledge.

Semantic Prototype Hypothesis. Rosch's position (Rosch & Mervis, 1975; Rosch et al., 1976) differs from the strong cognition hypothesis in three respects:

1. Semantic categories are determined by the correlational structure of attributes of real-world objects that people use to construct verbal and nonverbal hierarchical taxonomies with different levels of abstraction (i.e., basic level [common labels that people use to refer to objects] and nonbasic levels [superordinate, intermediate, and subordinate categories]).
2. Semantic categories are coded in terms of prototypes (superexemplars with internal representation of a central tendency that reflects the redundancy structure of a whole category).
3. Principles of semantic organization are universal, although their content varies across cultures.

Rosch's model was influenced by Brown's view (1977) of children's concept formation at an intermediate or basic taxonomic level. Rosch and colleagues (1976) claimed that these basic categories are stable across development, individuals, and cultures and that cultural and linguistic categorization systems differ at the two nonbasic levels. In relation to universality, Ijaz (1978) found that the prototypicality principle forms the basis of semantic category structure in all languages and influences the degree of difficulty in word meaning acquisition. Ijaz's finding that nonbasic semantic concepts constitute language-specific combinations of differentially weighted semantic dimensions may account in part for the different linguistic classifications of semantic concepts across languages. Rosch's model focused on the universal real-world correlation structure for manmade and natural objects for both comprehension and production, which was expanded to the nonbasic level categories by the constraint approach.

Modern Models. *Constraint Approach.* The constraint approach (Markman, 1981; Markman & Hutchinson, 1984; Waxman & Gelman, 1986) provides an explanation based on principles and constraints that children and adults use when they learn new word meanings. Different researchers have proposed different constraints such as the taxonomic constraint (Markman & Hutchinson, 1984; Waxman & Gelman, 1986) and the principle of mutual exclusivity (Markman & Watchel, 1988; Merriman & Bowman, 1989). The origins of the constraints can be innate or be induced from early language experience. The strong form of this model would hold that the constraints on word learning can help children learn new categories given a novel word. The weak form of the proposal would hold that children use the constraint to link a new word to a familiar categorical relation. This weak form is different from Whorf's (1956) linguistic determinism in that the former assumes that children who can acquire any language must share similar constraints on possible meanings for linguistic forms and that children would form categories without exposure to language.

Markman and Hutchinson (1984) proposed that children would shift their attention from thematic to taxonomic relations when more meaningful objects are used, if a label is provided. This approach uses novel variations of the linguistic stimuli presented at basic (i.e., the common labels that people use in everyday life for referring to objects) and nonbasic (i.e., the labels used for naming classes that can be at a superordinate, intermediate, or subordinate levels) level categories. Furthermore, Waxman and Gelman (1986) pointed to the contrast between children's ability to access superordinate relations in word learning and the difficulty in accessing superordinate relations in classification tasks. They explained this contradiction as a methodological problem in the open-ended traditional tasks, where children create thematic or other kinds of nontaxonomic relations due to the unnatural stimuli and verbal instructions used. According to Markman and Hutchinson (1984), the match-to-sample task (for which the instructions are, "See this? This is a sud. Find another sud that is the same as this sud") that is used in the constraint approach is more similar to a real-life situation where children are learning new words.

Several authors from the constraint approach (e.g., Markman, 1981; Waxman, 1990) have suggested the idea of universality (i.e., common concepts across cultures, subcultures, languages, and development) in relation to basic-level semantic categories of natural and cultural referents. However, it seems likely that objects belonging to basic-level semantic categories can also differ across natural and cultural environments. For instance, in English, the noun "berry" is at a basic level; however, the label *baya* in Spanish is not used frequently because the few berries that exist in the natural environment of Spanish-speaking countries have a nonbasic label that does not show the name of the category (e.g., *la fresa* [strawberry], *la mora* [blackberry], *la frambuesa* [raspberry]). Thus, the fact that the basic-level semantic category *baya* ("berry") in the Spanish language is seldom used is related to the nonexistence of the category suffix at the nonbasic-level semantic category (subcategories). This example illustrates the relationship between symbolic meanings of linguistic conventions made by the cultural community with the underlying linguistic structures and markers, and the semantic category formation at both the basic and nonbasic levels.

Another constraint provided by Markman and Hutchinson (1984) is the principle of mutual exclusivity, which hypothesizes that when children learn new words, they assume that nouns refer to mutually exclusive object categories. Au and Glusman (1990) conducted a series of experiments for exploring whether the principle of mutual exclusivity held for nouns across taxonomic categories, as well as across languages in children and adults. They found that monolinguals and bilinguals accept two names for the same object if the names clearly come from two different languages. That is, the metalinguistic knowledge that an object can have different labels in different languages helps monolinguals and bilinguals to avoid the mutual exclusivity principle. Thus, mutual exclusivity is not entirely useful in word learning because it is critical for children to learn when not to make this assumption across levels of a hierarchy and across languages.

In conclusion, children acquiring two languages will have the opportunity to gain metalinguistic awareness of similarities and differences in sociocultural conceptualizations underlying different labels across languages (see Gonzalez, 1991, 1994, 1995, for a broader discussion). Thus, the study of bilingual children may be useful for separating linguistic and conceptual factors in the intricate and subtle relationship between conceptual and semantic development. This is because different languages may or may not coincide in the specific taxonomic hierarchical level of object categories. It may be that these differences in the semantic conceptualization of the same object categories in different languages, such as in Spanish and English, will result in differences in bilingual children's verbal and nonverbal representational systems.

Sociocultural Content Knowledge Approach. Some authors (e.g., Miller & Stigler, 1987; Palermo, 1983) have outlined the important influence of sociocultural factors on concept development in terms of content and domain knowledge. Palermo (1983) suggested that children construct idiosyncratic meanings for the traditional classification tasks according to the context and their prior sociocultural experiences.

Some studies have focused on the two types of schemata described by Anderson (1985):

1. Organization by natural categories that are based on real-world phenomena, such as classification of plants, animals, minerals, quantities, and other aspects of the natural world
2. Organization by events, such as personal recollection of event sequences and the discourse organization of a story

For instance, Matsuyama (1983) showed that study scripts are influenced by cultural styles and social cognition in bilinguals. He concluded that the way in which declarative knowledge is organized and stored in memory suggests that concepts related to natural categories may be easier to transfer to the second language than are domain-specific cultural concepts.

In conclusion, there are different traditional and more modern models trying to solve the problem of how nonlinguistic meanings are mapped into linguistic forms. However, researchers are still discovering different multidimensional factors affecting this complex problem. Researchers are proposing holistic perspectives that include cultural and linguistic factors affecting the process of forming semantic categories. Thus, researchers from different models and approaches are conducting cross-cultural and multicultural studies in which bilingual children and adults are natural laboratories for gaining understanding on semantic category formation.

THE PROPOSED TRIPLE-INTERACTIONAL MODEL OF COGNITIVE, LINGUISTIC, AND CULTURAL VARIABLES

We present a multidimensional model that explains cognitive and language development in bilinguals and encompasses cognitive, cultural, and linguistic factors (see Gonzalez, 1991, 1995 for an extended explanation; and see Gonzalez, 1994 for a summary). Consider an example that is relevant to the influence of cognitive, cultural, and linguistic variables on the problem of knowledge representation (see Gonzalez, 1995, for an extended description of this and other examples). In his book, *Thought and Language*, Vygotsky (1962a) gave an example of the influence of sociocultural meanings on the linguistic structures and markers of different languages. He wrote about literal and grammatical translations of literary pieces from French and German into Russian. In the original languages, these literary pieces used grammatical feminine and masculine nouns referring to insects and trees as literary figures in order to express affective meanings. In Vygotsky's examples, the literal meaning was changed in the translation in order to convey the masculine or feminine gender required to communicate the symbolic sociocultural connotations of the metaphor used in the original versions of the literary pieces.

It is clear that linguistic structures and markers do not always correspond across languages, which may lead to a change in the symbolic meaning that a word connotes for a sociocultural community and the more abstract nonverbal semantic categories that gender for animate (e.g., animals) and inanimate (e.g., trees) objects can denote. Thus, a metaphor used in one language may have different sociocultural representations if it is translated literally to another language because of different underlying symbolic meanings and semantic categories. We propose that a multidimensional model that integrates cognitive, linguistic, and cultural factors will shed light on how bilingual children construct concepts and develop meanings in first and second languages. We do not know if bilingual children construct one or two representational systems when forming semantic categories in two languages. In this model we propose that the construction of representational systems is an active process because bilingual children develop cognitively through interiorization, transformation, and dual conceptual representations in verbal and nonverbal systems in the first and the second language. Thus the process of verbal and nonverbal concept formation in both languages can vary depending on the conceptual complexity and sociocultural context of use of the linguistic structures. Any language carries with it sociocultural symbolic meanings that can be reflected or absent in the linguistic structures of the language. Languages differ in what aspects of meaning they represent directly in their structures, and this fact influences the formation of symbolic meanings and semantic categories.

We selected gender as the linguistic structure to study in this triple-interactional model because the Romance languages have many markers for gender at the lexical level, where English has few or none. Note that gender is just one of the linguistic structures and markers that could be studied as an example of the influence of conceptual, linguistic, and cultural factors on conceptual and semantic development. In the triple-interactional model, it is hypothesized that in a bilingual child, whether the abstract categories that constitute nonverbal representations in both languages are common or unique depends on the similarities in symbolic meanings of linguistic conventions made by the sociocultural community, which sometimes are represented without the corresponding linguistic structures and markers. For instance, the English language does not have markers for the linguistic gender of inanimate objects, but some inanimate objects have symbolic gender, such as the noun "ship," which has a feminine cultural connotation. By contrast, the corresponding linguistic structures and markers sometimes do represent the symbolic meanings. For instance, in the English language, there are markers for the linguistic gender of animate referents such as people (e.g., "man" and "woman") and animals (e.g., "hen" and "rooster"). The Spanish language also has markers for the linguistic gender of animate referents such as people (e.g., *la mujer* and *el hombre*) and animals (e.g., *la gallina* and *el gallo*). However, the Spanish language also has linguistic gender markers for inanimate referents, such as food (e.g., *la tortilla* has the *-a* marker, which makes the noun feminine at a linguistic level). Whether a specific concept would be represented with a linguistic structure and marker and its corresponding symbolic meaning might depend on the cultural value that it has and might reflect the linguistic historical-social process.

In the triple-interactional model, it is proposed that the child learning a second language constructs concepts in three domains and at three different levels of representation:

1. Cognitive, with nonverbal, abstract categories, at the level of representation.
2. Symbolic, with sociocultural nonverbal representations that correspond to meanings of linguistic conventions made by the sociocultural community for different referents, at the level of representation.
3. Linguistic, with instantiations at one level of verbal representation.

There is no clear division between cognitive (nonverbal), symbolic, and linguistic (verbal) representations due to the common underlying instantiations and processes of representations that connect them. The cognitive level is operationalized as the hierarchical object level of the semantic categories (nonbasic [superordinate, intermediate, subordinate] and basic [everyday labels for objects]). The symbolic level is operationalized as the animate and inanimate object referents that are based on natural (physical) and arbitrary (linguistic and sociocultural conventions) gender, respectively. The cultural level is operationalized as the characteristics of the linguistic structures and markers of both languages (i.e., words that are familiar—similar, different, and no translation cases; and unfamiliar—translation and no translation cases). "Translation cases" are words that have literal parallel meanings in different languages. "No translation cases" are borrowed words adapted to the linguistic rules of another language (e.g., *tortilla* loses its linguistic gender when used as a borrowed word in English). The interaction of nonverbal conceptual development and semantic category formation is operationalized as verbal and nonverbal classification tasks. These include labeling, defining, nonverbal classification, verbal justification of the nonverbal classification, and category clues (for a description of these tasks, see Gonzalez, 1995; and Chapters 7, 8, and 9 in this book).

Moreover, it is important to differentiate abstract and semantic categories. Abstract categories are defined in the triple-interactional model as nonverbal symbolic representations that are instantiated in common structures and markers in the first and the second language. Semantic categories, on the other hand, are operationalized as verbal, symbolic, sociocultural representations that are instantiated in different linguistic structures and markers in the first and the second languages. This distinction has been made by other researchers as well. For instance, Bowerman (1988) considered the relationship between linguistic and nonlinguistic representational systems in terms of universal and language-specific semantic categories. Flavell (1970), in relation to the formation of concepts, pointed out that the difference between concepts and content knowledge was influenced by cultural and linguistic factors, as well as by classes or universal abstract objects of thought.

The triple-interactional model proposes that bilingual children may develop abstract categories better in one language than in the other due to the duplicity of the symbolic meanings of linguistic conventions made by the sociocultural community. If the linguistic structure and markers and/or symbolic meanings of linguistic conventions made by the sociocultural community exist in both languages, then the child may instantiate the nonverbal representation of the first into the second language (i.e., an assimilation process). In contrast, if the linguistic structure and markers and/or symbolic meanings of linguistic conventions made by the sociocultural community exist only in the second language, then the child might have to construct a new nonverbal representation that constitutes a new abstract category (i.e., an accommodation process).

These two cases are considered general conceptual learning processes, from which derive six cases of combinations of similarities and differences among conceptual, cultural, and linguistic factors (see Gonzalez, 1991, 1995, for an extended explanation of these six cases). The first derived case refers to equivalent (word-for-word translations) linguistic structures from one language into the other (e.g., "cow" and "bull" in English become *vaca* and *toro* in Spanish, two different words reflecting the existence of two physical genders). The second, third, and fourth derived cases are situations in which linguistic structures and markers differ from one language into the other. That is, there is no one-to-one word translation (e.g., "cat" in English is a neutral word that has no linguistic gender marker; in Spanish it becomes *la gata* or *el gato*, showing a feminine and masculine linguistic gender that reflects the physical gender of the animal). The last two derived cases refer to borrowed words, which are instantiated and adapted from one language into the other language's structures and markers (e.g., *la tortilla* in Spanish with a feminine conventional linguistic gender becomes "the tortilla" in English, losing its original article and disregarding the "a" ending that show feminine linguistic gender in Spanish). Thus, these six derived cases of combinations of similarities and differences among conceptual, cultural, and linguistic factors illustrate that the possibilities for contrasts and combinations of the first and second languages' semantic categories, symbolic meanings, and linguistic structures and markers are complex.

The model proposes a triple interaction among cognitive, linguistic, and cultural factors in the process of verbal and nonverbal concept representation given by abstract and semantic categories, which is related to general and gender-based classifications. The model proposes that children construct one representational system for abstract categories that are represented nonverbally and symbolically by the culture, and instantiated verbally and similarly across languages. At the same time, idiosyncratic linguistic structures and markers of each language, their sociocultural meanings for linguistic conventions, and their related underlying abstract and semantic conceptualizations influence verbal and nonverbal cognitive development differently across cultures and languages. The first representational system is common to both languages as the verbal, symbolic, and nonverbal representations coincide at the abstract level, and it is fairly well related to the children's language development in first and second languages and nonverbal conceptual development in both languages. This first representational system is nonverbal, abstract, and universal. Although it is abstract, the actual perceptual images and later conceptual networks have been established based on direct experience. This first conceptual representational system will be universal because there are commonalities between physical and cultural realities in which languages were developed. These common experiences are abstracted and transformed into conceptual networks by speakers of different languages. In contrast, the second representational system is specific to the Spanish language for the verbal, gender-based classification system, which is highly related to the language developmental level in Spanish and moderately related to the verbal conceptual level for the Spanish language. This second system is verbal or semantic, and thus culturally and linguistically bound.

To summarize, the triple-interactional model proposes that one universal and abstract representational system will be constructed when nonverbal, symbolic, and verbal concepts coincide in both languages. In contrast, two culturally bound and semantic representational systems will be constructed when nonverbal, symbolic, and verbal concepts are different across languages. In terms of the relationship between cognition and language, cognitive development precedes language development as a universal process of concept construction. That is, the universal and abstract representational system precedes the semantic representational system, which is linguistically and culturally bound.

The triple-interactional model has theoretical and educationally applied implications. At the theoretical level, the model explains how bilingual children construct nonverbal abstract and semantic concepts in first and second languages. At the educationally applied level, the model has as a product a qualitative assessment method (called QUEST, the Qualitative Use of English and Spanish Tasks; see Gonzalez, 1991, 1994, 1995; Gonzalez, Bauerle, & Felix-Holt, 1994; Gonzalez, Brusca-Vega, & Yawkey, 1997; and Chapters 7, 8, and 9 in this book) and an educational program (see Gonzalez et al., 1997) for evaluating and stimulating bilingual children's verbal and nonverbal conceptual development. Thus, this model can address the theoretical problem of how similar or different linguistic structures and sociocultural symbolic meanings in first and second languages influence bilingual children's cognitive and language development. This theoretical problem is related to a major educational and political issue currently: whether being bilingual is an advantage or a disadvantage for cognitive development and whether bilingual education has a positive effect on intelligence.

This model can also address the educational problem of lack of valid and reliable assessment instruments for bilingual children. The diagnosis of bilingual children's nonverbal intelligence and language development using standardized tests underestimates their nonverbal and verbal developmental levels. When these children are diagnosed using classification tasks of their verbal and nonverbal performance, they show a normal or above-normal verbal and nonverbal conceptual development (Gonzalez, 1991, 1994, 1995). Thus, standardized tests and qualitative measures lead to different classifications of children's cognitive and linguistic abilities. As a result, different conclusions will be reached when making a differential diagnosis regarding genuine disabilities and disabling conditions, giftedness, and the normal first and second language development.

THE INFLUENCE OF COGNITIVE, LINGUISTIC, AND CULTURAL FACTORS ON THE CONCEPTUAL AND SEMANTIC DEVELOPMENT OF BILINGUALS

Controversy has emerged from the literature on the relationship between conceptual and semantic development in bilinguals and monolinguals from different epistemological perspectives. This section looks at six major areas of controversy:

1. The direction of the mapping process between conceptual and semantic development
2. The interaction of verbal and nonverbal representational systems
3. Contradictory findings related to methodological differences in classification tasks
4. Problems with operational definitions of representational and mapping processes
5. Representational systems as structures versus category formation as a process
6. The influence of sociocultural factors on conceptual and semantic development

These areas of controversy are related because mapping is considered a categorization process that leads to different levels in the representation of meaning into images, symbols, words, and/or abstract concepts. As a result, problems with operational definitions of mapping and representational processes arise.

The Direction of the Mapping Process Between Conceptual and Semantic Development

The study of semantic category formation has been approached from three different perspectives that focus on the direction of the mapping process between conceptual and semantic development: (1) the influence of bilingualism on cognition; (2) the interaction between verbal and nonverbal representational systems, at the structural level; and (3) the mapping of nonverbal concepts into linguistic forms, at the process level.

The study of the relationship between cognition and language from a bilingual education perspective leads to the discussion of applied questions—

for example, Is bilingualism an advantage or a disadvantage for the child's intelligence? Are standardized intelligence tests culturally and linguistically biased for bilingual children? What are the major methodological flaws of studies relating bilingualism and intelligence?

The weight of the evidence supports the advantage of additive bilingualism in children in terms of increased mental flexibility, concept formation, creativity, and metalinguistic awareness. Historically, since the 1920s the direction of the mapping process between conceptual and semantic development has been studied from the perspective of advantages and disadvantages of bilingualism. From the perspective of educational psychology, the study of the direction of the mapping process between conceptual and semantic development in monolinguals has led to a debate since the 1950s. Within educational psychology, five major positions for the relationship between cognition and language have been proposed, all focusing on structures rather than the underlying semantic processes. On the other hand, the semantic process of mapping nonlinguistic meaning in linguistic forms has been studied within educational psychology in the literature on semantic category formation. The study of semantic category formation processes began with the study of monolinguals, but is beginning to include bilinguals as resources for shedding light on the intricate relationship between conceptual and semantic development. Thus, the study of semantic category formation processes is including not only cognitive and linguistic factors, but also cultural factors as important influences.

The direction of the mapping process between conceptual and semantic development can be enriched by considering how bilinguals construct nonverbal and verbal concepts. Bilinguals are natural laboratories for the interaction of cognitive, linguistic, and cultural factors and its influence on conceptual and semantic development. Different models within educational psychology studying verbal and nonverbal representational systems, and conceptual and semantic development have converged on the study of the process of becoming bilingual. At the same time, models within bilingual education have traditionally studied the relationship between intelligence and language development in bilinguals. Thus, research questions of a theoretical nature within educational psychology, and applied and psychometric issues within bilingual education, have converged on the study of the process of becoming bilingual. Different holistic models are being developed within educational psychology and bilingual education; these include cognitive, linguistic, and cultural factors that interact in the mapping process of nonverbal concepts into semantic categories. However, there are contradictory hypotheses that lead to different results and conclusions because of major differences in epistemological perspectives, methodologies, definitions, and applications between educational psychology and bilingual education.

The triple-interactional model has theoretical implications for educational psychology as well as theoretical and practical implications for bilingual education. This model has a multidisciplinary perspective that includes two languages and two cultures as new variables for enhancing the state of the art of the study of the relationship of cognitive and linguistic processes. In addition, bilingual education can be enriched by the triple-interactional model, a robust psycholinguistic model that explains cognitive and linguistic development in children who are immersed in a bicognitive, bilingual, and bicultural environment. This model also has practical implications for the field of bilingual education as it has as a product a new qualitative assessment method (QUEST) and an educational program that are currently being used for making diagnostic, placement, and instructional decisions, with very good results (see Gonzalez, Bauerle, & Felix-Holt, 1994; Gonzalez et al., 1997; Chapters 7, 8, and 9 in this book).

The Interaction of Verbal and Nonverbal Representational Systems

In relation to representational systems, it appears that the process of concept construction is dependent on languages. Researchers are still trying to understand and explain the complex interaction of verbal and nonverbal representational systems. Early models within the two traditional hypotheses from the mediation theory of semantics (Lambert et al., 1958) proposed that the construction of one or two representational systems was related to idiosyncratic language learning experiences in bilinguals. That is, they proposed that language learning history will lead to compound or coordinate types of bilingualism, differentiated in terms of having one or two representational systems. Later, an alternative bilingual dual-code model, proposed by Paivio (1983; Paivio & Desrochers, 1980; Paivio & Lambert, 1981), attempted to model the influence of types of concepts (i.e., concrete and abstract) and characteristics of linguistic structures (i.e., equivalents) in both languages on nonverbal representational systems.

This bilingual dual-code model can be related to the triple-interactional model. That is, different types of concepts (e.g., concrete, abstract, animate, and inanimate) lead to different or similar semantic underlying conceptualizations, and thus to one universal or two representational systems that are culturally and linguistically bound. The latter hypothesis is related to studies using the lexical decision paradigm (e.g., Palij, 1980), which indicated that bilingual cognition may in fact have features of language intermixture and separation independent from the language learning experiences, but in different areas of the cognitive system because of the influence of cultural and linguistic factors. Thus, cultural content knowledge that is represented similarly or differently across languages and cultures makes a difference in how these symbolic and abstract concepts will be represented verbally and nonverbally by bilinguals.

More recently, Clark and Paivio (1991) proposed a modified version of the dual-code theory suggesting that semantically equivalent words in different languages are encoded by distinct verbal and imaginal representations that do not converge on a single abstract code. These discrete verbal representations for different languages can be interpreted as semantic categories that are culturally and linguistically bound. However, as proposed by various models and approaches, such as the weak cognition hypothesis with the influence of sociocultural (e.g., Clark, 1973; Nelson, 1988) and linguistic factors (e.g., Bowerman, 1988), and the triple-interactional model (Gonzalez, 1991, 1994, 1995), common nonverbal and verbal representational systems can be constructed by a bilingual when conceptual, symbolic, and linguistic categories coincide across languages. This representational system would be universal, abstract, and nonverbal.

There is an increasing interest in the influence of sociocultural factors on the representation of verbal and nonverbal knowledge. The triple-interactional model that we propose suggests that each bilingual will represent concepts nonverbally—as abstract universal categories—and also verbally—as linguistically and culturally bound semantic categories. This first abstract representational system will still be based on direct experiences with the world, which tend to be common across physical and cultural realities. These common experiences are abstracted and transformed into conceptual networks by speakers of different languages. As a result, one universal representational system will be constructed when nonverbal, symbolic, and verbal concepts are parallel in both languages; two representational systems will be constructed when nonverbal, symbolic, and verbal concepts are different between languages (as findings from previous studies show; see Gonzalez, 1991, 1994, 1995). Thus, the representational process is more complex than previous researchers thought because of the interaction of multiple factors (stemming from cognitive, cultural, and linguistic variables) that influence the representation of knowledge in bilinguals. However, the issue of the interaction of verbal and nonverbal representations in bilinguals still requires further research to understand.

Methodological Differences in Classification Tasks

The categorization process has evolved within different models and approaches. Classification was traditionally studied within the strong cognition hypothesis model (Piaget, 1970; Piaget & Inhelder, 1947; Sinclair-de-Zwart, 1969) using production tasks with ambiguous open-ended verbal instructions ("Put together all the objects that go together"), and concrete objects that could be categorized only at a superordinate level (e.g., one banana, one apple, one orange for the category *fruit*). More recently, the prototype

(Rosch, et al., 1976; Ijaz, 1978) and constraint models (Callanan, 1990; Markman, 1981; Waxman, 1990) have used as a research methodology production and comprehension tasks where subjects are given specific verbal clues (English verbal labels or novel labels such as Japanese or nonsense syllables) and instructions that are more neutral and clear. That is, the subject is given concrete objects that can be categorized at different hierarchical levels (superordinate, basic level, intermediate, and subordinate).

Due to the different levels of cognitive processes tapped by the tasks used by the traditional and more recent models, results from research studies have been contradictory. There is evidence that the level of the cognitive variables, such as basic and nonbasic items, have made a difference in the conceptual nonverbal development of bilingual children. When children have been given basic and nonbasic stimuli, as in the characteristic-attribute model (e.g., Ijaz, 1978; Rosch, et al., 1976) and the constraint approach (e.g., Gelman & Taylor, 1984; Markman, 1981; Waxman, 1990), they have constructed subcategories with the nonbasic stimuli. Thus, as the constraint approach states, nonbasic semantic categories lead to a continuous process across developmental levels. In addition, Gonzalez (1991, 1994, 1995) found that kindergarten and first-grade bilingual Hispanic children who were given basic and nonbasic stimuli attained a concrete level (i.e., using categories and subcategories) in nonverbal conceptual classification tasks. These findings can be explained as the result of the control for methodological flaws of traditional Piagetian classification studies (Inhelder & Piaget, 1964; Piaget, 1964, 1967), in which children were given only basic-level stimuli. That is, the evidence in the literature suggests that young children, who are in the preoperational stage according to Piagetian theory, can form taxonomic categories if they are given basic and nonbasic stimuli.

Previous results obtained within the traditional paradigms are now being questioned because young children could not form taxonomic categories due to methodological limitations in earlier studies. Thus, theories stating that young children could not form taxonomic level concepts, such as the traditional Piagetian classification studies (Inhelder & Piaget, 1964; Piaget, 1964, 1967) and the weak cognition hypothesis with the influence of sociocultural factors (Clark, 1973; Nelson, 1988), have probably been tapping different categorization processes due to the use of different types or taxonomic levels of stimuli.

Problems with Operational Definitions of Representational and Mapping Processes

The controversy of mapping as a categorization process that leads to different levels of representation has generated a problem within and between the different disciplines. This problem stems from the absence of unique operational definitions for the constructs being studied (e.g., image, symbol, concept). This common problem in cognitive psychology is related to the characteristics of the phenomena being studied. One source of the problem in understanding how children represent knowledge is related to the different definitions of different authors. Different theoretical models emphasize different characteristics of the nature of knowledge or concepts, such as structures (Piaget, 1965), abstractness (Bruner & Olver, 1963; Flavell, 1970), utility (Brown, 1958), function (Clark, 1973), generality (Nelson, 1977; Rescorla, 1976), attributes (Rosch et al., 1976), categorical opposition (Bowerman, 1988), constraints (Markman, 1981; Waxman & Gelman, 1986), and prior cultural content knowledge (Miller & Stigler, 1987; Palermo, 1983). Because of these different definitions, the study of conceptual representational structures and mapping processes is ambiguous and confusing. How the different theoretical approaches relate to one another is unclear.

There are important differences in the epistemological assumptions concerning the nature of conceptual and semantic development: both mediational-constructivistic theories and innate constraint approaches are given a prominent place in the literature of cognitive psychology. For instance, many current theories in cognitive psychology assume that the individual constructs operations, concepts, or schemes that serve as cognitive tools for constructing new knowledge (e.g., Piagetian theory [Piaget, 1964, 1965, 1967], schema theory [Anderson & Pearson, 1984], and information processing theory [Lindsay & Norman, 1977]). In contrast, the constraint approach assumes the presence of innate default options, such as the principle of mutual exclusivity (e.g., see Au & Glusman, 1990; Merriman & Bowman, 1989), as the most important factor for semantic category formation and language acquisition of novel labels. However, as Au and Glusman pointed out, when mutual exclusivity is combined with novel labels referring to different object levels in a hierarchy (such as the superordinate term "animal" and the subordinate term "dogs"), more research studies need to be designed in order to find out whether results reflect a mutual exclusivity assumption about word meanings or merely differences in categorization skills.

In spite of different epistemological assumptions underlying mediational-constructivistic theories and the constraint approach, the same traditional question arises: How do children map words into concepts? Vice versa, the intricate relationship between conceptual and language development motivates researchers to try to resolve the apparent dilemma from different epistemological views that define mapping and representational processes differently.

Representational Systems as Structures Versus Category Formation as a Process

Although mediational-constructivist theories and innate constraint approaches hold different epistemological assumptions, they also hold underlying commonalities. As in the case of researchers studying nonverbal and verbal representational systems, researchers from the constructivist and constraint models are beginning to converge in the study of the influence of sociocultural factors on representational and mapping processes. Furthermore, both of these models within cognitive psychology are now studying bilinguals, who are influenced by two languages and two cultures for the formation of concepts. Across different theories and approaches, there are common underlying conceptual similarities that have been discussed at different levels (i.e., performance, structures, and processes), using different terminologies and methodologies, thus generating different applications. That is, across interdisciplinary theoretical approaches, there are common underlying conceptual similarities among what seem to be, at first glance, differences. Those underlying conceptual similarities are subsumed in the discipline of cognitive psychology as it studies cognitive structures and processes for the transformation of external objects (from the natural and cultural environment) into internal images, concepts, schemes, and hierarchical structures or networks, which are then expressed through verbal (language) and nonverbal representational systems in external behaviors (gestures, imitation, play, drawing). This transformation in conceptual similarities despite original physical or cultural differences, apparent at the perceptual level in the form of images or at the symbolic level in the form of cultural representations, is included in the first representational system of the triple-interactional model.

This transformation of external objects into internal mediational processes is what has been called by Karmiloff-Smith (1985) *cognitive reorganizational processes*, in which language generates (1) the construction of verbal and/or nonverbal representations and its connection with new or already existent nonverbal and/or verbal representations and (2) a mapping of these nonverbal and verbal representations with the corresponding linguistic forms. That is, the individual can re-represent or reorganize verbal and nonverbal representations at three different levels or stages (the discussion incorporates suggestions from Oller, personal communication, 1997):

1. At the perceptual or semiotic representational level, in the form of images and symbols, which are directly tied to physical and cultural experiences with the world.
2. At the semantic processes level, in the form of verbal and nonverbal logic conceptual relations, which are intermediate signs connected to both direct physical and cultural experiences with the world and to linguistic and symbolic meanings.
3. At the operational processes level, in the form of nonverbal logic concepts or hierarchical conceptual networks, which are abstractions or conceptual transformations of images and symbols into generalizations and rules.

The difficulty stems from the multidimensional characteristics that a concept can have, given by the influence of cultural and linguistic factors. Furthermore, the individual variations in meaning, representational verbal and nonverbal forms, accessibility of concepts, developmental stages, and the presence of two languages and cultures in bilinguals give concepts a peculiar complexity that no theory has yet been able to explain fully. Results of tests of the different theories are leading to a multidimensional interactional model in which cognitive, linguistic, and cultural factors interact in the mapping process of concepts into semantic categories. As a result, different terms used by different theories and approaches for naming constructs in educational psychology may in fact be just different labels for the same cognitive structures and processes at different levels of the transformational process.

The Influence of Sociocultural Factors on Conceptual and Semantic Development

Bilinguals offer a natural laboratory for studying the interaction of cognitive, linguistic, and cultural factors, because two cultures and languages influence their conceptual and semantic development. Other researchers too have pointed to the study of bilinguals for shedding light on basic issues in educational psychology. For instance, Schwanenflugel and Rey (1986) suggested that in order to understand the structure and processing of word meaning, it is important to study the representational process of the two languages in the bilingual lexicon. Hakuta (1988) also pointed out that although research on the relationship between cognition and language in second language learners is still quite limited (although see Brown, 1973; Ervin-Tripp, 1974; Hakuta, 1982; Lightbown, 1977; Rawen, 1986), available research evidence supports the efficacy of bilingual subjects for explaining the respective roles of cognitive and semantic development.

We think that the small number of research studies that focus on the importance of sociocultural and linguistic factors on cognitive development in bilinguals is related to the lack of consensus on the definitions of cognitive and linguistic knowledge processes. According to Alexander et al. (1991), how researchers explicitly or implicitly define constructs of cognitive and linguistic knowledge will influence their research. Researchers are still trying to impose their own general schemes derived from theories developed for monolinguals, with no consideration of how these models can be reformulated to encompass sociocultural aspects, such as the construction of meaning in bilinguals. Given that the process of conceptual and language development involves meaning construction, then including sociocultural variables in theoretical and applied research is a priority.

Moreover, theories of cognitive and language development generated for monolinguals cannot be directly applied in the case of bilingual children. We need to adapt or totally reconceptualize the models in order to include the more complex process of multidimensional interaction of two languages and cultures in bilingual children. That is, the specific sociocultural context of concept construction and mapping words into meaning varies for a monolingual and a bilingual child as they will sometimes represent the natural and social world events differently in the three domains—verbal, symbolic, and abstract—and other times the two languages and the two cultures may coincide. Thus, concept formation skills can be seen to transfer across languages (see Gonzalez, 1991, 1994, 1995). Learning the specific similarities and differences across languages and cultures is a case for conducting applied research. These applied studies would have the objective of reconceptualizing general models according to the specific characteristics of the cognitive, cultural, and linguistic development of bilingual children.

Conclusions

Different theoretical models are converging into a holistic and interactional model in which cognitive, linguistic, and sociocultural factors interact in the mapping process of nonverbal concepts into semantic categories. Different theoretical research issues from an educational psychology perspective have converged in the study of the process of becoming bilingual, such as the nature of verbal and nonverbal representational systems and the direction of the mapping process between conceptual and semantic development.

Traditionally, bilingual education researchers have studied the influence of bilingualism on cognition in the form of applied questions that now are converging in educational psychology. Although many studies have been conducted in the area of symbolic representation in bilinguals, the issue of whether bilinguals store knowledge in one or two systems is unknown. There is a general trend in recent work to a view positing an interdependence or interaction between the nonverbal and the two verbal representational systems in bilinguals. Researchers are realizing now that the issue is more complex than they had initially thought when conceptualizing the problem of knowledge representation, as they were mostly concerned with the representational structure in memory. Researchers studying knowledge representation have proposed various contradictory hypotheses and factors as causes for the different results and conclusions obtained. One possible reason for this is that the different retrieval demands of the tasks and stimuli used in the studies influenced the format of the representational systems accessed in memory. Because of this, different results were obtained that led to opposite conclusions. Thus, a multidimensional perspective that integrates these different approaches is needed for clarifying how bilinguals represent and process knowledge in two linguistic and cultural systems.

The explanation of the underlying semantic process of mapping nonlinguistic meaning in linguistic forms continues to be an issue of considerable interest. There are different traditional and more modern models trying to solve the problem of how meanings are mapped into words. However, researchers are still discovering different factors affecting this complex and multidimensional problem. Different models and approaches are now converging in holistic perspectives that include cultural and linguistic factors that affect the process of forming semantic categories. Thus, different models and approaches are now including cross-cultural and multicultural studies in which bilingual children and adults are natural laboratories for gaining understanding on semantic category formation.

Moreover, different applied research questions and psychometric issues in bilingual education have also converged on the study of the process of becoming bilingual, such as the study of:

1. Advantages and disadvantages on cognitive performance as an effect of first and second language learning
2. The effect of sociocultural and socioemotional processes on cognitive and metalinguistic processes resulting from learning two languages
3. Alternative assessments for bilingual children's cognitive and language development, and achievement levels taking into consideration cultural and linguistic differences

Although much of the research on bilingualism and bicognitivism is still in progress or has yet to be conducted, the weight of the evidence supports the positive influence of bilingualism on cognitive development. Research studies conducted by cognitive psychologists and bilingual educators have converged in the study of the process of becoming bilingual, but there are also differences in the approaches and underlying reasons for including bilingual subjects. Research studies conducted within the framework of cognitive psychology have used bilingual subjects as natural resources for solving methodological constraints of interfering variables when comparing monolingual groups. In addition, bilingual subjects have also been used for shedding some light on the intricate theoretical research question of the relationship between conceptual and semantic development. On the other hand, for the field of bilingual education, bilingual subjects per se are the focus of applied questions stated; they are not merely a methodological tool for attempting to solve basic research questions, as in the case of cognitive psychology. However, only a few researchers within cognitive psychology and bilingual education have combined a consideration of verbal and nonverbal representational systems, and the effect of linguistic and cultural factors on conceptual and semantic development in bilinguals.

The triple-interactional model has theoretical as well as educationally applied implications. At the theoretical level, the model explains how bilingual children construct nonverbal abstract and semantic concepts in first and second languages. Thus, this model can address the theoretical problem of how sociocultural symbolic meanings and linguistic structures that are similar or different in first and second languages influence cognitive and language development in bilinguals. This theoretical problem is related to current major educational and political issues: *Is being bilingual an advantage or a disadvantage for cognitive development?* and *Is bilingual education a positive influence for intelligence?* At the educationally applied level, the model has as a product a qualitative assessment method (QUEST, see Gonzalez, 1991, 1994, 1995; Gonzalez et al., 1997) and an educational program (Gonzalez et al., 1997) for evaluating and stimulating language-minority children's verbal and nonverbal conceptual development in first and second languages. This model can also address the current problem of a lack of valid and reliable assessment instruments for bilingual children.

REFERENCES

ALEXANDER, P. A., SCHALLERT, D. L., & HARE, V. C. (1991). Coming to terms with the terminology of knowledge. *Review of Educational Psychology, 61,* 315–343.

ANDERSON, J. R. (1978). Arguments concerning representations for mental imagery. *Psychological Review, 85,* 249–277.

ANDERSON, J. R. (1985). *Cognitive psychology and its implications* (2nd ed.). New York: Freeman Press.

ANDERSON, R. C., & PEARSON, P. D. (1984). A schema-theoretic view of basic processes in reading comprehension. In P. D. Pearson (Ed.), *Handbook of reading research* (pp. 255–293). New York: Longman.

ANGLIN, J. (1975, July). The child's first terms of reference. In S. Ehrlich & E. Tulving (Eds.), *Bulletin de Psychologie on Semantic Memory,* (pp. 129–166). [Special issue].

AU, T. K., & GLUSMAN, M. (1990). The principle of mutual exclusivity in word learning: To honor or not to honor? *Child Development, 61,* 1474–1490.

BARKE, E. M. (1933). A study of the comparative intelligence of children in certain bilingual and monoglot schools in South Wales. *British Journal of Educational Psychology, 3,* 237–250.

BATES, E., & MCWHINNEY, B. (1981). Second language acquisition from a functionalist perspective: Pragmatic, semantic, and perceptual strategies. In H. Winitz (Ed.), *Native language and foreign language acquisition* (pp. 190–214). New York: New Academy of Sciences.

BEN-ZEEV, S. (1977). The influence of bilingualism on cognitive strategy and cognitive development. *Child Development, 48,* 1009–1018.

BLANC, M. (1974). Cognitive functions of language in the preschool years. *Developmental Psychology, 10,* 229–245.

BLOOM, L. (1973). *One word at a time: The use of single-word utterances before syntax.* The Hague: Mouton.

BOWEN, J. D. (1977). Linguistic perspectives on bilingual education. In B. Spolsky & R. L. Cooper (Eds.), *Frontiers of bilingual education* (pp. 106–118). Rowley, MA: Newbury House.

BOWERMAN, M. (1976). Semantic factors in the acquisition of rules for word use and sentence construction. In D. Morehead & A. Morehead (Eds.), *Normal and deficient child language* (pp. 99–179). Baltimore: University Park Press.

BOWERMAN, M. (1977, July). *The structure and origin of semantic categories in the language learning child.* Paper presented at the Burg Wartenstein Symposium 74, Fundamentals of symbolism, Wenner-Gren Foundation for Anthropological Research, New York.

BOWERMAN, M. (1985). What shapes children's grammar? In D. I. Slobin (Ed.), *The crosslinguistic study of language acquisition* (pp. 153–186). Hillsdale, NJ: Lawrence Erlbaum Associates.

BOWERMAN, M. (1988). Inducing the latent structure of language. In F. S. Kessel (Ed.), *The development of language and language researchers: Essays in honor of Roger Brown* (pp. 23–49). Hillsdale, NJ: Lawrence Erlbaum Associates.

BROWN, A. L. (1977). Comments on cognitive development and the acquisition of concepts by Nelson. In R. C. Anderson, R. J. Spiro, & W. E. Montague (Eds.), *Schooling and the acquisition of knowledge* (pp. 241–263). Hillsdale, NJ: Lawrence Erlbaum Associates.

BROWN, R. (1958). How shall a thing be called? *Psychological Review, 65,* 14–21.

BROWN, R. (1965). *Social psychology.* New York: Free Press.

BROWN, R. (1973). *A first language: The early stages.* Cambridge, MA: Harvard University Press.

BRUNER, J. S. (1964). The course of cognitive growth. *American Psychologist, 19,* 1–15.

BRUNER, J. S., & OLVER, R. R. (1963). Development of equivalence transformation in children. In J. Wright & J. Kagan (Eds.), Basic cognitive processes in children. *Monograph of the Society for Research in Child Development, 28*(2), 125–142.

CALLANAN, M. A. (1990). Maternal speech strategies and children's acquisition of hierarchical category labels. *Genetic Epistemologist, 17*(2), 3–12.

CARLSON, H. B., & HENDERSON, N. (1950). The intelligence of American children of Mexican parentage. *Journal of Abnormal and Social Psychology, 45,* 544–551.

CHOMSKY, N. (1957). *Syntactic structures.* The Hague: Mouton.

CLARK, E. V. (1973). What's in a word? On the child's acquisition of semantics in his first language. In T. Moore (Ed.), *Cognitive development and the acquisition of language* (pp. 65–110). New York: Academic Press.

CLARK, E. V. (1977). Strategies and the mapping problem in first language acquisition. In J. Macnamara (Ed.), *Language learning and thought* (pp. 147–168). New York: Academic Press.

CLARK, J. M., & PAIVIO, A. (1991). Dual code theory and education. *Educational Psychology Review, 3*(3), 149–210.

CROMER, R. (1974). The development of language and cognition: The cognition hypothesis. In B. Foss (Ed.), *New perspectives in child development* (pp. 167–198). Harmondsworth: Penguin.

CROMER, R. F. (1988). The cognition hypothesis revisited. In F. S. Kessel (Ed.), *The development of language and language researchers: Essays in honor of Roger Brown* (pp. 223–248). Hillsdale, NJ: Lawrence Erlbaum Associates.

CUMMINS, J. (1978a). Metalinguistic development of children in bilingual education programs: Data from Irish and Canadian Ukranian–English programs. In M. Paradis (Ed.), *The Fourth Lacus Forum* (pp. 56–96). Columbia, SC: Hornbeam Press.

CUMMINS, J. (1978b). Bilingualism and the development of metalinguistic awareness. *Journal of Cross-Cultural Psychology, 9*(2), 131–149.

CUMMINS, J. (1979a). Cognitive/academic language proficiency, linguistic interdependence, the optimum age question and some other matters. *Working Papers on Bilingualism, 19,* 121–129.

CUMMINS, J. (1979b). Linguistic interdependence and the educational development of bilingual children. *Bilingual Education Paper Series, 3*(2), 112–126.

CUMMINS, J. (1989). Institutionalized racism and the assessment of minority children: A comparison of policies and programs in the United States and Canada. In R. J. Samuda, S. L. Kong, J. Cummins, J. Pascual-Leone, & J. Lewis (Eds.), *Assessment and placement of minority students* (pp. 95–107). Lewinston, NY: C. J. Hogrefe & Intercultural Social Sciences Publications.

D'ANGLEJAN, A., & TUCKER, G. R. (1973). Communicating across cultures. *Journal of Cross-cultural Psychology, 4,* 121–130.

DARCY, E. (1953). *Psycholinguistics.* Cambridge, MA: Harvard University Press.

DURGUNOGLU, A. D., & ROEDIGER, H. L. (1987). Test differences in accessing bilingual memory. *Journal of Memory and Language, 26,* 377–391.

ERVIN-TRIPP, S. (1974). Is second language learning like the first? *TESOL Quarterly, 8,* 11–127.

FATHMAN, A. (1975). *Language background, age, and the order of English structures.* Paper presented at the TESOL Convention, Los Angeles.

FELDMAN, C., & SHEN, M. (1971). Some language-related cognitive advantages of bilingual five-year-olds. *Journal of Genetic Psychology, 118,* 235–244.

FISHMAN, J. A. (1977). The social science perspective. In *Bilingual education: Current perspectives, I* (pp. 54–76). Arlington, VA: Center for Applied Linguistics.

FLAVELL, J. (1970). Concept development. In P. H. Mussen (Ed.), *Carmichael's manual of child psychology* (Vol. 1, pp. 983–1058). New York: Wiley.

FURTH, H. G. (1966). *Thinking without language: Psychological implications of deafness.* New York: Free Press.

GELMAN, S. A., & TAYLOR, M. (1984). How two-year-old children interpret proper and common names for unfamiliar objects. *Child Development, 45,* 469–473.

GENESEE, F. (1989). Early bilingual development: One language or two? *Journal of Child Language, 16,* 161–179.

GONZALEZ, V. (1991). *A model of cognitive, cultural, and linguistic variables affecting bilingual Spanish/English children's development of concepts and language.* Unpublished doctoral dissertation, University of Texas at Austin. (ERIC Document Reproduction Service No. ED 345 562)

GONZALEZ, V. (1994). A model of cognitive, cultural, and linguistic variables affecting bilingual Spanish/English children's development of concepts and language. *Hispanic Journal of Behavioral Sciences, 16*(4), 396–421.

GONZALEZ, V. (1995). *Cognition, culture, and language in bilingual children: Conceptual and semantic development.* Bethesda, MD: Austin & Windfield.

GONZALEZ, V., BAUERLE, P., & FELIX-HOLT, M. (1994). A qualitative assessment method for accurately diagnosing bilingual gifted children. *NABE '92–'93 Annual Conference Journal,* 37–52. Washington, DC, National Association for Bilingual Education (NABE).

GONZALEZ, V., BRUSCA-VEGA, R., & YAWKEY, T. D. (1997). *Assessment and instruction of culturally and linguistically diverse students with or at-risk of learning problems: From research to practice.* Needham Heights, MA: Allyn & Bacon.

GONZALEZ, V., & FELIX-HOLT, M. (1995). Influence of evaluators' prior academic knowledge on the diagnosis of cognitive and language development in bilingual Hispanic kindergartners. *New York State Association for Bilingual Education (NYSABE) Journal 10*(1), 34–45.

GOPNIK, A., & METTZOFF, A. N. (1984, July). *Some specific relationships between cognitive and semantic development: Disappearance words and the object concept and success/failure words and means-ends understanding.* Paper presented at the Third International Congress for the Study of Child Language, Austin, TX.

HAKUTA, K. (1975). *Becoming bilingual at age five: The story of Uguisu.* Unpublished senior honors thesis, Department of Psychology and Social Relations, Harvard University.

HAKUTA, K. (1976). A case study of a Japanese child learning English. *Language Learning, 26,* 321–351.

HAKUTA, K. (1982, June). *The second language learner in the context of the study of language acquisition.* Paper presented at the Society for Research in Child Development Conference on Bilingualism on Child Development, New York University.

HAKUTA, K. (1988). Why bilinguals? In F. S. Kessel (Ed.), *The development of language and language researchers: Essays in honor of Roger Brown* (pp. 299–318). Hillsdale, NJ: Lawrence Erlbaum Associates.

HARLEY, B. (1982). *Age-related differences in the acquisition of the French verb system by anglophone students in French immersion programs.* Unpublished doctoral dissertation, University of Toronto, Ontario, Canada.

HAUGEN, E. (1961). The bilingual individual. In S. Saporta (Ed.), *Psycholinguistics: A book of readings* (pp. 34–65) New York: Holt, Rinehart, & Winston.

IANCO-WORRAL, A. D. (1972). Bilingualism and cognitive development. *Child Development, 5,* 75–79.

IJAZ, I. H. (1978). Linguistic and cognitive determinants of lexical acquisition in a second language. *Language Learning, 36*(4), 401–451.

INHELDER, B., & PIAGET, J. (1964). *The early growth of logic in the child.* London: Routledge & Kegan Paul.

JACOBY, L. I., & DALLAS, M. (1981). On the relationship between autobiographical memory and perceptual learning. *Journal of Experimental Psychology: General, 3,* 306–340.

JONES, S. (1960). *Child-adult differences in second language acquisition.* New York: Harper & Row.

KANG, K. (1982). *The contexts in which errors of article usage occur and their implication for native-language transference.* Unpublished senior essay, Yale University.

KARMILOFF-SMITH, A. (1985). Language and cognitive processes from a developmental perspective. *Language and Cognitive Processes, 12,* 62–85.

KELLERMAN, E. (1978). Giving learners a break: Native language intuitions as a source of predictions about transferability. *Working Papers on Bilingualism, 15,* 60–92.

KELLERMAN, E. (1979). The problem with difficulty. *Interlanguage Studies Bulletin, 4,* 27–48.

KELLERMAN, E. (1983). Now you see it, now you don't. In S. M. Gass & L. Selinker (Eds.), *Language transfer in language learning* (pp. 112–134). Rowley, MA: Newbury House Publishers.

KIRSNER, K., SMITH, M. C., LOCKHART, R. S., KING, M. L., & JAIN, M. (1984). The bilingual lexicon: Language specific units in an integrated network. *Journal of Verbal Learning and Verbal Behavior, 23,* 519–539.

Kolers, P. A., & Brison, S. J. (1984). Commentary: On pictures, words, and their mental representation. *Journal of Experimental Psychology: Human Learning and Memory, 6*, 53–65.

Lambert, W. E. (1977). Culture and language as factors in learning and education. In A. Wolfang (Ed.), *Education of immigrant students* (pp. 59–67). Toronto: Ontario Institute for Studies in Education.

Lambert, W. E., Havelka, J., & Crosby, C. (1958). The influence of language acquisition context on bilingualism. *Journal of Abnormal Social Psychology, 56*, 239–244.

Lambert, W. E., & Tucker, S. (1972). The effects of bilingualism on the individual: Cognitive and socio-cultural consequences. In P. Hornby (Ed.), *Bilingualism: Psychological, social and educational implications* (pp. 154–187). New York: Academic Press.

Landry, R. G. (1974). A comparison of second-language learners and monolinguals on divergent thinking tasks at the elementary school level. *Modern Language Journal, 58*, 10–15.

Leopold, W. (1939). *Speech development of a bilingual child: A linguist's record*. Evanston, IL: Northwestern University Press.

Lightbown, P. (1977). *French L2 learner: What they're talking about*. Paper presented at the First Los Angeles Second Language Research Forum, UCLA.

Lindsay, P. H. & Norman, D. A. (1977). *Human information processing: An introduction to psychology* (2nd ed.). San Diego, CA: Harcourt, Brace, Jovanovich.

Lindsay, R. K. (1988). Images and inference. *Cognition, 29*, 229–250.

Macnamara, J. (1972). Cognitive basis of language learning in infants. *Psychological Review, 79*, 1–13.

Madler, G. (1980). Recognizing: The judgment of previous occurrence. *Psychological Review, 87*, 252–271.

Markman, E. M. (1981). Two different principles of conceptual organization. In M. E. Lamb & A. L. Brown (Eds.), *Advances in developmental psychology* (pp. 66–95). Hillsdale, NJ: Lawrence Erlbaum Associates.

Markman, E. M., & Hutchinson, J. E. (1984). Children's sensitivity to constraints on word meaning: Taxonomic vs. thematic relations. *Cognitive Psychology, 16*, 1–27.

Markman, E. M., & Watchel, G. A. (1988). Children's use of mutual exclusivity to constrain the meanings of words. *Cognitive Psychology, 20*, 121–157.

Matsuyama, V. K. (1983). Can story grammar speak Japanese? *Reading Teacher, 36*, 666–669.

Merriman, W. E., & Bowman, L. L. (1989). The mutual exclusivity bias in children's word learning. *Monographs of the Society for Research in Child Development, 54*, 223–250.

Miller, K. F., & Stigler, J. W. (1987). Counting in Chinese: Cultural variation in a basic cognitive skill. *Cognitive Development, 2*, 279–305.

Nelson, K. (1974). Concept, word, and sentence: Interrelationships in acquisition and development. *Psychological Review, 38*, 577–589.

Nelson, K. (1977). Cognitive development and the acquisition of concepts. In R. C. Anderson, R. J. Spiro, & W. E. Montague (Eds.), *Schooling and the acquisition of knowledge* (pp. 215–239). Hillsdale, NJ: Lawrence Erlbaum Associates.

NELSON, K. (1983). The conceptual basis for language. In T. B. Seiler & W. Wannenmacher (Eds.), *Concept development and the development of word naming* (pp. 173–188). Berlin, Germany: Springer-Verlag.

NELSON, K. (1987). Nativist and functionalist views of cognitive development: Reflections on Keil's review of making sense: The acquisition of shared meaning. *Cognitive Development, 2,* 237–247.

NELSON, K. (1988). Constraints in word learning? *Cognitive Development, 3,* 221–246.

OLLER, J. W., JR. (1991). *Language testing research: Lessons applied to LEP students and programs.* Paper presented at the First National Research Symposium on Limited English Proficient Students' Issues. Washington, DC: OBEMLA and OERI.

OLLER, J. W., JR. (1995). Adding abstract to formal and content schemata: Results of recent work in Peircean semiotics. *Applied Linguistics, 16*(3), 273–306.

OLLER, J. W., JR. (1996). How grammatical relations are determined. In T. Griffen (Ed.), *The 22nd Annual LACUS Forum* (pp. 37–88). Chapel Hill, NC: University of North Carolina Press.

OLLER, J. W., JR. (1997). Personal communication.

ORTIZ, A. A., & MALDONADO-COLON, E. (1986). Recognizing learning disabilities in bilingual children: How to lessen inappropriate referrals of language minority students to special education. *Journal of Reading, Writing, and Learning Disabilities International, 2*(2), 43–56.

ORTIZ, A. A., & YATES, J. R. (1983). Incidence of exceptionality among Hispanics: Implications for manpower planning. *Journal of the National Association for Bilingual Education, 7,* 41–53.

PAIVIO, A. (1971). *Imagery and verbal processes.* Hillsdale, NJ: Lawrence Erlbaum Associates.

PAIVIO, A. (1983). The empirical case for dual coding. In J. Yuille (Ed.), *Imagery, memory, and cognition: Essays in honor of Allan Paivio* (pp. 297–319). Hillsdale, NJ: Lawrence Erlbaum Associates.

PAIVIO, A. (1991). Mental representation in bilinguals. In A. G. Reynolds (Ed.), *Bilingualism, multiculturalism, and second language learning.* Hillsdale, NJ: Lawrence Erlbaum Associates.

PAIVIO, A., & DESROCHERS, A. (1980). A dual-coding approach to bilingual memory. *Canadian Journal of Psychology, 34,* 390–401.

PAIVIO, A., & LAMBERT, W. (1981). Dual coding and bilingual memory. *Journal of Verbal Learning and Verbal Behavior, 34,* 390–401.

PALERMO, D. S. (1983). Looking to the future: Theory and research in language and cognitive development. In Th. B. Seiler & W. Wannenmacher (Eds.), *Concept development and the development of word naming* (pp. 297–319). Berlin, Germany: Springer-Verlag.

PALIJ, M. (1980). *Semantic facilitation on a bilingual lexical decision task.* Stony Brook, NY: State University of New York.

PEAL, E., & LAMBERT, A. (1962). *Representational processes in early language acquisition.* Boston: Rowley.

PIAGET, J. (1964). *The early growth of logic in the child, classification, and seriation.* New York: Columbia University Press.

PIAGET, J. (1967). *Mental imagery in the child, a study of the development of imaginal representation.* New York: Oxford University Press.

PIAGET, J. (1970). Piaget's theory. In P. H. Mussen (Ed.), *Carmichael's manual of child psychology* (Vol. I, pp. 703–732). New York: Wiley.

PIAGET, J., & INHELDER, B. (1947). Diagnosis of mental operations and theory of the intelligence. *American Journal of Mental Deficiency, 51,* 401–406.

POTTER, M. C., SO, K. F, VON ECKARDT, B., & FELDMAN, L. B. (1984). Lexical and conceptual representation in beginning and proficient bilinguals. *Journal of Verbal Learning and Verbal Behavior, 23,* 23–38.

RAWEM, R. (1986). Language acquisition in a second language environment. *International Review of Applied Linguistics, 6,* 175–185.

RESCORLA, L. (1976). *Concept formation in word learning.* Unpublished doctoral dissertation, Yale University.

RICE, M. (1980). *Cognition to language: Categories, word meanings, and training.* Baltimore: University Park Press.

ROSCH, E. H., & MERVIS, C. B. (1975). Family resemblance and studies in the internal structure of categories. *Cognitive Psychology, 7,* 573–605.

ROSCH, E. H., MERVIS, C. B., GRAY, W., JOHNSON, D., & BAYES-BRAEM, P. (1976). Basic objects in natural categories. *Cognitive Psychology, 8,* 382–439.

SAER, D. J. (1923). The effects of bilingualism on intelligence. *British Journal of Psychology, 14,* 25–38.

SCHACHTER, J. (1974). An error in error analysis. *Language Learning, 24,* 205–214.

SCHLESINGER, I. M. (1974). Relational concepts underlying language. In R. L. Schiefelbusch & L. L. Lloyd (Eds.), *Language perspectives: Acquisition, retardation, and intervention* (pp. 129–151). Baltimore: University Park Press.

SCHLESINGER, I. M. (1977). The role of cognitive development and input in language acquisition. *Journal of Child Language, 4,* 153–169.

SCHWANENFLUGEL, P. J., & REY, M. (1986). Interlingual semantic facilitation: Evidence for a common representational system in the bilingual lexicon. *Journal of Memory and Language, 25,* 605–618.

SHIPLEY, E. F. (1989). Two types of hierarchies: Class inclusion hierarchies and kind hierarchies. *Genetic Epistemologist, 17*(2), 31–39.

SINCLAIR-DE-ZWART, H. (1969). Language acquisition and cognitive development. In T. E. Moore (Ed.), *Cognitive development and the acquisition of language* (pp. 78–134). New York: Academic Press.

SKUTNABB-KANGAS, T., & TOUKOMAA, P. (1976). Teaching migrant children's mother tongue and learning the language of the host country in the context of the sociocultural situation of the migrant family. (A report prepared for Unesco.) *Research Reports, 15* (pp. 88–99). University of Tampere: Tampere, Sweden.

SLOBIN, D. (1973). Cognitive prerequisites for the development of grammar. In C. Ferguson & D. Slobin (Eds.), *Studies in child language development* (pp. 175–208). New York: Holt, Rinehart, & Winston.

SNODGRASS, J. G. (1984). Concepts and their surface representation. *Journal of Verbal Learning and Verbal Behavior, 23,* 3–22.

TORRANCE, E. P., GOWAN, J. W., & ALIOHI, N. C. (1970). Creative functioning of monolingual and bilingual children in Singapore. *Journal of Educational Psychology, 61,* 72–75.

TUCKER, G. R. (1977). *The linguistic perspective in bilingual education: Current perspectives.* Arlington, VA: Center for Applied Linguistics.

VYGOTSKY, L. S. (1962a). *Thought and language.* Cambridge, MA: M.I.T. Press.
VYGOTSKY, L. S. (1962b). *Multilingualism in children.* Center for East European and Soviet Studies. Alberta, Canada: University of Alberta.
WAXMAN, S. R. (1990). Linking language and conceptual development: Linguistic cues and the construction of conceptual hierarchies. *Genetic Epistemologist, 17*(2), 13–20.
WAXMAN, S., & GELMAN, R. (1986). Preschoolers' use of superordinate relations in classification and language. *Cognitive Development, 1,* 139–156.
WELLS, G. (1974). Learning to code experience through language. *Journal of Child Language, 1*(2), 243–269.
WHORF, B. L. (1956). *Language, thought, and reality: Selected writings of Benjamin Lee Whorf.* Cambridge, MA: M.I.T. Press.
YOSHIOKA, J. G. (1929). A study of bilingualism. *Journal of Genetic Psychology, 36,* 473–479.

CHAPTER 3

Construction of a Phonological Development Test for Monolingual Spanish Preschoolers Learning English as a Second Language

VIRGINIA GONZALEZ

THIS CHAPTER OPENS THE CLUSTER OF STUDIES ON COGNITIVE AND LANguage development in bilingual children and adults. It highlights the second and third themes of the book: the need to construct assessments based on strong models that take into account the minority view of the interaction of cognition, culture, and language. (See the Preface for a description of the minority view.)

The study examined in this chapter had a twofold purpose. At the theoretical level, it responds to the need for robust psycholinguistic models that explain the relationship between cognitive and linguistic processes by exploring the relationship between phonological development and reading readiness. At the educationally applied level, it responds to the need for valid and reliable instruments for language-minority children by constructing a phonological development test in Spanish and English for assessing learning strategies that preschoolers use for acquiring articulation and auditory discrimination skills.

The first purpose of this research study is related to the need for robust psycholinguistic models that hold that the construct validity of assessment instruments depends on the consideration of cognitive, cultural, and linguistic variables (e.g., Cummins, 1989; Erickson & Iglesias, 1986; Gonzalez, 1994; Hakuta, 1988; Oller, 1983; Srihdar, 1981). In this study, a cognitive approach to the study of language, proposing that human beings construct symbolic representations instantiating meaning at the perceptual and memory levels in phonetic and phonological processes (Piaget, 1965, 1967) is endorsed. At the phonetic level, the individual articulates and discriminates sounds using sensation, motor schemes, and auditory perception. At the phonological level, cognitive processes take place as the child stores information using visual and auditory verbal memory processes, and then constructs symbolic representations of sounds at the level of constructive semantic memory. As a result, cognitive and linguistic processes are involved in perceptual, memory, and mediational transformational processes of sounds into meaningful symbols or phonemes.

In relation to the assessment of the area of phonological development, this study had the purpose of constructing a valid and reliable test in response to a major need for accurate instruments for bilingual children (De Avila & Havassy, 1974; Healey, Ackerman, Chappel, Perrin, & Stormer, 1981). More specifically, the test developed attempted to show construct validity as it was based on a model encompassing cognitive, cultural, and linguistic factors.

The test constructed for measuring phonological development in bilinguals had five goals:

1. To assess simultaneously articulation and auditory discrimination skills because they are an indissoluble expressive-receptive process that leads to the differential diagnosis between phonological and phonetic disorders
2. To generate a phonological developmental sequence for preschoolers whose first language is Spanish and who are in the process of learning English as a second language
3. To discover the most common learning strategies preschoolers use for acquiring Spanish and English using as a framework the distinctive features model (Jakobson, 1956) and the natural phonology theory (Stampe, 1969), which conceptualize errors as learning strategies
4. To develop parallel test versions tailored to the unique characteristics of Spanish and English, with the purpose of the assessment of phonological development in first and second languages
5. To generate additional criteria for the clinical assessment of readiness for reading and writing, visuo-motor coordination, and the association between visual and auditory perception

The literature review that follows looks at the two major theories used for the development of the phonological development test for bilingual children: (1) Jakobson's model of distinctive features, which provides a universal framework that can be applied to develop parallel test versions of phonological development in Spanish and English, and (2) the natural phonology theory, which explains phonological development as the application of learning strategies by children. The natural phonology theory departs from traditional approaches that offer only a framework for identifying and categorizing "errors" children make in articulation and auditory discrimination skills.

Review of the Literature

Jakobson's Model of Distinctive Features

The selection and categorization of items for the construction of this phonological development test for bilingual children was based on Jakobson's model (1956), which uses three major features for categorizing phonemes: mode of articulation, place of articulation, and voice. From these distinctive features, different universal categories of sounds, or phonemes, were derived. According to Jakobson, each sound is composed of some features that are related to acoustic properties of the sound and some that are related to the position of the lips, tongue, or velum. This distinctive features system is a binary one; each sound can be described in terms of a distinct number of characteristics that are either present or absent, or do not apply. The totality of these features is the minimum number of binary selections necessary for the specification of the phoneme.

For the phonological development test, an item consisted of two words that differed in one pair of phonemes and also in semantic meaning. The selected phonemes differed in one or two distinctive features. These pairs of words were called by Jakobson *minimal pairs*. For instance, the words *fast* and *past* form a minimal pair that differs in the semantic meanings conveyed due to only one pair of phonemes, /f/ and /p/, which are different in distinctive features.

According to Jakobson, maximum, or simple, contrasts are learned first, followed by minimum feature contrasts. Thus, the model of distinctive features led to the revelation that there might be a universal sequence of phonological acquisition because sounds of all languages appear to be able to be described using this system. Jakobson observed that young children acquiring new sounds, as well as adults with an established phonological system, presented the same kind of phonological attributes in their speech. Jakobson claimed that no matter what language a child was acquiring, where the child lived, or when the child acquired the language, the order of phonological acquisition would be the same. That is, Jakobson predicted that the child's sequence of phoneme acquisition would follow the phonological organization of the adult language. Jakobson's predictions about how children acquired sounds were very accurate, despite the fact that they were not originally supported by actual data.

Jakobson's (1956) predictions also included several specific observations in relation to sound acquisition by children. First, he suggested that a sound is acquired in direct relation to how widely the sound occurs in other languages. He discovered three commonalities for consonants and one for vowels, which he labeled the *laws of implication*. He noted that every language that has back consonants (such as the velars /k/ and /g/) also has front consonants (such as the labials /p/ and /b/). In addition, he noted that front consonants can exist without back consonants, but no language has back consonants alone. From this observation, he concluded that children first acquire front consonants, followed by back consonants. Thus, *place of articulation* (front and back) plays an important role in sound acquisition.

Jakobson (1956) also noticed that order of acquisition is related to the *manner of articulation* of sounds. He observed that all languages have stops (such as /t/ and /d/); however, not all languages have fricatives (such as /s/ and /z/). He believed that stops are acquired first, followed by fricatives. His third observation was that affricates, composed of a stop plus a fricative (such as the "ch" in "church"), exist in a language only if stops and fricatives are present. Furthermore, no language can have more affricates than it had fricatives. Affricates should be the last sounds to be acquired. Jakobson's observations were not limited to the acquisition of consonants. Regarding vowel development, he stated that the existence of back vowels (such as /u/) implies the existence of front vowels (such as /i/) of corresponding height. He believed that vowels develop vertically first, followed by a corresponding horizontal development.

As accurate as Jakobson's predictions have been, many details of his theory have not been confirmed by data-driven research findings. First, Ferguson, Freizer, and Weeks (1973) found that infants do not babble all possible sounds in a random fashion, as Jakobson stated. In addition, babbling plays an important role in the type of sounds acquired by children after 1 year of age (Oller, 1983). Some researchers have suggested that certain sounds occur more frequently in babbling because they occur in actual speech in a specific language. During the babbling stage, the infant produces the largest variety of sounds, nearly all of which are eliminated during the few words stage. These first distinctions, which tend to become significant, require phonic oppositions that are simple, clear, stable, and suitable to be imprinted in the memory (Oller, 1983).

Jakobson also neglected to talk about some aspects of sound combinations that have since been found to be very important (Oller, 1983). Jakobson did not mention the role that the position of a sound in a word plays in sound acquisition. In addition, the acquisition of sound clusters also appears to follow some specific kinds of rules that Jakobson failed to take into account (Ferguson et al., 1973). Another important point Jakobson avoided was the role that perception plays in learning sounds. Finally, Jakobson never defined what he meant by the word *acquired*. For instance, when he stated that stops were acquired before fricatives, it is not known whether he meant all stops and in all positions, and whether all clusters of two or more stops were mastered perfectly before the first fricatives appeared.

On the other hand, several of Jakobson's observations were correct. The most important observation that he made refers to the order in which children acquire sounds and how this is reflected in all languages. Jakobson also was correct about the fact that sounds used by the majority of languages are those that children acquire first and that sounds occurring rarely in languages are acquired late by children. Thus, Jakobson's theory has had a profound effect on our understanding of phonological development. When compared with data-driven studies on phonological development in children, many of Jakobson's predictions have proved to be correct. However, more data-driven studies will be needed before definite conclusions can be reached about the validity of Jakobson's model. The distinctive features model nevertheless offers much promise in helping us to understand phonological development.

The Natural Phonology Theory

The phonological strategies used for constructing the scoring system of this phonological development test were based on the theories of interactional discovery (Menn, 1976) and natural phonology (Stampe, 1969). Stampe gave the title *natural phonology* to what he believed is a universal system of phonological processes that respond to the innate limitations of the human speech capacity. Stampe believed that as the infant's phonological processes unfold, the adult phonological system, which is learned within a specific phonological system of the target language, places restrictions on this maturational process. This process shows plasticity, as every regular sound substitution (including assimilations, dissimilations, insertions, deletions, and metatheses) reflects the operation of a set of natural phonological processes.

A natural phonological process, according to Stampe (1969), is a mental operation that is applied to speech to substitute difficult sounds for an alternative identical class that lacks the difficult property. That is, natural processes are mediational substitutions for classes of sounds. Natural phonological processes are applied voluntarily and unconsciously, and they become explicit only when speakers find pronunciation difficulties. Thus, from a natural phonology perspective, children's errors are seen as steps along the path to acquisition rather than randomly inaccurate productions. The nature of errors rather than the age of correct production is the important organizational dimension. Compton (1976) suggested that both children who develop speech normally and those who do not use phonological processes go through various stages of omission and sound substitution patterns, which are subsequently dropped or replaced by others as the child moves from one stage to another. Some children, however, retain simplification patterns that normally developing children ordinarily discard.

In this test of phonological development, the specific strategies used that have been identified by the natural phonology theory include: (1) homonymy (Ingram, 1974; Priestly, 1980; Vihman, 1981); (2) reduplication (Ingram, 1974; Ferguson et. al., 1973); (3) deletion and cluster reduction (Ingram, 1970); (4) inversion (Ingram, 1974); (5) substitution (Ingram, 1970); and (6) linguistic transfer (Ingram, 1981). In the following description of these six phonological strategies, examples are presented in English and Spanish to illustrate how educators can identify the patterns of idiosyncratic strategies bilingual children use for phonological acquisition.

Homonymy. The strategy of homonymy provides information about the development of phonology and vocabulary as it refers to confounding the phonological characteristics of new words with words already present in the bilingual child's vocabulary. Creating a homonym involves reducing the number of different sound patterns of the new word to match a familiar word that differs in only one phoneme. This phonemic change can lead to misunderstanding in the communication process. For example, English "cuff" may be pronounced by the bilingual child as "cup," or Spanish *sapo* ("frog") may be produced as *"tapo"* ("I cover"). As illustrated by these two examples, the fricatives /f/ and /s/ of the new words are replaced by the stops /p/ and /t/. That is, the phonemes chosen for substitution are easier to pronounce because they correspond to lower levels of phonological development.

Reduplication. Reduplication is a general pattern in the early stages of phonological development that appears more frequently in bilingual children who are still in a monosyllabic rather than a multisyllabic type of development. When using the reduplication strategy, the bilingual child repeats two or more times only one or two syllables or variations of the syllables of the original word. For instance, English "bicycle" may become "bie bie," and Spanish *besito* may become *"pepi pepi."* Although monosyllabic bilingual children use more reduplication as a strategy for phonological development, all bilingual children appear to use this strategy for learning multisyllabic words (Ingram, 1974). If a bilingual child uses reduplication as a favorite strategy for acquiring multisyllabic words for a long period of time, further assessment of the possible cause of this problem may be needed. The overuse of reduplication can be due to a lack of ability to pronounce the second syllable of multisyllabic words with specific categories of phonemes, or any phonemes of middle syllables, or final syllables of multisyllabic words.

Deletion and Cluster Reduction. With deletion and cluster reduction, bilingual children omit phonemes that are difficult to produce because they have not acquired them yet. This is a strategy used frequently for multisyllabic words and for clusters acquired late in phonological development (Ferguson et al., 1973). For example, English "pretty" may be pronounced by the bilingual child as "petty," and in Spanish *mar* may be produced as *"ma."*

Inversion. Inversion involves a change in the sequence of contiguous or separate phonemes or syllables in a word. This learning strategy is especially used with phonemes that have not yet been acquired by the bilingual child (Vihman, 1981). For example, English "mine" may be pronounced by the bilingual child as "nime," and Spanish *chocolate* may become "cocholate."

Substitution. The phonological strategy of substitution involves the exchange of the correct phoneme of a word for an easier one that the bilingual child has already acquired. Here the child's utterance may not have any resemblance to a real word, so the meaning of the original word cannot easily be communicated. Bilingual children who use this strategy frequently and for a long period of time will develop their own "baby language" that only close family members can understand. For example, English "train" may be produced by the bilingual child as "fein," and Spanish *muñeca* may be pronounced as "*eca.*"

Linguistic Transfer. Linguistic transfer refers to errors caused by superimposing linguistic rules and structures from the first to the second language, or vice versa. These errors often result in misunderstanding of the meanings of words and overgeneralizations. For example, English "vase" may be pronounced by the bilingual child as "base" due to negative transfer from Spanish. In Spanish, typically no distinction in meaning is made between [b] and [v], whereas in English, the sounds /b/ and /v/ are phonemic, that is, substitution of one for the other will likely cause misunderstandings. In the same bilingual child, Spanish *perro* ("dog") may be produced as "*pero*" ("pear tree"). The transfer process from English to Spanish has occurred because the trilled /rr/ is nonexistent in English.

In summary, the natural phonology theory brings a new perspective for interpreting "errors" of articulation produced by young children. Instead of viewing problems producing sounds as errors, they are interpreted as the expression of mediational phonological strategies. Using the natural phonology theory in association with Jakobson's model of distinctive features is helpful because it provides a universal framework for categorizing phonemes and phonological strategies applicable across languages.

HYPOTHESES

To fulfill the purpose of this study, two hypotheses were stated:

1. There is a universal sequence in the acquisition of distinctive features between the Spanish and English languages in articulation and auditory discrimination abilities.
2. Older age groups will perform at a higher phonological developmental level in Spanish and English than younger age groups.

METHOD

Design

The main objective of this exploratory study was the construction of a test of phonological development in Spanish and English. Since the study investigated the relationship between linguistic and cognitive processes, the design was ex post facto.

Subjects

Subjects consisted of 75 preschoolers, age 3 to 5 years. They were monolingual Spanish speakers attending bilingual Spanish-English preschool settings in the metropolitan area of Lima, Perú, which served a middle-class population. These children were in the process of learning English as a second language. The examiner had had contact with the children for the entire academic year before selecting the subjects. All the subjects were average achievers and had normal cognitive and linguistic abilities, as measured by the Pupil Rating Scale (Myklebust, 1981) and the McCarthy Cognitive Scales (McCarthy, 1970). Subjects were also assessed in Spanish with the Peabody Picture Vocabulary Test (Dunn, 1982) and the researcher's own developmental scale of expressive vocabulary in English that matched curricular objectives. The children were divided into three age groups of 25 individuals each, resulting in a group of 3-year-olds, a group of 4-year-olds, and a group of 5-year-olds. The three age groups were compared in order to test the hypotheses.

Content Sample

A total of 8,475 responses were collected from the 75 preschoolers who participated in the study. Each child gave 32 responses in Spanish and 81 responses in English, for a total of 113 responses per child. The validity and reliability of the test of phonological development was later determined, using as a content sample the number of responses given by the 75 participants in the study.

Instruments

Minimal pairs that were part of the preschoolers' vocabulary were selected as *auditory stimuli*. Minimal pairs are words that differ in pronunciation by only one phoneme and have different meanings. These minimal pairs were recorded by an adult native speaker of each language and presented to the preschoolers using a tape recorder.

Schematic drawings in black and white, called *rebus symbols*, published as instructional materials by the American Guidance Service (AGS), were selected as *visual stimuli*.

Pilot Test

A pilot test of the minimal pairs serving as stimuli was administered to 15 subjects who had the same characteristics of the final sample. The purpose of the pilot test was to check the appropriateness of the administration procedures and the visual and auditory stimuli. The 15 preschoolers were selected at random and were subdivided in the same three age groups of the final study sample: five 3-year-olds, five 4-year-olds, and five 5-year-olds.

The pilot test encompassed six sequential procedures:

1. Assess Spanish and English articulation and auditory discrimination skills.
2. Transcribe the children's responses in Spanish and English.
3. Identify the most common phonetic errors and phonological strategies children used in the English and Spanish tests.
4. Categorize the most common minimal pairs in which children made errors in Spanish and English using Jakobson's model (1956) and the natural phonology theory (Stampe, 1969).
5. Score the children's responses in Spanish and English at the phonetic and phonological levels.
6. Assess the reliability of the scoring process by two bilingual linguists, two bilingual psychologists, and two bilingual educational diagnosticians who served as judges.

The pilot test of minimal pairs was successful and ensured content and construct validity of the instrument and study.

Procedure

Consent for participation in the study was obtained from children's parents and the preschool directors and teachers. Children were then assessed individually with six measurements: (1) the Wepman auditory discrimination test in English (Wepman, 1958) and in Spanish (Wepman, 1975); (2) the Batería Diagnóstica de la Madurez Lectora, a reading readiness test in Spanish (Molina, 1985); (3) the Pupil Rating Scale in Spanish (Myklebust, 1981); (4) the verbal scale of the McCarthy Cognitive Scales in Spanish (McCarthy, 1970); (5) the Peabody Picture Vocabulary Test in Spanish (Dunn, 1982); and (6) a developmental scale of expressive vocabulary in English that was developed by the researcher that matched curricular objectives. This testing was administered by the researcher in five sessions lasting a half-hour each. Testing occurred at the end of the school year within a two-month period. The purpose of this testing was twofold: (1) to ensure that the final sample for the study consisted of children who were average achievers with normal cognitive and linguistic abilities and (2) to use these measures for the psychometric analysis of validity and reliability of the phonological development test in Spanish and English constructed.

The researcher administered the phonological development test to the children in two half-hour sessions—one for Spanish, the other for English. The first part of the test measured children's articulation abilities. It consisted of presenting the children with the recorded auditory stimuli and asking them to imitate the words. The children's responses were written down and were also recorded on audiotape for further qualitative data analysis. The second part of the test measured children's auditory discrimination and consisted of presenting a recorded model of the pronunciation of one word and asking them to point to one of the two visual stimuli to indicate which the word was referring to. The child's motor responses for the auditory discrimination task were recorded on videotape.

Results and Discussion

There were three statistical procedures conducted in this research study: one was related to the test construction and its validity, one tested the reliability of the test, and one tested the hypotheses.

The first cluster of statistical procedures sought to determine the following:

1. The difficulty level of items using the Pearson correlation coefficient
2. The discrimination of items using the point biserial correlation
3. The criterion-related validity of the test constructed running correlational tests with other measures of cognitive and linguistic abilities (i.e., the Wepman in Spanish and English, the Peabody Picture Vocabulary test in Spanish, the verbal scale of the MacCarthy Cognitive Scales in Spanish, the Pupil Rating Scale in Spanish, and a test of expressive vocabulary constructed by the researcher)
4. The construct and content validity of the test constructed by conducting a six-step pilot test procedure in order to test the conceptual framework, the categorization of items by phonological clusters, and the scoring system for phonological strategies using experts as judges

The second cluster of statistical analysis included using the split-half procedure and the Kuder-Richardson formula for testing the internal consistency and reliability of the phonological development test. The third cluster for testing the two hypotheses stated in this study included using (1) a *t* test for an association between the phonological acquisition sequence in Spanish and English and the child's lexical developmental level in English (Hypothesis 1) and (2) a correlation test for the possibility of differences in phonological developmental levels in first and second language in the three age groups (Hypothesis 2).

Item Analysis

Difficulty Level of Items. The difficulty level of items was obtained through the Pearson correlation coefficient. The items removed were those that presented a .05 level of significance. The percentages of correct responses given by the children in Spanish and English to the phonological test are presented in Tables 3.1 and 3.2. As these tables show, results indicated that the test constructed had a normal distribution of the difficulty level of items in both languages. For the Spanish test, a mean score of 13.83 and a standard deviation (SD) of 8.01 were obtained (see Table 3.1). For the English test, a mean score of 11.05 and an SD of 7.78 were obtained (see Table 3.2). One item from the Spanish test and 11 items from the English test were deleted because they did not correlate with the phonological categories they were placed in.

TABLE 3.1 Percentage of Correct Responses According to Category on the Phonological Development Test in Spanish

Category	Percentage of Correct Responses
Vowels	
Front vowels vs. back vowels	28.0%
Consonants	
Voiced stops vs. voiceless fricatives	40.0
Voiceless stops vs. nasals	42.0
Voiceless stops	52.0
Voiceless stops vs. voiced stops	53.8
Nasals	56.0
Voiced stops vs. nasals	42.0
Voiced stops vs. voiceless fricatives	60.0
Voiced stops	52.0
Liquids	74.5
Consonant clusters	
Voiced stops	81.3
Voiceless stops	88.0

TABLE 3.2 Percentage of Correct Responses According to Category on the Phonological Development Test in English

Category	Percentage of Correct Responses
Vowels	
Front vowels vs. back vowels	66.0%
Consonants	
Voiced stops vs. voiceless fricatives	94.5
Voiceless occlusives	90.7
Voiceless stops vs. voiced stops	76.5
Nasals	84.0
Voiceless stops vs. voiceless fricatives	94.5
Voiced stops vs. voiced fricatives	40.0
Voiceless fricatives	90.4
Voiceless fricatives vs. voiced affricates	90.4
Voiceless fricatives vs. voiced fricatives	94.5
Voiceless affricates vs. voiced affricates	94.5
Consonant clusters	
Consonant clusters that do not exist in Spanish in initial position	79.9
Consonant clusters that exist in Spanish in initial position	63.3
Consonant clusters that exist in Spanish in final position	79.9

Based on these results, four patterns are observed:

1. The order of phonological acquisition of the distinctive features in Spanish and English corresponded to Jakobson's model (Jakobson, 1956).
2. Vowels were acquired before nasals in Spanish and English.
3. Stops in voiceless-voiced contrasts appeared before the contrast stops-nonstops (e.g., /d/-/s/, /t/-/m/) in both Spanish and English.
4. Affricates appeared before fricatives in English, and affricates and the liquids appeared after consonants and vowels in Spanish.
5. In Spanish, consonant clusters appeared later in phonological development, and in English consonant clusters in initial position appeared before the ones in final position (the latter category not existent in Spanish).

In addition, preschoolers in the process of learning English as a second language performed better for the phonemes that were common to both Spanish and English than in the phonemes that were unique to English. This pattern shows a sequential, rather than a simultaneous, phonemic acquisition in both languages. Moreover, children need to be mature in their phonological development in their first language in order to learn a second language.

Validity of Items. The discrimination of items was obtained through the point biserial correlation. The minimum value for an acceptable item-test coefficient was .3 (Reid, Zhang, Nie, & Ding, 1986). The best items were selected at $p < .05$, or $p < .001$. There were 94 percent of acceptable item-test coefficients for Spanish and 90 percent for English. This percentage of correlation of items with the total score on the test was the result of many items with correct responses (100 percent, 90 percent, or 80 percent) in both languages, which makes $r = 0$.

Criterion-Related Validity

Concurrent Validity. Concurrent validity showed a significant correlation between the test of phonological development constructed in Spanish ($r = .2170, p < .05$) and in English ($r = .1779, p < .1$), and the developmental scale of expressive vocabulary in English constructed by the researcher. This finding suggested the need to have a maturational level in phonological development in the first language before beginning the process of learning vocabulary in English.

In addition, the scores on the Spanish and English form of the test of phonological development were correlated with the scores of the test that measured cognitive and linguistic abilities, with the following results:

1. There was a significant correlation with the reading readiness test in Spanish ($r = .3907, p < .05$).
2. There was a significant correlation with the Test of Auditory Discrimination in Spanish and English ($r = .2743, p < .05$).
3. There was a significant correlation with the Peabody Picture Vocabulary Test in Spanish ($r = .1416, p > .05$).
4. There was not a significant correlation with the verbal scale of the McCarthy Cognitive Scales in Spanish ($r = .3002, p < .05$).

There was no correlation between performance on the Spanish developmental test with verbal ability as measured by the McCarthy Cognitive Scales (general cognitive score and IQ categories). This might be due to the independence of the phonological development with other aspects of language development, such as verbal fluency, vocabulary development, and verbal concept formation (measured by the verbal scale of the McCarthy Cognitive Scales). This could mean that if children have a problem in the phonological development of articulation and auditory discrimination, they may not show a delay in cognitive and language developmental areas (e.g., verbal fluency, vocabulary, syntax, concept formation). If low levels of development do exist in other areas of language acquisition, it could be that there are other problems in the area of visuomotor coordination, the interface between visual and auditory perception, or concept formation processes. These problems can generate developmental delays in language and in learning how to read and write.

Construct and Content Validity. The selection of items was based on Jakobson's model (1956) of distinctive features (based on mode and place of articulation and voice). The phonological strategies were based on the theory of interactional discovery (Menn, 1976) and natural phonology (Stampe, 1969). These two theoretical frameworks ensured construct validity for the test of phonological development.

Seven phonological categories were observed in the pilot studies:

1. Processes related to the syllabic structures of language, such as insertion, omission, reduplication, and interchange
2. Assimilation processes that affected voice, and place and mode of articulation
3. Dissimilation
4. Distortion
5. Strengths and weaknesses in mode and place of articulation
6. Change in the mode or place of articulation
7. Problems for articulating vowels

These seven categories corresponded to the six phonological strategies of homonymy, reduplication, deletion and cluster reduction, inversion, substitution, and linguistic transference. The six stages of the pilot study served as evidence for construct and content validity. The first through the third stages (assessment of articulation and auditory discrimination skills in Spanish and English, and transcription and categorization of responses in phonetic errors and phonological strategies) were mainly related to test construct validity. For these first three stages, the conceptual framework served as a basis for the selection of the test items. The fourth through the sixth stages (categorization of errors, scoring responses at the phonetic and phonological levels, and assessing reliability of the scoring) were related to content validity because the methods used relied on expert judgment to assign test items to the phonetic and phonological categories defined by the conceptual framework. During the fourth step of the pilot test, the items with no correlation with their own categories were removed, using the Pearson correlation coefficient ($p < .05$). One item was removed from the Spanish test and eight items were removed from the English test.

Intercorrelations among categories of phonemes were used to support that the test measured a single distinctive feature or contrast on each category. During the last step of the pilot test, the categorization system developed was tested at a practical level by six judges. There was a high reliability (82 percent) among the six judges' categorizations of phonetic errors and phonological strategies. Although the six steps of the pilot test procedure can be separated tentatively, there is not an exact limit between content and criterion-related evidence for demonstrating the validity of tests (APA, 1986).

Reliability

The internal consistency of the overall test was tested by the split-half procedure, using the Kuder-Richardson formula. The first component of each minimal pair of phonemes was correlated with the second component of the same minimal pair. The correlations for the Spanish ($r = 0.93$, $p < .05$) and the English tests ($r = 0.89$, $p < .05$) were high. Both languages showed high correlation coefficients, especially taking into consideration that the phonological development test was individually administered. Thus, the test showed reliability, ensuring accurate measurement of articulation and auditory discrimination skills when used for test-retest purposes.

Test of Hypotheses

The first hypothesis tested the universal sequence of acquisition of distinctive features between two languages, with dominance in the first language. The test rejected the null hypothesis in English ($t = 1.000$, $p < .01$) and in Spanish ($t = -.560$, $p < .01$). The following observations can be made regarding the first hypothesis. First, the data confirmed Jakobson's law of sequential acquisition: English fricative and affricates are acquired later in the developmental sequence. Second, a related fact was the existence of a higher number of contrasts between fricative phonemes and stops, and between affricate phonemes and stops in English. Therefore, because fricative and affricate phonemes are more numerous in English than in Spanish and are acquired later in the developmental sequence, a higher level of phonological readiness in Spanish is necessary for the acquisition of fricative and affricate phonemes in English.

A third observation is that the existence of a higher number of fricatives and affricates contrasts in English may explain the higher level of phonological development achieved by children in Spanish than in English. However, only Spanish has the category of liquids (they are not present in English), which are of higher difficulty than the fricative and affricate phonemic categories present mostly in English. A possible explanation for the higher level of phonological development achieved by children in Spanish may be the tendency to mature phonologically earlier in the first language, and then to transfer their language abilities to the second language. An educational implication of these findings is that in order to begin learning English as a second language, children need to have already achieved phonological readiness in their first language.

Although most findings in this research study confirmed Jakobson's (1956) developmental sequence, there were also some differences. It was found that children acquired early difficult phonemes when they existed in both the Spanish and the English languages. For instance, an almost similar percentage of correct responses within categories of stops, fricatives, and consonant clusters common to English and Spanish was found.

The second hypothesis tested the possibility of differences in phonological developmental levels in first and second language in the three age groups. The correlation among the scores for the three age groups was significant at the .05 level, thus rejecting the null hypothesis. Results showed significant differences in phonological development across age groups.

Five sequential developmental patterns of acquisition occurred:

1. Consonant clusters in final position
2. Consonant clusters in initial position
3. Contrasts of voiceless and voiced stops
4. Contrasts of fricatives and affricates
5. Contrasts of stops and nonstops

These developmental patterns showed bilingual children's tendency to acquire phonemes that were common between Spanish and English and then, later, to acquire phonemes that were unique to the Spanish or the English language. Although this same developmental pattern was present in the three age groups, the Spanish phonological acquisition patterns present in the 3-year-olds were more similar to Jakobson's (1956) sequence of phonological acquisition than observed in the older groups.

In a comparison of Spanish phonological development among 3- and 4-year-olds, a difference was found with respect to the contrast voiceless-voiced and the consonant clusters. In addition, the same sequential order of acquisition of fricatives and affricates was present in the Spanish and English languages. Further, distinctive features were acquired earlier when within-group comparisons (e.g., voiced stops such as /b/ and /d/) rather than intergroup comparisons (e.g., voiced stop versus voiceless fricatives such as /d/ and /s/) were made. Moreover, children mastered phonemes in initial, medial, and final positions before phonemic contrasts and also before vowels and consonant clusters.

In relation to Jakobson's (1956) developmental order, the comparison of the phonological performance of the three age groups showed that the model was confirmed. Five-year-olds showed better performance than 3- and 4-year-olds, especially at the distinctive features and consonant cluster level for the phonemes that were similar in Spanish and English. However, children showed a better performance in the consonant clusters than in the vowels. The performance improved from younger to older children quantitatively in terms of percentage of correct articulations. In addition, the performance of children also improved qualitatively because there was a reorganization within the categories that reflected more stable and universal patterns of phonological acquisition. Moreover, each child demonstrated an internal coherence in phonological errors and strategies as he or she acquired phonological patterns.

A practical implication derived from testing the second hypothesis is that when preschoolers demonstrate a normal phonological development in Spanish, it does not necessarily mean that they will achieve at the same level in English. English has several phonemes that do not exist in Spanish, and its articulation and sounds do not correspond to its graphic representations (i.e., English is not a phonetic language). Therefore, a better than normal level of phonological development in Spanish is required in order to master the articulation and auditory discrimination of English sounds.

Implications for Diagnosis

The first implication for improving the assessment process of bilingual children derived from the results of this study concerns the fact that normal second language learners make errors in the production of phonemes of the second language that do not exist in the first language and also have linguistic transfer effects (either positive or negative). For bilingual children, there are different rates of development compared to monolinguals; moreover, the process is an idiosyncratic one. For instance, Swain (1977) suggested that a child in a bilingual or monolingual environment uses a single set of rules in learning a language. He pointed out that bilingual language development is four to five months behind monolingual language development, because the bilingual child has more language units to acquire and differentiate than the monolingual child does. The difficulties of Spanish-dominant children when learning phonemic contrasts that are unique to the English language can be explained because contrasts must be automatically recognized, and just not merely intellectually learned. For instance, many English sounds have no counterparts in Spanish; several phonemes common to Spanish and English never appear in word-final position in Spanish but do so often in English, and English has word-final consonant clusters whereas Spanish has none. Therefore, native-Spanish-speaking children cannot pronounce some sounds unique to the English language because they cannot hear the relevant distinctions. These apparent articulatory problems in Spanish-dominant children who are learning English as a second language are in fact problems in auditory discrimination.

A second implication of this study refers to the fact that errors that children in the process of normal second language learning make in Spanish and English can be confounded with errors that monolingual Spanish or monolingual English children with genuine articulation or auditory discrimination problems make. Bilingual children can present developmental delays or mispronunciations if they are compared with a native speaker of their second language but not if compared to a native speaker of their first language. However, if they are compared to children learning English as a second language, they will show normal first and second language acquisition patterns. Therefore, only bilingual children who present developmental delays and pathological patterns in their first language, in comparison to other bilingual children of their same characteristics, will show genuine speech and language problems. Thus, the comparison between bilingual children's phonological development in the parallel Spanish and English versions of the phonological test constructed can show whether in fact there are speech (alterations in the motor schemes for articulation) or language problems (alterations in the auditory discrimination of phonemic categories). A phonological approach to the study of speech problems provides a functional view of language development that includes meaning and context for communication purposes in natural settings.

A third implication based on the results of the study shows that specific phonological patterns in bilingual children assessed in both Spanish and English consistently discriminates between genuine speech and language problems from normal second language development. Bilingual children with genuine problems use shorter utterances, simpler syntactical structures, and fewer and simpler types of verb tenses. It is very important to analyze the qualitative characteristics of the responses in order to determine if there are delays or pathological patterns uncommon to bilingual children.

Conducting a differential diagnosis of articulation problems is difficult because the cause of the problem needs to be identified. The problem may be due to the difficulty of formation of phonetic motor schemes (as modes and places of articulation), visual and auditory perception problems, auditory memory problems (especially at the sequential short-term level), or deeper cognitive processes level problems involving thinking (as an ability of concept formation for the construction of meaning and the transformation of sensorial schemes of sounds into phonological representations).

Phonemes in English and Spanish

Following is a description, from an applied educational perspective, of common phonemes in English and Spanish for which bilingual children use phonological strategies. This description, derived from the 75 children who participated in this study, offers a framework for understanding the phonological learning strategies that bilingual Spanish/English children commonly present and for developing educational programs for these children.

English Language. Bilingual Spanish/English children tend to make the following pronunciations:

- /st/ for /est/: *Phonetic error:* addition; *phonological strategy:* linguistic transference. This transfer occurs in initial word positions because the syllabic consonant-vowel structure of the Spanish language means that no words start with two consonants (besides clusters present in the language).
- /sh/ for /ch/: *Phonetic error:* change in the mode of articulation (a fricative for an affricate); *phonological strategy:* linguistic transfer. This transfer occurs because the sound /sh/ does not exist in Spanish, and it is substituted for the most similar one in Spanish; both phonemes are voiceless linguopalatals in terms of place of articulation.
- /b/ for /v/: *Phonetic error:* change in place and manner of articulation (a fricative is converted into an occlusive); *phonological strategy:* linguistic transference. This transfer occurs because the sound /v/ is pronounced in Spanish as /b/.
- /f/ or /s/ for /th/: *Phonetic error:* change in the place and manner of articulation (to a labiodental for /f/ and to a linguoalveolar for /s/); *phonological strategy:* linguistic transference. This transfer occurs because the /th/ does not exist in Spanish and is substituted for phonemes that have the same manner of articulation and voice.
- /d/ for /b/ and /t/ for /th/: *Phonetic error:* change in place and manner of articulation (a voiceless occlusive for a voiceless fricative); *phonological strategy:* linguistic transference. This transfer occurs because the phoneme /th/ does not exist in Spanish, and the /d/ and /t/ phonemes are pronounced with different points and manners of articulation in Spanish than in English.
- /ch/ for /dz/: *Phonetic error:* change in voice (a voiceless for a voiced phoneme); *phonological strategy:* linguistic transference. This transfer occurs because the sound /dz/ does not exist in Spanish.
- /n/ for /ing/: *Phonetic error:* change in place of articulation (a voiced linguoalveolar for a voiced linguopalatal); *phonological strategy:* linguistic transference. This transfer occurs because the phoneme /ing/ does not exist in Spanish.
- /ch/ for /th/: *Phonetic error:* change in mode of articulation (a voiceless affricate for a voiceless fricative); *phonological strategy:* linguistic transfer. This transfer occurs because the phoneme /th/ does not exist in Spanish.
- /ks/ for /rks/, /f/ for /lf/, /n/ for /nd/, /n/ for /nt/, and /s/ for /st/: *Phonetic error:* reductions of consonant clusters in final position; *phonological strategy:* avoidance. This occurs because the /ks/, /rks/, /lf/, /nt/, and /st/ phonemes do not exist in Spanish, due to its consonant-vowel syllabic structure

Spanish Language. Bilingual Spanish/English children tend to make the following pronunciations:

- /l/ for /ll/: *Phonetic error:* change in place of articulation; *phonological strategy:* linguistic transfer. This transfer occurs because the phoneme /ll/ does not exist in English.

- /l/ for /r/ and /rr/: *Phonetic error:* change in the mode of articulation; *phonological strategy:* substitution. This occurs because the thrilled "r" is a difficult phoneme to acquire in Spanish, and therefore it is mastered late by normally developing children. In addition, this phoneme does not exist in English.
- /d/ for /r/ and /rr/: *Phonetic error:* change in mode of articulation; *phonological strategy:* substitution. This occurs because the "rr" is a difficult phoneme to acquire in Spanish, and therefore it is mastered late by normally developing children. In addition, this phoneme does not exist in English.
- /r/ for /rr/: *Phonetic error:* change in mode of articulation; *phonological strategy:* substitution. This occurs because the "rr" is a difficult phoneme to acquire in Spanish, and therefore it is mastered late by normally developing children. In addition, this phoneme does not exist in English.
- /t/ for /tr/, /d/ for /dr/, and /k/ for /kr/: *Phonetic error:* reductions of consonant clusters; *phonological strategy:* avoidance. This occurs because clusters are difficult phonemes to acquire, and therefore they are acquired late by children developing normally. This process can happen in both Spanish and English.
- /tl/ for /tr/, /pl/ for /pr/, and /kl/ for /kr/: *Phonetic error:* change in mode of articulation; *phonological strategy:* substitution. This occurs because clusters are difficult phonemes to acquire, and therefore they are acquired late by children developing normally. This process can happen in both Spanish and English.
- /ch/ for /sh/: *Phonetic error:* change in mode of articulation; *phonological strategy:* substitution. This occurs because children make a linguistic transfer from English into Spanish.

OTHER ADMINISTRATIONS OF THE PHONOLOGICAL DEVELOPMENT TEST

Experimentations with two other versions of administration of the phonological development test were conducted: a copy of minimal pairs for exploring visual perception and visuomotor coordination and a dictation of minimal pairs for exploring the capacity of transformation of auditory schemes into graphic-visual representations. For instance, the child was asked to copy minimal pairs of words for assessing visual perception as a visuomotor coordination ability at a fine level, or the evaluator dictated minimal pairs of words to the child in order to assess the child's ability for associating auditory and visual perception. The dictation task requires the child to construct auditory schemes and transform them into grapho-visual representations. For instance, children who have visuoperceptual deficits and cannot copy graphic models but who do not have auditory perception problems can achieve a good level of performance when the phonological test is administered by dictation. And children who have auditory perception problems and cannot transform auditory schemes into graphic representations at the level of visuomotor coordination can achieve a good level of performance when the phonological test is administered at the copy level. These procedures provide the evaluator with qualitative data for making a differential diagnosis between phonological and phonetic disorders and for developing individualized educational programs.

When these additional administration forms were used, it became clear that the test of phonological development is useful for diagnosing reading and visual or auditory perceptual problems. It is important to use a phonological development test for assessing the interface between visual and auditory perception present in the encoding (phonemes) and decoding (graphemes) of sounds in the reading and writing process. Phonological disorders constitute problems in the auditory discrimination skill, a disorder in the phonemic categorization. Perhaps the child has difficulty in building phonetic motor schemes or has a learning disability. The latter is a deeper problem in the areas of visual and auditory perception, auditory memory (especially at a sequential short-term level), or cognitive abilities (i.e., the construction of phonemic symbolic representations at the semantic level which involves meaning construction). In contrast to phonological problems, phonetic disorders constitute problems in the articulation process, that is, only surface-level problems in the motor coordination ability for pronouncing the sounds.

Diagnostic Categories

Four diagnostic categories were generated as a result of the qualitative analysis of the children's performance on the phonological test:

Level 1: Superior. The child achieves mastery (approximately 100–90 percent correct responses) of all the minimal pairs in which bilingual children use phonological strategies in the articulation and auditory discrimination skills for his or her first language and age.

Level 2: Normal. The child achieves mastery (approximately 90–80 percent correct responses) of almost all the minimal pairs in which bilingual children use phonological strategies in the articulation and auditory discrimination skills for his or her first language and age. There are isolated errors in some phonemes in difficult positions.

Level 3: Delayed. The child does not achieve mastery (approximately 78–60 percent correct responses) of some of the minimal pairs in which bilingual children use phonological strategies in articulation and auditory discrimination skills for his or her first language and age. The child makes errors in the phonemes that are acquired earlier in phonological development (voiced occlusives as /b/, /d/, /g/; voiceless occlusives as /p/, /t/, /k/; and nasals as /m/ and /n/) because he or she has not yet developed automatic motor schemes for correctly uttering the phonemes. In most cases, the child uses a preferred strategy to cope with the more difficult phonemes. These children need an individualized educational program with emphasis in weak areas, for the stimulation of articulation and auditory discrimination of the phonemes in which the child has problems.

Level 4: Disordered. The child does not achieve mastery (approximately 50 percent or less correct responses) of most of the minimal pairs in which bilingual children use phonological strategies in articulation and auditory discrimination skills for his or her first language and age. Furthermore, the errors are made in all the phonemes and positions, and a preferred phonological strategy does not exist. The child makes all types of phonetic errors, and uses all kinds of phonological strategies, thus there is not a systematic pattern of errors.

Conclusions

This study demonstrated that every bilingual child presents an internal coherence in his or her phonological errors and strategies, as evidenced in the patterns of phonological acquisition used. In addition, the universal model of Jakobson (1956) was confirmed: older children presented a higher developmental level than younger children. Moreover, the phonological developmental sequence in first and second language is not simultaneous, but sequential. This finding can be the result of cognitive learning factors associated with phonological development, or of the different phonetic and phonological characteristics of the Spanish and English languages. As a result, a child who is learning English as a second language can have a higher level of phonological development in Spanish than in English.

The fact that there was no correlation between bilingual children's performance on the phonological development test constructed in Spanish and English supported the differences between the two languages in terms of their phonological characteristics. Many sounds the child has not yet learned in the first language cannot be learned in the second language. Thus, children must have attained a certain maturational level in phonological development in their first language according to their chronological and developmental ages before they can begin learning a second language. For instance, the mastery of some phonological categories in English, such as fricatives and affricates, requires a maturational phonological level in Spanish because these phonemes appear later in development and do not exist in Spanish. Moreover, there are developmental trends that each age group showed, and thus specific qualitative diagnostic categories of phonological development (i.e., superior, normal, delayed, and disordered) are suggested for conducting a differential diagnosis.

The test of phonological development was found to have validity and reliability for the assessment of the areas of articulation and auditory discrimination in both Spanish and English. This test correlated with standardized tests of reading readiness; thus, it can be used for an early diagnosis in bilingual children in order to prevent problems in reading and writing. Given that the test showed validity and reliability, another study involving older Mexican-American bilingual 6- and 7-year-olds was conducted (see Gonzalez, 1991). Finally, the phonological test provides qualitative data for developing individualized educational programs in order to stimulate phonological development at expressive (articulation) and receptive (auditory discrimination) levels in bilingual Spanish/English children.

REFERENCES

AMERICAN PSYCHOLOGICAL ASSOCIATION. (1986). *Standards for educational and psychological testing* (3rd ed.). Washington, DC: APA.

COMPTON, A. (1976). Generative studies of children's phonological disorders: Clinical ramifications. In D. Morehead & A. Morehead (Eds.), *Normal and deficient child language* (pp. 61–96) . Baltimore: University Park Press.

CUMMINS, J. (1989). Institutionalized racism and the assessment of minority children: A comparison of policies and programs in the United States and Canada. In R. J. Samuda, S. L. Kong, J. Cummins, J. Pascual-Leone, & J. Lewis (Eds.), *Assessment and placement of minority students* (pp. 95–107). Lewinston, NY: C. J. Hogrefe.

DE AVILA, E. A., & HAVASSY, B. E. (1974). Piagetian alternative to IQ: Mexican-American study. In N. Hobbs (Ed.), *Issues in the classification of exceptional children* (pp. 246–265). San Francisco: Jossey-Bass.

DUNN, L. M. (1982). *Peabody Picture Vocabulary Test (PPVT)*. Circle Pines, MN: American Guidance Service.

ERICKSON, J. G., & IGLESIAS, A. (1986). Assessment of communication disorders in non–English proficient children. In O. L. Taylor (Ed.), *Nature of communication disorders in culturally and linguistically diverse populations*. San Diego, CA: College Hill Press.

FERGUSON, C., FREIZER, D., & WEEKS, T. (1973). Model and replication in the phonological development of the first words of a child. *Lingua, 31*, 35–65.

GONZALEZ, V. (1991). Construction of a phonological development test in Spanish and English (PHDeSE) for bilingual children. In Malavé (Ed.), *Annual Conference Journal NABE 1988–1989* (pp. 171–184). Washington, DC: National Association for Bilingual Education (NABE).

GONZALEZ, V. (1994). A model of cognitive, cultural, and linguistic variables affecting bilingual Spanish/English children's development of concepts and language. *Hispanic Journal of Behavioral Sciences, 16*(4), 396–421.

HAKUTA, K. (1988). Why bilinguals? In F. S. Kessel (Ed.), *The development of language and language researchers: Essays in honor of Roger Brown* (pp. 299–318). Hillsdale, NJ: Lawrence Erlbaum Associates.

HEALEY, W. C., ACKERMAN, B. L., CHAPPEL, C. R., PERRIN, K. L., & STORMER, J. (1981). *The prevalence of communication disorders: A review of the literature.* Rockville, MD: American Speech-Language-Hearing Association.

INGRAM, D. (1970). Some suggestions on the role of systematic phonemics in child phonology. *PRCLD, 1,* 43–55.

INGRAM, D. (1974). Phonological rules in young children. *Journal of Child Language, 1,* 233–241.

INGRAM, D. (1981). *Procedures for the phonological analysis of child language.* Baltimore: University Park Press.

JAKOBSON, R. (1956). *Fundamentos del lenguaje.* Madrid, Spain: Ciencia Nuevas.

MCCARTHY, D. (1970). *McCarthy Scales of Children's Abilities.* Cleveland, OH: Psychological Corporation.

MENN, L. (1976). *Pattern, control and contrast in beginning speech.* Unpublished doctoral dissertation, University of Illinois.

MOLINA, S. (1985). *BADIMALE: Batería Diagnóstica de la Madurez Lectora.* Madrid, Spain: CEPE.

MYKLEBUST, H. R. (1981). *Pupil Rating Scale.* Cleveland, OH: Psychological Corporation.

OLLER, J. W., JR. (1983). Testing proficiencies and diagnosing language disorders in bilingual children. In D. R. Omark & J. G. Erickson (Eds.), *The bilingual exceptional child* (pp. 78–123). San Diego: College Hill Press.

PIAGET, J. (1965). *Mental imagery in the child, a study of the development of imaginal representation.* New York: Oxford University Press.

PIAGET, J. (1967). Piaget's theory. In P. H. Mussen (Ed.), *Carmichael's manual of child psychology* (Vol. 1, pp. 703–732). New York: Wiley.

PRIESTLY, T. (1980). Homonimy in child phonology. *Journal of Child Language, 7,* 413–427.

REID, C., ZHANG, Y., NIE, H , & DING, B. (1986). The ability to manipulate speech sounds depends on knowing alphabetic spelling. *Cognition, 24,* 31–44.

SRIHDAR, K. K. (1981). Pragmatics and language assessment. In J. G. Erickson & D. R. Omark (Eds.), *Communication assessment of the bilingual bicultural child.* Baltimore: University Park Press.

STAMPE, D. (1969). The acquisition of phonetic representation. *Proceedings of the Fifth Regional Meeting of the Chicago Linguistic Society, 5,* 443–454.

SWAIN, M. K. (1977). Bilingualism, monolingualism, and code acquisition. In W. F. Mackey & T. Anderson (Eds.), *Bilingualism in early childhood* (pp. 28–35). Rowley, MA: Newbury House.

VIHMAN, M. (1981). Phonology and the development of the lexicon. *Journal of Child Language, 8,* 239–265.

WEPMAN, J. M. (1958). *Wepman Auditory Discrimination Test* (English version). Chicago: Language Research Associates.

WEPMAN, J. M. (1975). *Test de Discriminación Auditiva de Wepman* (Spanish version). Lima, Perú: Universidad Católica.

CHAPTER 4

Models for the Relationship Among Language, Relative Degree of Bilingualism, Phonological Strategies, and Reading Readiness in Bilingual Spanish/English Children

VIRGINIA GONZALEZ

THIS CHAPTER, THE SECOND IN THIS PART, FOCUSING ON STUDIES OF cognitive and language development in bilingual children and adults, highlights the theme of including a multidimensional view on the assessment of cognition and language in bilingual children. In addition, the chapter highlights the second theme of the book by clearly demonstrating the need for a theoretical framework that includes an interface among cognition, culture, and language when assessing these children.

The objective of the study presented in this chapter was to find support for the hypothesis of a cause-and-effect relationship between independent and dependent linguistic and cognitive variables. The linguistic variables were the characteristics of the Spanish and English languages and the teachers' ratings of the bilingual children's relative degree of bilingualism. The cognitive variables were phonological strategies and reading readiness in bilingual children. Based on our objective, it was our intent to develop psychoeducational principles that have practical implications for the assessment, diagnosis, and instruction of bilingual children. This objective is closely related to a major need in the field of bilingual education: the development of robust psycholinguistic models for constructing alternative assessments of cognitive and first and second language processes. This study has practical implications for developing valid alternative assessments for bilingual children based on the theoretical model that identifies the cause-and-effect association between cognitive and linguistic processes. This study can also shed some light on the association between cognitive (e.g., phonological strategies and reading readiness) and linguistic (e.g., characteristics of the Spanish and English languages and relative degree of bilingualism) processes when bilingual children are assessed with alternative and standardized measures of language proficiency.

THE ASSESSMENT OF COGNITIVE AND LANGUAGE DEVELOPMENT IN BILINGUAL CHILDREN

The literature review that follows critically analyzes the measurement of cognitive and language development in bilingual children and discusses it in relation to three major problems:

1. The need for alternative assessments
2. The need to differentiate between assessment and diagnosis
3. The need to assess bilingual children in first and second languages

The discussion of these three major problems is followed by a literature review on the other variables included in this study:

4. Phonological development in bilingual children
5. Phonological development and reading readiness in bilingual children

Need for Alternative Assessments

Several authors have pointed to the need to construct alternative assessments:

- For making a differential diagnosis among genuine disabling conditions, the normal process of second language learning, and giftedness in bilingual children (e.g., Bernal, 1975; Cummins, 1981; De Avila & Havassy, 1975; Erickson, 1981; Erickson & Iglesias, 1986; Kamin, 1974; Mercer, 1979; Ortiz, 1987; Srihar, 1980; Taylor & Payne, 1983);
- For making accurate placement decisions for bilingual children in regular, bilingual, or bilingual special education (e.g., Cummins, 1979a, 1979b; Fishman, 1977; Oller, 1991; Oller & Perkins, 1978; Zirkel, 1976).

Thus, the construction of robust psycholinguistic models that explore the relationship between cognitive and linguistic processes in bilingual children is important for developing alternative assessments. Several authors from different disciplines (linguistics, cognitive psychology, psycholinguistics, psychometrics, bilingual education) have pointed to this need. For instance, Erickson and Iglesias (1986) and Srihar (1980) emphasized the need for models that consider linguistic and cultural variables and their influence on cognitive performance. Wagner (1980) pointed to the need for studies that relate individual differences in language proficiency to cognitive skills in bilinguals. Oller (1979, 1991) outlined the need to generate theories assessing the semiotic representational systems underlying first and second language learning.

The need for alternative assessments based on robust psycholinguistic theories stems from a lack of validity and reliability in standardized tests for bilingual children. For instance, bilingual children given standardized tests of intelligence are put at risk because of the high probability that the results will be inaccurate predictors for placement and instructional decisions. The weight of the evidence points to the fact that standardized tests underestimate children's cognitive and linguistic development due to the lack of an underlying psycholinguistic model that explains the relationship of cognitive, linguistic, and cultural factors in bilingual children. For instance, Erickson and Iglesias (1986) and Srihar (1980) have suggested that the construct validity of assessment instruments depends on the existence of an underlying robust psycholinguistic model that considers cognitive, cultural, and linguistic variables.

Furthermore, there is evidence demonstrating that standardized tests that measure language proficiency may not be reliable or valid (Bernal, 1975; De Avila & Havassy, 1975; Kamin, 1974; Mercer, 1979; Taylor & Payne, 1983) due to the association with cognitive and verbal processes. Evidence in the literature shows that language proficiency tests contain tasks that measure not linguistic skills per se but cognitive processes applied to verbal performance commonly measured by intelligence tests (Anderson & Pearson, 1984; Alexander, Schallert, & Hare, 1991). For instance, tests of pronunciation, which are considered to be measures of linguistic skills, may in fact measure auditory discrimination based on cognitive and linguistic processes, such as verbal perception. In addition, reading comprehension is included as a measure of linguistic skills when research (e.g., Anderson & Pearson, 1984) suggests that it is instead a constructive cognitive process. Finally, vocabulary, often presented as a linguistic ability, is very much based on cognitive and linguistic processes (Alexander, Schallert, & Hare, 1991) because it is dependent on verbal conceptual development.

Oller (1991) pointed to the fact that tests of intelligence and achievement (e.g., reading vocabulary and comprehension and writing proficiency) have as an implicit objective the measurement of primary language skills and verbal intelligence. According to Oller, these tests in the primary language also have many deficit-oriented categories, such as language disorders, mental retardation, and learning disabilities. Oller (1991) stated, "What traditional intelligence tests measure best are acquired primary language skills" (p. 8). As a result, Oller pointed out, American educators are misinterpreting a lack of English proficiency as a second language as a widespread intelligence deficit among non-native–English-speaking children and adults.

Thus, in this study, our objective was to understand how the performance of bilingual children in cognitive measurements, such as reading readiness, relates to linguistic measurements, such as their scores on standardized tests of language proficiency in Spanish and English. According to the literature, standardized measurements of cognitive and linguistic variables will show associations, given that the relationship between these factors is being tested. By mapping the association between cognitive and linguistic variables, we can shed light on the construction of some models for explaining first and second language learning and intelligence development in bilingual children. The construction of models explaining the association between cognitive and linguistic factors in bilingualism will also have practical implications for the generation of new qualitative or alternative methods that can measure the interaction of cognition, culture, and language.

Need to Differentiate Between Assessment and Diagnosis

Asher (1990) has noted an awareness of the psychometric biases of standardized and psychological tests for assessing bilingual children and has pointed out a major and well-known psychological principle for assessment calling for a battery of instruments: A diagnosis, placement, or instructional decision has to be based on a battery of psychoeducational tests and additional criteria from multiple sources and areas of information (medical history, parents' interview, teacher's ratings, class observations, functional or pragmatic use of the language by the child, etc.). This psychological principle leads to an important distinction: the conceptual differences among testing, assessment, and diagnosis. *Testing* is the process of test taking by students, and test administration and scoring by an evaluator. *Assessment* involves the interpretation of scores and the identification of potential problems or exceptional cases such as giftedness or learning disabilities. *Diagnosis* is the process of reaching a conclusion on the presence or absence of an intrinsic or extrinsic psychoeducational problem for the child, developing placement and instructional recommendations, therapy, and other suitable responses.

The diagnostic process, based on extended information derived from a battery of tests, including qualitative assessments across contexts using multiple informants, demands (1) deep knowledge on the underlying cognitive and linguistic processes being examined, (2) an awareness of the influence of cultural and linguistic factors on cognitive and learning processes, and (3) an extensive acquaintance with the individuals being assessed and diagnosed. Evaluators also have to be aware of the influence of their own attitudes, ideologies, value systems, beliefs, and general cultural identity on the assessment and diagnostic process. The analysis of a case study conducted by Gonzalez and Felix-Holt (1995) presented evidence demonstrating that reaching a diagnostic conclusion required the evaluator to go through an inferencing and interpretation process of a subjective nature. By virtue of the nature of the assessment and diagnostic process, decision making involves subjective judgments on the part of evaluators. This is especially the case in assessments of bilingual children because qualitative methods and standardized tests present

contradictory evidence. Thus, evaluators' personal biases influence the beliefs they hold on theoretical constructs that they are measuring using instruments derived from different assessment models (see Gonzalez & Felix-Holt, 1995, and Chapter 9 of this book). The result can be contradictory diagnostic and placement decisions across evaluators with different personal and academic backgrounds. Thus, the evaluator undertaking the diagnostic process puts together multidisciplinary pieces of information in order to solve the puzzle. Moreover, taking into account the lack of valid and reliable assessment instruments for bilingual children and the absence of underlying robust psycholinguistic models for the assessment instruments that are available, it is better to conceptualize the diagnostic process as an art rather than a technique.

This psychological assessment principle that differentiates between assessment and diagnosis is an important issue when the purpose is to make a differential diagnosis between the normal process of second language learning and genuine disabilities in the bilingual child. For instance, Duran (1989) reported that Hispanic bilinguals were diagnosed as "mentally retarded" when cut-off scores were used on IQ tests, with no additional data to support this diagnosis. Gonzalez (1991b, 1994, 1995) found that standardized tests of nonverbal intelligence (Test of Non-verbal Intelligence, TONI; Brown, Sherbenou, & Dollar, 1982) underestimated first-grade bilingual Hispanic children's cognitive abilities, and as a result these children were labeled "mentally retarded." In fact these same bilingual children showed normal-superior cognitive development levels when assessed by an alternative instrument based on classification problem-solving tasks, including linguistic and cultural factors (Gonzalez, 1991b, 1994, 1995). As a result, the product of biased assessment instruments leads to the overrepresentation of minority children in special education classes (Maestas, 1981; Ortiz & Maldonado-Colon, 1986; Ortiz & Yates, 1983).

Clearly, we need to develop alternative assessment approaches that can accurately measure the potential for learning of "at-risk bilingual children," and not only the external cultural factors associated with constructs measured. For instance, socially created constructs such as intelligence and its standardized measurements reflect the amount of information a child has learned in a particular cultural context rather than neuropsychological factors. However, the fallacy is that these intelligence or other standardized tests are interpreted as genuine measurements of internal factors in majority and minority children. The unfairness of this inaccurate assumption is even more acute and damaging for bilingual children, given that their intelligence (especially verbal and, to a lesser degree, their nonverbal abilities) is dramatically influenced by the cultural and linguistic factors affecting their representational and conceptual higher-level cognitive abilities. Diagnosis, appropriately done, reflects the interaction of both internal and external factors in the cognitive and linguistic development of bilingual children.

Need to Assess Bilingual Children in Their First and Second Languages

Asher (1990) pointed out that evaluators who rely only on tests administered in a single language may not be able to develop an empirical or hypothetical direction for interpreting or diagnosing on the basis of those scores. Thus, the need for assessing bilingual children in both their first and second languages is widely acknowledged (e.g., Cummins, 1981; Erickson, 1981; Oller, 1979; Ortiz, 1987; Zirkel, 1976). Assessment in first and second languages will give necessary information to the evaluator for making the differential diagnosis between the normal process of the acquisition of English as a second language and genuine disabilities. In support, Erickson (1981) suggested that collecting information on a child in both languages would allow the evaluator to differentiate among children who may have exhibited delays or problems in their native language and may need special education services from those who are developing satisfactorily. This need to assess bilingual children in both their first and second languages has been stated by the American Educational Research Association, the American Psychological Association, and the National Council on Measurement in Education (APA, 1986) in *Standards for Educational and Psychological Testing*, which point out that the administration of English-language tests to non-English-proficient children will assess only language proficiency in English or any other language, not achievement in a subject domain. These standards also underline the need to assess English-language proficiency by more than multiple-choice, paper-and-pencil tests.

Showing a developmental delay in language learning, even in the first language, is not sufficient for assuming the cause to be the presence of internal problems. Language developmental delays in the first language can also be the product of external factors, such as teaching problems or a home environment lacking appropriate language models. It is difficult to differentiate genuine learning problems based solely on the results of standardized tests, even when they are administered in both the first and second languages. A more appropriate strategy for differentiating genuine disabling conditions in bilingual children from the normal process of learning English as a second language is to use alternative assessments. Qualitative methods measuring verbal and, especially, nonverbal intelligence using problem-solving tasks are especially recommended for making an accurate differential diagnosis in bilingual children (see Gonzalez, 1994; Gonzalez & Yawkey, 1993).

There is evidence as well for the need to differentiate between problems in surface aspects of language (e.g., articulation) and deeper language disorders (e.g., aphasia or genuine learning disabilities). Skutnabb-Kangas and Toukomaa (1976) initially drew attention to the distinction between surface fluency in language and academically related aspects of language proficiency. Cummins (1979a, 1980) formalized the distinction in terms of basic interpersonal communication skills (BICS) and cognitive/academic language proficiency skills (CALPS). The distinction between BICS and CALPS was expressed in order to highlight the difference between viable, quantifiable, formal aspects of language (e.g., pronunciation, vocabulary, and grammar) and the less visible and less easily measurable aspects dealing with semantic and pragmatic aspects of proficiency (e.g., cultural connotations, idiomatic expressions, dialectal variations in vocabulary, and so forth). Oller (1983) assembled considerable evidence to show that academic and cognitive variables are strongly related to at least some measure of all general language skills (listening, speaking, reading, and writing) and pointed out that school personnel attributed lack of academic English proficiency to deficient cognitive or personality traits in bilingual students. Oller (1991) recommended deep rather than surface assessment through discourse-based and real-life performances.

The need to differentiate between problems in the surface and deeper aspects of language through the use of alternative assessments has been addressed by Ortiz (1987), who reported the characteristics of Hispanic limited-English-proficient (LEP) students in programs for the learning disabled, mentally retarded, and speech disabled in three urban school districts in Texas. The major reasons for referral were articulation and language problems. Ortiz reported that most speech and language testing seemed to address the student's mastery of surface aspects of language, described erroneously as articulation problems. She concluded that without data in both languages, it was impossible to determine whether the student's poor performance in syntax and grammar reflected LEP or a genuine speech-language disorder. High error rates on English discrete tests appeared to be used to justify recommendations for special education rather than to validate the student's LEP.

Thus, evaluators who are assessing bilingual children need to conduct a dual-language assessment that targets the deep levels of language proficiency that are connected to cognitive processes. When using only surface-level, discrete-point standardized tests, the deep connection between cognitive-linguistic processes is disintegrated. Qualitative assessments offer the best alternative for measuring deep-level cognitive and linguistic processes.

In summary, there are two major, connected needs in the field of bilingual education. The first need refers to the development of alternative assessment approaches that should be derived from strong theoretical models. The second need refers to improving the state of the art of the differential diagnosis between genuine disabling conditions and disabilities, giftedness, and the normal process of second language learning by using dual-language and alternative assessments.

Phonological Development in Bilingual Children

According to Stampe (1969), bilingual children use errors in articulation and auditory discrimination processes as phonological strategies for first and second language acquisition. A natural phonological process, Stampe proposed, is a mental operation that is applied in speech to substitute a different class for an alternative class of sound sequences that is almost identical but lacks the difficulty property. Using this natural phonology theory as a framework, Gonzalez (1986, 1988,1991a; see also Chapter 3 in this book) identified phonological strategies used by bilingual Spanish/English children. Several authors have reported a description of the most common phonological strategies bilingual Spanish/English children use: homonymy (Ingram, 1981; Priestly, 1980; Vihman, 1981), reduplication (Ingram, 1974; Ferguson, Freizer, & Weeks, 1973), substitution (Ingram, 1970), incongruent generalization (Gonzalez, 1986, 1991a), and inversion (Ingram, 1970).

According to findings in previous research (Gonzalez, 1986, 1988, 1991a; see also Chapters 3 and 7), the phonological strategies that bilingual children use follow an idiosyncratic and coherent pattern that is sequential with respect to first and second languages. Thus, they present a higher level of development in their first language than in their second language. These findings could be the result of cognitive learning factors associated with phonological development or the different phonetic and phonological characteristics of the Spanish and the English languages. Gonzalez's studies (1986, 1988, 1991a) have confirmed the universal model of Jakobson (Jakobson & Halle, 1956). Gonzalez (1988, 1991a) suggested that the fact that there is no correlation between bilingual children's performance on phonological development in Spanish and English supports the differences between the two languages in terms of their phonological characteristics and distinctive features. Gonzalez's findings (1986, 1988, 1991a) provided evidence for a sequential rather than a simultaneous phonological acquisition pattern among Spanish/English bilingual children. That is, sounds that the child has not yet learned in the first language cannot be learned in the second language either. As a result, bilingual children must have achieved a maturational level in phonological development in the first language before the process of learning the second language begins. Thus, phonological strategies used for coding the data of this research study were based on previous empirical studies (Gonzalez, 1986, 1998, 1991a), a feature that gives methodological strength to this study.

Articulation and auditory discrimination are two linguistic processes related to phonological strategies, considered to be cognitive abilities. Research shows that phonological development is a sequential rather than a simultaneous process that requires dual-language assessment. Evaluators who are assessing phonological development in both the first and second languages should not focus on the amount of articulation and auditory discrimination "errors," but rather on the study of the learning processes the bilingual child uses.

Phonological Development and Reading Readiness in Bilingual Children

There is ample evidence in the literature for the possibility of an association among language proficiency, phonological strategies, and reading readiness. For instance, Gonzalez (1986, 1988, 1991a) showed that the process of using phonological strategies for learning articulation and auditory discrimination skills is related to the process of learning how to read and write. She (1991a) interpreted these findings as the presence of an underlying common symbolic representational process of meaning construction in both cognitive processes (learning articulation and auditory discrimination skills, and learning how to read and write). Thus, in both cognitive processes, there is an interface between visual and auditory perception for encoding phonemes and decoding graphemes, and also for the transformation of these symbols into semantic representations (Menn, Shankweiler, & Smith, 1984).

Research studies conducted in the area of phonological development and its relationship to reading readiness have led to contradictory findings. The main difficulty arises due to the multidimensional variables involved in learning how to articulate and discriminate sounds, on the one hand, and how to read, on the other hand. Another difficulty is related to the multiple definitions associated with the term *phonological development*. As a result, there are three major positions in the literature.

The first position refers to the presence of a significant positive correlation between phonological development and reading readiness. The direction of the relationship, however, is not clear; it is still not known if phonological development or reading readiness is the cause or the effect. According to Bowey and Francis (1991), phonemic analysis can be a cause and an effect of alphabetic literacy because it is mediated by comprehension of the alphabetic principle. They found that children showed low performances on phoneme oddity tasks even after six months of reading instruction.

Within this first position, different areas of the relationship between phonological development and reading readiness have been studied, including the following:

- The positive effect of teaching children phonemic awareness for improving their reading skills (e.g., Ludberg, Frost, & Peterson, 1988)
- The predictive relationship between phonological segmentation and reading ability (e.g., Bradley & Bryant, 1985)
- The relationship between poor phonemic segmentation and reading problems (e.g., Jorm & Share, 1983; Snowling, 1987)

The second position refers to studies finding lack of influence of phonological deficits as explaining factors for reading difficulties (e.g., Bishop, 1991; Bishop & Butterworth, 1980). In addition, Bryant (1991) has noted a difference between "developmental prerequisites" and "developmental precursors." The former are essential abilities that need to be developed previously, and the latter are optional abilities that can help achieve a high performance on related abilities. There is some evidence supporting the concept of phonological skills acquired as developmental precursors of reading (e.g., Kirtley, Bryant, MacLean, & Bradley, 1989; Treiman, 1985).

Bryant (1991) supported the idea of idiosyncratic differences on the level of influence of phonological development on reading skills. Thus, for some children, phonological development can be a precursor, for others it can be a prerequisite, and for others it can have no relationship at all. Bryant also supported the idea of the influence of multiple interactional factors on what role phonological development plays on reading readiness, such as the pedagogical method used for teaching how to read. For instance, Seymour and Elder (1986) have shown that the whole language approach to teaching children how to read is only minimally related to phonological development levels and other relevant skills for reading readiness. Thus, Bryant (1991) believed that phonological development levels are only one among the many existing precursors of reading.

The third position on the relationship between phonological development and reading readiness states the existence of the inverse cause-and-effect relationship—that is, reading ability influences phonological awareness (e.g., Mann, 1986; Morais, Cary, Alegria, & Bertelson, 1979; Read, Zhang, Nie, & Ding, 1986). These authors also question the idea of considering phonological development as a causal variable for reading achievement levels.

The cause-and-effect relationship between phonological development and reading readiness needs to be clarified. The research study reported in this chapter can help to clarify this relationship because it takes into account cognitive and linguistic processes such as relative degree of bilingualisms. Furthermore, the study of bilingual children can help shed light on the relationship between cognitive and linguistic processes, because bilinguals are natural laboratories for the interaction of cognitive, cultural, and linguistic variables.

The exploratory research reported in this chapter studied the association among Spanish- and English-language proficiency, phonological strategies, and reading readiness in bilingual children. It sought to strengthen the hypothesized cause-and-effect relationship between independent and dependent factors, though not to prove it. Another purpose of the study was to derive some educational implications of the findings, such as psychopedagogical principles that can be used as guidelines for developing educational programs and for assessing, diagnosing, and placing bilingual Spanish/English children.

METHOD

Research Questions

This study set out seven research questions hypothesized as log-linear models; the first two were analyzed using symmetric models, and the following five were analyzed using asymmetric models. See Figure 4.1 for a graphic representation of the seven models tested.

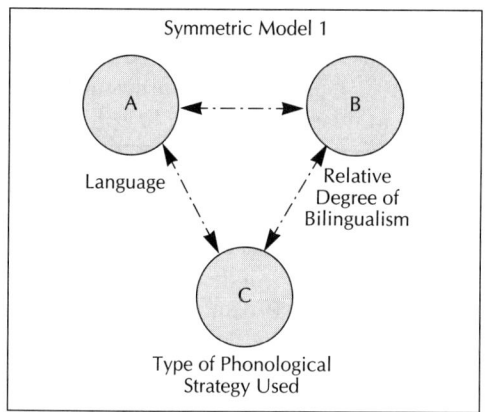
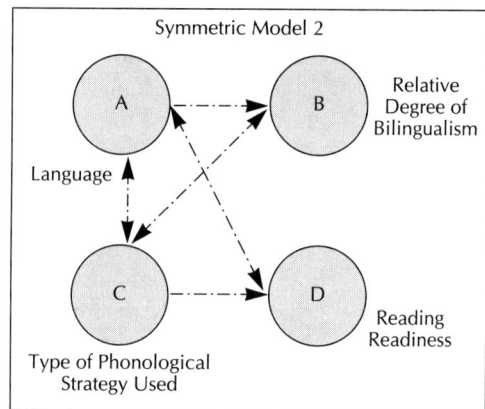
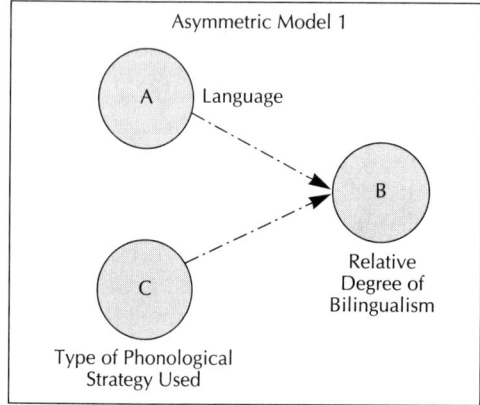
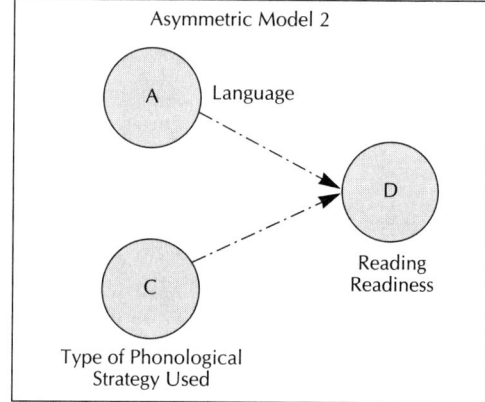
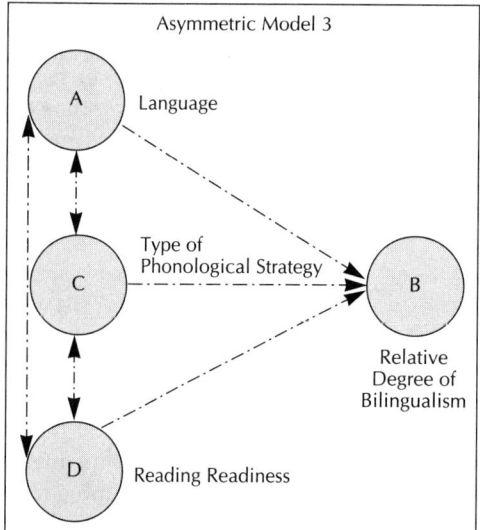
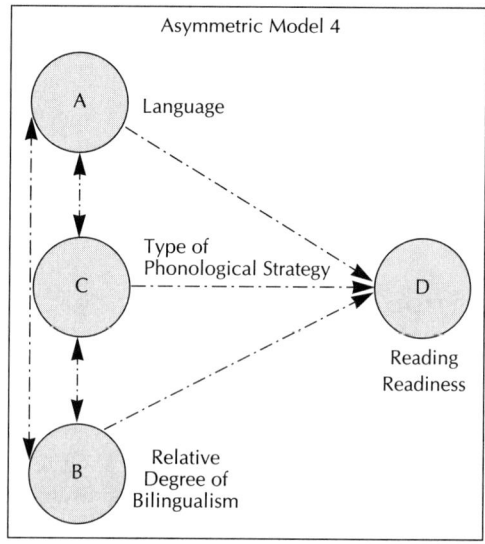

(*Continued*)

Chapter 4 Relationship Between Language and Other Factors

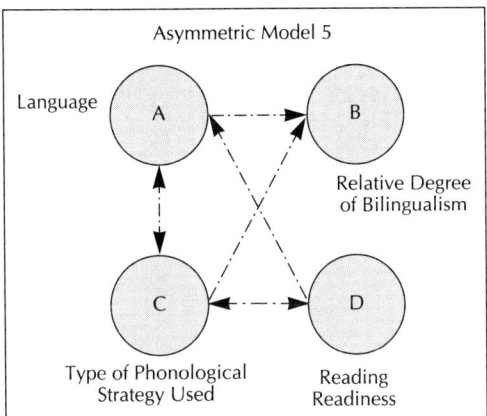

A = Language:
  A1 = Spanish, A2 = English.
B = Relative degree of bilingualism:
  B1 = Fluent bilinguals,
  B2 = Limited Spanish proficient.
C = Type of phonological strategy used:
  C1 = Homonymy,
  C2 = Reduplication,
  C3 = Substitution,
  C4 = Incongruent generalization,
  C5 = Avoidance, C6 = Inversion.
D = Reading readiness levels:
  D1 = Immature,
  D2 = Middle range,
  D3 = Mature.

FIGURE 4.1 Symmetric and asymmetric models for studying the association between language, language proficiency, type of phonological strategy used, and reading readiness in bilingual children.

Symmetric Models

1. Is there an association among language, relative degree of bilingualism, and types of phonological strategy (independent variables) that bilingual children use?
2. Is there an association among language, relative degree of bilingualism proficiency, types of phonological strategy, and reading readiness (independent variables) in bilingual children?

Asymmetric Models

1. Is there an association between language, type of phonological strategy (independent variables), and relative degree of bilingualism (dependent variable) in bilingual children?
2. Is there an association among language, type of phonological strategy (independent variables), and level of reading readiness (dependent variable) in bilingual children?
3. Is there an association among language, type of phonological strategy, level of reading readiness (independent variables), and relative degree of bilingualism (dependent variable) in bilingual children?
4. Is there an association among language, relative degree of bilingualism, and type of phonological strategy (independent variables), and level of reading readiness (dependent variable) in bilingual children?
5. Is there an association between language and type of phonological strategy (independent variables), and relative degree of bilingualism and level of reading readiness (dependent variables) in bilingual children?

Research Design

The study used an exploratory paradigm for investigating the association among four variables present in bilingual children:

1. Use of Spanish and English languages
2. Relative degree of bilingualism
3. Phonological strategy used
4. Level of reading readiness

The study's objective was to identify the causal or independent variables and the effects or dependent variables. The statistical technique that makes possible the identification of causal factors or effects for qualitative data is the procedure of fitting symmetric and asymmetric log-linear models to the data. In this case, the use of log-linear models is made only as a regression analysis for categorical data. Fitting symmetric and asymmetric log-linear models to the data was used for identifying cause-and-effect factors for qualitative data. However, the factors were not experimentally manipulated, so no attributions of causality resulted from this study.

The Models Explored

This study focused on symmetric and asymmetric log-linear models (see Figure 4.1 for a graphic representation of all seven models tested). For the symmetric model, the study explored two models with different dimensions:

Model 1: An association among three independent variables: language (with two levels: A1 = Spanish and A2 = English), relative degree of bilingualism (with two levels: B1= fluent bilinguals, and B2 = limited Spanish proficient), and types of phonological strategies (with six levels: C1 = homonymy, C2 = reduplication, C3 = substitution, C4 = incongruent generalization, C5 = avoidance, and C6 = inversion).

Model 2: An association among four independent variables—all those included in the three-dimensional model plus a fourth variable, reading readiness (with three levels: D1 = immature, D2 = middle-range performance, but still maturation has not been achieved, and D3 = mature).

For the asymmetric model, this study explored five models with different independent and dependent variables and dimensions:

Model 1: The presence of an association between two independent variables—language (A1, A2) and type of phonological strategy (C1–C6)—and a dependent variable—relative degree of bilingualism (B1, B2).

Model 2: The presence of an association between two independent variables—language (A1, A2) and type of phonological strategy (C1–C6)—and a dependent variable—level of reading readiness (D1–D3).

Model 3: The possibility of an association among three independent variables—language (A1, A2), type of phonological strategy (C1–C6), and level of reading readiness (D1–D3)—and one dependent variable—relative degree of bilingualism (B1, B2).

Model 4: The possibility of an association among three independent variables—language (A1, A2), relative degree of bilingualism (B1, B2), and type of phonological strategy (C1–C6)—and a dependent variable—level of reading readiness (D1–D3).

Model 5: The possibility of an association among two independent variables—language (A1, A2) and type of phonological strategy (C1–C6)—and two dependent variables—relative degree of bilingualism (B1, B2) and level of reading readiness (D1–D3).

Operational Definitions of Variables

Variable A, language, is defined as the specific language used for testing the children on the phonological strategies identified for language acquisition. There are two languages: A1 = Spanish and A2 = English.

Variable B is defined as the relative degree of bilingualisms. There are two groups: B1 = fluent bilinguals, with equally high levels in Spanish and English; and B2 = limited Spanish proficient, with low levels of language proficiency in Spanish and high levels of language proficiency in English.

Variable C is defined as the type of phonological strategy used for acquisition of the Spanish and English language. Six types of phonological strategies are identified based on previous research studies: C1 = homonymy, C2 = reduplication, C3 = substitution, C4 = incongruent generalization, C5 = avoidance, and C6 = inversion.

Variable D is defined as the level of reading readiness achieved. There are three levels: D1 = immature, D2 = middle-range performance, but still maturation has not been achieved, and D3 = mature.

Variables B and D separate naturally between groups of subjects. Variables A and C are within-subjects variables, so in an asymmetrical model, A and C can be considered independent variables and B and D can be considered dependent variables.

Subjects

Bilingual teachers of the bilingual classrooms selected at random for the study rated the children's language dominance and relative degree of bilingualism.

Teachers were provided with a description of the characteristics of the two groups of children that were of interest for the study (A1 = fluent bilinguals and A2 = limited Spanish proficient). Children identified by the teachers were tested on language proficiency and language dominance using the Language Assessment Scales in Spanish and English (De Avila & Duncan, 1986) and also on nonverbal intelligence using the TONI (Brown, Sherbenou, & Dollar, 1982). Children selected for the study had a normal nonverbal intelligence score. Two groups of bilinguals were selected for this study—10 children, 5 per group (B1 and B2).

Procedure

The children participated in two 30-minute assessment sessions. All were assessed on reading readiness using the BADIMALE (a readiness test in Spanish constructed by Molina, 1985). For the assessment of types of phonological strategies used for first and second language acquisition, all children were administered a test of phonological development in Spanish and English (Gonzalez, 1986, 1988, 1991a; see Chapter 3).

RESULTS AND DISCUSSION

Two major models were examined, symmetric and asymmetric, for acceptability of fit to the data. For both models, three-dimensional and four-dimensional tables were considered: ABC and ABCD. Variable D, reading readiness, was added because of the possibility of an association in the semantic nature of cognitive processes involved for all the variables included in the model. Tables 4.1 and 4.2 show the observed frequencies in the data used in this study for the three- and four-dimensional log-linear models. The zeroes in the tables are random zeroes.

Symmetric Model

For the three-dimensional table (ABC) presented in Table 4.3, a hierarchical log-linear model was considered in order to test the independence and three final models with significance of fit to data. The best model was the independent plus AB and BC model, a first-order interaction model indicating the presence of A and B effects. Although the significance level was low, the model was retained for further exploration (because of the small sample, the results were not very powerful). Thus, for gaining power, a low alpha level ($p < .025$) was considered appropriate. However, the procedures for sample selection were random, so that the assumptions for the symmetrical model were not violated. The best model (Independent + AB + AC) showed that there was an A

Chapter 4 Relationship Between Language and Other Factors

TABLE 4.1 Observed Frequencies by Language, Relative Degree of Bilingualism, and Type of Phonological Strategy

		C1	C2	C3	C4	C5	C6
A1	Spanish						
B1	Fluent bilinguals	10	0	13	0	0	2
B2	Limited Spanish proficient	12	2	33	0	11	16
A1	Spanish						
B1	Fluent bilinguals	31	4	43	2	2	3
B2	Limited Spanish proficient	20	1	5	0	1	3

effect that made a difference, which means that there was an association between language used (Spanish or English) and relative degree of bilingualism and also between language used (Spanish or English) and type of phonological strategy used, with a language main effect. In addition, as suggested by the second-best model (Independent + AB + BC), there was an association between language used (Spanish or English) and relative degree of bilingualism and between relative degree of bilingualism and type of phonological strategy used.

TABLE 4.2 Observed Frequencies by Language, Relative Degree of Bilingualism, Type of Phonological Strategy, and Level of Reading Readiness

		C1			C2			C3			C4			C5			C6		
		D1	D2	D3	D1	D2	D3	D1	D2	D3	D1	D2	D3	D1	D2	D3	D1	D2	D3
A1 Spanish B1 Fluent bilinguals		0	0	10	0	0	0	0	0	13	0	0	0	0	0	0	0	0	2
B2 Limited Spanish proficient		2	7	3	1	1	0	9	17	7	0	0	0	3	3	5	2	2	2
A1 Spanish B1 Fluent bilinguals		0	5	26	0	0	4	0	6	37	0	0	2	0	0	2	0	2	1
B2 Limited Spanish proficient		4	5	11	0	1	0	8	22	21	0	0	0	0	1	0	0	2	1

TABLE 4.3   Summary of Three-Dimensional Models (ABC)

Model	G2	df	Gain in G2	Gain in df	p
Independent	107.2487	16			< .0001
Independent + AB	54.65	15	52.5987	1	< .0001
Independent + AB + BC	30.6894	10	23.9706	5	< .01
Independent + AB + BC	28.7206	10	1.9688	0	< .025

G2 = log-linear model test
df = degrees of freedom

Based on this three-dimensional (ABC) model, two patterns can be observed:

1. Each bilingual child uses a different type of phonological strategy in Spanish and English according to the degree of bilingualism attained.
2. The Spanish and English languages require children to use different phonological strategies.

For the four-dimensional table (ABCD), a hierarchical log-linear model was carried out, getting the independent model and only one more final model with significance of fit to data, which are presented in Table 4.4. The

TABLE 4.4   Summary Table for Four-Dimensional Models: ABCD, ACDB, ACBD, and AC, DB

Model	G2	df	Gain in G2	Gain in df	p
ABCD model					
Independent	168.2028	62			< .0001
Independent + BD	82.5152	60	85.69128	2	< .050
ACDB model					
D × A, D × C, B	149.4981	58			< .001
C × D, C × A, B	143.0355	55	6.4626	3	< .001
ACBD model					
A × C, D	154.9564	64			< .001
B × A, B × C, D	138.483	63	16.4734	1	< .001
C × A, C × B, D	136.2063	59	2.2767	4	< .001
AC, DB model					
A × C, B, D	151.3477	63			< .001

G2 = log-linear model test
df = degree of freedom

best model was the first-order interaction model (independent model plus BD), which indicated the presence of BD effects. This model was significant at $p < .050$, a very respectable level, given that the sample was small. The best model (Independent + BD) shows an association between language proficiency and reading readiness levels that made a difference in the model. Adding the reading readiness variable was helpful for the analysis. It is suggested that each relative degree of bilingualism was associated with different levels of reading readiness. Based on these empirical observations, a hypothesis can be stated: *In order to achieve reading readiness, a bilingual child needs to achieve maturational levels in first and second language proficiency according to his or her chronological age.* This association was the only one that achieves significance in the four-dimensional symmetric level, so further asymmetric models were explored, taking variables B and/or D as dependent variables (i.e., language proficiency associated with reading readiness, or just one variable or the other).

Asymmetric Model

We decided to examine an asymmetric model because for the four-dimensional, log-linear models, only one first-order model had significance of fit to date. Thus, as the dimensionality of the tables increased from three to four variables, so did the likelihood that the inquiry was asymmetrical.

For the first three-dimensional table (AC, B), a hierarchical log-linear model was tested, getting one final first-order interaction model with significance of fit to data, which is presented in Table 4.5. The best model showed an interaction between the independent variables A and C on the dependent variable B, suggesting an association between language and type of phonological strategy used that made a difference with respect to relative degree of bilingualism. For the second three-dimensional table (AC, D), a hierarchical log-linear model was carried out, getting one final first-order interaction model with significance of fit to data. The model in Table 4.5 showed an interaction between the independent variables A and C on the dependent

TABLE 4.5 Summary Table for Three-Dimensional Tables: AC, B and AC, D

Model	G2	df	Gain in G2	Gain in df	p
A × C, B	239.4154	65			< .001
A × C, D	159.9564	64			< .001

G2 = log-linear model test
df = degree of freedom

variable D. The best model suggested an association between language and type of phonological strategy that made a difference with respect to level of reading readiness.

For the first four-dimensional table (ACDB), a hierarchical log-linear model was examined, getting two final first-order interaction models. The first model showed an interaction between the independent variables D and A, and D and C, with D effects, on the dependent variable B. The first model suggested an association between level of reading readiness and language and between level of reading readiness and type of phonological strategy used that made a difference with respect to relative degree of bilingualism. There was thus a level of reading readiness effect. The second model showed an interaction between the independent variables C and D, and C and A, with a C effect, on the dependent variable B. This second model is the best model that suggested an association between type of phonological strategy used and level of reading readiness and between type of phonological strategy used and language (Spanish and English), which made a difference with respect to relative degree of bilingualism. There was thus a type of phonological-strategy-used effect with respect to relative degree of bilingualism. These two final first-order interaction models are shown in Table 4.4.

For the second four-dimensional table (ABCD), a hierarchical log-linear model was tested, getting three final first-order interaction models shown in Table 4.4. The first model showed an interaction between the independent variables A and C, on the dependent variable D. The second model showed an interaction between the independent variables B and A, and B and C, with B effects, on the dependent variable D. The third model showed an interaction between the independent variables C and A, and C and B, with a C effect, on the dependent variable D. The third model was considered the best one. This best model suggested an association between type of phonological strategy used and language (Spanish and English); and between phonological strategy used and relative degree of bilingualism, which made a difference with respect to level of reading readiness. So there was a type of phonological-strategy-used effect with respect to level of reading readiness. Finally, for the third four-dimensional table (AC, BD), a hierarchical log-linear model was carried out, getting one final first-order interaction model. The model showed an interaction between the independent variables A and C and the dependent variables B and D, as shown in Table 4.4. This best model suggested an association between language and type of phonological strategy used (independent variables), which made a difference with respect to relative degree of bilingualism and level of reading readiness (dependent variables).

In summary, it can be observed that there was an association among the variables considered in the three- and four-dimensional models examined and that asymmetrical models fit the data better than symmetrical models.

Conclusions

It can be concluded that there is an association among language, relative degree of bilingualism, type of phonological strategy, and level of reading readiness, which varies according to the dimensions included and whether the variables are considered independent or dependent. Asymmetric models fit the data better than symmetric models. This outcome suggested that some independent variables make a difference with respect to other dependent variables.

Based on the three-dimensional symmetric models that fit the data, we can conclude that each bilingual child used a different combination of phonological strategies in Spanish and English according to the relative degree of his or her bilingualism. Based on the four-dimensional symmetric model, it can be concluded that the relative degree of bilingualism was associated with different levels of reading readiness. In addition, based on the three-dimensional asymmetric models that fit the data, we can conclude that there was an association between language and type of phonological strategy used that made a difference with respect to relative degree of bilingualism and reading readiness.

Based on the four-dimensional asymmetric models that fit the data, we can conclude that there was an association between type of phonological strategy used and level of reading readiness, and between type of phonological strategy used and language (Spanish and English), which made a difference with respect to relative degree of bilingualism. Thus, there was a phonological-strategy effect with respect to relative degree of bilingualism. In addition, there was an association between type of phonological strategy used and language (Spanish and English) and also between type of phonological strategy used and relative degree of bilingualism, which made a difference with respect to level of reading readiness. Thus, there was a type of phonological strategy effect with respect to level of reading readiness.

Based on the conclusions reported for each asymmetric and symmetric model tested, it can be observed that the four-dimensional asymmetric model fits the data best. This best model suggests an association between language and type of phonological strategy used (independent variables), which made a difference with respect to relative degree of bilingualism and level of reading readiness (dependent variables). Thus, the practical implications for bilingual children's assessment of cognitive and linguistic processes derived from the results found in this study include the following:

1. There is a need to assess phonological development in bilingual children in their first language because they will use different phonological strategies in comparison to their second language.
2. There is a need to assess first and second language proficiency in bilingual children because different levels of language learning will be associated with different phonological learning patterns and strategies used.

3. There is a need to assess reading readiness in bilingual children because it is associated with relative degree of bilingualism attained and type of phonological strategy used.

Bilingual children showed a different pattern of phonological strategies when assessed in their first and second languages. As a result, it is important when making a differential diagnosis between genuine disabling conditions and disabilities, giftedness, and the normal process of second language learning to take into account the children's language dominance and first and second language phonological similarities and differences. These two latter factors are important because they affect the language proficiency and reading readiness levels of bilingual children.

This study has some methodological weaknesses, including the small sample tested in the log-linear models hypothesized, the number of models run with this small sample and the fact that some cells were missing in the data, the subjectivity of the teachers rating the first and second relative degree of bilingualisms of the children, and the standardized tests used for measuring reading readiness. Even though results were significant at high levels of probability, because of the limitations of this study, generalization of results should be made with caution.

REFERENCES

ALEXANDER, P. A., SCHALLERT, D. L., & HARE, V. C. (1991). Coming to terms with the terminology of knowledge. *Review of Educational Psychology, 61,* 315–343.

AMERICAN PSYCHOLOGICAL ASSOCIATION. (1986). *Standards for educational and psychological testing.* (3rd ed.). Washington, DC: APA.

ANDERSON, R. C., & PEARSON, P. D. (1984). A schema-theoretic view of basic processes in reading comprehension. In P. D. Pearson (Ed.), *Handbook of reading research* (pp. 255–293). New York: Longman.

ASHER, S. R. (1990). Recent advances in the study of peer rejection. In S. R. Asher & J. D. Coie (eds.), *Peer rejection in childhood* (pp. 3–16). Cambridge, England: Cambridge University Press.

BERNAL, E. M. (1975). A response to "Educational uses of tests with disadvantage students." *American Psychologist, 30,* 93–95.

BISHOP, D. V. M. (1991). Developmental reading disabilities: The role of phonological processing has been overemphasized. *Mind and Language, 6*(2), 97–101.

BISHOP, D. V. M., & BUTTERWORTH, A. (1987). Verbal-performance discrepancies: Relationship to birth risk and specific reading retardation. *Cortex, 16,* 375–389.

BOWEY, J. A., & FRANCIS, J. (1991). Phonological analysis as a function of age and exposure to reading instruction. *Applied Psycholinguistics, 12,* 91–121.

BRADLEY, L., & BRYANT, P. E. (1985). Rhyme and reason in reading and spelling. *IARLD Monographs, 1, 120–135.* Ann Arbor: University of Michigan Press.

BROWN, L., SHERBENOU, R. J., & DOLLAR, S. J. (1982). *Test of Nonverbal Intelligence* (TONI). Austin, TX: Pro-Ed.

BRYANT, P. E. (1991). Phonological awareness is a pre-cursor, not a pre-requisite, of reading. *Mind and Language 6*(2), 102–106.

CUMMINS, J. (1979a). Cognitive/academic language proficiency, linguistic interdependence, the optimum age question and some other matters. *Working Papers on Bilingualism, 19,* 121–129.

CUMMINS, J. (1979b). Linguistic interdependence and the educational development of bilingual children. *Bilingual Education Paper Series, 3*(2), 233–255.

CUMMINS, J. (1980). Psychological assessment of immigrant children: Logic or intuition? *Journal of Multilingual and Multicultural Development, 1,* 97–111.

CUMMINS, J. (1981). The role of primary language development in promoting educational success for language minority students. In California State Department of Education, *Schooling and language: Minority children* (pp. 3–49). Los Angeles: California State University.

DE AVILA, E. A., & DUNCAN, S. H. (1986). *Language Assessment Scales.* Monterey, CA: Macmillan/McGraw-Hill.

DE AVILA, E. A., & HAVASSY, B. E. (1975). Piagetian alternative to IQ: Mexican-American study. In N. Hobbs (Ed.), *Issues in the classification of exceptional children* (pp. 246–265). San Francisco: Jossey-Bass.

DURAN, R. P. (1989). Assessment and instruction of at-risk Hispanic students. *Exceptional Children, 5*(2), 154–158.

ERICKSON, J. G. (1981). Communication assessment of the bilingual bicultural child. In J. G. Erickson & D. R. Omark (Eds.), *Communicative assessment of the bilingual/bicultural child: Issues and guidelines* (pp. 1–21). Baltimore: University Park Press.

ERICKSON, J. G., & IGLESIAS, A. (1986). Assessment of communication disorders in non-English proficient children. In O. L. Taylor (Ed.), *Nature of communication disorders in culturally and linguistically diverse populations.* San Diego, CA: College Hill Press.

FERGUSON, C. A., FREIZER, D. B., & WEEKS, T. E. (1973). Model and replication in the phonological development of the first words of a child. *Lingua, 4,* 35–65.

FISHMAN, J. A. (1977). The social science perspective. *Bilingual education: Current perspectives* (Vol 1). Arlington, VA: Center for Applied Linguistics.

GONZALEZ, V. (1986). *Test of phonological development in Spanish and English (TPhDeSE) for preschoolers.* Unpublished bachelor's thesis, Catholic University of Perú, Lima.

GONZALEZ, V. (1988). *Construction of a phonological development test in Spanish and English (PhDeSE) for bilingual children.* Unpublished master's report, University of Texas at Austin.

GONZALEZ, V. (1991a). Construction of a phonological development test in Spanish and English (PHDeSE) for bilingual children. In L. Malavé (Ed.), *Annual Conference Journal NABE 1988–1989* (pp. 171–184). Washington, DC: National Association for Bilingual Education (NABE).

GONZALEZ, V. (1991b). *A model of cognitive, cultural, and linguistic variables affecting bilingual Spanish/English children's development of concepts and language.* Unpublished doctoral dissertation, University of Texas at Austin. (ERIC Document Reproduction Service No. ED 345 562).

GONZALEZ, V. (1994). A model of cognitive, cultural and linguistic variables affecting bilingual Hispanic children's development of concepts and language. *Hispanic Journal of Behavioral Sciences, 16*(4), 396–421.

GONZALEZ, V. (1995). *Cognition, culture, and language in bilingual children: Conceptual and semantic development.* Bethesda, MD: Austin & Windfield.

GONZALEZ, V., & FELIX-HOLT, M. (1995). Influence of evaluators' prior academic knowledge and beliefs on the diagnosis of cognitive and language development in bilingual Hispanic kindergartners. *New York State Association for Bilingual Education Journal, 10*(1), 34–45.

GONZALEZ, V., & YAWKEY, T. D. (1993). Assessment of culturally and linguistically different students: Celebrating change. *Educational Horizons, 72*(1), 41–49.

INGRAM, D. (1970). Some suggestions on the role of systematic phonemes in child phonology. *PRCLD I,* 43–55.

INGRAM, D. (1974). Phonological rules in young children. *Journal of Child Language, 1,* 49–64.

INGRAM, D. (1981). *Procedures for the phonological analysis of child language.* Baltimore: University Park Press.

JAKOBSON, R., & HALLE, M. (1956). *Fundamentos del lenguaje.* Valencia, Spain: Editorial Ciencias Nuevas.

JORM, A. F., & SHARE, D. L. (1983). Phonological recoding and reading acquisition. *Applied Psycholinguistics, 4,* 103–147.

KAMIN, L. J. (1974). *The science and politics of IQ.* New York: Wiley.

KIRTLEY, C., BRYANT, P., MACLEAN, M., & BRADLEY, L. (1989). Rhyme, rime and the onset of reading. *Journal of Experimental Child Psychology, 48,* 224–245.

LUNDBERG, I., FROST, J., & PETERSON, O. (1988). Effects of an extensive program for stimulating phonological awareness in preschool children. *Reading Research Quarterly, 23,* 263–284.

MAESTAS, J. (1981, March). *The participation of Hispanics in special education.* Paper presented at the Institute for Educational Leadership, Washington, DC.

MANN, V. A. (1986). Phonological awareness: The role of reading experience. *Cognition, 24,* 65–92.

MENN, L., SHANKWEILER, D., & SMITH, S. (1984). The association between comprehension of spoken sentences and early reading ability: The role of phonetic representation. *Journal of Child Language, 2,* 627–643.

MERCER, J. R. (1979). A policy statement on assessment procedures of the rights of children. *Harvard Educational Review, 44,* 125–141.

MOLINA, S. (1985). *BADIMALE: Batería Diagnóstica de la Madurez Lectora.* Madrid, Spain: CEPE.

MORAIS, J., CARY, L., ALEGRIA, J., & BERTELSON, P. (1979). Does awareness of speech as a sequence of phones arise spontaneously? *Cognition, 7,* 323–331.

OLLER, J. W., JR. (1979). *Language tests at school.* London: Longman.

OLLER, J. W., JR. (1983). Testing proficiencies and diagnosing language disorders in bilingual children. In D. R. Omark & J. G. Erickson (Eds.), *The bilingual exceptional child* (pp. 78–123). San Diego, CA: College-Hill Press.

OLLER, J. W., JR. (1991). *Language testing research: Lessons applied to LEP students and programs.* Paper presented at the National Research Symposium on Limited English Proficient (LEP) Students' Issues: Focus on Evaluation and Measurement. Washington, DC: OBEMLA and OERI.

OLLER, J. W. JR., & PERKINS, K. (1978). *Language in education: Testing the tests.* Rowley, MA: Newbury House.

ORTIZ, A. A. (1987). Communication disorders among limited English proficient Hispanic students. *Bilingual Special Education Newsletter* (University of Texas at Austin), 5.

ORTIZ, A. A., & MALDONADO-COLON, E. (1986). Reducing inappropriate referrals for language minority students to special education. *Journal of Reading, Writing, and Learning Disabilities International, 2*(1), 43–56.

ORTIZ, A. A., & YATES, J. R. (1983). *Incidence of exceptionality among Hispanics: Implications for manpower planning.* Unpublished manuscript, University of Texas, Department of Special Education, Austin.

PRIESTLY, T. (1980). Homonymy in child phonology. *Journal of Child Language, 7,* 413–427.

READ, C., ZHANG, Y., NIE, H., & DING, B. (1986). The ability to manipulate speech sounds depends on knowing alphabetic spelling. *Cognition, 24,* 31–44.

SEYMOUR, P. K., & ELDER, L. (1986). Beginning reading without phonology. *Cognitive Neuropsychology, 3,* 1–36.

SKUTNABB-KANGAS, T., & TOUKOMAA, P. (1976). *Teaching migrant children's mother tongue and learning the language of the host country in the context of the sociocultural situation of the migrant family.* (UNESCO Research Report No. 15). Tampere, Sweden: University of Tampere.

SNOWLING, M. (1987). *Dyslexia: A cognitive developmental perspective.* Oxford: Blackwell.

SRIHAR, K. K. (1980). Language testing in bilingual education: A critical analysis. *Bilingual Resources, 3,* 30–36.

STAMPE, D. (1969). *The acquisition of phonetic representation.* Paper presented at the fifth regional meeting of the Chicago Linguistic Society, Chicago.

TAYLOR, O. P., & PAYNE, K. T. (1983). Culturally valid testing: A proactive approach. *Topics in Language Disorders, 3,* 1–7.

TREIMAN, R. (1985). Onsets and rimes as units of spoken syllables: Evidence from children. *Journal of Experimental Child Psychology, 39,* 161–181.

VIHMAN, M. (1981). Phonology and the development of the lexicon. *Journal of Child Language, 8,* 239–265.

WAGNER, A. L. (1980). Cognitive perspectives on bilingualism in children. *International Review of Applied Psychology, 29,* 31–41.

ZIRKEL, P. A. (1976). The "why's" and ways of testing bilinguality before teaching bilingually. *Elementary School Journal 3,* 323–330.

CHAPTER 5

Why Is It *Una Persona* and Not *Un Persona?*
Influence of Linguistic and Cultural Variables on Conceptual Learning in Second Language Situations*

VIRGINIA GONZALEZ, DIANE L. SCHALLERT,
SONIA DE RIVERA, MARTHA FLORES,
AND LORRI M. PERRODIN

CHAPTER 5 HIGHLIGHTS THE MAJOR THEME OF THE BOOK: THE CULTURAL and linguistic influence on the construction of semantic representations in bilingual learners. In the study reported in this chapter, we were interested in exploring the application of a conceptual learning model to adults learning a second language. The objective of this study was to validate a multidimensional model that represents the triple interaction of cognitive, cultural, and linguistic factors in second language concept formation. We used an exploratory-interpretative, data-gathering approach to shed light on the relationship between language and thought, since our argument is that second language learning situations are fruitful for highlighting the processes reflecting how thought is influenced by language and cultural factors. The focus of

---

*Preparation of this article was supported in part by a Small Grant given by the Office of the Vice President for Research in conjunction with the University of Arizona Foundation. Partial results of the study reported in this chapter have been presented at the American Educational Research Association annual meetings (see Gonzalez & Schallert, 1993; Gonzalez, Schallert, Flores, Perrodin, & de Rivera, 1994).

this study is on monolingual English college students who were developing new gender concepts, unique to the Spanish language and culture, that reflect the interaction of linguistic structures, cultural symbolic meanings, and abstract conceptual categories. In our model, the process of second language concept formation is influenced by the presence of both common and different first and second language structures, cultural symbolic meanings, and cognitive and metacognitive processes.

Consider the following example. A monolingual English college student is facing a problem-solving task in which he must explain to his instructor (the interviewer) why he made certain linguistic choices as he wrote answers on an assignment for a first-year intensive Spanish course:

INTERVIEWER: (reading from student's paper) *El joven es un persona que no tiene mucho años.* This is right. *El joven.* Why did you pick *el* and not *la*?

STUDENT: Hm. I was thinking of a young boy.

INTERVIEWER: If you were thinking of a young girl, which article would you use?

STUDENT: I would use *la joven.*

INTERVIEWER: *La joven.* Okay. So, *joven* would not change?

STUDENT: Yes.

INTERVIEWER: Okay. (reading from student's paper) *El joven es un persona.* Why *un persona?*

STUDENT: *Un persona* is masculine.

INTERVIEWER: How come you have *un persona?*

STUDENT: Because you have *el joven.*

INTERVIEWER: Okay. *Un* reflects *el joven.*

STUDENT: Yes.

INTERVIEWER: So if I have *la joven*, it would be, *La joven es* . . . ?

STUDENT: *Sí*, es *una persona.*

INTERVIEWER: Okay, so you are making the difference, right? Feminine or masculine. (reading from student's paper) *El joven es un persona que no tiene mucho años.* Why *mucho* and not *mucha*?

STUDENT: *Mucho* is like *el joven, un persona, es masculino.*

INTERVIEWER: Okay, *mucho* is reflecting *el joven.*

STUDENT: Ah . . . *Sí, o un persona.*

INTERVIEWER: So everything is reflecting . . .

STUDENT: Yes.

INTERVIEWER: So, you have (reading from student's paper) *La joven es una persona que no tiene* . . .

STUDENT: Hm . . . *mu, mucha* . . . No, I couldn't do that, because it would be *mucha años* . . . (laughs).

INTERVIEWER: So are you kind of confused? If you put *la joven*. Just guessing, which one would you pick? If that would be *la joven*.

STUDENT: First, I think it should be *muchos*.

INTERVIEWER: Uh-huh, because *años* is plural?

STUDENT: Yeah . . . and I don't think it would change. It would be *muchos años*.

INTERVIEWER: Okay, so here there is a difference, and they would be the same.

STUDENT: Yes.

INTERVIEWER: Actually, you are right. *El joven y la joven* can both happen.

The student is facing a common situation: learning to be sensitive to a linguistic distinction that Spanish makes that is not relevant in his native (English) language. The task he faces requires the simultaneous consideration of intralinguistic and extralinguistic knowledge. For instance, when he must decide which article to use with the word *joven*, he must tap extralinguistic topic knowledge to decide if the feminine or masculine article is appropriate to capture his intended meaning or imagined referent. When the interviewer asks him to justify his incorrect use of the masculine article with *persona*, he reveals that he is overextending a rule and applying it to a collective noun that is an exception to the rule. In fact, the application of gender to nouns and modifiers in Spanish follows a complex set of rules, and for any one noun, different combinations of rules apply, reflecting linguistic, cultural, and cognitive dimensions. An English speaker learning Spanish must understand which rules apply in which context. This student is a typical intermediate learner: he overgeneralizes some rules and lacks knowledge of other rules and their restrictions. He also creates false hypotheses, which consider only unidimensional and insufficient factors and do not include the multidimensional combinations of rules reflecting linguistic, cultural, and cognitive factors. When the interviewer pushes him to consider how he would use the linguistic gender-appropriate adjective with the word *años*, he realizes that he has overextended a rule and reaches a higher level of metacognitive awareness and self-evaluation. He laughs.

We have already argued that second language acquisition involves constructing conceptual and cultural knowledge representations, as well as linguistic knowledge (Gonzalez, 1991, 1994; see Chapter 2 of this book). Understanding how second language learners represent language-related concepts is a complex issue with important educational implications. Although it has been the focus of much research, it has yet to be solved. Past research studies (e.g., Bialystock, 1978; Karmiloff-Smith, 1979, 1985, 1986; O'Malley, Russo, Chamot, & Stewner-Manzanares, 1988) have only partially considered the interface of cognitive, cultural, and linguistic factors, which may explain the contradictory results that have been reported. In addition, contradictory results may derive from researchers' using different levels of analysis: the process and product levels. In other words, an analysis centered on cognitive underlying *processes* may yield a different understanding of second language learning than an analysis focusing on the verbal *products*.

The study of second language learning at the cognitive processes level can be enlightened by the use of introspective report methods that focus on concept formation. Involving the learner as an active, knowing informant is a key factor for discovering underlying cognitive processes in second language learning. Also, the presence of theoretical contrasts in the analysis of second language learning (at the process and product levels) is reflected in the difficulty of labeling, stating operational definitions, and measuring concept formation processes. To alleviate these difficulties, we use introspective report methods that provide access to a psychological dimension of metacognitive and metalinguistic processes, viewing the learner as an insightful co-researcher. Moreover, we propose that the interface of cognition, culture, and language can be studied through problem-solving tasks that require the learner to articulate the underlying concept formation processes through verbal reports. Through the use of verbal reports, we can access the process of language-related concept construction, reflecting how meaning is represented at the linguistic, symbolic, and abstract levels by the learner.

Finally, we anticipate that individuals learning a second language will show varying levels of sophistication in their cognitive and metacognitive processes and their linguistic, cultural, and conceptual knowledge, depending on what content they are learning. That is, the same learner can be at different points in his or her development depending on the linguistic, cultural, and conceptual characteristics of the content to be learned. Thus, we propose that there will be an interaction between the cultural and linguistic characteristics of the content to be learned and the learner's specific language learning strategies and preexisting knowledge.

The following sections present an integration of three literature paradigms that have been generated by Bialystock's (1978) model of language learning processes and forms of knowledge, Karmiloff-Smith's (1979, 1985, 1986) model of knowledge representation, and O'Malley and colleagues' (1988) categorization of language learning strategies. We then discuss the methodological problems that have plagued previous studies as a springboard to formulating specific design and methodological features for the study reported in this chapter. We focus on methodological dichotomies between introspective report methods and experimental or quantitative research methods, and between a product- versus a process-oriented research design. Next, we integrate this literature review on cognitive processes and methodological dichotomies with the model of the cognitive, linguistic, and cultural factors influencing concept formation proposed by Gonzalez (1991, 1994, 1995). Finally, we illustrate this integration with the results of an exploratory-interpretive study of college-level students learning Spanish through the concept formation approach (experimental group) and a traditional approach (control group).

Concept Construction and Strategy Use in Second Language Learning

The theoretical framework of our study is derived from models developed by Bialystock (1978), Karmiloff-Smith (1979, 1985, 1986), and O'Malley and colleagues (1988). The integration of these three models is reflected in the content categories used for our data analysis, focusing on cognitive processes used for concept construction at three different levels: (1) forms of knowledge, (2) developmental phases, and (3) metacognitive, cognitive, and social-affective language learning strategies. This framework makes a distinction between *intralinguistic knowledge*—that is, first and second language knowledge—and *extralinguistic knowledge*, such as sociocultural knowledge. These two types of knowledge can be represented on a continuum ranging from a vague, implicit, and insecure form to a clear, explicit, and secure form. Finally, in the framework, intralinguistic and extralinguistic knowledge merge in the semantic categories for gender, encompassing general, regular, and irregular cases.

Language Learning Processes and Forms of Knowledge

Bialystock (1978) presented a model of second language learning that was intended to account for discrepancies in individual achievement in different semantic domains. The model is explained in terms of learning processes and strategies that are organized in three levels: input, knowledge, and output. The knowledge level assumes that information about a language may be represented in three ways: explicit linguistic knowledge, implicit linguistic knowledge, and other knowledge. This last category refers to all other information the learner brings to the language task explicitly or implicitly (e.g., knowledge of the native language or other languages, information about the culture associated with the target language, and knowledge of the world). Thus, having access to other knowledge is important because the meaning of linguistic knowledge is sometimes dependent on particular cultural connotations. That is, whereas the use of the word in appropriate contexts is implicit, the specific cultural aspects of the meaning and its occasions for use may be articulated explicitly.

The difference between explicit and implicit linguistic knowledge refers to whether the language learner can access internal representations. *Explicit linguistic knowledge* contains all the conscious facts the learner has about the language that can be expressed verbally. *Implicit linguistic knowledge* is the intuitive information upon which the language learner operates in order to produce responses at the comprehension or production levels in the target language. The content of explicit and implicit linguistic knowledge may include some grammar rules, vocabulary items, and pronunciation rules.

Bialystock (1978) assigned three functions to the explicit linguistic knowledge source:

1. To act as a buffer for new information about language, some of which may eventually become automatic and be transferred to implicit linguistic knowledge
2. To act as a store for information that is always represented explicitly
3. To act as an explicit articulatory system

By contrast, only one function is ascribed to the implicit linguistic knowledge form: a working system containing all the information about the target language necessary for most spontaneous comprehension and production tasks.

Developmental Phases in Language Learning

Early conceptions of the nature of the cognitive processes involved in language learning often used dichotomies for explaining phenomena, such as implicit and explicit, procedural and declarative, unconscious and conscious, representational and metarepresentational. Karmiloff-Smith (1979, 1985, 1986), however, argued that such conceptions did not capture the complex nature of the processes involved. Instead, she proposed that knowledge is made up of modules, each representing a domain. *Domains* consist of knowledge represented in different codes. Instead of using categories of codes, Karmiloff-Smith proposed that the codes were on a continuum of accessibility, with verbal and nonverbal representations at each end. Learners would progress on this continuum from lower nonverbal representations to higher verbal representations. The possibility of representing knowledge through different continuous domains gives access to higher-order concepts, propositional thinking, logical reasoning, and metaknowledge. Thus, language, the most abstract representational system for cognition, makes possible higher forms of thinking such as metaknowledge.

Karmiloff-Smith (1986) presented a three-phase multidimensional model to explain the relations between implicit, or unconscious, and explicit, or conscious, metacognitive processes. These phases apply to specific domains rather than across domains and are loosely age related. Thus, phases are recurrent cycles of processes that are repeated as the different aspects of the linguistic system develop. Language learning is a sequential rather than simultaneous process of rule learning that is influenced by recurrent transformations of knowledge in different domains. In the first phase, the stimulus is encoded linguistically, resulting in the formation of one-to-one mappings of form and function without rules or access to consciousness. In the second phase, networks of semantic representations of linguistic structures in different contexts are explicitly defined. Robinett and Schachter (1983) presented different developmental errors of second language rule learning, including overgeneralization, ignorance of rule restrictions, incomplete application of rules, and false concepts. The student in our introductory example showed all four of these developmental errors and would thus be at the second developmental phase. In the third phase, the learner is able to transform or re-represent nonverbal into verbal codes and to connect abstract codes with verbal meta-knowledge that becomes explicitly linked by a common code. As a result, the learner has constructed a cognitive system that is very flexible and can be explicitly related and accessed through semantic networks.

Language Learning Strategies

O'Malley and colleagues (1988) presented a classification system of three types of language learning strategies: metacognitive, cognitive, and social-affective (see the data analysis section of this chapter for the operational definitions). In general, "metacognitive strategies" refers to the learner's conscious access to his or her own perceptual, attention, memory, or higher-level thought processes (e.g., creativity or problem-solving abilities). "Cognitive strategies" refers to internal mental processes that are used automatically for learning (e.g., perception, attention, memory, problem-solving, and so forth). "Social-affective strategies" refers to internal emotional processes that are learned within a particular sociocultural reality. (The first two strategies were adapted from Brown & Palinscar, 1982, and the third from O'Malley et al., 1988.) Our argument is that the use of these strategies is related to the forms of knowledge suggested by Bialystock (1978) and the developmental phases proposed by Karmiloff-Smith (1978, 1985, 1986). That is, the language learning strategies that individuals use vary according to idiosyncratic preference and developmental level, and also according to the linguistic and cultural content being learned. In our framework, metacognitive strategies correspond to explicit knowledge and are the prime indicator that a learner has reached the third developmental phase because the learner is able to access consciously a verbal explanation for the production of linguistic structures. Some of the cognitive language learning strategies O'Malley and colleagues (1988) identified correspond to an implicit form of knowledge, where the learner uses automatic processes for producing or comprehending language. Other cognitive language learning strategies correspond to explicit knowledge processes because the learner is able to access verbally the internal representational processes required. Learners at all three developmental phases use social-affective language learning strategies along with the cognitive strategies.

METHODOLOGICAL PROBLEMS

The Exploratory-Interpretative Paradigm

The aim of the exploratory-interpretative paradigm applied to second language learning situations is to understand how learners reconstruct language processes, the view of self as a language learner, and of learners' extralinguistic knowledge. According to Grotjahn (1987), researchers themselves become research instruments by virtue of their role of interpreters. Thus, in the study reported in this chapter, the researchers' interpretations and reconstructions of the learners' introspective reports, cognitions, and personal theories were restated during the interviews to the learners for their agreement or disagreement. That is, the researchers attempted to validate the communication procedure used in the interviews because, according to Grotjahn, the validity of introspection as a data collection method is related to the researchers' conceptualization of language and theoretical model. Because the objective of this study is to explain the influence of cognitive, cultural, and linguistic variables on concept formation in second language learning, with the goal of developing a model and raising research questions, we adopted the exploratory-interpretative paradigm.

Methods of Data Analysis

Historically, some second language learning research methods focus on product and others focus on process in data analysis (i.e., quantitative and qualitative paradigms). Product-centered techniques (according to Færch & Kasper, 1987) are based on the learner's performance and include contrastive, error, and performance analysis, all focusing on observable language behaviors. One limitation of these techniques is that language utterances produced by two different language learners may look the same at the observable level. By contrast, qualitative or introspective process-centered techniques can access the different possible underlying representations at the metacognitive and metalinguistic levels in responses that otherwise seem similar. When learners are asked to analyze their utterances at the introspective level, their participation as active, knowing informants may reveal the strategies and cognitive processes they are using that cannot be observed at the performance product level. That is, introspective report methods give access to psychological data and to metacognitive and metalinguistic processes. Thus, according to Grotjahn (1987), an epistemological learner model can contribute to a richer understanding of a phenomenon.

In addition to allowing access to the internal processes involved in language learning, asking learners to explain the whats, hows, and whys of their language performance touches on a dichotomy: declarative versus procedural knowledge. Færch and Kasper (1987) borrowed this dichotomy from cognitive psychology and used it to explain language learning. These authors defined *declarative knowledge* as articulated and structured macroprocesses that can be brought to the learner's attention for explaining metalinguistic judgments. *Procedural knowledge* was defined as automatic cognitive and interactional microprocesses that the language learner is not conscious of. However, Færch and Kasper argued that procedural knowledge could be brought to consciousness by problem-solving tasks that involve slow and controlled processing, causing a breakdown of automatic processing. For example, tasks that make the language learner face a problem in reception or production due to a lack of relevant declarative linguistic or other knowledge initiates the production of linguistic intuitions, revealing new metalinguistic knowledge. Complementing Færch and Kasper's argument about gaining conscious access to procedural knowledge is our own observation that when second language learners are stimulated to think about linguistic problems and when researchers probe their linguistic utterances, the learners may gain new insights or construct new knowledge through inferential reasoning.

Thus, we believe that problem-solving tasks used with verbal reports can help researchers to understand the relation between cognitive processes and strategies, forms of knowledge, and the linguistic and cultural content represented. At the same time, the process of interviewing learners helps them gain access to internal metacognitive and metalinguistic processes that accelerate their language learning due to the presence of the conceptual connections and inferences they make during the verbal report. Moreover, when the same learner reconstructs the language processes, the researcher can get at a deeper level of analysis; that is, the same learner is attempting to explain what metacognitive and cognitive processes are taking place when he or she produces observable verbal behaviors in the second language. Thus, the utterances produced in the second language by the learner acquire new objective meaning when they are explained by the learner, because the researcher is not overimposing her or his own explanation of the utterances or simply classifying the learner's utterances according to the type of linguistic errors made at the performance level.

THE PROPOSED MULTIDIMENSIONAL MODEL

The use of verbal reports opens up the possibility of understanding the influence of cognitive processes and cultural symbolic meanings on concept construction in second language learning. Gonzalez's (1991, 1994, 1995; see Chapter 2 of this book) model of the conceptual, cultural, and linguistic factors affecting concept formation is applied in this study to the active construction of different forms of knowledge at different developmental phases and to the use of metacognitive, cognitive, and affective strategies by second language learners. We propose that the learner develops cognitively through internalization, transformation, and concept re-representations in terms of cognitive, cultural, and linguistic factors. That is, the interface of linguistic structures, nonverbal concepts, and cultural concepts influences the formation of concepts at four levels:

1. Conceptual knowledge about linguistic structures that can be expressed at both implicit and explicit levels
2. Knowledge of cultural conventions for using linguistic structures that is expressed as language proficiency at the pragmatic level
3. Knowledge of nonverbal sociocultural symbolic meanings that is expressed as cultural nonverbal concepts used at the pragmatic level
4. The multidimensional interaction of language, cognition, and culture when constructing new concepts in a second language (see Figure 5.1)

The process of concept formation in first and second languages can vary depending on the conceptual complexity and the symbolic sociocultural context in which linguistic structures are used. Whether a specific concept would be represented with a linguistic structure and marker and its corresponding symbolic meaning might depend on the cultural value that it has, and might reflect the sociohistorical development of the language. Languages differ in what aspects of meaning they represent directly in their linguistic structures, and this

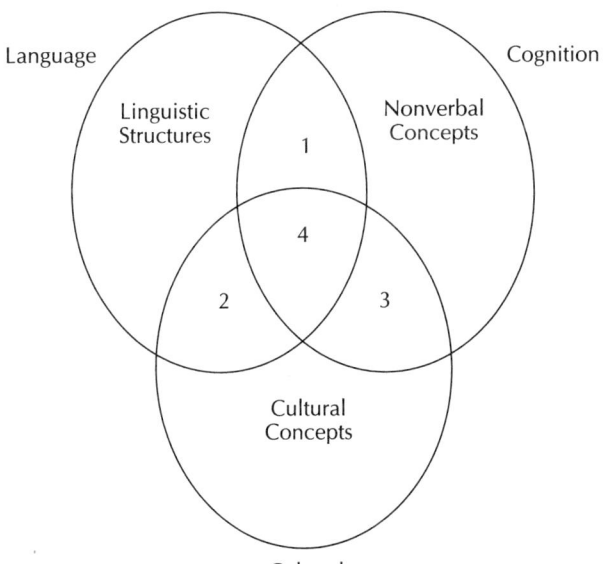

FIGURE 5.1   Multidimensional interaction of language, cognition, and culture for the construction of concepts.

fact influences the formation of symbolic meanings and semantic categories. We decided to focus on the linguistic feature of gender because Romance languages have many markers at the morphological and syntactic levels to represent gender, whereas English has few or none. Gender is just one example of many linguistic structures and markers that are different between Spanish and English. Thus, native English speakers learning Spanish must experience two kinds of conceptual development. For situations where gender is expressed similarly in both languages, they must assimilate the second language concepts into the first language concepts. And for those aspects of the second language that are unique and not represented in the first, they must construct a new, nonverbal representation that constitutes a new concept.

Thus, we propose that learning a second language leads to the construction of new representations that are linguistically and culturally bound. We proposed two basic language learning processes:

1. *Assimilation.* The abstract concepts and cultural and linguistic representations coincide in both the first and second languages.
2. *Accommodation.* The new abstract concepts, with their correspondent cultural and linguistic symbolic representations, need to be constructed because they are different between the first and the second languages.

Gonzalez (1991, 1994, 1995) conducted a study using this model of the influence of cognitive, cultural, and linguistic factors affecting concept and language development. As with the study reported here, the linguistic structure of gender was studied using problem-solving tasks. She found that bilingual kindergarten and first-grade Hispanic Spanish/English children represented concepts in two different systems. The first representational system was common to both languages, nonverbal, abstract, and universal. The second representational system was verbal or semantic, specific to the Spanish language for the verbal gender-based cases, and culturally and linguistically bound. Thus, one universal and abstract representational system was constructed when nonverbal and verbal concepts coincided in both languages. In contrast, two culturally bound and semantic representational systems were constructed when nonverbal and verbal concepts were different across languages. In terms of the relationship between cognition and language, the abstract representational system was always at a higher developmental level than the semantic representational system. Thus, Gonzalez concluded that cognitive development precedes language development as a universal process of concept construction. In addition, there was a difference in the conceptual developmental level attained in animate and inanimate content knowledge domains.

The study we report here reflects an attempt to integrate previous research findings, theoretical formulations, and methodological insights. Using an exploratory-interpretative, data-gathering approach, introspective verbal reports, and problem-solving tasks, we applied the model of second language learning to adults developing new gender concepts that are unique to the Spanish language and culture.

METHOD

Design

This is an exploratory-interpretative study that uses two samples, an experimental and a control group, for revealing how second language processes reflect the way in which language and culture influence thought. The experimental group was taught by the researcher-interviewer and first author of this study, who used a conceptual learning approach emphasizing students' gaining metalinguistic awareness of the relationship of sociocultural symbolic meanings, conceptual categories, and linguistic structures and markers of the Spanish language. "Linguistic structures" refers to grammatical rules, while "markers" refers to syntax (e.g., prefixes, suffixes, word roots, or word endings). The control group was taught using a traditional grammar-oriented approach by an assistant instructor who acted also as a researcher-interviewer and as a third coauthor for this study. Intralinguistic, extralinguistic-cultural, and cognitive factors influencing concept formation in second language learning situations were included, which were analyzed at the utterance and cluster levels by three judges (the first, fourth, and fifth coauthors). Data interpretation was done within a qualitative framework that identifies theses, themes, and topics (Bodgan & Biklen, 1982).

Research Questions

Five research questions were posed as guidelines for data analysis and interpretation of this study:

1. Is the nature of second language learning processes affected by different forms of knowledge (intralinguistic and extralinguistic) and semantic categories (animate and inanimate object referents)?
2. Can the same learner use different forms of knowledge and be at different developmental phases in relation to different semantic categories?
3. Does the conceptual learning approach stimulate in learners the use of higher-level forms of knowledge and learning strategies in comparison to the traditional grammar approach?
4. Do the particular questions used in the interviews help the learner to use higher-level learning strategies?
5. Are there idiosyncratic characteristics associated with the process of second language learning?

Subjects

Experimental Group. Seven students from a lower-division intensive Spanish class at the University of Texas at Austin volunteered to participate in the study. Personal background data were collected at the beginning of the semester by giving students open-ended questions regarding their major, rank, age, second or foreign language background, and personal objective for studying Spanish as a second language. All five female students were from an Anglo ethnic background, one male student was from a Hispanic background, and another male student was from an African-American background. All students were English native speakers in the process of learning Spanish as a second language, and the majority had some background in learning a second language. All students were between the ages of 19 and 21. Five students were freshmen and two students were juniors. None of the students were Spanish majors. When asked about their expectations for the Spanish class at the beginning of the semester, students reported that they expected to acquire a strong knowledge of the language and the culture.

Given that this study focuses on in-depth analysis of individual cases, we consider it important to include additional relevant characteristics of the subjects. (Pseudonyms are used.)

- Karen was a 19-year-old freshman majoring in psychology. She had studied French for four and a half years in high school and had recently spent two months in rural Ecuador. She had received two years of Spanish tutoring prior to her trip to Ecuador. Her motivation to study Spanish was related to her goal of returning to a small village in Ecuador.
- Jessica was a 19-year-old junior majoring in journalism. She had taken some French and some high-school-level Spanish. Both of her parents spoke some Spanish. When asked about her motivation for learning Spanish, Jessica reported that she would like to communicate with native speakers and the Spanish-speaking population in her area.
- Helen was an 18-year-old freshman majoring in communications. She had had two years of high school Spanish and had traveled extensively in Mexico. She reported that learning Spanish would better serve her travel needs.
- Heather was a 21-year-old junior majoring in psychology. She had had two years of high school Spanish and anticipated traveling in Spanish-speaking countries in the near future.
- Lynn was an 18-year-old freshman, whose major was bilingual education. She had taken high school Spanish for two years and considered learning how to speak Spanish a mandatory skill for bilingual education.
- Robert was a 19-year-old freshman, who had not yet chosen his major. He had had two years of Spanish in high school and had maternal grandparents who spoke to him only in Spanish when he was a child. Due to

Robert's background in the Spanish language, his comprehension level of the Spanish language was higher than his production level, and his pronunciation was good. In addition, he was intrinsically motivated to learn Spanish because he had a positive attitude toward the Hispanic culture and the Spanish language.
- Michael was an 18-year-old freshman from an African-American background, majoring in computer science. He had not taken any Spanish classes in high school; neither had he been exposed informally to Spanish before. Thus, he was the only student with no prior background in the Spanish language. At the beginning of the semester, Michael reported that he expected to speak Spanish fluently and to understand native speakers. He thought that learning Spanish would be easy.

Control Group. Eight undergraduate students from an intensive Spanish class at the University of Arizona volunteered to participate in the study. Personal background data were collected before the interview by giving students open-ended questions regarding their major, rank, age, second or foreign language background, and personal objective for studying Spanish as a second language. All six female students were Anglo, one of the male students was Hispanic, and the other one was Anglo. All students were English native speakers in the process of learning Spanish as a second language, and the majority of the students had some background in learning a second language. The only Hispanic subject did not speak Spanish as a native language. Seven students were between the ages of 18 and 20; the other was 25 years old. Three students were freshmen, three were sophomores, one was a junior, and one was a senior. None of the students were majoring in Spanish. When asked about their expectations for the Spanish class at the beginning of the semester, four students reported that they enjoyed learning the language and culture and they wanted to communicate with native speakers. The other four gave reasons related to the need of speaking Spanish in their future professions (e.g., nursing) and also mentioned that taking a foreign language was a requirement for their majors.

Given that this study focuses on in-depth analysis of individual cases, we consider it important to include additional relevant characteristics of the subjects. (Pseudonyms are used.)

- Paul was a 20-year-old Anglo sophomore, who had taken four years of Spanish in high school. He was majoring in accounting, and Spanish was a requirement for the College of Business.
- Alfredo was a 19-year-old Hispanic sophomore majoring in jazz studies. He had taken Spanish for two years in high school. Although his father was from a Hispanic background, he had not been taught Spanish at home. He expressed an interest in "learning more about the language and to communicate *con latinos.*"

- Steve was an 18-year-old Anglo freshman whose major was political science. Steve had taken Spanish in high school for two years. Spanish was a requirement for his major; also, he was planning on studying in Europe during his junior year.
- Linda was a 20-year-old Anglo junior majoring in general biology. She had taken three years of Spanish in high school. Foreign language was a requirement for her major, but she also said she enjoyed Spanish and believed knowledge of the language is important.
- Carol was a 19-year-old Anglo sophomore who was majoring in prenursing. She reported being offered Spanish classes from elementary school through high school. In addition, she had visited the Dominican Republic for three weeks as an exchange student when she was in high school. Carol expressed an intrinsic motivation for learning Spanish: "I would like to speak Spanish so that I can work with Hispanics who do not speak English. Even though it does not help my major directly, I think as a nurse it would be important to speak Spanish."
- Patricia was a 25-year-old Anglo senior majoring in ecology. She had taken intensive courses in Latin during her first three years at the university level and had taken one Spanish course before. She explained that "she had a genuine interest in learning to speak, write, and understand Spanish."
- Sarah was a 19-year-old Anglo freshman majoring in education. She had taken two years of Spanish in high school and had spent one summer in Spain. She had taken also one semester of French and one semester of Spanish. She was studying Spanish because "I enjoy learning Spanish and I eventually want to be fluent."
- Christine was an 18-year-old Anglo freshman whose major was in premedicine. She had taken one year of Spanish in high school. She stated "personal reasons to learn Spanish" and reported, "I really would like to master the language and be able to speak it as well as English."

Instructional Method

Experimental Group. The instructional method used to teach Spanish to the experimental class focused on concept construction at the linguistic, cultural, and abstract levels. This conceptual approach, developed by Gonzalez (1991, 1994, 1995), offered learners the possibility of discovering and understanding the underlying symbolic sociocultural meanings and different conceptual classifications of the world given by different linguistic structures in the second language. That is, learners were stimulated to discover the underlying cultural meanings and conceptual classifications when learning new linguistic structures. The instructor acted as a facilitator for modeling how to think with the Spanish language in order to discover the culturally bound semantic categories. (It is important to note that the instructor and first author of this chapter is a native speaker of the Spanish language, who is also bilingual—Spanish/English—and bicultural.) Students were presented with linguistic cases and were stimulated to discover the underlying linguistic and semantic rules. For instance, in the case of gender, the linguistic rule is related to cultural and abstract classifications that call for using extralinguistic knowledge of natural gender (i.e., physical) for animates and nonnatural gender (i.e., sociocultural linguistic conventions) for inanimates. Thus, this conceptual approach was meant to stimulate learners to understand that the general linguistic rule for assigning gender to nouns (nouns ending in *o* are masculine and nouns ending in *a* are feminine) is connected with cultural extralinguistic knowledge (i.e., symbolic connotative meanings of nouns) and abstract classifications in the Spanish language (i.e., animates can have two genders due to the presence of a natural origin gender, and inanimates can have only one gender that is given by a linguistic convention) that are semantic in nature (i.e., meanings of words are culturally and linguistically bound).

According to Collins and Stevens (1982), good teachers have three major hierarchical goals: (1) to teach students the facts and concepts of a domain of knowledge, (2) to teach students a particular rule or theory underlying a domain of facts and concepts, and (3) to teach students how to derive a new theory for a domain of knowledge. The goal of the conceptual approach is to stimulate students to understand that for the content knowledge domain of second language learning, only a theory that considers multiple factors—stemming from the linguistic, cultural, and cognitive dimensions—will be successful for constructing new concepts. Thus, according to Collins and Stevens's theory, a second higher goal is pursued in the conceptual approach used in this study for second language learning with three subgoals for the student:

1. To analyze different cases in order to derive the rule or theory that the teacher has in mind
2. To confront incorrect learning hypotheses through eliciting and "debugging" incorrect rules or theories
3. To make novel predictions based on the rule or theory discovered

In the verbal reports used in this study, the interviewer has a double role of an instructor and a researcher whose goal was to stimulate students to form second language concepts at higher levels. In order to achieve this goal, the interviewer used probing strategies that led students to make new inferences and interrelate multidimensional factors stemming from the linguistic, cultural, and cognitive domains.

Good teachers, according to Collins and Stevens (1982), use a number of entrapment strategies to make students reveal their misconceptions about a knowledge domain. They stated, "Some of these misconceptions exist prior to the teacher's inquiry, but some are in fact created by the inquiry" (p. 81). In fact, we proposed that our methodology of introspective verbal reports can act as a data collection instrument as well as a technique for stimulating students to construct second language concepts at higher levels. The interviewer probes students' ideas by offering counterexamples when misconceptions and insufficient factors are taken into consideration, or false hypotheses are made for solving the language problems presented. Collins and Stevens referred to these cases of probing as teaching strategies used when students propose a rule or make a prediction based on one or more insufficient factors. This case of using counterexamples for insufficient factors also happens in second language learning situations when students consider only isolated unidimensional factors and as a result construct misconceptions or false hypotheses. Second language problems can be solved only when students, with the scaffolding help of the interviewer, can make inferences and note relations between intralinguistic and extralinguistic knowledge, resulting in a multidimensional interaction of factors stemming from the linguistic, cultural, and cognitive domains. The use of counterexamples for insufficient factors and the scaffolding role of the interviewer when probing the student is illustrated in the example on pages 105–106, which we continue later in this chapter.

Control Group. The traditional grammar-oriented instructional method commonly used for second language learning in adults was implemented for the control group. The instructor for this Spanish class was an international master's student of bilingual education whose first language is Spanish and who is the third author of this chapter. She had been teaching Spanish to college students for a year before she taught this class. The major instructional strategies used in this control class were grammar explanations based on linguistic rules, irregular cases, and exceptions. Some explanations based on semantic conventions and pragmatic use of the language were also provided, but with a focus on intralinguistic reasons only. Students were not stimulated to think about underlying extralinguistic reasons for intralinguistic explanations. And although appropriate models of language use were offered, no models for the use of learning strategies were provided. Thus, students were left to implement their own study skills for producing meaningful sentences with the new structures they learned in the Spanish language.

Instructional media were used frequently for modeling language use by native speakers within a real-life cultural context. Students read stories and poetry; watched videos; used realia; listened to songs; engaged in games, contests, and role-plays; and conducted interviews with native Spanish speakers. In addition, the instructor aimed to motivate students to learn Spanish by offering interactive and cooperative activities that focused on listening, speaking, and writing abilities. The instructor's objective was to create a "stress-free" environment that would encourage students to use the Spanish language and to establish pragmatic communication. Thus, the instructor created an active environment in which students could use the Spanish language pragmatically within a cooperative learning context.

Tasks

For the data analyzed and reported here, two problem-solving tasks were designed for conducting verbal reports in order to access metacognitive, cognitive, and affective language learning processes. The first task consisted of defining three nouns denoting specific linguistic gender cases for animates in Spanish. Subjects were required to produce the appropriate article for the noun and to use categories and descriptions to fill in the complement part of the definition. The first and second nouns corresponded to neutral gender cases in which the article defines if the animate referent has a feminine or masculine linguistic gender (e.g., *el/la joven, el/la cliente*). The third noun corresponded to a collective noun for animates that is a special case (generally nouns ending in *e* tend to be masculine, but *gente* is linguistically feminine—*la gente*) and, moreover, is counter to a general related linguistic rule stating that masculine prevails over feminine linguistic gender (*gente* is linguistically feminine and encompasses both physical genders). Students were asked to write at least five words per definition and to define the word so that their classmates could guess the word being defined.

The second task was to provide the students with a real-life context for communicating functionally with the Spanish language. The following directions were given: "You are at a Mexican restaurant, and you are very hungry. You would like to accomplish three actions: (1) call the attention of the waitress; (2) order seven items: tortillas, chicken, rice, tomatoes, flan, and apple pie; and (3) ask for the bill." Subjects were asked to write three complete sentences, one for each action, with at least five words per sentence. They were to concentrate on what they would say in order to accomplish the three actions, *not* to write a dialogue between themselves and the waitress. Both tasks were familiar to the students; they had often engaged in similar assignments as part of regular class activity.

Students were interviewed individually in the instructor's office. As they arrived, they were given the two tasks written on paper and received instructions in English. They were reminded to supply the correct gender form in their written answers. Immediately after they had completed both tasks, the students were interviewed with "thinking-aloud protocols." They were asked to explain why a particular linguistic form they had supplied in their written work was correct or incorrect, focusing on linguistic gender markers. Verbal reports were audiotaped for subsequent analysis.

Both general open-ended questions common to all subjects and specific questions used to follow the train of thought of each specific subject were used. The researcher always used a general question referring to the underlying reason that the subject had for producing a specific linguistic structure of interest for the study—for example: "Why did you use _____ [specific linguistic structure]?" The researcher would repeat the question or clarify the answers given by the subject. Restating the answers was considered important so that correct interpretation and categorization of the subjects' explanations could be accomplished during data analysis. It was also important to probe subjects, asking them if a change in the linguistic gender of the noun could be made. Probing stimulated some subjects to state new insights, suggesting that they had constructed new knowledge during the interview. The conversation was closely controlled by the focus of our research: linguistic gender assignment for nouns and strategies used for constructing extralinguistic and intralinguistic knowledge forms and their interactions. However, students were always given the freedom to bring up topics naturally and to follow their own ideas during their verbal reports. Structure to the responses was provided later by the researchers through content analysis. Thus, the focus of the researcher's questions was on the reason that a particular linguistic structure had been produced by learners, and on the learners' level of understanding of linguistic structures in relation to underlying cultural symbolic meanings and abstract knowledge categories.

Data Analysis

Three factors influencing concept formation in second language learning situations were taken into consideration in this study: intralinguistic, extralinguistic-cultural, and cognitive (see Table 5.1). Intralinguistic factors include the linguistic function that categorizes students' responses at the morphological syntactic level in reference to linguistic gender. Extralinguistic-cultural factors include two subcategories of variables:

1. By origin, encompassing natural physical gender, which includes animates (animals and people), and nonnatural linguistic gender, which includes inanimates (objects and abstract concepts)
2. By language, encompassing sociocultural symbolic meanings at the connotative level and linguistic structures and markers at the denotative level (both levels can include cases that are common to Spanish and English or unique to Spanish)

Intralinguistic and extralinguistic-cultural factors merge in semantic categories for gender including general rules, and regular and irregular cases. Cognitive factors encompass forms of knowledge, developmental phases, and language learning strategies. Bialystock's model (1978) was used for adapting five nominal categories of forms of knowledge:

1. Extralinguistic general knowledge—explicit justifications by reference to general knowledge outside the linguistic task (i.e., real-world, sociocultural, and pragmatic knowledge)
2. Extralinguistic topic knowledge—explicit justifications by reference to specific object knowledge outside the linguistic task

TABLE 5.1 Factors Influencing Concept Formation

Intralinguistic Factors	Extralinguistic-Cultural Factors	Cognitive Factors
By linguistic function	**By language**	**Forms of knowledge**
Nouns	Sociocultural symbolic meanings	**Third developmental phase**
Articles	Connotative level	1. Extralinguistic general
Adjectives	Common to Spanish and English	2. Extralinguistic topic
Adverbs	Unique to Spanish	3. Explicit relation between extralinguistic topic knowledge and intralinguistic knowledge
Numerals	Linguistic structures and markers	
Indefinite pronouns	Denotative level	**Second developmental phase**
Demonstrative pronouns	Common to both Spanish and English	4. Explicit intralinguistic knowledge (system and marker)
Subject pronouns	Unique to Spanish	
Direct object pronouns	By origin	**First developmental phase**
Indirect object pronouns	Natural physical gender: Animates (including people and animals)	5. Implicit intralinguistic knowledge (system and marker)
	Nonnatural origin gender: Inanimates (including objects and abstract concepts)	**Second language learning strategies**
		Metacognitive: Explicit knowledge
		Cognitive: Explicit and implicit knowledge
		Social-affective: Implicit knowlege

By semantic function: Semantic categories*
General rule
  By origin: For inanimates, and for inanimates
  By language: Unique to Spanish
Regular cases
  By origin: For inanimates
  By language: Common to Spanish and English and unique to Spanish
Irregular cases
  By origin: For inanimates
  By language: Common to Spanish and English and unique to Spanish

*Note that semantic categories merge intralinguistic and extralinguistic-cultural factors, so that column is centered below the other two.

3. Explicit relation between extralinguistic general or topic knowledge and intralinguistic knowledge at the system (linguistic categories) or marker (specific linguistic cases) levels—justification by reference to the relationship between knowledge outside the linguistic task and linguistic knowledge
4. Explicit intralinguistic knowledge at the system or marker levels—justification of responses by making explicit reference to linguistic categories or specific cases
5. Implicit intralinguistic knowledge at the system or marker levels—correct responses involving linguistic structures or cases with no further explanation

These five categories were combined with Karmiloff-Smith's model (1979) referring to the three developmental phases (see Table 5.1). The first three forms of knowledge indicated that the learner was at the third developmental phase. Especially the third form of knowledge, indicating a relation between extralinguistic and intralinguistic knowledge, was considered to reveal the construction of new conceptual relations or insights by the language learner (e.g., a metacognitive strategy of inferencing). The fourth form of knowledge was considered to indicate that the learner was at the second developmental phase; she could access consciously linguistic knowledge of rules and specific cases; however, no relationship was made with extralinguistic knowledge. The fifth form of knowledge indicated that the learner was at the first developmental level; she could not access verbally the underlying strategies and forms of knowledge used for learning linguistic structures or markers (see Table 5.1).

Second language learning strategies were adapted from the categorization made by O'Malley and colleagues (1988) that differentiates metacognitive, cognitive, and social-affective strategies. O'Malley and colleagues differentiated nine metacognitive strategies:

1. Advance organizers—making a general but comprehensive preview of the concept or principle in an anticipated learning activity
2. Directed attention—deciding in advance to attend in general to a learning task
3. Selective attention—deciding in advance to attend to specific details of a learning task
4. Self-management—understanding the conditions that help one learn and arranging for the presence of those conditions
5. Functional planning—planning for and rehearsing linguistic components necessary to carry out an upcoming language task
6. Delayed production—consciously deciding to postpone speaking to learn initially through listening comprehension
7. Self-evaluation—checking the outcomes of one's own language learning against an internal measure of completeness and accuracy

8. Monitoring—bringing explicit knowledge of word meanings and structures to a language task for examining or correcting the response
9. Inferencing—generating an explicit linguistic hypothesis about a previously unknown linguistic structure

O'Malley and colleagues differentiated fourteen cognitive strategies:

1. Repetition—initiating a language model, including overt practice and silent rehearsal
2. Directed physical response—relating new information to physical actions used as directives
3. Imagery—relating new information to visual concepts in memory by familiar and easily retrievable visualizations
4. Auditory representation—retaining the sound of a linguistic sequence
5. Key word—remembering a new word by linking it with a familiar linguistic sequence, image, or concept
6. Resourcing—expanding a word or concept through the use of the target language reference materials
7. Translation—using the first language as a basis for understanding or producing the target language
8. Grouping—reclassifying and labeling the new linguistic material based on common attributes
9. Note taking—writing down the main ideas, outlining, or summarizing target language materials in a written or oral form
10. Deduction—consciously applying rules to produce or understand the second language
11. Recombination—constructing a meaningful language sequence by combining known elements in a new way
12. Contextualization—placing a word or phrase in a meaningful language sequence
13. Elaboration—relating new information to other concepts in memory
14. Transfer—using previously acquired linguistic and/or conceptual knowledge to facilitate a language learning task

In addition, we used four second language learning cognitive strategies proposed by Robinett and Schachter (1983) for data analysis:

1. Overgeneralization—creating a deviant structure on the basis of experience with other linguistic structures in the target language in order to avoid redundancy
2. Ignorance of rule restrictions—failing to observe the restrictions of existing linguistic structures when applying them to new contexts
3. Incomplete application of rules—lacking accurate and complete knowledge of linguistic rules

4. False concepts hypothesized—making developmental errors resulting from faulty comprehension, distinctions, or contrasts in the target language

These four strategies were considered to be characteristic of a learner at the second developmental phase, who could show only explicit forms of knowledge.

Finally O'Malley and colleagues (1988) had four categories of social-affective strategies:

1. Cooperation—working with peers to obtain feedback, look for information, or model a language activity
2. Question for clarification—asking an instructor or other native speaker for repetition, paraphrasing, explanation, and/or examples
3. Formal practice—attempting to increase exposure to the target language or asking for information about the rules of the linguistic structures and markers to represent meaning
4. Functional practice—using the target language in communicative situations

All nine metacognitive strategies correspond to explicit forms of knowledge, the first five cognitive strategies correspond to implicit knowledge levels, and the following nine cognitive strategies correspond to explicit levels of knowledge. In addition, the four social-affective strategies correspond to explicit forms of knowledge. That is, we have attempted to integrate the categorization of language learning strategies adapted by O'Malley and colleagues (1988) with Bialystock's (1978) implicit and explicit levels of knowledge, which in turn were integrated also with Karmiloff-Smith's (1986) developmental levels.

We propose that three factors—intralinguistic, extralinguistic-cultural, and cognitive—merge in the semantic function of language, represented in this study by the semantic categories for linguistic gender (see Figure 5.1, Table 5.1, and Appendix 5A). Thus, these semantic categories, created by Gonzalez for this study, reflect the multidimensional interrelationship among cognition, culture, and language for the construction of second language concepts. We used theory triangulation in interpreting a single set of data from different integrated theoretical perspectives associated with specific variables of interest and theoretical and applied objectives in this study. Data analysis was carried out by means of interpretative procedures (i.e., qualitative content analysis of nominal categories) in order to find associations or patterns among variables revealed in subjects' productions. We let the data speak to us, as just some research questions were pointed out in relation to some theoretical perspectives. Thus, a qualitative data analysis approach was taken in this study, in which theory was tested with heuristic and applied implications.

Two levels of analysis were differentiated in this study: utterance and cluster levels. The *utterance level* was considered a single idea conveyed by the subject. Each utterance was coded independently in relation to cognitive variables (forms of knowledge, developmental phases, and language learning strategies). Utterances referring to the same word being discussed throughout the verbal reports were considered a second level of analysis that we called *clusters*. Each cluster was categorized independently in relation to gender cases that included linguistic and semantic functions. Following the evolution of the discussion of the same cluster by the subject was considered particularly important because new levels of understanding of the same cluster emerged throughout the verbal report. Thus, the cluster as a unit of analysis can provide evidence for the argument that verbal reports are not only data collection tools, but also an instructional method for developing new conceptual knowledge at higher developmental levels. These two levels of data analysis can reveal some common or different patterns in the specific forms of knowledge, developmental phases, and language learning strategies that may be related to the interaction of intralinguistic, extralinguistic-cultural, and cognitive variables. These two data analysis levels were anticipated to be a potential source for discovering patterns regarding the influence of linguistic and cultural factors on the process of second language concept formation. We derived this system of data analysis from the actual context of data, having an open-minded attitude, and letting the data speak to us in order to develop a structure for data analysis based on nominal categories derived from the same data bank.

Three judges (the third, fourth, and fifth authors) independently categorized each subject across all nominal categories. Judges were trained by the first author during a six-week period in order to gain familiarity with the theoretical framework underlying the nominal categories, and also for achieving a high reliability coefficient between judges. Before data analysis was conducted, a high reliability across judges ($r = .81$) was established, ensuring that the operationalization and understanding of the nominal categories was consistent and clear among judges. Any disagreement obtained during the process of training for coding data was discussed among the first author and the three judges. When the final data analysis was done, the few disagreements arising were also discussed among the three judges in order to arrive at a common categorization.

RESULTS AND DISCUSSION

Data are reported and interpreted using a two-level data analysis adapted for this study: the utterance and cluster levels. Following is a case study illustrating data interpretation and integration. With the purpose of integrating the summary of this data report, data interpretation will follow the three types of focus suggested by Bogdan and Biklen (1982):

1. Thesis or propositions related to the integration of literature and the model proposed
2. Themes that encompass theoretical formulations emerging from data analysis in the form of patterns or abstract conceptual categories
3. Topics that include descriptions of specific findings

With the purpose of illustrating the procedure that we followed for getting from the data analysis to the results and conclusions, we expand on the example used at the beginning of this chapter. Robert exemplifies a good language learner who participated in the experimental group. He is at the second developmental phase; he is trying to understand explicitly his already acquired implicit linguistic knowledge. Both language problem-solving tasks are included, since the definition task focuses on animate object referents and the role-playing task includes primarily cases of inanimate object referents. The example that follows is divided into the two levels of data analysis used in this study. In addition, we include semantic categories for gender, reflecting the interrelation of intralinguistic and extralinguistic-cultural factors (see Table 5.1) and the coding system reflecting cognitive factors (i.e., forms of knowledge, developmental phases, and language learning strategies). The interpretation and connection with the multidimensional model proposed in this study is also included in the emerging thesis, topics, and themes section.

Definition Task

Cluster 1: *Tienda.* Semantic categories. Intralinguistic factors, by linguistic function—noun; by semantic function—general rule. Extralinguistic-cultural factors, by language—linguistic structures and markers at the denotative level that are unique to the Spanish language; and by origin—nonnatural origin gender for inanimates.

INTERVIEWER: You picked *la tienda*. Why *la* and not *el*? (The interviewer was trying to stimulate the student to refer explicitly to the general rule for assigning linguistic gender to nouns. See Appendix 5A.)

(Utterance 1) STUDENT: Because *tienda* is feminine.

INTERVIEWER: Okay. How do you know?

(Utterance 2) STUDENT: Because of the a *en tienda*, just that. (Form of knowledge: Explicit intralinguistic knowledge Markers. Second developmental phase. Cognitive strategy: Deduction; Robert is applying the linguistic rule to a specific case.)

Cluster 2: *Persona.* Semantic categories. Intralinguistic factors, by linguistic function—noun; by semantic function, regular cases. Extralinguistic-cultural factors, by language—sociocultural symbolic meanings at the connotative level that are unique to the Spanish language, and linguistic structures and markers at the denotative level that are unique to the Spanish language; and by origin—natural physical gender for animates.

INTERVIEWER: So, how come? What happens in *persona?* This is an *a*. You know, *persona.*

(Utterance 3) STUDENT: *Persona.* I thought it would just stay. You know like . . . I'm trying to think of an example of an ending *a*, like *la tortilla.* (Form of knowledge: Explicit intralinguistic knowledge—system, because Robert is pointing out a category of words that correspond to the general rule for inanimate objects. Second developmental phase. Cognitive strategy: Deduction, as Robert is trying to illustrate the general rule through an example, *tortilla*, in which only one linguistic gender for the suffix can be applied. However, the example was not completely appropriate for explaining the case of *persona*, because in *tortilla*, the article is always linguistically feminine and can never be changed since there is no natural physical gender in the referent. Instead, for the word *persona*, even though there is a natural physical gender, only one conventional linguistic gender applies. Robert's hypothesis was that for the noun *persona*, the *a* ending will always stay, and that the article will indicate if the linguistic gender was feminine or masculine.)

INTERVIEWER: Okay. So that would be kind of an exception. *Tortilla* would be another example. Is that an exception?

(Utterance 4) STUDENT: Yes.

INTERVIEWER: Well, actually this is *una persona* in both cases. Does it make sense to you? (Robert nods.) Why? (The interviewer was pointing out the correct linguistic gender as a counterexample in order to ask Robert for an explanation.)

(Utterance 5) STUDENT: Because *una persona* is always feminine, so *una persona* does not match. So it would be *una* for feminine or masculine. (Form of knowledge: Explicit relation between intralinguistic marker and extralinguistic topic knowledge—markers, because Robert stated that the article and the suffix *a* of *persona* do not have to match in gender with the actual feminine or masculine gender of the referent. Third developmental phase. Metacognitive strategy: Inference; Robert is realizing at this point that the general rule does not apply for this specific case.)

Robert has progressed from using cognitive to metacognitive strategies with the help of the scaffolding role of the interviewer. The interview process has stimulated Robert to think at higher levels, leading him to an insightful conclusion made through inferential reasoning.

Cluster 3: *Cliente.* Semantic categories. Intralinguistic factors, by linguistic function—noun; by semantic function—regular cases. Extralinguistic-cultural factors, by language—sociocultural symbolic meanings at the connotative level that are unique to the Spanish language, and linguistic structures and markers at the denotative level that are unique to the Spanish language; and by origin—natural physical gender for animates.

INTERVIEWER: *Muy bien. El cliente.* Why did you pick *el* and not *la?*

(Utterance 6) STUDENT: Because I thought it was masculine. (laughs) (Form of knowledge: Extralinguistic topic knowledge. Third developmental phase. Cognitive strategy: Imagery; Robert is laughing now because he realizes that there was not any linguistic hint in the directions given for the task indicating that the marker should be masculine.)

INTERVIEWER: So you are actually thinking of a man. A man as a customer?

(Utterance 7) STUDENT: Yes.

INTERVIEWER: Okay. How about if I have a woman who is a customer?

(Utterance 8) STUDENT: It would be the same: *la cliente.* (Form of knowledge: Implicit intralinguistic knowledge—markers, because Robert is just pointing out what would be the linguistic form for this specific case, without referring to any linguistic rule or further explanation. First developmental phase. Cognitive strategy: Deduction; Robert is correctly applying the linguistic rules for regular cases.)

Cluster 4: *Algo.* Semantic categories. Intralinguistic factors: by linguistic function—pronoun; by semantic function—regular cases. Extralinguistic-cultural factors: by language—linguistic structures and markers at the denotative level that are unique to the Spanish language; and by origin—nonnatural origin gender for inanimates.

INTERVIEWER: Okay. *Alguien que compra algo.* (reading from student's paper) Okay. Why do you have *algo* and not *alga?*

(Utterance 9) STUDENT: Because it is not used in *alga* form. It is always *algo*, "something." (Form of knowledge: Explicit intralinguistic knowledge—markers, because Robert is referring to a specific pronoun explaining the reason that he cannot change the linguistic gender. Second developmental phase. Cognitive strategy: Translation; it also happens that in English "something" is a neutral pronoun that does not refer to an object that has a specific linguistic gender.)

INTERVIEWER: Okay. If you buy, for example, *la gasolina. Algo* would apply to *la gasolina?*

(Utterance 10) STUDENT: *Sí.*

INTERVIEWER: Okay, so it doesn't matter if this is feminine?

(Utterance 11) STUDENT: No, it doesn't matter.

Cluster 5: *Gente.* Semantic categories. Intralinguistic factors, by linguistic function—noun; by semantic function—regular cases. Extralinguistic-cultural factors, by language—sociocultural symbolic meanings at the connotative level that are unique to the Spanish language, and linguistic structures and markers at the denotative level that are unique to the Spanish language; and by origin—natural physical gender for animates.

INTERVIEWER: Okay, *gente.* How did you know *gente* is masculine? (*Gente* is actually feminine, an irregular case.)

(Utterance 12) STUDENT: Well, because of the majority of the people, even if there was only one man, in a group of women; it wouldn't matter, it will be always masculine. And if there is only a big group of just women, then it would be *la.* (Form of knowledge: Explicit intralinguistic knowledge—system, because Robert is pointing out a regular case that applies to a category of objects. Second developmental phase. Cognitive strategy: Overgeneralization and ignorance of rule restrictions; Robert does not know that *gente* is an irregular case, and thus an exception for the regular case that he is pointing out.)

INTERVIEWER: Okay, if you have only feminine, you would make that difference.

(Utterance 13) STUDENT: Yes.

INTERVIEWER: *La*, right?

(Utterance 14) STUDENT: Yes.

INTERVIEWER: And if you have a bunch of people of both genders, it would be . . .

(Utterance 15) STUDENT: Masculine.

Cluster 6: *Hermanos, tías,* and *abuelos.* Semantic categories. Intralinguistic factors, by linguistic function—noun; by semantic function—general rule. Extralinguistic-cultural factors, by language—sociocultural symbolic meanings at the connotative level that are unique to the Spanish language, and linguistic structures and markers at the denotative level that are common to Spanish and English; and by origin—natural physical gender for animates.

INTERVIEWER: (reading from student's paper) *De la familia.* You told me the ending *a.* (reading from student's paper) *Son personas que no tienen hermanos, tíos, abuelos, primos. Muy bien.* Why are you picking everything in the masculine?

(Utterance 16) STUDENT: *No, tías.*

INTERVIEWER: Is this *tías?* Okay, so why is *hermanos* masculine and *tías* feminine?

(Utterance 17) STUDENT: I wanted to include *hermanos y hermanas, tías.* I just pick then, I guess. (Form of knowledge: Implicit intralinguistic knowledge—

markers; Robert cannot explain why he decided to use different linguistic genders. First developmental level. Cognitive strategy: Imagery; Robert just imagined and pointed out a specific gender.)

INTERVIEWER: Okay, so both can happen.

(Utterance 18) STUDENT: For *abuelos*, I just used it for talking about both, but *el masculino* changed everything to *abuelos*. (Form of knowledge: Explicit relation between extralinguistic topic knowledge and intralinguistic marker knowledge; Robert could explain the specific regular case that made him use the linguistic masculine gender for referring to the physical gender of the animate objects that he had in mind. Third developmental phase. Metacognitive strategy: Inferencing.)

Cluster 7: *Primos*. Semantic categories. Intralinguistic factors, by linguistic function—noun; by semantic function—general rule. Extralinguistic-cultural factors, by language—sociocultural symbolic meanings at the connotative level that are unique to the Spanish language, and linguistic structures and markers at the denotative level that are unique to the Spanish language; and by origin—natural physical gender for animates.

INTERVIEWER: How about *primos*?

(Utterance 19) STUDENT: You can have a lot of cousins, and some females and some males. (Form of knowledge: Extralinguistic topic knowledge; Robert is pointing out that the specific animate object referents have natural physical gender. Third developmental phase. Metacognitive strategy: Inferencing; Robert could understand that the linguistic gender was reflecting the physical natural gender of the animate referents.)

Return to Cluster 5: *Gente*.

INTERVIEWER: Okay, Everything is correct except this. You see, the only case is *la gente*. Does it make sense to you? (The interviewer wanted to provide the correct linguistic gender in order to probe Robert's comprehension of this irregular case.)

(Utterance 20) STUDENT: Hmm ... Yes.

INTERVIEWER: Why?

(Utterance 21) STUDENT: I wasn't sure. I guess I wasn't sure like in *la gente*; this is just a part of *personas*, and it relates to people. But it is just used in the *la* form. (Form of knowledge: Explicit relation between extralinguistic general knowledge and intralinguistic marker knowledge. Robert is able to relate his previous understanding that *gente* refers to both feminine and masculine animate referents with his realization that the category people—*personas*—could refer to animate referents of both physical genders. Third developmental phase. Metacognitive strategy: Inferencing and monitoring; Robert realized at this point in the interview that there was a connection between *gente* and *personas*, since both had the same animate referent—the category "people" in English. Robert is having a major insight, bringing his higher level of understanding achieved earlier in the interview to shed light on getting at a higher form of knowledge, developmental phase, and learning strategy.)

INTERVIEWER: Okay. Even if you have *la gente*, do you think that refers to men also?

(Utterance 22) STUDENT: Well, I was trying to think if I use it in the general form, and I know I used the *la* before, but I just used *el* anyway, but I wasn't sure. (Form of knowledge: Explicit intralinguistic knowledge—system; Robert is pointing to the existence of a general rule and a specific regular case; however, he is confused as to which one would apply in this case. Second developmental level. Metacognitive strategy: Self-evaluation. Cognitive strategy: Overgeneralization and ignorance of rule restrictions; Robert knows the existence of a general rule and of a regular case, but he cannot realize that *gente* is an exception.)

INTERVIEWER: So you were actually trying to tap both—masculine and feminine?

(Utterance 23) STUDENT: Yes.

INTERVIEWER: But was there any hint in the *gente* form that tells you that *gente* may be masculine?

(Utterance 24) STUDENT: Yes, just ending in *e*, like that, or *a* or any other ... *ción*, or anything like that, it is obvious that it is the *la* form. It makes it clear that the masculine linguistic gender is incorrect, just because of the way it looks. (Form of knowledge: Explicit intralinguistic knowledge—system; Robert is relating the general rule to regular cases in which a specific linguistic gender is indicated by the suffix. Second developmental phase. Cognitive strategy: Deduction; Robert is applying linguistic rules.)

INTERVIEWER: Okay, but when you say "the way it looks," what specifically are you talking about?

(Utterance 25) STUDENT: The ending *a* is feminine, but if it looks like *o* or *e* is masculine. (Form of knowledge: Explicit intralinguistic knowledge of the target language—markers; Robert is pointing out specifically the ending as relevant to deciding what linguistic gender to apply. Second developmental phase. Cognitive strategy: Deduction.)

INTERVIEWER: *O* or *e*. So this is ending in *e*. How come this is feminine?

(Utterance 26) STUDENT: This is just an exception. (Form of knowledge: Explicit intralinguistic knowledge. Second developmental phase. Metacognitive strategy: Inferencing; Robert is arriving at the conclusion that *gente* is an exception based on the scaffolding help of the interviewer. This is another point in the interview in which we can observe how the interviewer's probing questions helped the student to use higher-level language learning strategies, from cognitive to metacognitive levels.)

Role-Playing Task

Cluster 1: *Camarera.* Semantic categories. Intralinguistic factors, by linguistic function—noun; by semantic function—general rule. Extralinguistic-cultural factors: by language—sociocultural symbolic meanings at the connotative level that are common to Spanish and English, and linguistic structures and markers at the denotative level that are common to Spanish and English; and by origin—natural physical gender for animates.

INTERVIEWER: (reading from the student's paper) Here, number one, *perdón camarera. Me gustaría pedir. Yo tengo mucho hambre. Muy bien.* Everything is correct. Why are you specifically using *camarera?*

(Utterance 1) STUDENT: Hm... because is the waitress, *femenino*, and if it would be male, then you would use *camarero*. (Form of knowledge: Extralinguistic topic knowledge; Robert is pointing out the natural physical gender of the object referent that is reflected in the linguistic gender selected. Third developmental phase. Cognitive strategy: Translation—in this case translating to the English "waitress" helps Robert to understand that there are two linguistic gender forms related to this noun.)

Cluster 2: *Hambre.* Semantic categories. Intralinguistic factors, by linguistic function—noun; by semantic function—irregular cases. Extralinguistic-cultural factors, by language—linguistic structures and markers at the denotative level that are unique to the Spanish language; and by origin—nonnatural origin gender for inanimates.

INTERVIEWER: Why did you use *mucho hambre?*

(Utterance 2) STUDENT: Because the situation is telling you that you are hungry. So, I used *mucho hambre* and... it relates to *hambre. Hambre* is masculine, I suppose... Yes. (Form of knowledge: Extralinguistic topic knowledge and intralinguistic marker knowledge. Second developmental phase. Cognitive strategy: Ignorance of rule restrictions; Robert is making a linguistic error when he is considering *hambre* to be a regular case, when in fact it is an irregular case. Metacognitive strategy: Self-evaluation; he is checking if his response is correct.)

INTERVIEWER: This is one where colloquially people make lots of errors. It is *mucha hambre.* You thought it was masculine, you were telling me. Do you relate it to something that we talked before?

(Utterance 3) STUDENT: Yes—*gente*. (Form of knowledge: Explicit intralinguistic knowledge—markers, in which he pointed out earlier in the interview that *gente* was an irregular case that was counter regular cases. Third developmental phase. Metacognitive strategy: Elaboration, relating previous discussed cases of rule restrictions.)

INTERVIEWER: *Gente*. Okay. That's a very good intuition, and that happens to be feminine, so now does it makes sense?

(Utterance 4) STUDENT: Wouldn't it be *mucha hambre?* (Form of knowledge: Implicit intralinguistic knowledge—marker. First developmental phase. Social-affective strategy: Question for clarification.)

INTERVIEWER: Uh-huh. *Mucha hambre*. But does it makes sense to you?

(Utterance 5) STUDENT: Are you saying *el hambre?* It would be *la hambre?* (Form of knowledge: Implicit intralinguistic knowledge—marker. First developmental phase. Social-affective strategy: Question for clarification.)

INTERVIEWER: Actually this is masculine, but in this case it is *mucha hambre*. Does it make sense?

(Utterance 6) STUDENT: Yes. It is an exception. (Form of knowledge: Explicit intralinguistic knowledge—marker. Third developmental phase. Metacognitive strategy: Elaboration, relating previous discussed cases of rule restrictions.)

Cluster 3: *Pollo.* Semantic categories. Intralinguistic factors, by linguistic function—noun; by semantic function—regular case. Extralinguistic-cultural factors, by language—linguistic structures and markers at the denotative level that are unique to the Spanish language; and by origin—nonnatural origin gender for inanimates.

INTERVIEWER: (reading from student's paper) *Deseo pollo y arroz con tomates en el lado*. There are no errors here. Everything is correct. There is no need for an article here, but let's pretend there is. Which one would you pick?

(Utterance 7) STUDENT: Hmm . . . *el*, no, *un* . . . no, it would be *un pollo*. (Form of knowledge: Implicit intralinguistic knowledge—marker. First developmental phase. Metacognitive strategy: Self-evaluation; he is checking if his response is correct against an internal measure of accuracy.)

Cluster 4: *Arroz* and *tomates.* Semantic categories. Intralinguistic factors, by linguistic function—noun; by semantic function—regular cases. Extralinguistic-cultural factors, by language—linguistic structures and markers at the denotative level that are unique to the Spanish language; and by origin—nonnatural origin gender for inanimates.

INTERVIEWER: How about *arroz* and *tomates?*

(Utterance 8) STUDENT: *El arroz* and *los tomates*, I guess. I guess *un arroz* would be just one. (laughs) (Form of knowledge: Implicit intralinguistic knowledge. First developmental level. Metacognitive strategy: Self-evaluation.)

INTERVIEWER: Okay. How did you know *arroz* is masculine?

(Utterance 9) STUDENT: Hm. I guess that the ending to me is more masculine. I learn the article with the word. (Form of knowledge: Explicit intralinguistic knowledge; Robert is pointing to the suffix for explaining his response. Second developmental phase. Metacognitive strategy: Selective attention.)

Cluster 5: *Mano*. Semantic categories. Intralinguistic factors: by linguistic function—noun; by semantic function—irregular cases. Extralinguistic-cultural factors: by language—linguistic structures and markers at the denotative level that are unique to the Spanish language; and by origin—nonnatural origin gender for inanimates.

INTERVIEWER: How about *mano*? Which is the gender for *mano*?

(Utterance 10) STUDENT: *La*.

INTERVIEWER: Okay. For this kind of exceptions. You know that the gender of the article does not match the gender of the noun. How did you deal with those when you study?

(Utterance 11) STUDENT: When I study, before I look at the meaning of the word, first I look at the article. If I just know that first, it helps a lot. Then after I make sure which article is right, I'll go ahead and find the meaning. (Form of knowledge: Explicit intralinguistic knowledge. Second developmental level. Metacognitive strategy: Selective attention, functional planning, and monitoring.)

Cluster 6: *Pastel*. Semantic categories. Intralinguistic factors, by linguistic function—noun; by semantic function—regular cases. Extralinguistic-cultural factors, by language—linguistic structures and markers at the denotative level that are unique to the Spanish language; and by origin—nonnatural origin gender for inanimates.

INTERVIEWER: (reading from the student's paper) *Además voy a desear flan y un pastel de manzanas* Muy bien. No need for an article, but I would like you to . . .

(Utterance 12) STUDENT: *El pastel*. Usually the *n* in *flan* and *l* in *pastel* are masculine. I studied it. (Form of knowledge: Explicit intralinguistic knowledge. Second developmental phase. Metacognitive strategy: Selective attention. The student has already learned the procedure followed in the interview, and thus he can access explicit levels of knowledge and higher metacognitive strategies more easily than at the beginning of the interview.)

Cluster 7: *Listo.* Semantic categories. Intralinguistic factors, by linguistic function—adjective; by semantic function—general rule. Extralinguistic-cultural factors, by language—linguistic structures and markers at the denotative level that are unique to the Spanish language; and by origin—nonnatural origin gender for inanimates.

INTERVIEWER: Okay. *Muy bíen.* Now, how do you know this is *listo* and not *lista?*

(Utterance 13) STUDENT: I am referring to myself. (Form of knowledge: Extralinguistic topic knowledge. Third developmental phase. Metacognitive strategy: Monitoring. Robert is relating his response to the appropriateness of the extralinguistic context.)

Cluster 8: *Tortillas.* Semantic categories. Intralinguistic factors, by linguistic function—noun; by semantic function—general rule. Extralinguistic-cultural factors, by language—linguistic structures and markers at the denotative level that are unique to the Spanish language; and by origin—nonnatural origin gender for inanimates.

INTERVIEWER: Masculine. Okay. I want to ask you one more thing. If I have *las tortillas*, can I have *los tortillos?*

(Utterance 14) STUDENT: No, because there is no gender in *tortillas*—no masculine or feminine. They are just known as *las tortillas*. (Form of knowledge: Explicit relation between extralinguistic topic and intralinguistic topic knowledge. Third developmental phase. Metacognitive strategy: Inferencing; Robert is generating an explicit linguistic hypothesis about a previously unknown meaning.)

Return to Cluster 1: *Camarera.*

INTERVIEWER: Aha. How about here? How come I can interchange *camarero* and *camarera* according to the situation?

(Utterance 15) STUDENT: Because of the fact you have *persona*, they can change—masculine or feminine according to the person. (Form of knowledge: Explicit relation between extralinguistic general and intralinguistic system knowledge. Third developmental phase. Metacognitive strategy: Inferencing, grouping, and elaboration; Robert is combining previous knowledge made explicit in the interview with new words that belong to the same category.)

Return to Cluster 3: *Pollo.*

INTERVIEWER: How about *pollo?* Can I have *la polla?*

(Utterance 16) STUDENT: No. Even though there is feminine and masculine chicken, this is known as *pollo*, and you don't use *la polla*. That is not right. (Form of knowledge: Explicit relation between extralinguistic topic and intralinguistic marker knowledge. Third developmental phase. Metacognitive strategy: Monitoring; Robert is checking the correctness of the linguistic form in relation to the specific case.)

INTERVIEWER: You are trying to refer to food, right? How about animals in a farm? Can I have *la polla?*

(Utterance 17) STUDENT: No, even though they are not considered food, because they are still kicking around, they are not considered persons—masculine or feminine. They are just considered as *pollo* for referring to feminine and masculine. You know there is no *el vaco*. (Form of knowledge: Explicit relation between extralinguistic topic knowledge and Intralinguistic knowledge—system. Third developmental phase. Metacognitive strategy: Inferencing, grouping, and elaboration; Robert is combining previous knowledge made explicit in the interview with new words that belong to the same category; and incomplete application of rules. Robert is referring at this point to previous knowledge inferred in the interview process. That is, at several points during the interview Robert has explicitly pointed out that people can have both natural physical genders in the real world and that this fact may or may not be reflected in the linguistic gender forms due to the presence of general rules and regular and irregular cases. However, he is still applying this relation between extralinguistic and intralinguistic knowledge incompletely [only for extralinguistic topic knowledge such as the case of the category "people"—*personas* and *gente* in Spanish], as he fails to understand that this same knowledge can be transferred to the extralinguistic general knowledge level, that is, animal referents, as both people and animals are animate objects.)

INTERVIEWER: So this happens only in the feminine: *la vaca?*

(Utterance 18) STUDENT: Which is only a female animal. (Form of knowledge: Explicit extralinguistic topic knowledge. Third developmental phase. Metacognitive strategy: Inferencing.)

INTERVIEWER: Okay. How about if I want to point to the masculine?

(Utterance 19) STUDENT: It would be *el toro*. Some do have different names according to the gender. (Form of knowledge: Explicit relation between extralinguistic general knowledge and intralinguistic system knowledge; he is pointing to the existence of a category of words that have different stems for pointing to the feminine or masculine natural genders. Third developmental phase. Metacognitive strategy: Inferencing.)

INTERVIEWER: So if you are talking about *pollo*, you would not make the difference between the feminine and the masculine chicken?

(Utterance 20) STUDENT: Oh—I think there is a feminine for chicken. I suppose, a rooster for masculine, but I am not sure. Well, even if the chickens are feminine, they are called *pollos*. (Form of knowledge: Explicit relation between extralinguistic general knowledge and intralinguistic system knowledge. Third developmental phase. Metacognitive strategy: Monitoring, inferencing, and translation since in this case, both English and Spanish have the same regular case for using words that have different stems for reflecting linguistically the natural physical gender of animates.)

INTERVIEWER: *Muy bien. Muchas gracias.*

Robert is at the second developmental phase because he could produce and comprehend only some specific cases of the relation between intralinguistic and extralinguistic knowledge. Although he is using metacognitive, cognitive, and social-affective strategies, he could not always generalize his knowledge of the explicit relation between extralinguistic and intralinguistic knowledge from the topic to the general level. However, during the interview process, he was able to move to the third developmental phase for some concepts using monitoring and inferencing metacognitive strategies to relate intralinguistic system and extralinguistic general knowledge. It appears that the interviewer's scaffolding role helped him to gain explicit knowledge of the Spanish language, to move to higher developmental phases, and to use higher-level metacognitive language learning strategies.

Emerging Theses, Themes, and Topics

Adaptation of Learning Strategies to Linguistic and Semantic Content. The first, and most important, emerging thesis was the presence of unidimensional and multidimensional language learning processes. At the linguistic-unidimensional level, learners used lower-level implicit cognitive strategies that corresponded to the implicit intralinguistic form of knowledge applied to semantic categories reflecting regular cases for assigning gender to inanimate referents (i.e., at the marker level). At the semantic-simultaneous level, learners used higher-level explicit cognitive and metacognitive strategies that corresponded to the explicit relationship between intralinguistic and extralinguistic forms of knowledge applied to semantic categories reflecting the general rule for assigning gender to animate referents (i.e., at the system level). As a result, the presence of unidimensional and multidimensional language learning processes coming from the cognitive domain illustrates the complex influence of intralinguistic and extralinguistic-cultural factors, which varies with different kinds of words. The extralinguistic-cultural variable specifying the origin of semantic-gender cases classified as inanimates and animates leads the learner to make a conceptual distinction between physical gender (extralinguistic knowledge) and linguistic gender (intralinguistic knowledge) given by sociocultural conventions.

In sum, we propose the thesis that second language concept formation involves two hierarchical processes: at the linguistic level, the construction of unidimensional representations for specific linguistic cases; and at the semantic level, the construction of multidimensional representations for semantic categories that reflect the complex interaction of variables stemming from the cognitive, cultural, and linguistic domains. In other words, our thesis is that second language learning involves the construction of linguistic and semantic categorical representations that reflect culturally and linguistically bound concepts. Cohen (1987) stated that "categorization tasks are an integral part of second-language learning, as in the learning of agreement between subject and verb in person, number, and gender" (p. 90).

Moreover, the two second language learning processes stated by Gonzalez (1991, 1994, 1995) in relation to assimilation of concepts that are similar between languages and the need for accommodation processes for concepts that are different between languages was also present in this first emerging theme. In previous studies, Gonzalez found the presence of one universal representational system for abstract concepts that coincided across cultural symbolic and linguistic representations and two representational systems for semantic concepts that were culturally and linguistically bound. As a result, this first thesis emerging from the data suggested that learners think at different developmental phases in relation to the complex interaction of cognitive, cultural, and linguistic factors reflected in the content knowledge domain of the second language. In relation to this first theme, Karmiloff-Smith (1986) proposed the presence of two representational systems: a semantic one, related to specific knowledge domains; and an abstract one, formed by re-representations that explicitly link first and second language domain knowledge.

Furthermore, in this unidimensional and multidimensional language learning thesis, we could observe a first theme or pattern that indicated a complex interaction of variables stemming from the cognitive, cultural, and linguistic domains. That is, the same individual showed both unidimensional and multidimensional language learning processes, and the presence of one or the other depended on the interrelation between intralinguistic and extralinguistic-cultural factors, clustered in the semantic categories for gender (see Tables 5.2 and 5.3).

To see this first emerging thesis and theme, refer back to Robert's responses. If we compare Robert's response for the word *tienda* (Utterance 2 for the definition task) and his response for the word *persona* (Utterance 5 for the definition task), a clear difference in the language learning process used arises. For the word *tienda*, a unidimensional representational process suffices; only the application of the general-semantic rule coming from the intralinguistic domain is needed to solve this inanimate object-referent case. In contrast, for the word *persona*, a multidimensional representational process is needed in order to reflect the interaction of cognitive, cultural, and linguistic domains for solving this more complex semantic case. At the cognitive level, the word *persona* illustrates the need to take into consideration both intralinguistic and extralinguistic-cultural factors. Moreover, this word reflects a sociocultural

TABLE 5.2   Frequency of Language Learning Strategies, Forms of Knowledge, and Developmental Phases in the Experimental Group (*N* = 7)

Strategy *(Frequency)**	*Form of Knowledge†* *(Frequency)*	*Developmental Phase*
Gente: Irregular case for the semantic function for gender		
Deduction (16)	4b (10)	Second
	5b (6)	First
Inferencing (6)	3 (3)	Third
	4b (2)	Second
	2 (1)	Second
Question for clarification (4)	4b (1)	Second
	5a (1)	First
	5b (2)	First
Selective attention (4)	5a (1)	First
	3 (1)	Third
	4b (1)	Second
	4a (1)	Second
Auditory representation (7)	5a (7)	First
Repetition (2)	3 (2)	Third
Translation (2)	4b (2)	Second
Imagery (1)	5a (1)	First
Key word (1)	5a (1)	First
Monitoring (1)	3 (1)	Third
Joven: Special case for the semantic function for gender		
Deduction (16)	4a (2)	Second
	4b (14)	Second
Imagery (4)	5b (4)	First
Auditory representation (4)	4b (4)	Second
Grouping (2)	4a (1)	Second
	4b (1)	Second
Elaboration (1)	4b (1)	Second
Inferencing (1)	4b (1)	Third

*The frequencies for some strategies do not equal the number of subjects because some subjects used certain strategies more than once in their responses, while others did not use certain strategies at all.

†Forms of knowledge are as follows:
1 = General extralinguistic knowledge
2 = Extralinguistic topic knowledge
3 = Explicit relation between extralinguistic topic knowledge and intralinguistic knowledge
4a = Explicit intralinguistic knowledge at the system level
4b = Explicit intralinguistic knowledge at the marker level
5a = Implicit intralinguistic knowledge at the system level
5b = Implicit intralinguistic knowledge at the marker level.

These numbers correspond to the code used in Column 3 (Cognitive Factors) of Table 5.1.

TABLE 5.3 Frequency of Language Learning Strategies, Forms of Knowledge, and Developmental Phases in the Control Group ($N = 8$)

Strategy (Frequency)*	Form of Knowledge† (Frequency)	Developmental Phase
Gente: Irregular case for the semantic function for gender		
Self-evaluation (12)	4b (10)	Second
	4a (2)	Second
Auditory representation (8)	5a (8)	First
Delayed production (4)	4b (4)	Second
Imagery (2)	5a (2)	First
Recombination (2)	5b (2)	First
Directed physical response (2)	5b (2)	Second
Question for clarification (2)	5b (2)	First
Joven: Special case for the semantic function for gender		
Deduction (18)	4a (4)	Second
	4b (14)	Second
Auditory representation (8)	5a (3)	First
	5b (5)	First
Imagery (4)	3 (4)	First

*The frequencies for some strategies do not equal the number of subjects because some subjects used certain strategies more than once in their responses, while others did not use certain strategies at all.
†Forms of knowledge are as follows:
1 = General extralinguistic knowledge
2 = Extralinguistic topic knowledge
3 = Explicit relation between extralinguistic topic knowledge and intralinguistic knowledge
4a = Explicit intralinguistic knowledge at the system level
4b = Explicit intralinguistic knowledge at the marker level
5a = Implicit intralinguistic knowledge at the system level
5b = Implicit intralinguistic knowledge at the marker level.
These numbers correspond to the code used in Column 3 (Cognitive Factors) of Table 5.1.

convention (extralinguistic-cultural domain) that the linguistic marker for gender (intralinguistic domain) does not reflect; *persona* shows only one linguistic gender, but it refers to both feminine and masculine natural genders. The same processes were present in the control group subjects, but the higher-level semantic processes for the most complex words were used to a lesser extent than the experimental group subjects (see Tables 5.2 and 5.3).

Adaptation of Learning Strategies to Level of Difficulty of Linguistic Content.
A second thesis we observed was the influence of intralinguistic and extralin-

guistic-cultural factors, merged in the semantic categories for gender, on different forms of knowledge and developmental phases that were used by the same language learner. This thesis leads to the formulation of the second theme: that words that corresponded to the general semantic rule evoked lower-level cognitive strategies in every learner. In contrast, words that corresponded to regular and irregular semantic cases evoked higher-level cognitive and metacognitive strategies. Descriptions of specific findings or topics illustrate this second thesis and theme.

For instance, the word *gente* ("people") required of learners a higher frequency of cognitive and metacognitive strategies, and they also had to make an explicit relation between intralinguistic and extralinguistic-cultural knowledge (see Tables 5.2 and 5.3). In contrast, the word *joven* ("youth") elicited in learners a lower frequency of metacognitive strategies and an explicit intralinguistic form of knowledge (see Tables 5.2 and 5.3). Thus, the word *gente* corresponded to an irregular semantic case that required the multidimensional consideration of intralinguistic and extralinguistic-cultural factors because it was further away from the general rule in comparison to the word *joven*. The word *gente* denotes an animate referent that extralinguistically has natural physical gender and therefore should reflect the general semantic rule. However, it is a collective noun that has a neutral linguistic gender, and therefore it is an irregular semantic case that is also a counterexample of two other regular semantic cases:

1. Nouns ending in *e* tend to have a masculine linguistic gender.
2. Masculine prevails over feminine linguistic gender when the referents include both natural genders.

Thus, although the word *gente* is linguistically feminine and singular (intralinguistic domain), it refers to both genders at the symbolic-cultural convention level (extralinguistic-cultural domain) and is conceptually a collective noun encompassing both physical genders referring to animates (i.e., cognitive domain). Therefore, a unidimensional linguistic conceptual-formation process does not suffice for it; the concept-formation problem will be solved only if the three cognitive, cultural, and linguistic factors are taken into account simultaneously, and therefore multidimensionally, by the learner.

At the linguistic and semantic levels, the word *gente* calls for the construction of a new concept at a higher form of knowledge and developmental phase because it is an irregular semantic case and goes against the general semantic rule and two regular semantic cases. Therefore, the learner needs to use metacognitive strategies at the highest forms of knowledge and developmental levels in order to construct a concept that encompasses the multidimensional interaction of linguistic, cultural, and cognitive factors merging in the semantic representation of knowledge. Robert's reaction to the semantic complexity of the word *gente* is a common one: "I guess I wasn't sure like in *gente*, that is just a part of *personas* ["people" in English] and it relates to people, but it is used just in the *la* form" (Utterance 28 for the definition task). This response illustrates the use of monitoring and inferencing metacognitive strategies, relating explicitly extralinguistic topic knowledge and intralinguistic knowledge at the marker level, and the construction of concepts at the third developmental phase.

Moreover, for the word *persona* (Utterance 5 for the definition task), Robert showed an explicit relation between intralinguistic and extralinguistic knowledge, he was at the third developmental phase, and he used the metacognitive strategy of inferencing. In contrast, his response for the word *tienda* (Utterance 2 for the definition task) is an example of lower-level concept-formation processes needed, as only a unidimensional consideration of intralinguistic factors suffices for this inanimate object referent that conforms to the general semantic case. Robert showed an explicit intralinguistic form of knowledge at the marker level, he was at the second developmental phase, and he used the cognitive strategy of deduction. As these examples show, the same learner can use lower- or higher-level language learning strategies and forms of knowledge and be at different developmental phases in relation to the unidimensional or multidimensional characteristics of different content domains of knowledge representations. In contrast, the control group had a much lower use than experimental group subjects of higher-level metacognitive processes for their explanations (see Tables 5.2 and 5.3).

Stimulation of Higher-Level Learning Strategies Through the Interview Process. The third thesis was the appearance of new insights and new access to explicit knowledge, and the construction of new forms of knowledge (new relations across linguistic concepts, new intralinguistic-extralinguistic connections, new inferences at a higher cognitive level) during the course of the interview for the group of experimental subjects only. When analyzing experimental subjects' interviews, we found that the verbal reports gave us access to "invisible" or internal language learning processes, as if we were opening a window to the students' minds that generated the occurrence of language learning processes before us. Thus, in the process of trying to explain the reason that a particular linguistic structure was produced, the language learner could understand new forms of knowledge, a learning process that was stimulated by the scaffolding role of the interviewer, who used counterexamples and probing. As a result, a third theme emerging from data analysis was that some learners could reveal in their verbal reports how they formed new concepts by re-representing knowledge from lower to higher developmental phases. That is, this third theme emerging from data analysis in experimental subjects supports the thesis that the kind of questions the interviewer used was related to the level of knowledge accessed by the learner.

Control subjects, in contrast, could not access higher levels of knowledge during the course of the interview. In fact, the interviewer's probing and questioning *confused* learners who had not been exposed to the use of conceptual second language learning strategies. They felt confused about linguistic gender assignments when the interviewer probed, and they tended to adopt the interviewer's probings as if they were true statements. Also they had a tendency to "correct" their previous responses.

This third thesis and theme found in experimental subjects can be portrayed by descriptions of specific findings or topics by comparing Robert's responses for the word *gente* on two different occasions during the interview process. The first response that Robert gave for explaining the linguistic gender of the word *gente* portrays a unidimensional representational process (Utterance 17 of the definition task): "Well, because of the majority of the people, even if there was only one man, in a group of women; it wouldn't matter, it will be always masculine. And if there is only a big group of just women, then it would be *la*." Robert showed an explicit intralinguistic knowledge at the system level, a second developmental phase, and the use of the cognitive strategies of overgeneralization and ignorance of rule restrictions. In contrast, when Robert explained the linguistic gender for this same word by the middle of the interview (Utterance 28 of the definition task), Robert said: "I wasn't sure. I guess I wasn't sure like in *la gente*; this is just a part of *personas*, and it relates to people. But it is just used in the *la* form." This response shows the presence of an explicit relation between extralinguistic-cultural topic knowledge and intralinguistic knowledge at the marker level, a third developmental phase, and the use of the metacognitive strategies of inferencing and monitoring. At this point in the interview, Robert is able to relate his previous understanding that *gente* refers to both feminine and masculine animate referents to his realization that the category *personas* can refer to animate referents of both physical genders. Thus, Robert realized that there is a connection between *gente* and *personas*: both have the same animate referent—the category "people" in English. As a result, Robert is having a major insight, achieving at a higher level of understanding, a higher form of knowledge and developmental phase, and using more complex learning strategies.

This third thesis, that the introspective report method for eliciting verbal reports can stimulate the learner to think at higher levels, can be also portrayed by using descriptions of specific findings or topics. At the beginning of the interview, Karen, an experimental subject, explained her correct choice of masculine gender for the word *cliente* ("client") as follows: "I wasn't sure if it was masculine or feminine, but with an *e* it could be either one. I wasn't sure, and it was kind of a guessing game. Usually I think it's going to be masculine if it ends in an *e*." In the middle of the interview, Karen was asked again if the word *cliente* can be only masculine. Before, she had explained that the word *gente* can have only one gender, and that idea was influencing her following utterance in relation to the word *cliente*: "I would think you could make it feminine, just because it has an ending that you don't need to mess with." When comparing both utterances referring to the same word at different points in the interview, we can observe a progression in the level of learning strategies used: from a cognitive strategy of deduction, as Karen was explicitly applying the linguistic rule, to a metacognitive strategy of inferencing, as she was constructing a new explicit hypothesis of a previously unknown meaning in the second language. It is important to note that the word *cliente* also deviates from the general rule that words ending in *e* tend to be masculine. The word *cliente* is a regular semantic case; animate referents can have both physical gender in relation to symbolic sociocultural conventions.

Thus, the learner needs to construct a new concept that considers the multidimensional factors of cognitive, cultural, and linguistic domains. An interviewer who uses thought-provoking questions for eliciting verbal reports can help the learner to think with language at higher levels. Nevertheless, the issue of whether the level of knowledge accessed by the learner is related to the type of questions used is a controversial one. There are different positions regarding the validity of data collected through verbal reports. Some authors argue that it is not possible to access internal language learning processes and representations through verbal reports (Selinger, 1983). In sum, our thesis is that the researcher's questions will make a difference in what level of knowledge is accessed: language use (How do learners use the language at the pragmatic and implicit level?) versus language learning (How do learners represent language, and what strategies do they use for producing and understanding language at the explicit level?).

Several authors support our thesis that the types of questions influence the knowledge level accessed. According to Cohen (1987), we were asking for a verbalization of the learning process that resulted in a description of internal language processes (i.e., language learning strategies and forms of knowledge used), as well as a description of the study skills that learners used. White (1980) pointed out that researcher's questions and tasks for generating verbal reports will influence how much attention learners could pay to their cognitive processes. Hayes and Flowers (1983) suggested that although some thinking processes are unconscious, nevertheless, we can still explore and collect evidence on cognitive processes that are not available in overt language performance. Dechert (1987) stated that part of human cognitive processes are accessible for verbalization (declarative knowledge) and part are not accessible (procedural knowledge).

Thus, it is our thesis that the types of questions used in eliciting verbal reports in this research study served as an opportunity for language learners to access new, insightful knowledge at higher developmental levels. Verbal reports can serve as a psychopedagogical tool for increasing accessibility to declarative knowledge by the language learner. Dechert (1987) views verbal reports in second language research as tools for documenting the structure and rules of language processing. We propose that through verbal reports, we can discover how second language learners represent knowledge through language and can study the relation between language and thought. However, subjects in the experimental group were trained throughout the semester to focus on concept formation and accessing implicit knowledge through reflection for re-representing their procedural or implicit knowledge in an explicit form. This conceptual approach to teaching Spanish may have had an influence on the presence of new inferences and the re-representation of knowledge at higher levels that we could observe during the interviews. Moreover, the use of verbal reports may stimulate language learners to gain conscious access to procedural or explicit knowledge in the process of second language concept formation. That is, higher levels of knowledge attained during the process of interviewing learners could have been influenced by the researcher's questions and probing in the verbal reports. Thus, verbal reports may stimulate second language learners to gain consciousness to their own procedural or explicit knowledge in the process of concept formation. The analysis of a control sample is important because these learners were exposed to a standard grammar approach, not a conceptual instructional approach.

In general, subjects in the control group performed at lower levels in comparison to the experimental subjects. If we compare control with experimental subjects for words that required higher- (e.g., *gente*) or lower-level (e.g., *joven*) knowledge forms and learning strategies, we can observe the presence of much lower learning processes used by control subjects (see Tables 5.2 and 5.3). For instance, for the words *gente* and *joven*, control subjects used primarily an implicit intralinguistic form of knowledge at the marker level and learning strategies at the auditory and visual levels, leading mainly to a first developmental phase (see Tables 5.2 and 5.3). In contrast, for the same words, experimental subjects used a higher-level form of knowledge, explicit intralinguistic knowledge at the marker level, and also higher-level metacognitive strategies, including deduction and inferencing. Thus, experimental subjects performed mainly at the second and third developmental phases (see Table 5.2), and control subject performed generally at the first and second developmental phases (see Table 5.3).

Consider Linda, who participated in the control group. During the course of the interview, when asked about why she had chosen the feminine linguistic gender for *gente*, she replied, "Because I remember *la gente*. I don't know why. There is no clue. It is just one of those words that you have to remember." Clearly Linda was performing at an intralinguistic implicit knowledge level for markers because she used primarily cognitive strategies for memorizing specific cases of linguistic gender assignment. For this particular case of the word *gente*, she was using the cognitive strategy of auditory representation, and she was performing at the first developmental phase.

A second example can be portrayed by using Alfredo's responses, another participant in the control group. When Alfredo was probed by the interviewer about the linguistic gender assignment for the noun *persona*, he replied, "I don't know. I have never seen *un persona* or *un persono* before, so I am not sure." Actually, the only gender assignment for *persona* is feminine, but it refers to both feminine and masculine referents. Thus, *persona* is a complex case because it is an exception to the semantic convention stating that masculine prevails over feminine when only one linguistic gender is assigned to nouns. In this case, Alfredo was using visual representation as the primary basis of his responses. His performance can also be characterized as being in the first developmental phase because he was using primarily cognitive strategies at the implicit intralinguistic level only.

A third example is portrayed by Paul, who also participated in the control group. When Paul was asked why he had chosen the masculine linguistic gender for *joven*, he responded, "Why *el joven*, because it's masculine, because it doesn't have an *e* at the end, and it is talking about a young person in general, so I need to use *el*." Paul is using the cognitive strategy of deduction for applying a general rule referring to suffixes, the *e* ending, for deciding the linguistic gender assignment of nouns. However, he has a misunderstanding of this linguistic rule, because it actually points to nouns ending in *e* as generally having a masculine linguistic assignment. Moreover, Paul shows a misunderstanding of a semantic convention that points to masculine prevailing over feminine for assigning linguistic genders to plural nouns. Paul is applying this semantic convention incorrectly to singular nouns. His performance showed false concepts hypothesized; he was making developmental errors that stemmed from a faulty comprehension of linguistic general rules and semantic conventions of the Spanish language. His performance is typical of learners at the second developmental phase, who show only explicit forms of knowledge.

Accessibility of Metacognitive and Cognitive Strategies Through the Interview Process. The fourth emerging thesis was that the interview process and the scaffolding role of the interviewer helped subjects in the experimental group to gain access to metacognitive and cognitive strategies used as study skills for second language learning. That is, the fourth emerging theme was that verbal reports revealed the underlying cognitive, metacognitive, and metalinguistic processes used as study skills by second language learners. Robert's response for the role-playing task (Utterance 9) portrays this thesis and theme emerging from descriptions of specific findings or topics. His response reveals the study skill that he used for learning this kind of word while trying to explain the reason that he had selected the masculine linguistic gender for the word *arroz* ("rice" in English): "Hm. I guess that the ending to me is more masculine. I learn the article with the word." Robert focused his attention on the specific gender of the article associated with the new word that he was trying to learn, a study skill that was coded as a cognitive strategy named selective attention. Another example in relation to study skills is given by Michael, who also used selective attention for dealing with irregular semantic cases exemplified by the word *gente:* "So you just have to make a special note that this word is just masculine or this word is just feminine." In these examples, the metacognitive strategy of selective attention relates to study skills that second language learners had developed for dealing with irregular semantic categories for gender.

Individual Differences and Cognitive and Extralinguistic Cultural Factors Influencing Second Language Learning. Three more related themes emerged from data analysis in both the control and experimental groups. The fifth emerging theme was the presence of individual learning approaches associated with a tendency to use specific language learning strategies that appeared more frequently in relation to specific forms of knowledge and the developmental phase at which the learner tended to perform. The sixth emerging theme was the use of a limited or a vast repertoire of language learning strategies in a specific learner, which was also related to the preferred form of knowledge used and developmental phase achieved. The seventh emerging theme was the relation between learners' specific strategies, forms of knowledge, and developmental phases and their personal experiences with the Spanish language (e.g., contact with the Spanish language during early childhood and context of second language learning). These three related themes stemmed from the same thesis: Second language learners present unidimensional tendencies to use learning strategies and forms of knowledge and to perform at a specific developmental phase due to the influence of cognitive and extralinguistic-cultural factors. The fifth theme pointed to a cognitive factor: the presence of idiosyncratic second language learning approaches. It also portrayed an extralinguistic-cultural factor showing how personal background experiences with the target language could influence the expression of cognitive factors (i.e., forms of knowledge, developmental phases, and learning strategies). The sixth theme also pointed to a cognitive factor that revealed individual differences in how second language learners use learning strategies.

The following descriptions of specific findings or topics help to illustrate the fifth, sixth, and seventh emerging themes. For the explicit knowledge form, learners preferred the higher-level cognitive strategies of deduction and elaboration, indicating the application of rules for concepts that were different between Spanish and English. For the implicit knowledge form, learners preferred the lower-level cognitive strategies of auditory representation, visual imagery, repetition, and key words. Robert, an experimental subject, functioned at the second developmental phase, with some potential to achieve at the third developmental phase with the scaffolding help of the interviewer, and he used implicit and explicit knowledge forms. In addition, Robert tended to use the cognitive strategies of deduction and question for clarification, corresponding to an implicit knowledge form, and the metacognitive strategies of selective attention and self-evaluation, corresponding to an explicit knowledge form.

These three related themes can be illustrated by comparing the individual learning approaches of Robert and Jessica, both experimental subjects, which are different and yet similar at the same time. Robert primarily used the second developmental phase, in relation to both implicit and explicit forms of knowledge; however, he had the potential to achieve at the third developmental phase with the help of the scaffolding role of the interviewer. His individual learning style was different from that of the other learners; he demonstrated a broad spectrum of learning strategies and displayed the largest vocabulary and topic knowledge. Robert used cognitive (translation, grouping, deduction, recombination, imagery, key word, and contextualization), metacognitive (selective attention, self-evaluation, and inferencing), and social-affective strategies (question for clarification) for second language learning. Although Jessica also showed a broad range of developmental phases, she consistently used a limited repertoire of cognitive (deduction, auditory representation, and contextualization) and social-affective strategies (question for clarification), and she showed the emergence of some metacognitive strategies (i.e., monitoring and inferencing). Thus, although both learners had a common pattern in relation to the broad range of developmental phases at which they can be stimulated to perform, they also showed unique profiles in relation to the variety, frequency, and level of the learning strategies they used.

Robert and Jessica can also serve as examples to illustrate the seventh theme, because their language learning background histories can shed some light on our interpretation of their individual learning approaches. Robert had used Spanish for communication with his grandparents during his early childhood. As a result, he had some implicit knowledge of the language as a former native speaker, as well as some explicit knowledge as an adult second language learner in a formal context. Jessica had had some background in learning French and Spanish as a second language only in formal contexts, and thus she used frequently explicit intralinguistic forms of knowledge at both the rule and specific cases levels.

Conclusions

There is a multidimensional interaction of cognitive, cultural, and linguistic factors affecting concept construction in second language learning. The verbal reports revealed that concept construction is a complex process, encompassing unidimensional and multidimensional processes in relation to the linguistic or semantic levels of content knowledge domains in second languages. The linguistic level of concept construction occurred when learners accessed implicit intralinguistic forms of knowledge at a first developmental phase. The semantic level of concept construction occurred when learners accessed explicit intralinguistic and extralinguistic-cultural forms of knowledge at second and third developmental phases. Thus, the same learner could access higher or lower forms of knowledge and perform at different developmental phases in relation to the particular semantic and linguistic characteristics of the second language content knowledge. Moreover, we found that learners could benefit from the use of the proposed conceptual learning approach and the scaffolding role of the interviewer; experimental subjects performed at higher developmental phases and used higher-level forms of knowledge and learning strategies in comparison to control subjects. Learners could gain implicit or explicit (or both) knowledge of the relations between intralinguistic and extralinguistic-cultural knowledge, and they could gain access to cognitive and metacognitive learning strategies used as study skills.

We also found individual tendencies to use learning strategies and forms of knowledge and to perform at specific developmental phases that were related to cognitive (idiosyncratic learning approaches, and a limited or a vast repertoire of learning strategies) and extralinguistic-cultural factors (the second language learner's individual history). The most advanced students could produce and comprehend the relations between intralinguistic and extralinguistic-cultural knowledge at a general level. In contrast, the less advanced learners could not produce or comprehend the relations of intralinguistic and extralinguistic-cultural knowledge forms. They showed only an implicit intralinguistic knowledge. Some learners were at an intermediate level of explicit production and comprehension of the relations between intralinguistic and extralinguistic-cultural knowledge. They could produce and comprehend some specific cases of the relation between extralinguistic and intralinguistic knowledge but could not generalize their explicit knowledge (i.e., topic knowledge).

This study is relevant from theoretical and applied perspectives. Theoretically, it presents a model for gaining understanding of the influence of linguistic and cultural factors on conceptual learning in second language situations in adults. It leads to insights on how these adults develop concepts for new linguistic structures and symbolic cultural meanings. At an applied level, the study suggests a new educational approach for teaching second languages through conceptual learning using verbal reports for gaining higher-level knowledge and study skills. The main educational implication is the optimization of second language learning processes by using conceptual learning as a method for instruction beginning with middle school students.

References

Bialystock, E. (1978). A theoretical model of second language learning. *Language Learning, 28*(1), 69–83.

Bogdan, R. C., & Biklen, S. K. (1982). *Qualitative research for education: An introduction to theory and methods.* Needham Heights, MA: Allyn & Bacon.

Brown, A. L., & Palinscar, A. S. (1982). Inducing strategies learning from texts by means of informed, self-controlled training. *Topics in Learning and Learning Disabilities, 2,* 1–17.

Collins, A., & Stevens, A. L. (1982). Goals and strategies of inquiry teachers. In R. Glaser (Ed.), *Advances in instructional psychology* (Vol. 2, pp. 65–119). Hillsdale, NJ: Lawrence Erlbaum.

Cohen, A. D. (1987). Using verbal reports in research on language learning. In C. Færch & G. Kasper (Eds.), *Introspection in second language research* (pp. 82–95). Clevedon, England: Multilingual Matters.

Dechert, H. W. (1987). Analyzing language processing through verbal protocols. In C. Færch & G. Kasper (Eds.), *Introspection in second language research* (pp. 96–112). Clevedon, England: Multilingual Matters.

Færch, C., & Kasper, G. (1987). From product to process: Introspective methods in second language research. In C. Færch & G. Kasper (Eds.), *Introspection in second language research* (pp. 5–23). Clevedon, England: Multilingual Matters.

Gonzalez, V. (1991). *A model of cognitive, cultural, and linguistic variables affecting bilingual Spanish/English children's development of concepts and language.* Unpublished doctoral dissertation, University of Texas at Austin. (ERIC Document Reproduction Service No. ED 345 562)

Gonzalez, V. (1994). A model of cognitive, cultural, and linguistic variables affecting bilingual Spanish/English children's development of concepts and language. *Hispanic Journal of Behavioral Sciences, 16*(4), 396–421.

Gonzalez, V. (1995). *Cognition, culture, and language in bilingual children: Conceptual and semantic development.* Bethesda, MD: Austin & Windfield.

Gonzalez, V., & Schallert, D. L. (1993, April). *Influence of linguistic and cultural factors on conceptual learning in second-language situations.* Paper presented to the Second Language Special Interest Group at the annual meeting of the American Educational Research Association, Atlanta, GA.

Gonzalez, V., Schallert, D. L., Flores, M., Perrodin, L., & de Rivera, S. (1994, April). *Concept formation in second-language learning situations: A conceptual approach versus a natural approach.* Paper presented to the Second Language Special Interest Group at the annual meeting of the American Educational Research Association, New Orleans, LA.

Grotjahn, R. (1987). On the methodological basis of introspective methods. In C. Færch & G. Kasper (Eds.), *Introspection in second language research* (pp. 56–81). Clevedon, England: Multilingual Matters.

Hayes, J. R., & Flowers, L. (1983). Uncovering cognitive processes in writing. In P. Mosenthal (Ed.), *Research in writing: Principles and methods* (pp. 207–220). New York: Longman.

Karmiloff-Smith, A. (1979). Micro and macrodevelopmental changes in language acquisition and other representational systems. *Cognitive Science, 3,* 91–118.

Karmiloff-Smith, A. (1985). Language and cognitive processes from a developmental perspective. *Language and Cognitive Processes, 1*(1), 61–85.

Karmiloff-Smith, A. (1986). From meta-processes to conscious access: Evidence from children's metalinguistic and repair data. *Cognition, 23,* 95–147.

O'Malley, J. M., Russo, R. P., Chamot, J. M., & Stewner-Manzanares, G. (1988). Applications of learning strategies by students learning English as a second language. In C. E. Weinstein, E. T. Goetz & P. Alexander (Eds.), *Learning and study strategies: Issues in assessment, instruction, and evaluation* (pp. 215–231). San Diego, CA: Academic Press.

Robinett, B. W., & Schachter, J. (1983). *Second language learning: Contrastive analysis, error analysis, and related aspects.* Ann Arbor, MI: University of Michigan Press.

Selinger, H. W. (1983). The language learner as linguist: Of metaphors and realities. *Applied Linguistics, 4*(3), 179–191.

White, P. (1980). Limitations on verbal report of internal events. *Psychological Review, 87*(1), 105–112.

Appendix 5A: Semantic Categories for Gender

General Rule

There is only one general rule stating that nouns ending in *a* (suffix) are linguistically feminine and that nouns ending in *o* (suffix) are linguistically masculine. The corresponding definite (*el* for masculine, *la* for feminine) or indefinite (*un* for masculine, *una* for feminine) article should match the linguistic gender of the noun.

General Rule for Inanimates, Different. These nouns have only one linguistic gender due to sociocultural linguistic conventions that are usually independent of the intrinsic nature of the object. Here the general rule applies: an *a* ending or suffix implies feminine linguistic gender, and an *o* ending or suffix implies masculine linguistic gender.

General Rule for Animates, Different. People and animals generally take a feminine and a masculine linguistic form, according to the natural physical gender of the referent. This change of gender in the markers of nouns happens only occasionally in English.

Regular Cases for Inanimates

Regular Case for Inanimates 1, Common. Some historical linguists propose a cultural connotative meaning that points to the cultural symbolic meaning of the object—for example, "the land"/*la tierra* being linguistically feminine in Spanish. In addition, the symbolic meaning is also feminine (and thus the connotative meaning) across languages and cultures. This feminine symbolic meaning may not be present in the linguistic structure and its markers in the English language (the denotative meaning). However, the connotative meaning can exist independent of the denotative meaning (sometimes there is a commonality between Spanish and English in connotative but not denotative meanings).

Regular Case for Inanimates 2, Different. Nouns ending in *tad*, *dad*, *ción*, and *sión* are linguistically feminine and thus require a feminine article. Some of these nouns can be abstract concepts—for example, *la libertad* ("liberty"), *la responsabilidad* ("responsibility"). Other nouns are concrete objects—for example, *la composición* ("a composition"), *la televisión* ("a television"). When collective nouns refer to categories of objects (inanimates), usually they cannot be made plural, because they are considered mass nouns—for example, *la ropa*, ("clothes") and *la comida* ("food").

Regular Case for Inanimates 3, Different. When the linguistic gender of some inanimate nouns changes, the meaning of the word also changes—for example, *el libro* means "book" and *la libra* means "the pound," *el manzano* means the "apple tree" and *la manzana* means "the apple" (fruit), *el televisor* means "the electric appliance" and *la televisión* means "the media." For other inanimate nouns, a change in linguistic gender can occur without affecting the meaning of the word—for instance, *el refrigerador* and *la refrigeradora* (both mean "refrigerator").

Regular Case for Inanimates 4, Different. Some inanimate nouns have a plural form, but the corresponding article is singular—for example, *el lavaplatos* ("a dishwasher"), *el espantapájaros* ("a scarecrow"), and *el cumpleaños* ("a birthday").

Regular Case for Inanimates 5, Different. Inanimate nouns ending in *e* tend to be linguistically masculine—for instance, *el accidente* ("an accident"), *el cine* ("the movies"), *el nombre* ("a name"), *el norte* ("north"), *el tomate* ("a tomato"), and *el restaurante* ("a restaurant").

Regular Case for Inanimates 6, Different. Inanimate nouns ending in a consonant (e.g., *l, n, r, z*) tend to be linguistically masculine—for instance, *el papel* ("a piece of paper"), *el flan* ("a flan"), *el televisor* ("a television"), *el arroz* ("rice").

Irregular Cases for Inanimates 1, Different. There are a number of exceptions for inanimates, such as *el problema* ("a problem"), *el sofá* ("a sofa"), *la carne* ("meat"), and *el agua* ("water").

Regular Cases for Animates

Regular Case for Animates 1, Different. Collective nouns take only one linguistic gender. The collective noun will be feminine if the word ends in *a*, according to the general intralinguistic rule (e.g., *la familia*—"a family") and if the word ends in *tad, dad, ción*, and *sión*, according to the specific intralinguistic cases (e.g., *las profesiones*—"professions"). The collective noun is linguistically masculine if the word ends in a consonant (e.g., *el animal*—"an animal"). Collective nouns referring to people (animates) sometimes can be pluralized (e.g., *las profesiones*—"professions," and *las personas*—"people"); for other words, only the singular form exists (e.g., *la gente*—"people," *el público*—"an audience," and *el ser humano*—"a human being").

Regular Case for Animates 2, Different. Some nouns use variable suffixes and common stems. Linguistically masculine nouns tend to end in a consonant; for forming the feminine, add an *a* suffix—for example, for "people": *el alemán* (masculine)—*la alemana* (feminine), both corresponding to a German person; and for animals: *el león* (masculine)—*la leona* (feminine), both corresponding to a lion.

Regular Case for Animates 3, Different. Some words are used for both the feminine and masculine referents, but use different articles. These nouns tend to end in an *e* suffix. However, there are also some nouns ending in other vowels (*a* and *o*) or in a consonant (*n, r,* and *d*). The linguistic gender for these nouns is marked by the definite or indefinite article—for example, *el/la cliente* ("a client"), *el/la turista* ("a tourist"), *el/la testigo* ("a witness"), and *el/la huesped* ("a visitor").

Regular Case for Animates 4, Different. When pluralizing animate nouns, masculine linguistic gender prevails over feminine when referring to a group of individuals or animals. For example, *los estudiantes* will refer to both female and male students; *los profesores* will refer to both female and male teachers. When you specifically point to the linguistically feminine case, then only female individuals or animals are included. For example, *las estudiantes* will refer only to a group of female students.

Regular Case for Animates 5, Common. Nouns referring to roles, professions, and occupations sometimes exist in both linguistic genders, following the regular cases already explained—for example, *el profesor/la profesora* ("a teacher"), *el/la estudiante* ("a student"), and *la madre/el padre* ("mother/father"). Sometimes the nouns exist only in feminine or masculine linguistic forms, due to sociocultural reasons (professions, occupations, and roles that can only be feminine or masculine in the sociocultural context of language use). This is changing very rapidly. For example, *la mujer policía* ("a policewoman") is a recent noun, created to reflect societal changes. The same is true for *la doctora* ("the female doctor") and *la ingeniera* ("the female engineer"). Some professions or occupations remain only in one gender—for example, *el mecánico* ("a mechanic"), *el ama de casa* ("a housewife"), and *el plomero* ("a plumber").

Regular Case for Animates 6, Different. Some nouns for labeling animals or people show only one linguistic gender, corresponding to the actual ending of the word—for example, *el pájaro* ("a bird"), *el pinguino* ("a penguin"), *la jirafa* ("a giraffe"), and *la persona* ("a person"). These nouns for animals that have only one linguistic gender refer to both female and male cases. For specifying the gender of the animal, an adjective can be added, such as *macho* for male animals (e.g., *el elefante macho*—"the male or he elephant"), and *hembra* for female animals (e.g., *el elefante hembra*—"the female or she elephant").

Regular Case for Animates 7, Common. Some nouns use different words or stems from the masculine to the feminine form—for example, for people: *el padre/la madre* ("father/mother"), *el hombre/la mujer* ("man/woman"); and for animals: *el toro/la vaca* ("bull/cow"), and *el caballo/la yegua* ("horse/mare").

Regular Case for Animates 8, Different. These nouns share the prefix; the suffix is different when feminine and masculine linguistic forms are produced—for instance, *señor/señorita* ("sir/miss"), *gallo/gallina* ("rooster/hen").

Irregular Cases for Animates, Different. There are a number of exceptions to the general rule and the specific cases—for example, *actor/actríz* ("actor/actress"), *la reyna/el rey* ("queen/king"), *la jefa/el jefe* ("a boss").

CHAPTER 6

Conceptualizations of *Ser* and *Estar* by College Students Learning Spanish as a Second Language and Adult Spanish Native Speakers

VIRGINIA GONZALEZ AND SONIA DE RIVERA

THIS CHAPTER HIGHLIGHTS THE MAJOR THEME OF THE BOOK: THE CULtural and linguistic influence on the construction of semantic representations in bilingual learners. The qualitative study presented focuses on linguistic structures that are different between Spanish and English so that learners must construct new semantic representations reflecting cultural meanings.

There is a need for studies with adult first and second language learners to explain the cognitive processes involved in learning semantic functions of linguistic structures in Spanish. Learning semantic functions involves constructing meaningful hierarchical conceptual structures, a psycholinguistic process in which cognition and language interact. Several authors (e.g., Sera, 1992; VanPatten, 1985) with both linguistic and cognitive psychology perspectives have stated this need.

The purpose of the qualitative study presented in this chapter was to increase the understanding of some possible similarities or differences in the explicit and implicit knowledge that adult native Spanish speakers and adult second language learners could articulate in their explanations of their conceptualizations of the semantic functions of *ser* and *estar* forms. It thus investigated the relationship between cognition and language because people who are learning semantic functions of linguistic structures have to form new concepts to accommodate cultural meanings. This study used different semantic categorizations of *ser* and *estar* illustrated in some correct and incorrect statements presented to eight Spanish native speakers and five college students learning Spanish as a second language. These thirteen subjects were asked by a bilingual Spanish/English interviewer (the second author of this chapter) to explain the conceptual reasoning underlying their choices using a "thinking-aloud" protocol methodology. The probing questions used had the objective of understanding the implicit or explicit forms of knowledge that subjects had constructed for the semantic functions of *ser* and *estar* forms. (See Chapter 5 for a similar study of linguistic gender in Spanish.)

The chapter begins with a critical literature review that discusses different semantic categorizations of *ser* and *estar* made by linguists (De Mello, 1979; Franco, 1984; Higgs, 1985; Pountain, 1984; Ruggeri Marchetti, 1985). It then reviews the developmental stages found in previous research studies (Finnemann, 1990; Garreton & Medley, 1985; Guntermann, 1992; VanPatten, 1985) in the acquisition process of *ser* and *estar* and refers to the concept formation process of *ser* and *estar*, reviewed from a cognitive psychology perspective (Sera, 1992). The last section of the literature review focuses on educational methodologies that can stimulate second language learners to form explicit knowledge of the semantic functions of the *ser* and *estar* forms.

The results and discussion section presents patterns found throughout the cases for both adult Spanish native speakers and second language learners; examples of explicit and implicit forms of knowledge are given to illustrate similarities and differences between the groups. Conclusions are formulated for both the theoretical knowledge gained about cognitive processes and learning strategies used by adult Spanish native speakers and second language learners, and for the educational implications of how instructors can present semantic functions of linguistic forms in Spanish textbooks and in the classroom.

LITERATURE REVIEW

The literature review that follows served as a framework for developing the data coding design used for qualitatively analyzing the data in our study. The data coding system separates semantic and grammatical functions of *ser* and *estar*, and divides semantic functions into classification, identification, and location in reference to animate and inanimate objects and events. An analysis of the subjects' explicit and implicit knowledge forms and strategies will also be conducted. The objective of the data coding system derived from this theoretical framework is to reveal individual differences as well as group patterns that may be similar or different between adult native Spanish speakers and second language learners. Some educational methodological practices will be derived from the findings.

Semantic Categories in Ser *and* Estar

According to Higgs (1985), "The basic communicative functions of '*ser*' include identifying, defining, and classifying" (p. 410). The more difficult function to learn, says Higgs, is classifying because both *ser* and *estar* forms can be syntactically correct. However, when these words are used for classification purposes, a different meaning is conveyed, which De Mello (1979) calls "a different semantic value" (p. 338). According to Higgs, *"ser"* + adjective conveys the meaning of "commitment to a classification" (p. 410), while *"estar"* + adjective refers only to "reporting an observation or a reaction" (p. 410). Ruggeri Marchetti (1985) and De Mello noted that both *ser* and *estar* mean "to exist" or "to take place," but *estar* in addition can convey a temporal or situational meaning. In addition, De Mello held that the contrast *ser* and *estar* also functions as a distinction between different opposite meanings such as "permanent (*ser*) vs. transitory (*estar*), quality (*ser*) vs. state (*estar*), [and] inherent (*ser*) vs. accidental (*estar*)" (p. 340).

Pountain (1982) noted that *estar* "represents a state through which a subject [or object] is passing . . . [or] . . . an impression made on the speaker" (p. 141). A speaker using *estar* must have had experience with the object, whereas the use of *ser* is associated with a semantic process of classification in which language influences cognition. In addition, De Mello (1978) held that "any word which may be interpreted to refer either to an action or to a physical object may be used with *ser* and *estar*, depending on whether reference is to an occurrence (*ser*) or to a location (*estar*)" (p. 338). When *ser* and *estar* are used as auxiliaries for forming the past or present participle used as an adjective in a passive voice in Spanish (e.g., *ha sido lavado, está siendo lavado*), the linguistic forms of *ser* and *estar* lose their semantic value to acquire a grammatical one.

Regarding the semantic nature of the distinction between *ser* and *estar*, Pountain (1982) stated, "My interpretation of the use of *ser* and *estar* . . . is that both are possible with animate and inanimate subjects in the context of a locative adverbial complement" (p. 152). Moreover, Franco (1984) proposed that both *ser* and *estar* can be used to refer to location—for example, *ser* when referring to inanimates that are placed permanently in a specific site (e.g., a building, a room, an exit door, *la clase es en el salón B*) and *estar* when referring to inanimates that do not have a definite place (objects that can be moved, such as a pen or car—as in *El carro está en el garage*), inanimates in relation to finding out their location (e.g., *Dónde está el salón de clases?*), and animates that can change location (e.g., a dog, a boy, *El niño está en la escuela*).

Higgs (1985) recommended that second language learners of Spanish assume that the use of *ser* and *estar* is a problem-solving situation and to use questions to make the correct choice, such as: "Am I classifying a person or object by type? If the answer is 'Yes' *ser* is used; if not *estar*" (p. 411). Thus, the process of learning *ser* and *estar* requires second language learners to construct new concepts associated with the semantics of Spanish. Then one of the difficulties for language learners when deciding whether to use *ser* or *estar* is that the contrast is based on semantics (contextual pragmatic meaning), not on grammatical rules. For most cases, both *ser* and *estar* would be semantically and pragmatically correct, but only one would be contextually adequate.

Ruggeri Marchetti (1985) proposed that the decision of whether to use *ser* or *estar* is a psychological one because the possible meanings conveyed by the speaker refer to idiosyncratic thoughts and emotions. The same sentence using *ser* or *estar* may mean different things to different speakers, depending on the semantic value that he or she may want to communicate. The choice of *ser* and *estar* therefore is related to the construction of connotative (subjective or affective) meanings. De Mello (1978) noted that when a speaker uses *estar*, he has the idea of change, "either because a change has taken place (*Juan está alto = Juan ha crecido—Juan is tall = Juan has grown*) or because a change could take place (*Juan está enfermo* [Juan is sick] implies the near future possibility of *Juan está bien* [Juan is well])" (p. 340). De Mello also held that change implies that the speaker is making an evaluation and forming an opinion based on personal experiences with the objects or subjects that he is referring to. Thus, both Ruggeri Marchetti and De Mello referred to the subjectivity involved when different speakers use *ser* and *estar* to convey different connotative meanings.

Moreover, Ruggeri Marchetti (1985) noted that learning Spanish can be as difficult for Italian native speakers as for English native speakers, given that both Italian and English have only one form of the verb "to be" (*essere* in Italian). According to Pountain (1982), modern Spanish, derived from Castilian, is "able to make overt a distinction [*ser* and *estar* forms of the verb "to be"] which in many languages, English included, is covert" (p. 140).

Developmental Stages for Acquiring Ser *and* Estar

According to VanPatten (1985), second language learners may develop the same sequential patterns of acquisition as in their first language. VanPatten noted that there is a sequence of transitional stages for grammatical structures in English that appear to be universal; several authors have found the same acquisition sequence in children and adults (Dulay & Burt, 1974; Krashen, 1981; Larsen-Freeman, 1976). Nevertheless, more data-driven studies need to be conducted for documenting the stages that second language learners go through when acquiring specific grammatical structures.

Guntermann (1992) interviewed Peace Corps volunteers in order to study their mastery level of the *ser* and *estar* forms in Spanish. The author presented lower-level second language Spanish speakers questions about their interests and their future work. They used primarily *ser* to convey many different meanings, such as introducing topics or a longer description, presenting a general idea when they did not know the specific vocabulary (circumlocution), providing reasons for actions in a brief way, and explaining ideas by using impersonal expressions. When these same subjects were interviewed later, after they had reached higher levels of Spanish mastery, their repertoire of impersonal expressions with *ser* had increased, but their use of them had decreased. In addition, these subjects generally demonstrated correct use of *estar* in the functions of location, condition, and progressive.

Guntermann (1992) identified seven stages of acquisition of the *ser* and *estar* forms in these second language Spanish learners:

> Stage 1, novice plus. Subjects used *estar* incorrectly when the context called for *ser*, and used *ser* with very reduced utterances and as a filler when literal English translations of the verb "to be" were made.
>
> Stage 2, intermediate from low to moderate. Subjects primarily used *ser* "for describing qualities, identifying and asking for identifications, indicating existence, and expressing ideas using impersonal expressions" (p. 1300).
>
> Stage 3, intermediate high. Subjects generally used *estar* accurately and could use *ser* in a larger number of ways, including to express reasons, origins, purpose, temporal goal, and age. During this stage, the progressive form using *estar* also appeared.
>
> Stage 4, advanced. Subjects used *estar* mostly accurately for location. They also showed an increase in the use of the progressive form, and their omission errors disappeared.
>
> Stage 5, advanced plus. Subjects could use *ser* generally in a correct manner.
>
> Stages 6 and 7, superior. Subjects correctly used all the functions of the *ser* and *estar* forms, including the passive voice.

VanPatten (1985) found that college students learning Spanish as a second language acquired *ser* before *estar* within their first year of studies. From his data, VanPatten noted that " 'ser' is acquired first and overgeneralized" (p. 400) and that "learners would acquire 'estar' with adjectives later than other syntactic/semantic functions" (p. 403). Some of these students' preferred strategies were simplification, communicative value, frequency of input, and whether transfer from the first language could be made. Van Patten identified three stages of learning *ser* and *estar* that appeared in a sequential and predictable manner:

1. Overgeneralization of *ser* in *estar* locative and conditional contexts, leading toward acquisition of *ser* first
2. Use of *estar* with locatives
3. Use of *estar* with adjectives of condition and in progressive verb constructions

The learning strategies of transference from first language, overgeneralization, and simplification that VanPatten found are similar to a description of monolingual children's second stage (Garreton & Medley, 1986). In relation to these second language learning strategies, Guntermann (1992) asserted that "all learners need to 'simplify' the language at the beginning—that is, use the fewest forms and rules to express the most meaning—but... [that when using] simplification... learners do not seek to reduce the language, but rather to expand their ability to use it to the point where they are comfortable with their expertise" (p. 1303). Guntermann explained the early acquisition of *ser* by adult second language learners to be due to similarities with the form "to be" in English in its singular present tense form.

Guntermann (1992) also acknowledged the presence of individual differences in the order of acquisition of the *ser* and *estar* forms and explained them as the result of personality factors affecting the second language learning process in adults. In addition, according to Finnemann (1990), second language learner differences also include their learning strategies such as being form oriented or attending to meaning, which in turn interact with the linguistic and semantic characteristics of the structures to be learned. Finnemann noted that form-oriented learners attended to the markers present in the linguistic forms to be learned, while learners who attended to meaning focused on the pragmatic use of the language. Finnemann stated, "In the case of *ser* and *estar*, which is a semantic contrast, meaning-based learners should be more inclined than form-based learners to experiment with *estar*" (p. 1295).

Garreton and Medley (1986) described the stages that children learning their first language go through. These stages are sequential, relate cognitive with language development, and present similarities with adult second language learners. These sequential developmental stages, described in parallel for the monolingual child and the adult second language learner, share many characteristics with Piagetian theory. According to Garreton and Medley, two factors influence the level at which an individual is able to use language: the person's cognitive developmental stage, and the level of cultural and linguistic knowledge of the target language mastered.

Garreton and Medley (1985) described the first language stage that monolingual children go through as a comprehension phase in which the child is not yet able to produce meaningful speech but does understand communication. During this stage, the child cannot yet form categories of words that are related by common meanings. The child links objects and referents at random, resulting in the use of the same word to convey different meanings. Thus, the verbal concept formation process is not yet possible, resulting in syncretic relationships and the misuse of nouns and other lexical units. Garreton and Medley say that the novice second language learner resembles a child learning his first language because he "communicates largely with memorized phrases, one-word utterances, and non-verbal strategies" (p. 25).

Garreton and Medley (1986) characterized the second stage as an overgeneralization of meaning and the presence of only explicit language knowledge. They stated that there may be a "correct use of many grammatical forms without an awareness of or attention to the logical operations necessary to generate those forms" (p. 12). That is, children can form concepts solely with language at the preconceptual level. When adult second language learners reach an intermediate stage, they present many of the characteristics of the second-stage child learning his first language; both are able to use full sentences for communication, but they speak primarily about concrete issues because their still-sparse grammar knowledge centers on the present tense. Both are overgeneralizing their constructed hypotheses and use strategies that demonstrate an incomplete understanding of the semantic nature of *ser* and *estar*. Relatedly, many adult Spanish native speakers may know the correct form of *ser* and *estar* explicitly but cannot explain linguistically or semantically their underlying reasons for using these forms. Thus, the parallel among second-stage children learning their first language, adult second language learners, and native Spanish speakers is that all are unaware of the conceptual and linguistic rules guiding the process of concept construction. They have implicit but not explicit knowledge.

During the third stage, children learning their first language are able to form verbal concepts by "abstracting and singling out elements of an experience, [and can] view those elements apart from the experiences as a whole, [can] draw conclusions, [and can] synthesize and analyze, all based upon a process of reasoning" (Garreton & Medley, 1986, p. 15). According to Garreton and Medley, the advanced adult second language learner, like the third-stage child learning his first language, can connect sentences into meaningful paragraphs, describe and discuss abstract issues, and refer to temporally and spatially removed and unfamiliar issues, such as past and future tense. Advanced adult learners can explicitly understand how concept formation is related to language use in particular cultural contexts of use of the Spanish language, making possible the explicit connection between intralinguistic and extralinguistic knowledge (Bialystock, 1978). Intralinguistic knowledge refers to understanding the grammatical and syntactic rules based on which linguistic structures and markers are used by the speaker. Extralinguistic knowledge refers to awareness that linguistic structures and markers refer to meanings of objects and subjects present in the cultural environment. Thus, advanced second language learners are able to think in a culturally appropriate manner.

Despite the similarities among monolingual Spanish children, adult second language learners, and adult native Spanish speakers, there are also many differences. Adult second language learners have already developed the conceptual schemata necessary to understand language at a symbolic level and are familiar implicitly with the learning strategies necessary to learn a language. Nevertheless, if their first language is English, they must develop explicit knowledge of the semantic and linguistic forms of *ser* and *estar* in Spanish, which are absent in English. Then they need to form a verbal conceptual knowledge of new linguistic structures and markers representing unique cultural semantic meanings in the new language. That is, they have to start thinking in a culturally appropriate manner with the second language. That is why adult second language learners show similarities with monolingual children: both have to form new concepts associated with new cultural and semantic meanings. In most cases, children whose first language is Spanish will show an implicit knowledge of the correct semantic and pragmatic use of *ser* and *estar*. In contrast, adult second language learners of Spanish generally have an explicit theoretical or grammatical knowledge of the uses of *ser* and *estar*, but not an explicit semantic understanding of their correct pragmatic use.

In contrast, adult Spanish native speakers, who learned their first language in childhood, can use the *ser* and *estar* forms correctly in a cultural context. Although they may have never been exposed directly to an explicit explanation of how the *ser* and *estar* forms differ semantically and how to use them correctly pragmatically, they have implicit knowledge of their language. Franco (1984) noted that native Spanish speakers may not be able to explain the difference between sentences that use *ser* and *estar* within pragmatically correct or incorrect contexts; however, they know which forms are used correctly and that these forms are not identical.

Learning Ser *and* Estar *as a Concept Formation Process*

According to Sera (1992), studies that compare linguistic structures offer an opportunity to see how language relates to cognition: "Languages of the world differ in the ways they classify experiential attributes... The distinctions expressed in different languages offer a 'window' through which one can examine the structure of underlying cognition" (p. 408). Concept formation is related to the semantic categories present in the linguistic structures that help speakers to engage in class inclusion processes in which categories and subcategories in a hierarchical order emerge. Concept formation processes such as semantic contrasts and class inclusion are present when native speakers or second language learners try to explain the *ser* and *estar* forms in Spanish. Thus, learning how and when to use *ser* and *estar* is a problem-solving task of a semantic nature for both native and second language learners. For instance, when native Spanish speakers choose to use *ser* or *estar* forms with adjectives, we construct different conceptual meanings (e.g., related to permanent or temporary conditions) that are related to the particular situational cultural contexts in which we use the language.

Different classifications have been proposed by different authors (De Mello, 1979; Franco, 1984; Higgs, 1985; Pountain, 1982; Ruggeri Marchetti, 1985) for the semantic meanings based on which *ser* and *estar* forms are separated. As Sera (1992) stated, "The controversy and debate among linguists about the meaning of 'ser' and 'estar' parallels the controversy and debate among cognitive psychologists on the organization of categories." (p. 411). However, although the linguistic controversy has generated several classifications of the *ser* and *estar* forms, our thorough search of the literature from a cognitive psychology perspective turned up only one study, Sera's (1992). She found differences in meaning as used by native Spanish speakers when asked to use *ser* and *estar* with adjectives that referred to objects and events. Subjects were children between 3 and 9 years of age and adults living in Madrid, Spain. No information is given regarding the level of their language proficiency, which is a limitation of this study since some confounding effects given by the level of language proficiency may affect the results. When describing and defining attributes of objects that differed in texture, size, color, and shape, these native Spanish speakers preferred to use *ser*. We believe that these findings may suggest that the different linguistic markers for *ser* and *estar* have different semantic categories or meaning loadings that may lead to nonverbal conceptual differences.

According to Sera (1992), "The difference between objects and events has recently been proposed to play an important role in conceptual structure" (p. 410). Sera also found, in a second experiment, that these adult and children native Spanish speakers used *ser* when they were given sentences referring to events and *estar* when the sentences referred to objects. The subjects, said Sera, were not aware of these differences in their use of *ser* and *estar*. And although they could make the distinction, they could not explicitly explain their choice. We believe that these subjects were unaware of the semantic categorizations underlying the use of *ser* and *estar* with events and objects. They showed no metalinguistic awareness (i.e., the ability to explain verbally their automatic use of the language) or explicit knowledge forms. Nevertheless, they had learned the verbal and nonverbal conceptual differences, indicating that culture and language influence the formation of verbal and nonverbal concepts.

In a third experiment testing for the use of *ser* and *estar* for marking location, Sera (1992) found a difference between children and adults. All children could use *estar* when referring to location of objects, but they could not understand the use of *ser* for referring to the location of events; adults, however, could use both *estar* and *ser* appropriately. Based on the results of these experiments, Sera concluded that "children's uses (of "*ser*" and "*estar*") have a less semantic basis than adults' uses" (p. 424). Sera also interpreted the results as showing that children first tend to use syntactic, rather than semantic, criteria for making categorical choices of words. She mentioned the possibility that children could not differentiate objects from events not because of a linguistic developmental trend considering syntactic and not semantic criteria, but because of cognitive developmental factors.

Second Language Learning Methodologies

Higgs (1985) wrote that instructors who are teaching a second languge must stimulate students to understand and represent the meaning underlying the linguistic structures. "A grammar," he stated, "is not a collection of forms and paradigms but a system for converting meaning into speech" (p. 407). He sought to dispel the misconceptions and myths that beginning second language learners hold, such as the idea that a literal automatic translation strategy suffices to decode messages from one language into the other. Since misconceptions are part of beliefs and other cognitive-affective processes, instructors need to guide students toward a change of attitude regarding second language learning. Higgs called this misconception "the 'lexical analog hypothesis' according to which the universal constant across languages is held to be the individual word" (p. 407).

Higgs (1985) proposed giving students some parallel concepts in English that correspond to the meanings underlying the structures of the target language. For students to start thinking using the conceptual structure of the target language, they need a transition period in which they can still think in their first language. Even though no parallel linguistic structure exists for *ser* and *estar* in English, some analogs could be given in functional or semantic areas. Higgs developed a system based on pairs of sentences in English that show that "sentences that answer different questions proceed from different meanings and/or structures ... [and that] ... different words are needed to express them in Spanish" (p. 409). With these pairs of sentences, Higgs wanted to communicate to the second language learner that "to be" in English opens up in *ser* and *estar* meanings in Spanish, and that these different meanings respond to different questions. Higgs proposed an instructional approach that included presenting students "with challenging, but comprehensible learning problems [rather] than ... arbitrary lists to be memorized" (p. 410). Thus, Higgs's approach is similar to what Gonzalez (see Chapter 5) has called "conceptual learning," in which linguistic cases are discussed as problems to be solved using high-level cognitive processes and strategies.

Garreton and Medley (1986) proposed that higher-level thinking processes are related to the formation of verbal concepts. They argued that an understanding of how second language learners assign "a word to a category of meanings" (p. 11) can improve teaching methodologies. Following their belief, we can view learning *ser* and *estar* as a verbal concept formation process because it is based on learning semantic relations. Most Spanish instructors, however, do not emphasize the semantic functions of *ser* and *estar*, and concentrate on the grammatical or general semantic uses of these linguistic forms. Franco (1984) noted that when teaching Spanish as a second language, only the semantic function of *estar*, referring to location, is emphasized in explanations given by textbooks and instructors. Roldán (1974) also noted that "the rules about the use of '*ser*' and '*estar*' that appear in most Spanish textbooks suffer from lack of generality" (p. 74). Moreover, most explanations in Spanish textbooks are incomplete and full of exceptions or unexplained cases.

Guntermann (1992) asserted that the differences in strategies showed by second language learners of Spanish can be explained by the different instructional methodologies that they had been exposed to. For instance, Guntermann referred to the fact that "the distinctions between '*ser*' and '*estar*' for locating entities are almost never explained to learners" (p. 1302). When studying Spanish second language learners, she found individual differences in their order of acquisition of the *ser* and *estar* forms, which showed little relation to the order of presentation and study in most textbooks and courses. Guntermann indicated that "while '*estar*' appears first in the textbooks, for conditions and locations, it is not controlled until much later . . . [and that] while '*ser*' describing qualities appears very early and accurately in the data" (p. 1302), it was not presented until much later in the textbooks. Guntermann asserted that "only the progressive forms show a relationship between presentation and use" (p. 1302).

Method

Design

This is an exploratory-interpretative study that uses two samples: five college students learning Spanish as a second language and eight adult native Spanish speakers. These two samples can help us understand how culture and language influence the process of verbal concept formation. The seven college students were enrolled in an intensive second-year Spanish course. Four of the adult native Spanish speakers were associated with the university setting (two graduate students, one professor, and one secretary). The other two adult native Spanish speakers were school teachers.

Intralinguistic, extralinguistic-cultural, and semantic and grammatical factors influencing verbal concept formation were included and were analyzed at the utterance and cluster levels. An introspective report method of data analysis, "thinking-aloud protocols," was used. Data interpretation was done within a qualitative framework that identifies theses, themes, and topics (Bodgan & Biklen, 1982). This research design is parallel to the one used in Chapter 5 for the study of linguistic gender in Spanish. Thus, the same multidimensional model of the triple interaction of cognitive, linguistic, and cultural factors on semantic concept formation developed by Gonzalez (1991, 1994, 1995) is used.

Research Questions

Five research questions were analyzed in a qualitative manner (the last four are parallel to the ones for the study presented in Chapter 5):

1. Is there a difference between adult native Spanish speakers and second language learners in their explicit and implicit knowledge about *ser* and *estar* forms?

2. Do different semantic categories (animate and inanimate object referents) affect the form of knowledge (intralinguistic and extralinguistic) constructed for *ser* and *estar* forms?
3. Can the same learner use different forms of knowledge and be at different developmental phases in relation to different semantic categories of *ser* and *estar*?
4. Do the particular questions asked in the interviews help learners to use higher-level learning strategies?
5. Are there idiosyncratic characteristics associated with the process of verbal concept formation?

Subjects

The first sample of subjects consisted of five undergraduate college students, all native English speakers, taking an intermediate-level Spanish course. They attended a major state university in the Southwest; four were females and one was male, and their age ranged between 19 and 28 years. Two were majoring in psychology, one was an education major, one was a women's studies major, and one was a merchandising major. Three were seniors and two were juniors. All were enrolled in an intensive second-year Spanish course.

The second sample consisted of eight adults who were native Spanish speakers and whose second language was English. They were either graduate students, professors, or staff at a major state university in the Southwest. They have been living in the United States from 2 to 11 years and were originally from different countries in Central and South America and from Mexico.

Given that this study focuses on an in-depth analysis of individual cases, we consider important to include additional relevant characteristics of the subjects. (Pseudonyms are used.)

Students Learning Spanish as a Second Language. Amy was a 20-year-old white female senior majoring in women's studies. She had already taken two semesters of Spanish and one semester of German. She thought that it was easier for her to learn Spanish in order to fulfill the foreign language requirement and said that "learning intensive Spanish was the fastest way to get the requirement over with."

Blanca was a 25-year-old Hispanic female senior majoring in psychology. She had lived in the Philippines as a child, and since her parents were fluent in Spanish, they had taught her the language. However, she had forgotten Spanish when they moved to the United States. She had a personal interest in learning Spanish, besides the fact that it was a requirement for her degree.

Jennifer was a 28-year-old white female senior majoring in education. She had taken two years of Spanish at a different major Southwest university because of her English-as-a-second-language endorsement. She had also visited

Mexico twice: first with a study-abroad program and then for her six-month student teaching requirement. In addition, she had worked as a teacher's aide with Spanish-speaking children for four years. She wanted to minor in Spanish and to become fully bilingual.

Wendy was a 26-year-old white female senior majoring in psychology. She had taken two semesters of Spanish as a requirement for graduation.

Anthony was a 19-year-old white male junior majoring in merchandising. He had taken three years of Spanish in high school and three semesters of Spanish as an undergraduate at the time of the interview. He planned to minor in Spanish. He reported that he was trying to speak Spanish to others as much as possible.

Adult Spanish Native Speakers. Renato was a 24-year-old master's student of Spanish, who was originally from Bolivia and had lived in the United States for six years.

Sofía was a 37-year-old psychologist working as a special education teacher. She was originally from Mexico and had lived in the United States for nine years.

Fernando was a 38-year-old doctoral student of anthropology. He was originally from Mexico and had lived in the United States for nine years.

Teresa was a 30-year-old elementary school teacher originally from Spain. She had lived in the United States for two years.

Pilar was a 42-year-old secretary originally from Ecuador. She had lived in the United States for five years.

José was a 41-year-old teacher's aide originally from El Salvador and had lived in the United States for two years. He held a bachelor's degree in tourism from a university in Brazil.

Carlos was a 35-year-old professor of engineering who was originally from Costa Rica and had lived in the United States for 11 years.

Monica was a 35-year-old secretary. A Mexican-American, her first language was Spanish. She reported using her Spanish language skills every day at work and in her family life.

Stimuli

Twenty-eight pairs of sentences were developed based on 10 categories of semantic functions of *ser* and *estar*. Each pair of sentences presented both forms within the same context (the chapter appendix lists the sentences). The sentences were developed based on the most frequent semantic functions of *ser* and *estar* presented in Spanish textbooks, and in fact came from the textbook used by the college students in the Spanish-intensive course that they were taking during the semester in which they were interviewed: *Puntos de Partida:*

An invitation to Spanish (Knorre, Dorwick, VanPatten, & Villareal, 1989). These 10 categories of semantic functions were divided into two groups. The first group encompassed the semantic functions of *ser* and *estar*:

1. Adjectives (5 items), corresponding to the function of classification
2. Permanent versus temporary events (5 items), corresponding to the function of classification
3. Nationality or origin (4 items), corresponding to the function of classification
4. To express for whom something is intended (2 items), corresponding to the function of classification
5. Possession (1 item), corresponding to the function of classification
6. To tell the time (2 items), corresponding to the function of classification
7. Nouns (3 items), corresponding to the function of location

The second group encompassed the grammatical function of *ser* and *estar:*

8. To form generalizations (2 items)
9. Present progressive forms (2 items)
10. Idiomatic expressions (2 items)

Procedure

All subjects were interviewed individually in a small, quiet office. The interviews were scheduled at each subject's convenience during a period of three months. Each subject was interviewed once for one hour. As subjects arrived, they were explained the task in their native language. They were reminded to choose one of the two sentences that the interviewer read for them—the one they thought used correctly the *ser* or *estar* form.

Immediately after each selection, subjects were interviewed with "thinking-aloud protocols." They were asked to explain why the particular sentence they had chosen was grammatically correct or incorrect. The questions used in the verbal reports included general open-ended questions common to all subjects and also some specific questions used to follow each subject's train of thought. The interviewer always used a general question referring to the underlying reason that the subject had for choosing a sentence—for example: "Why did you choose _____ [specific *ser* or *estar* form]?" The researcher would repeat the question or clarify the subject's answers. Restating the answers was considered important to ensure correct interpretation and categorization of the subjects' explanations during data analysis. It was also considered important to probe subjects by asking them if a change in the *ser* and *estar* form could be made. Probing stimulated some subjects to state new insights, suggesting that they had constructed new knowledge during the interview. The conversation was closely controlled by the focus of our research, but subjects were always free to bring up topics and to follow their own ideas. Structure to the responses was provided later by the researchers through content analysis. Verbal reports were audiotaped for subsequent analysis.

Data Analysis Design

Three factors influencing verbal concept formation were taken into consideration in this study: intralinguistic, extralinguistic-cultural, and semantic (see Table 6.1). These same factors and a similar data analysis coding system were employed for the analysis of linguistic gender in college students learning Spanish as a second language presented in Chapter 5. This parallel will make it possible to compare second language learning studies focusing on different linguistic structures (linguistic gender and the *ser* and *estar* forms). This comparison can reveal the presence of similarities and differences in the process of verbal concept formation in relation to different linguistic knowledge domains in second language learning.

Intralinguistic factors include the grammatical function in reference to *ser* and *estar* forms, which were described in relation to three developmental phases (see Table 6.1).

Extralinguistic-cultural factors include three semantic functions (see Table 6.1):

1. Classification of events and objects of opposite meanings
2. Location in relation to inanimate and animate referents
3. Subjective (connotative) versus cultural (denotative) meanings

Cognitive factors encompass forms of knowledge (implicit and explicit), developmental phases, and language learning strategies. Bialystock's model (1978) was used for adapting five nominal categories of forms of knowledge (see Table 6.1):

1. Extralinguistic general knowledge—explicit justifications by reference to general knowledge outside the linguistic task (i.e., real-world, sociocultural, and pragmatic knowledge)
2. Extralinguistic topic knowledge—explicit justifications by reference to specific object knowledge outside the linguistic task
3. Explicit relation between extralinguistic general or topic knowledge and intralinguistic knowledge at the system (linguistic categories) or marker (specific linguistic cases) levels—justification by reference to the relationship between knowledge outside the linguistic task and linguistic knowledge

TABLE 6.1 Interrelation of Factors When Constructing Verbal Concepts for *Ser* and *Estar* Forms

Intralinguistic Factors	Extralinguistic-Cultural Factors	Cognitive Factors
By grammatical function (focus on form)	**By semantic function: Contextual pragmatic meaning**	**Forms of knowledge**
Third stage	**Classification**	**Third developmental phase**
Use of *ser* and *estar* abstractly with past, future, and progressive tense and passive voice (temporally-spatially removed and unfamiliar issues)	*Ser* + adjective = Classification (events) *Estar* + adjective = Observation/reaction/experience (objects)	1. Extralinguistic general 2. Extralinguistic topic 3. Explicit relation between extralinguistic and intralinguistic knowledge (system and marker)
Think in culturally appropriate manner, with conceptual verbal formation	**Opposite meanings**	
Relation between intralinguistic and extralinguistic knowledge	*Ser* = Permanent vs. *estar* = Transitory *Ser* = Inherent vs. *estar* = Accidental *Ser* = Quality vs. *estar* = State	**Second developmental phase**
Second stage	**Location**	4. Explicit intralinguistic knowledge (system and marker)
Use of *ser* and *estar* concretely with present tense only	*Ser* = Inanimates placed in a permanent state with no permanent place *Estar* = Inanimates with questions for finding place *Estar* = Inanimates *Estar* = Animates that change location	**First developmental phase**
Reduced grammar knowledge		5. Implicit intralinguistic knowledge (system and marker)
Incomplete understanding of semantic functions		
Explicit linguistic knowledge only	**Subjective vs. cultural meanings**	**Second language learning strategies**
Preconceptual verbal formation	Connotative (subjective) meanings of *ser* and *estar* Denotative (cultural) meanings of *ser* and *estar*	Metacognitive explicit knowledge (**semantic**)
Overgeneralization of meaning and constructed hypotheses		
First Stage		Cognitive: Explicit and implicit knowledge (**grammatical**)
One-word utterances		
Communication with memorized phrases		
Cannot form verbal concepts		
Misuse of meanings		
Use *estar* incorrectly		
Use *ser* with reduced utterances and as a filler for translating literally from English ("to be")		

4. Explicit intralinguistic knowledge at the system or marker levels—justification of responses by making explicit reference to linguistic categories or specific cases
5. Implicit intralinguistic knowledge at the system or marker levels—correct responses involving linguistic structures or cases with no further explanation

These five categories were combined with Karmiloff-Smith's model (1979) referring to three developmental phases (see Table 6.1). According to our conception, the first three forms of knowledge indicate that the learner is at the third developmental phase. Especially the third form of knowledge, indicating a relation between extralinguistic and intralinguistic knowledge, reveals the construction of new conceptual explicit relations or insights by the language learner (e.g., a metacognitive strategy of inferencing). This third developmental phase thus includes explicit semantic knowledge. The fourth form of knowledge indicates that the learner is at the second developmental phase because she can access explicitly linguistic knowledge of rules and specific cases; however, no relationship was made with extralinguistic knowledge. That is, the second developmental phase includes explicit grammatical knowledge. The fifth form of knowledge indicates that the learner is at the first developmental level; she cannot verbally access the underlying strategies and forms of knowledge used for learning linguistic structures or markers (see Table 6.1). Thus, the first developmental phase includes only implicit grammatical knowledge.

Second language learning strategies were adapted from the categorization made by O'Malley and colleagues (1988) that differentiates between metacognitive and cognitive strategies. Only three of the many metacognitive strategies differentiated by O'Malley and colleagues were used by the native speakers and second language learners in this study:

1. Self-evaluation—checking the outcomes of one's own language learning against an internal measure of completeness and accuracy
2. Monitoring—bringing explicit knowledge of word meanings and structures to a language task for examining or correcting the response
3. Inferencing—generating an explicit linguistic hypothesis about a previously unknown linguistic structure

Five of the many cognitive strategies differentiated by O'Malley and colleagues were used by the native speakers and second language learners in this study:

1. Auditory representation—retaining the sound of a linguistic sequence
2. Translation—using the first language as a basis for understanding or producing the target language
3. Deduction—consciously applying rules to produce or understand the second language

4. Contextualization—placing a word or phrase in a meaningful language sequence
5. Elaboration—relating new information to other concepts in memory

In addition, three second language learning cognitive strategies proposed by Robinett and Schachter (1983) were used for data analysis. These three strategies were considered to be characteristic of a learner at the second developmental phase, who can show only explicit forms of knowledge:

1. Ignorance of rule restrictions—failing to observe the restrictions of existing linguistic structures when applying them to new contexts
2. Incomplete application of rules—lacking accurate and complete knowledge of linguistic rules
3. False concepts hypothesized—making developmental errors resulting from faulty comprehension, distinctions, or contrasts in the target language

The three metacognitive strategies used by the subjects in this study correspond to explicit forms of knowledge, the first two cognitive strategies correspond to implicit knowledge levels, and the following three cognitive strategies correspond to explicit levels of knowledge. In this data coding system, we attempted to integrate the categorization of language learning strategies adapted by O'Malley and colleagues (1988) with Bialystock's (1978) implicit and explicit levels of knowledge, which were integrated with Karmiloff-Smith's developmental levels. (See Chapter 5 of this book for an extensive discussion of the models in Bialystock, 1978; Karmiloff-Smith, 1979; O'Malley et al., 1988; and Robinett & Schachter's, 1983.)

In sum, we propose that three factors—intralinguistic, extralinguistic-cultural, and cognitive—merge in the semantic function of language, represented in this study by the semantic categories for *ser* and *estar* forms (see Table 6. 1). These semantic categories reflect the multidimensional interrelationship of cognition, culture, and language for the construction of verbal concepts. Thus, we used theory triangulation in interpreting a single set of data from the different integrated theoretical perspectives (Bialystock, 1978; Karmiloff-Smith, 1979; O'Malley et al., 1988) associated with specific variables of interest and theoretical and applied objectives in this study. Data analysis was carried out by means of interpretative procedures (qualitative content analysis of nominal categories) in order to find associations or patterns among variables that were revealed in subjects' productions. We let the data speak to us, as just some research questions were pointed out in relation to some theoretical perspectives. Thus, a qualitative data analysis approach was taken in this study, in which theory was tested with heuristic and applied implications.

Two levels of analysis were differentiated in this study: utterance and cluster levels. The utterance level was considered a single idea conveyed by the subject. Each utterance was coded independently in relation to cognitive variables (i.e., forms of knowledge, developmental phases, and language learning strategies). Utterances referring to the same word being discussed throughout the verbal reports were considered a second level of analysis that we called *cluster*. Each cluster was categorized independently in relation to *ser* and *estar* forms that included linguistic and semantic functions. Following the evolution of the discussion of the same cluster by the subject was considered particularly important because new levels of understanding of the same cluster emerged throughout the verbal report. Thus, the cluster as a unit of analysis can provide evidence for the argument that verbal reports are not only data collection tools, but also an instructional method for developing new conceptual knowledge at higher developmental levels. These two levels of data analysis can reveal some common or different patterns in the specific forms of knowledge, developmental phases, and language learning strategies that may be related to the interaction of intralinguistic, extralinguistic-cultural, and cognitive variables. Thus, these two levels were anticipated to be a potential source for discovering patterns of the influence of linguistic and cultural factors on the process of verbal concept formation. We derived this system of data analysis from the actual context of data, having an open-minded attitude, and letting the data speak to us in order to develop a structure for data analysis based on nominal categories derived from the same data bank.

Two judges (the first author and an independent trained rater) categorized each subject independently across all nominal categories. The second judge was trained by the first author during a one-week period in order to gain familiarity with the theoretical framework underlying the nominal categories, and also for achieving a high reliability coefficient between judges. Before data analysis was conducted, a high reliability across judges ($r = .85$) was established, ensuring that the operationalization and understanding of the nominal categories were consistent and clear between the judges. Any disagreement obtained during the process of training for coding data was discussed by the judges. When the final data analysis was done, the few disagreements arising were also discussed by the judges to achieve a common categorization.

RESULTS AND DISCUSSION

Data are reported and interpreted in relation to the five research questions using the two-level data analysis of the utterance and cluster levels. We also include some quotations for illustrating data interpretation and integration. In addition, with the purpose of integrating the summary of this data report, data interpretation will follow the three types of focus suggested by Bogdan and Biklen (1982):

1. Thesis or propositions related to the integration of literature and the model proposed in this chapter

2. Themes that encompass theoretical formulations emerging from data analysis in the form of patterns or abstract conceptual categories
3. Topics that include descriptions of specific findings

Table 6.2 presents an overall descriptive summary of the forms of knowledge, developmental phases, and learning strategies used by second language learners for the two major functions of *ser* and *estar* forms: semantic and grammatical. This descriptive table was then used for condensing information in subsequent tables in relation to the specific research questions.

In relation to the first research question, a difference was found between adult native Spanish speakers and second language learners in the forms of knowledge that they constructed about *ser* and *estar* (see Table 6.3). The theme or pattern emerging from the data refers to the finding that native Spanish speakers constructed mainly explicit extralinguistic topic and general knowledge (coded as forms of knowledge 1 and 2), placing them in the first and most advanced developmental phase. In contrast, second language learners constructed mainly implicit intralinguistic general knowledge (form of knowledge 4), with the exception of one subject, Wendy, who constructed explicit extralinguistic topic knowledge (form of knowledge 2). Thus, most of the second language learners were constructing *ser* and *estar* concepts at the third developmental level.

The thesis emerging from previous findings in the literature for this first research question coincides with these results because beginning and intermediate second language learners have been found to have an incomplete understanding of the semantic nature of *ser* and *estar* forms, showing an implicit form of knowledge only (see e.g., Garreton & Medley, 1985). In relation to this thesis, Sera (1992) differentiated between two levels of concept formation in *ser* and *estar* forms: (1) a lower implicit or grammatical knowledge level and (2) a higher explicit or semantic knowledge level in which second language learners can relate intralinguistic (grammatical rules) and extralinguistic (pragmatic or cultural) knowledge. The specific finding or topic referring to the one exception found among the second-language learners, the subject who could form explicit forms of knowledge, can be explained based on the thesis emerging from the literature pinpointing that advanced learners can understand explicitly the conceptual and pragmatic rules guiding the process of concept construction for *ser* and *estar* forms (see e.g., Garreton & Medley, 1986).

Regarding the second research question, it was found that animate and inanimate object referent semantic categories affect the intralinguistic or extralinguistic form of knowledge constructed by native Spanish speakers and second language learners (see Table 6.4). The theme or pattern emerging from the data showed that native Spanish speakers used explicit extralinguistic general and topic knowledge (coded as forms of knowledge 1 and 2) more frequently for inanimate than for animate words, and consequently they used implicit intralinguistic knowledge (coded as forms of knowledge 4 and 5) less

TABLE 6.2 Forms of Knowledge, Developmental Phase, and Learning Strategies Used by Second Language Learners for Semantic and Grammatic Functions of "Ser" and "Estar"

Semantic function cluster	Amy	Blanca	Jennifer	Wendy	Anthony
Casada (classification)	4/second phase/resourcing*	4/second phase/deduction, contextualization*	4/second phase/resourcing, contextualization*	2/third phase/resourcing*	4/second phase/deduction, monitoring, self-evaluation*
Joven (classification)	4/second phase/resourcing	1/first phase/resourcing	4/second phase/contextualization, incomplete application of rules	4/second phase/incomplete application of rules	4/second phase/deduction
Profesora (classification)	4/second phase/resourcing	1/first phase/deduction	4/second phase/deduction, contextualization, false concepts hypothesized	4/second phase/resourcing, translation	4/second phase/resourcing, auditory representation
Alto (classification)	4/second phase/resourcing	1/first phase/contextualization, translation	4/second phase/contextualization, false concepts hypothesized	4/second phase/resourcing, translation	4/second phase/deduction
Limpio (classification)	2/third phase/false concepts hypothesized	1/first phase/contextualization, translation	2/third phase/contextualization	2/second phase/resourcing, deduction	4/second phase/ignorance of rule restrictions
Sur America (location)	5/first phase/Self-Evaluation	5/first phase/false concepts, hypothesized	4/second phase/deduction	5/first phase/translation	4/second phase/deduction
Arizona (location)		4/second phase/ignorance of rule restrictions		5/first phase/translation	
Lapiz (location)	4/second phase/deduction	2/third phase/false concepts hypothesized	4/second phase/deduction	5/first phase/translation	4/second phase/deduction
Café (classification)	2/second phase/deduction, contextualization	2/third phase/contextualization	2/third phase/resourcing, contextualization, inferencing	2/second phase/deduction	4/second phase/monitoring, ignorance of rule restrictions, inferencing
Sopa (classification)	2/third phase/contextualization, deduction		2/third phase/contextualization, resourcing		4/second phase/translation, ignorance of rule restrictions
Agua (classification)	2/third phase/contextualization, inferencing	4/third phase/deduction, contextualization, resourcing	4/second phase/deduction	2/second phase/deduction	4/second phase/deduction
Día (classification)	5/first phase/deduction, contextualization, false concepts hypothesized	4/third phase/deduction, contextualization, resourcing	2/third phase/contextualization	2/second phase/deduction	4/second phase/deduction, self-evaluation
Enferma (classification)	2/third phase/deduction	4/third phase/deduction, translation, resourcing	2/third phase/contextualization	2/second phase/deduction, contextualization	4/second phase/inferencing, translation, false concepts hypothesized
Argentina (location, classification)	4/second phase/resourcing	4/third phase/resourcing, translation, deduction	2/third phase/resourcing, contextualization	5/first phase/incomplete application of rules	5/first phase/translation, false concepts hypothesized

Semantic function cluster	Amy	Blanca	Jennifer	Wendy	Anthony
Paraguay (location, classification)	4/second phase/resourcing, contextualization	4/third phase/self-evaluation, monitoring	2/third phase/resourcing	2/second phase/resourcing, translation	4/second phase/translation, self-evaluation, monitoring
Mesa (classification)		4/third phase/resourcing	4/second phase/translation	2/third phase/Contextualization, false concepts hypothesized	5/first phase/ignorance of rule restrictions
Puerta (classification)				2/third phase/contextualization	
Libro (classification)	4/second phase/translation, deduction, monitoring, self-evaluation, auditory representation	5/first phase/translation, false concepts hypothesized	4/second phase/translation	5/first phase/translation, resourcing	5/first phase/auditory representation
Carro (classification)	5/first phase/translation	4/third phase/translation, resourcing	4/second phase/translation	5/first phase/translation, resourcing	5/first phase/translation, auditory representation
Tarde	4/second phase/resourcing	2/third phase/resourcing, deduction, translation	5/first phase/translation	2/third phase/ignorance of rule restrictions	4/second phase/deduction
Clase	4/second phase/resourcing			2/third phase/resourcing, translation	4/second phase/deduction, false concepts hypothesized
Estudiar	5/first phase/auditory representation	4/second phase/false concepts hypothesized	5/first phase/translation	5/first phase/auditory representation	5/first phase/false concepts hypothesized
Trabajar	5/first phase/auditory representation	4/second phase/false concepts hypothesized	5/first phase/translation	5/first phase/auditory representation	5/first phase/deduction
Comiendo		4/second phase/translation, resourcing	4/second phase/resourcing	5/first phase/translation	5/first phase/ignorance of rule restrictions
Bailando			4/second phase/translation	5/first phase/translation, resourcing	
Cuadros	4/second phase/resourcing	2/third phase/resourcing, translation	4/second phase/resourcing	2/third phase/resourcing, deduction	4/second phase/deduction, translation
Rayas	4/second phase/resourcing	2/third phase/resourcing	4/second phase/resourcing	2/third phase/resourcing, deduction	5/first phase/auditory representation, translation

*The notations in the table body refer, in order and separated by slashes, to forms of knowledge, developmental phase, and learning strategy.

TABLE 6.3   Frequency and Percentage of Forms of Knowledge Used by Native Speakers and Second Language learners for *Ser* and *Estar* Forms: Descriptive Data Related to Research Questions

	Frequency for Level of Knowledge*						Percentage for Level of Knowledge*				
Name	1	2	3	4	5	Total	1	2	3	4	5
Native Speakers											
Renato	10	**12**	1	—	—	23	43.5	**52.2**	4.3	—	—
Sofía	5	**10**	1	—	6	22	22.7	**45.5**	4.5	—	27.3
Fernando	8	**10**	2	—	1	21	38	**47.6**	9.5	—	4.8
Teresa	4	**16**	—	—	1	21	19	**76.2**	—	—	4.8
Pilar	3	**13**	2	—	7	25	12	**52**	8	—	4.8
José	**12**	5	3	—	1	21	**57.2**	23.8	14.3	—	4.8
Carlos	**18**	1	—	1	1	21	**85.7**	4.8	—	4.8	4.8
Monica	1	**11**	—	7	2	21	4.8	**52.4**	—	33.3	9.5
Second Language Learners											
Amy	—	5	—	**12**	5	22	—	22.7	—	**54.5**	22.7
Blanca	1	2	3	**12**	2	20	5	10	15	**60**	10
Jennifer	—	7	—	**14**	3	24	—	29.2	—	**58.3**	12.5
Wendy	—	**13**	—	3	10	26	—	**50**	—	11.5	38.5
Anthony	—	—	—	**16**	8	24	—	—	—	**66.7**	33.3

*Highest scores for each learner are indicated in boldface type. Forms of knowledge are as follows:

1 = General extralinguistic knowledge
2 = Extralinguistic topic knowledge
3 = Explicit relation between extralinguistic topic knowledge and intralinguistic knowledge
4 = Explicit intralinguistic knowledge (system and marker level)
5 = Implicit intralinguistic knowledge (system and marker level)
A dash indicates that there were no responses for that form of knowledge.

frequently for inanimate words. For second language learners the forms of knowledge used most frequently were implicit intralinguistic knowledge (coded as forms of knowledge 4 and 5) for both animate and inanimate words and explicit extralinguistic topic knowledge (coded as form of knowledge 2) for inanimate words. In contrast, they less frequently used explicit extralinguistic general knowledge (coded as form of knowledge 1) for inanimate words, and they did not use at all the relationship between intralinguistic and extralinguistic forms of knowledge (coded as form of knowledge 3) for either inanimate or animate words.

This second theme can be related to the thesis emerging from the literature referring to a connection between semantic categorizations pertaining to the origin of object referents (animate and inanimate) and concept construction of *ser* and *estar* as a problem-solving process (Higgs, 1985; Pountain, 1982). That

CHAPTER 6 CONCEPTUALIZATIONS OF *SER* AND *ESTAR*   179

is, the *ser* and *estar* contrast is based on semantic (i.e., contextual and pragmatic meaning) rather than on linguistic or grammatical rules. We believe that the decision of whether to use *ser* and/or *estar* forms is an ill problem-solving situation because the semantic meaning conveyed depends on culturally adequate concepts (denotative aspect of meaning) and subjective interpretations (connotative

TABLE 6.4 Frequency and Percentage of Forms of Knowledge for Animate and Inanimate Object Referents for Native Speakers and Second Language Learners for *Ser* and *Estar* Forms: Descriptive Data for Research Question 2

Word	Form of Knowledge for Native Speakers*					Form of Knowledge for Second Language Learners*				
	1	2	3	4	5	1	2	3	4	5
Frequency for Semantic Function for Animates										
Casada	3	5	—	—	—	—	1	—	—	4
Joven	5	6	—	—	1	1	—	—	4	—
Profesora	3	—	3	1	2	1	—	—	4	—
Alto	4	1	—	1	2	1	—	—	4	—
Enferma	4	3	1	—	—	—	3	—	2	—
Frequency for Semantic Function for Inanimates										
Limpio	6	1	1	—	—	1	3	—	1	—
Sur America	—	2	—	1	1	—	—	—	2	3
Lápiz	5	1	—	—	2	—	1	—	3	1
Café	2	4	1	—	—	—	4	—	1	—
Sopa	4	4	—	—	—	—	2	—	1	—
Agua	3	5	—	—	—	—	2	—	1	—
Diá	2	5	1	—	—	—	2	—	2	1
Argentina	4	4	—	—	—	—	1	—	2	2
Paraguay	2	2	—	—	—	—	2	—	3	—
Mesa	2	5	—	—	1	—	1	—	2	1
Libro	3	4	—	—	1	—	—	—	2	3
Carro	2	4	—	—	2	—	—	—	2	3
Frequency for Grammatical Function for Animates										
Estudiar	2	3	—	1	2	—	—	—	1	3
Comiendo	2	2	1	—	—	—	1	—	2	—
Frequency for Grammatical Function for Inanimates										
Tarde	1	1	—	—	3	—	2	—	2	1
Clase	2	—	1	1	1	—	1	—	2	—
Cuadros	1	5	1	—	—	—	2	—	3	—
Rayas	1	4	—	1	—	—	2	—	2	1

TABLE 6.4   (continued)

	Form of Knowledge				
	1	2	3	4	5
Total for Semantic Function: Animates					
Frequency	3	4	—	18	—
Percentage	12	16	—	72	—
Total for Semantic Function: Inanimates					
Frequency	1	18	—	24	14
Percentage	1.8	31.6	—	42.1	24.6
Total for Grammatical Function: Animates					
Frequency	—	—	—	3	6
Percentage	—	—	—	33.3	66.6
Total for Grammatical Function: Inanimates					
Frequency	—	7	—	9	2
Percentage	—	38.9	—	50	11.1
Total for Both Semantic and Grammatical Function: Animates					
Frequency	3	4	—	21	6
Percentage	6.5	8.7	—	45.7	13
Total for Both Semantic and Grammatical Function: Inanimates					
Frequency	1	15	—	33	14
Percentage	1.4	34.3	—	45.2	19.2

*Forms of knowledge are as follows:
1 = General extralinguistic knowledge
2 = Extralinguistic topic knowledge
3 = Explicit relation between extralinguistic topic knowledge and intralinguistic knowledge
4 = Explicit intralinguistic knowledge (system and marker level)
5 = Implicit intralinguistic knowledge (system and marker level)
A dash indicates that there were no responses for that form of knowledge.

aspect of meaning). That is, both forms require concept formation processes that are culturally adequate, corresponding to the denotative aspect of meaning, and at the same time are based on subjective interpretations corresponding to the connotative aspect of meaning. In addition, we can hypothesize that the different linguistic forms of *ser* and *estar* may lead to a double concept formation process: (1) different nonverbal concepts that are based on abstract meanings such as inanimate concepts (e.g., liberty, beauty) and (2) different verbal concepts that are based on symbolic networks of hierarchies of categories and subcategories of concepts such as animate concepts (e.g., chair, furniture).

The third research question referred to whether the same learner could be at different developmental phases in relation to the semantic categories of classification and location of *ser* and *estar* forms. Data showed that both native Spanish speakers and second language learners were at different developmental phases in relation to different semantic categories (see Table 6.5). In addition, we found that the same learner differed in the form of knowledge and learning strategies that she or he used for the semantic and grammatical functions of *ser* and *estar* forms (see Table 6.5). Most native Spanish speakers more frequently used the explicit extralinguistic forms of knowledge (coded as 1 and 2) for both the classification and location semantic function. For the grammatical function, native Spanish speakers differed in the form of knowledge they preferred to use: one subject used mostly the explicit extralinguistic general form of knowledge (coded as 1), three subjects used mostly the explicit extralinguistic topic knowledge form (coded as 2), two subjects used the relationship between extralinguistic and intralinguistic forms of knowledge (coded as 3), and two subjects preferred to use the implicit intralinguistic form of knowledge (coded as 5; see Table 6.5). In contrast, most second language learners more frequently used the implicit intralinguistic forms of knowledge (coded as 4 and 5) for the semantic function, including both the classification and location forms, and also for the grammatical function. Thus, there was a within- and between-group difference in the preferred forms of knowledge that native Spanish speakers and second language learners had for the semantic and grammatical functions of *ser* and *estar* forms.

The literature shows that the semantic function of *ser* and *estar* forms is the more difficult to learn because in many pragmatic contexts, both forms can be grammatically correct (Higgs, 1985) but simultaneously have a different connotative or subjective, and denotative or pragmatic meaning (De Mello, 1979). Ruggeri-Marchetti (1985) believed that the decision of whether to use the *ser* or *estar* form is a psychological one because meaning conveys idiosyncratic thoughts and emotions that involve subjective or connotative meanings. Moreover, Franco (1984) pointed out that the use of *ser* and *estar* forms is associated not only with semantic functions, such as location, but also with whether animate or inanimate objects were the referents.

The fourth research question referred to whether the particular questions used in the interviews help learners to use higher-level learning strategies. The analysis of responses of all subjects shows that the thinking-aloud protocols stimulated subjects to think at higher levels and to become aware of their implicit knowledge. The following dialogue between Anthony (a second language learner) and the interviewer illustrates the process Anthony went through in order to realize the semantic meaning of the use of *estar*.

INTERVIEWER: *Linda está enferma o Linda es enferma?* ("Linda is sick" for both cases in English.)
ANTHONY: *Es enferma.*

TABLE 6.5 Frequency and Percentage of Forms of Knowledge in Relation to Semantic Classification and Location Functions and the Grammatical Function by Native Speakers and Second Language Learners: Descriptive Data for Research Questions 3 and 5

	Classification					Location				
	Frequency for Forms of Knowledge					Frequency for Forms of Knowledge				
Name	1	2	3	4	5	1	2	3	4	5
Semantic Function for Native Speakers										
Renato	3	9	1	—	—	2	1	—	—	—
Sofía	5	7	1	—	—	2	—	—	—	1
Fernando	7	2	—	—	1	3	—	—	—	—
Teresa	3	9	—	—	—	—	4	—	—	—
Pilar	1	7	2	—	4	2	—	—	—	2
José	7	6	—	—	—	4	—	—	—	—
Carlos	12	1	—	—	1	3	—	—	2	—
Monica	—	9	—	2	2	1	2	—	—	—
Semantic Function for Second Language Learners										
Amy	—	5	—	6	3	—	—	—	3	—
Blanca	4	1	—	6	1	—	—	—	3	1
Jennifer	—	5	—	8	—	—	2	—	2	—
Wendy	—	8	—	3	2	—	1	—	—	—
Anthony	—	—	—	10	3	—	—	—	3	1
Grammatical Function for Native Speakers										
Renato	5	2	—	—	—					
Sofía	—	2	1	—	4					
Fernando	1	5	—	—	—					
Teresa	1	3	—	—	1					
Pilar	—	6	—	—	1					
José	1	1	3	—	1					
Carlos	—	—	3	—	—					
Monica	—	—	—	4						
Grammatical Function for Second Language Learners										
Amy	—	—	—	2	4					
Blanca	—	3	—	3	—					
Jennifer	—	—	—	4	3					
Wendy	—	—	—	4	4					
Anthony	—	—	—	3	4					

*Forms of knowledge are as follows:
1 = General extralinguistic knowledge
2 = Extralinguistic topic knowledge
3 = Explicit relation between extralinguistic topic knowledge and intralinguistic knowledge
4 = Explicit intralinguistic knowledge (system and marker level)
5 = Implicit intralinguistic knowledge (system and marker level)

A dash indicates that there were no responses for that form of knowledge.

INTERVIEWER: Why?

ANTHONY: It's a description of her condition. She's sick.

INTERVIEWER: She is always sick?

ANTHONY: No, not always. Ahh ... then, no. I would say *es enferma* if it is a condition of a person who is always sick. Now that I think about it ... of course, I could be wrong.

INTERVIEWER: *Linda está enferma o Linda es enferma?*

ANTHONY: *Está enferma* if she is sick today, or for a week I would say *está enferma*, but if she is always sick, then I would say *es*.

The interviewer asking Anthony a probing question—"She is always sick?"—makes him think and realize that actually there are two semantic meanings associated with the use of *ser* and *estar*. At the beginning Anthony was using direct translation from English as a strategy; only with the help of the interviewer for being stimulated to think did Anthony progress to a higher level of knowledge in Spanish. On several similar occasions, we saw that posing probing questions and counterexamples helped the subjects to analyze the sentences at deeper levels and to use inferencing and resourcing as learning strategies.

In relation to research question 5, analyzing Tables 6.2 and 6.5 we can see that even though there were some patterns across all subjects for the use of forms of knowledge and strategies, each subject had specific preferences or tendencies for the use of *ser* and *estar* forms. These idiosyncrasies are the result of the influence of personality factors such as the subjectivity involved in the interpretation of pragmatic meanings.

For example, when Fernando was asked about the correctness of the *Maria es casada o Maria está casada* utterances (in English, only one form is used: "Maria is married"), he replied (translated from Spanish): "I would use *Maria está casada* because it is a condition or state that she has. However, I could also use *Maria es casada* but in a general way, but I would use only *es* in a specific way like, *Maria es casada con José.*" In this example the specific versus general meaning that Fernando, a native Spanish speaker, interprets in the *ser* and *estar* contrast of these utterances is highly personal or subjective. This interpretation refers only to the connotative aspect of meaning within the semantic function of language, and not at all to the linguistic rules underlying the use of language. The subjectivity involved in concept formation can also be observed in the use of learning strategies that most subjects made when interpreting the *ser* and *estar* forms. For instance, Fernando also used the strategy of false concepts hypothesized when he was asked to explain the correctness of *Pedro es alto o Pedro está alto*. Fernando replied (translated from Spanish): "*'Pedro es alto'* [Pedro is tall] defines the height of Pedro. *'Pedro está alto'* [Pedro is tall also in English, but a different connotation in Spanish] defines if Pedro has climbed to a tall object, like a building. Then if I want to refer to Pedro's height, I would say *'Pedro es alto.'*" Fernando had his own subjective interpretation of the conceptual difference between *ser* and *estar*, which he illustrated in his explanation. Generally *estar* refers to a temporal state, and *ser* refers to a more permanent state, but not necessarily to the specific applications in Fernando's example.

Another example of the subjectivity involved in the interpretation of the meaning of *ser* and *estar* is portrayed by another native Spanish speaker, Cristina. When she was asked about whether *Maria es casada* or *Maria está casada* is correct, she replied: "I think that both can be exchanged and used. I think 'being married' is a state that can or cannot be continued in the future. Some people use *estar*. Other people consider that 'being married' is a permanent state that will continue for life, so they prefer to use *ser*. I prefer to use *ser*." In this explanation, it is clear that Cristina is using the semantic strategies of subjective or cultural meaning and resourcing for getting to her final answer. She is aware that different connotative meanings can be interpreted by different people who may have different conceptualizations of the topic "being married." Thus, she makes her own decision based on her own beliefs about the topic.

Other kinds of examples are portrayed by second language learners who are unaware of the cultural connotations of the uses of *ser* and *estar*, as well as some of the semantic or linguistic rules that apply to some cases. For example, when Blanca was asked whether she would use *el lápiz es en la mesa* or *el lápiz está en la mesa* ("the pencil is on the table" in English for both sentences), she replied: "It could be both. It depends. If it is a desk your pencil is always going to be on, I would use *es*. But if it is just a table, I would go with *está*." Blanca has developed her own personal explanation, a false concept that she has hypothesized, which does not correspond to the cultural connotation that most Spanish speakers are aware of. That is, the particular place in which an object is located does not have any relationship with the decision of whether to use *ser* or *estar*. For this case, a semantic rule applies given that location always requires *estar*. Blanca also has a problem with understanding that the use of *estar* is not related to timing or duration of occurrence of events. Another example is portrayed by Amy, when she was asked whether she would use *el libro es para John* or *el libro está para John* ("the book is for John" for both sentences), she replied: "You can use both. The first one means it's John's, and the second one means John has it [the book] right now or today." Amy is using the strategies of translation and false concepts hypothesized because her explanation is not correctly based on any cultural connotations of the semantic use of *ser* and *estar*. She has created a new concept that does not follow the cultural meaning given that *el libro está para John* is an unidiomatic use of *estar*.

Conclusions

This second language learning study poses heuristic questions that advance theoretical knowledge in this field by applying methodology from cognitive psychology. This study broadens the understanding of the specific thinking processes that adult native Spanish speakers and second language learners go through when analyzing semantic structures that are different between Spanish and English, such as *ser* and *estar* forms. Asking subjects to become collaborators with researchers for discovering the learning strategies and the forms and levels of knowledge that they construct when facing cultural connotative meanings in Spanish expands the objectivity of our investigation. We do not have to guess or interpret subjectively what subjects' responses meant; rather, the subjects uncovered or accessed their internal processes for us in order to study them. Like other studies investigating many different dimensions of knowledge (not only those restricted to second languages), this study also shows that content domain (such as whether animate or inanimate object referents are used) does make a difference in the kinds and levels of learning strategies and forms of knowledge used when using *ser* and *estar*, and level of expertise (such as being a native speaker or a second language learner) makes a difference in the level of knowledge of the target language.

Practical applications refer to the use of conceptual learning methodologies for stimulating second language learners to understand that any language has an important cultural dimension that carries with it semantic connotative meanings. That is, learning a second language involves acquiring a new underlying culture that forms the bases for thinking directly in this new way of conceptualizing the world. Learning a second language goes beyond being exposed to grammatical and syntactic rules, to include becoming immersed in forming new cultural concepts that will enhance thought processes. In addition, affective processes are also involved in learning second languages, given that the learner needs to be motivated to form new cultural knowledge that opens up a whole new world of attitudes, belief systems, visions, or perspectives of a new cultural reality, and in general a whole new world of conceptualizations. Thus, the second language classroom needs to offer learners a creative, open, active, and dynamic environment in which they are allowed to discover new cultural concepts and to expand their cognitive and affective processes in order to think in different cultural ways like native speakers.

This collection of case studies has too few subjects, thus making the generalization of findings a difficult and limited task. We consider this to be a pilot study that explores new research questions; follow-up studies with more subjects and a statistical analysis of data need to be conducted. However, a qualitative analysis of data would also need to be made in larger statistical studies in order to code the nominal categories included in the categorization of responses. We believe that the most powerful research design would combine a qualitative and quantitative analysis of data.

References

Bialystock, E. (1978). A theoretical model of second language learning. *Language Learning, 28*(1), 69–83.

Bogdan, R. C., & Biklen, S. K. (1982). *Qualitative research for education: An introduction to theory and methods.* Needham Heights, MA: Allyn & Bacon.

De Mello, G. (1979). The semantic values of "ser" and "estar." *Hispania, 62,* 338–341.

Dulay, H. C., & Burt, M. K. (1974). Natural sequences in child second language acquisition. *Language Learning, 24,* 37–53.

Finnemann, M. D. (1990). Markedness and learner strategies: Form-and-meaning-oriented learners in the foreign language context. *Modern Language Journal, 24,* 176–187.

Franco, F. (1984). "Ser" and "estar" + locatives en español. *Hispania, 67,* 74–79.

Garreton, M. T., & Medley, F. W., Jr. (1986). *Developmental stages in functional language proficiency.* Unpublished document. (ERIC Document Reproduction Service No. ED 336 990)

Gonzalez, V. (1991). *A model of cognitive, cultural, and linguistic variables affecting bilingual Spanish/English children's development of concepts and language.* Unpublished doctoral dissertation, University of Texas at Austin. (ERIC Document Reproduction Service No. ED 345 562)

Gonzalez, V. (1994). A model of cognitive, cultural and linguistic variables affecting bilingual Spanish/English children's development of concepts and language. *Hispanic Journal of Behavioral Sciences, 16*(4), 396–421.

Gonzalez, V. (1995). *Cognition, culture, and language in bilingual children: Conceptual and semantic development.* Bethesda, MD: Austin & Windfield.

Guntermann, G. (1992). An analysis of interlanguage development over time: Part II, "ser" and "estar." *Hispania, 75,* 1294–1303.

Higgs, T. V. (1985). Ser or not ser: That is the question. *Hispania, 68,* 407–411.

Karmiloff-Smith, A. (1979). Micro- and macrodevelopmental changes in language acquisition and other representational systems. *Cognitive Science, 3,* 91–118.

Knorre, M., Dorwick, T, VanPatten, B., & Villareal, H. (1989). *Puntos de Partida: An invitation to Spanish* (3rd ed.). New York: Random House.

Krashen, S. (1981). *Second language acquisition and second language learning.* New York: Pergamon.

Larsen-Freeman, D. (1976). An explanation for the morpheme accuracy order of English as a second language. *Language Learning, 26,* 125–135.

O'Malley, J. M., Russo, R. P., Chamot, J. M., & Stewner-Manzanares, G. (1988). Applications of learning strategies by students learning English as a second language. In C. E. Weinstein, E. T. Goetz, & P. Alexander (Eds.), *Learning and study strategies: Issues in assessment, instruction, and evaluation* (pp. 215–231). San Diego, CA: Academic Press.

Pountain, C. (1982). Essere/stare as a romance phenomenon. In N. Vincent & M. Harris (Eds.), *Studies in the Romance verb* (pp. 138–160). London: Croom Helm.

ROBINETT, B. W., & SCHACHTER, J. (1983). *Second language learning: Contrastive analysis, error analysis, and related aspects.* Ann Arbor, MI: The University of Michigan Press.

ROLDÁN, M. (1974). Toward a semantic characterization of "ser" and "estar." *Hispania, 57,* 68–75.

RUGGERI-MARCHETTI, M. (1985). La lingüística aplicada a la relación paradigmática entre los verbos "ser" y "estar." *Rassegna Italiana di Linguistica Aplicata, 9*(12), 65–74.

SERA, M. D. (1992). To be or not to be: Use and acquisition of the Spanish copulas. *Journal of Memory and Language, 31,* 408–427.

VANPATTEN, B. (1985). The acquisition of "ser" and "estar" by adult learners of Spanish: A preliminary investigation of transitional stages of competence. *Hispania, 68,* 399–406.

APPENDIX 6A: SENTENCE PAIRS USING *SER* AND *ESTAR*

Semantic Function

Category 1: Adjectives

1. Maria es casada
   Maria está casada.
2. Juan es joven.
   Juan está joven.
3. Julia es profesora.
   Julia está profesora.
4. Pedro es alto.
   Pedro está alto.
5. La casa es limpia.
   La casa está limpia.

Category 2: Permanent Versus Temporary Events

6. El café es caliente.
   El café está caliente.
7. La sopa es rica.
   La sopa está rica.
8. El agua es fría.
   El agua está fría.
9. El día es frío.
   El día está frío.
10. Linda es enferma.
    Linda está enferma.

Category 3: Nationality or Origin

11. Daniela es argentina.
    Daniela está en Argentina.
12. Carlos es de Paraguay.
    Carlos está en Paraguay.
13. La mesa es de plástico.
    La mesa está de plástico.

Category 4: To Express for Whom Something Is Intended

14. El libro es para Sara.
    El libro está para Sara.

Category 5: Possession

15. El carro es de Pedro.
    El carro está de Pedro.

Category 6: To Tell Time

16. *Es la una de la tarde.*
    Está la una de la tarde.
17. *La clase de español es a las diez de la mañana.*
    La clase de español está a las diez de la mañana.

Category 7: Location

18. *Argentina es en Sud América.*
    Argentina está en Sud América.
19. *El lápiz es en la mesa.*
    El lápiz está en la mesa.

Grammatical Function

Category 8: To Form Generalizations

20. *Es necesario estudiar.*
    Está necesario estudiar.
21. *Es importante trabajar.*
    Está importante trabajar.

Category 9: Present Progressive

22. *Manual es comiendo.*
    Manuel está comiendo.
23. *Carolina es bailando.*
    Carolina está bailando.

Category 10: Idiomatic Expressions

24. *La camisa es de cuadros.*
    La camisa está de cuadros.
25. *El pantalón es de rayas.*
    El pantalón está de rayas.

CHAPTER 7

Alternative Assessment Models of Language-Minority Children
Is There a Match with Teachers' Attitudes and Instruction?

MARIA FELIX-HOLT AND VIRGINIA GONZALEZ

THIS CHAPTER HIGHLIGHTS THE THIRD AND FOURTH THEMES OF THE book, referring to the need to represent the minority perspective in multiple measures of cognition and language in bilinguals. It also represents the fifth and sixth themes of the book, referring to the need to include in the construct validity of measures of bilinguals the subjectivity and responsibility of evaluators to assume an advocacy role. In addition, this study highlights the major theme of the book: the sociocultural context for assessment and a socioeducational framework to view evaluation. Within this sociocultural-socioeducational perspective, materials and tests need to be analyzed because evaluators use them subjectively.

STUDY OVERVIEW

The objective of this exploratory qualitative study was to examine the effect of teachers' beliefs and knowledge on the placement and instruction of language-minority children. This study was a follow-up of 13 language-minority kindergartners assessed using standardized (Language Assessment Scales [LAS], De Avila & Duncan, 1987) and alternative measures (Qualitative Use of English and Spanish Tasks [QUEST], Gonzalez, 1991, 1994a, 1995) during the

1992–1993 academic year. QUEST, developed by Gonzalez (1991, 1994a, 1995) based on a model that explains cognitive and language development in bilingual children, has proved to have construct and predictive validity (see, e.g., Gonzalez, Bauerle, & Felix-Holt, 1996). Based on the results of these assessments, these 13 language-minority children were placed into first-grade gifted English or regular bilingual English/Spanish classrooms during the 1993–1994 academic year. This study was conducted when the children were attending first grade in three public elementary schools located in a low socioeconomic status (SES) neighborhood in a Hispanic "barrio" in the southwest region of the United States. The children's first-grade teachers were interviewed in order to obtain information about their attitudes and knowledge levels, their perceptions of each child's educational development, and their recommendations for the future educational placement of these children. Classroom observations were conducted in order to compare the teachers' beliefs articulated during the interviews with their actual instructional methodologies, and also for analyzing the match between the teachers' instructional styles and the children's learning styles.

This study explored three major research questions:

1. Is there a relationship between teachers' personal backgrounds and their beliefs and knowledge about intelligence and language assessment theories in language-minority children?
2. Is there a relationship between teachers' beliefs and knowledge about intelligence, language, and assessment theories and the actual instructional strategies that they use when teaching language-minority children in their classrooms?
3. Is there a relationship between the teachers' ratings of children's cognitive and language development and the LAS results, and the teachers' and QUEST independent evaluators' placement recommendations for language-minority children?

STATEMENT OF THE PROBLEM

The American school system is confronting an important problem with social, cultural, and educational implications: culturally and linguistically different children are being misdiagnosed and incorrectly placed in educational programs that do not provide them with adequate and fair education (Baca & Cervantes, 1989; Gonzalez, 1991). Moss (1992) pointed out that it becomes important to study the social, ethical, and educational implications of the validity of assessment models for language-minority children. The assessment instruments that are currently being used with these children lack validity and reliability (Frasier, 1987; Oller, 1991; Santos de Barona & Barona, 1991; Snow, 1992), resulting in their overrepresentation and inaccurate placement in special education programs (French, 1992; Plata, 1986) and their underrepresentation in gifted programs (Smith, La Rosa, & Clasen, 1991). The three most commonly used intelligence standardized tests—Wechsler Intelligence Scales for Children–Revised (Wechsler, 1991), the Kaufman Assessment Battery for Children (Kaufman & Kaufman, 1983), and the Stanford-Binet IV (Thorndike, Hagen, & Sattler, 1986a, 1986b)—are normed to assess primarily mainstream, white, middle-class children.

It becomes a major concern of the American educational reform movement to implement assessment procedures that will overcome the biases that exist for language-minority children when they take standardized tests. These tests tend to be inaccurate for identifying and placing language-minority children; the tests lack construct validity represented in an underlying medical model that cannot explain the children's cognitive and linguistic development (for an extended revision of the characteristics of the medical model, see Gonzalez & Yawkey, 1993). Thus, there is need for culturally sensitive theories that take language and culture into consideration when assessing and instructing language-minority children (Gonzalez, 1993, 1994a; Santos de Barona & Barona, 1991). Concerns about assessment, placement, and diagnosis of these children have prompted educators to call for reforming our educational system. For instance, Baker (1992) pointed out three areas of needed change encompassing curriculum, instruction, and staff development. Change in the education of language-minority children is badly needed because diagnoses made on the basis of standardized test scores do not provide accurate information for developing appropriate educational plans and implementing successful educational strategies and curriculum.

Change is needed as well in teacher education models because educators have been endorsing standardized tests that have led to tracking minority students, who are placed in low-level academic programs (Hadaway & Marek-Schoroer, 1992). Bennet and Ragosta's findings (cited by French, 1992) showed that many teachers refer students to special education programs based on such extraneous factors as their race, sex, physical appearance, and SES, rather than their psychological and neurological needs. Hamayan and Damico (1991) stated that because teachers are the referring agents and consumers of the assessment results, if the currently used assessment models are to be changed, teachers need to change their attitudinal belief systems and support alternative assessments. According to Bialystock (1990) beliefs are formed by underlying philosophies and idiosyncratic ideas resulting from prior experience and knowledge expressed in the instructional strategies that teachers select. Therefore, this study can contribute to the goal of making teachers aware of their belief systems so that they can create better educational opportunities for children of different cultures and languages. These are the reasons why research needs to be conducted on the teachers' theoretical beliefs regarding assessment and instruction, endorsed when serving the unique population of language-minority children.

Theoretical Framework

The theoretical framework used in this study comes from the "ethnic researcher" perspective and from developmental assessment models (Gonzalez & Yawkey, 1993) that differ from mainstream intelligence theories and standardized tests. The alternative assessment model conceptualizes language-minority children's cognitive and language development as influenced by the interaction of both internal and external factors (Gonzalez & Yawkey, 1993). Gonzalez, Bauerle, and Felix-Holt (1994) recognized that cognitive and language development needs to be measured using qualitative descriptors and multiple informants in order to obtain a multidimensional view of language-minority children's developmental factors and examine the relationship of assessment, placement, and instruction. The most important theoretical assumption of the ethnic researcher model (Gonzalez & Yawkey, 1993) is that educators' attitudes, values, beliefs, prior knowledge, and personal backgrounds have a major impact on the placement and instructional decisions they make for language-minority children.

Literature Review

Many variables affect the assessment and education of language-minority children considered in this study. The literature review that follows begins by discussing the socioeducational, second language learning model that Robert Gardner and his colleagues developed (Gardner, Lalonde, & Pierson, 1983); it emphasizes the way that teachers' attitudes influence the assessment and instruction of language-minority children. The second section examines the modifications that we made in the socioeducational model to adapt it to this study. The third section presents an overview of factors influencing second language learning: how teachers' beliefs and attitudes toward second language learning can influence how they teach language-minority children; intelligence development and its assessment as it relates to the underrepresentation of language-minority children in gifted educational programs; and second language learning theories and instruction, bilingualism, and multicultural education issues. The first and second sections address the first and second research questions correspondingly. The final two sections address the third research question.

Gardner's Socioeducational Model

In order to understand the interrelated variables discussed in this literature review, we have used the socioeducational model of second language learning (Gardner et al., 1983). Baker (1992) described the four stages of the socioeducational model: (1) cultural background, (2) individual differences, (3) learning context, and (4) outcomes.

In stage 1, external factors are considered to influence second language learning. The model acknowledges that children grow up in communities that transmit beliefs and attitudes about language and culture. Other authors have also made this claim. For example, Hamers and Blanc (1992) stated that in the socialization process, individuals have a life-long interaction with their social environment. Then, the role of society will have the strongest impact on each person's values and beliefs.

In stage 2 of the model, four variables interact: (1) individual differences; (2) intelligence, defined as how quickly an individual understands explanations provided about a second language such as rules; (3) language aptitude, described as the individual's talents for learning a second language, which includes the motivation, affect, effort, and desire for learning; and (4) situational anxiety, described as a potential inhibitor for learning a second language. That is, Gardner's model includes attitudes and personality differences in this second stage.

In stage 3 of the model, the learning context can be either formal or informal. In the formal context of the classroom, there is an intent or purpose to transmit the target language to the individual, who learns by drilling, practicing, using audiovisual materials, translating, and doing grammar exercises. Informal second language learning is defined by Gardner and colleagues (1983) as an unintentional outcome because the individual may be learning a second language by talking to a friend or watching a movie in another language. The purpose of an informal learning context is social communication or entertainment. There are some differences between the formal and informal contexts of second language learning, but they do overlap.

Finally, in stage 4 of the model, according to Baker (1992), Gardner and his colleagues suggested that there are two final outcomes when individuals are learning a second language: (1) linguistic outcomes, such as becoming a fluent bilingual (with good vocabulary, pronunciation, and grammar), and (2) nonlinguistic outcomes, such as modifications in attitudes, self-concept, cultural values, and beliefs. The socioeducational model of second language acquisition has been tested using a causal model technique, Linear Structural Relationship Analysis (LISREL). According to Baker (1992), the socioeducational model has been proved to be valid by these studies and therefore has empirical validity.

Modified Version of Gardner's Model

We have modified Gardner's model in order to emphasize the role of teachers' attitudinal belief systems influencing the assessment and instruction of language-minority children. It becomes appropriate to adapt this model since it also examined beliefs as related to second language learning processes. In the original model, within the first stage, the cultural environment surrounding the individual was acknowledged as influencing second language learning. We have adapted this influence from the cultural environment to explain how teachers' backgrounds relate to their teaching methods when instructing language-minority children (see Figure 7.1). Teachers come from varied cultural and educational backgrounds and therefore have different attitudes and beliefs toward language-minority children. We have maintained the emphasis on individual differences in the modified model; however, the focus in our version is on the teachers' individual differences, such as their personal backgrounds, beliefs, and knowledge levels of intelligence and second language develop-

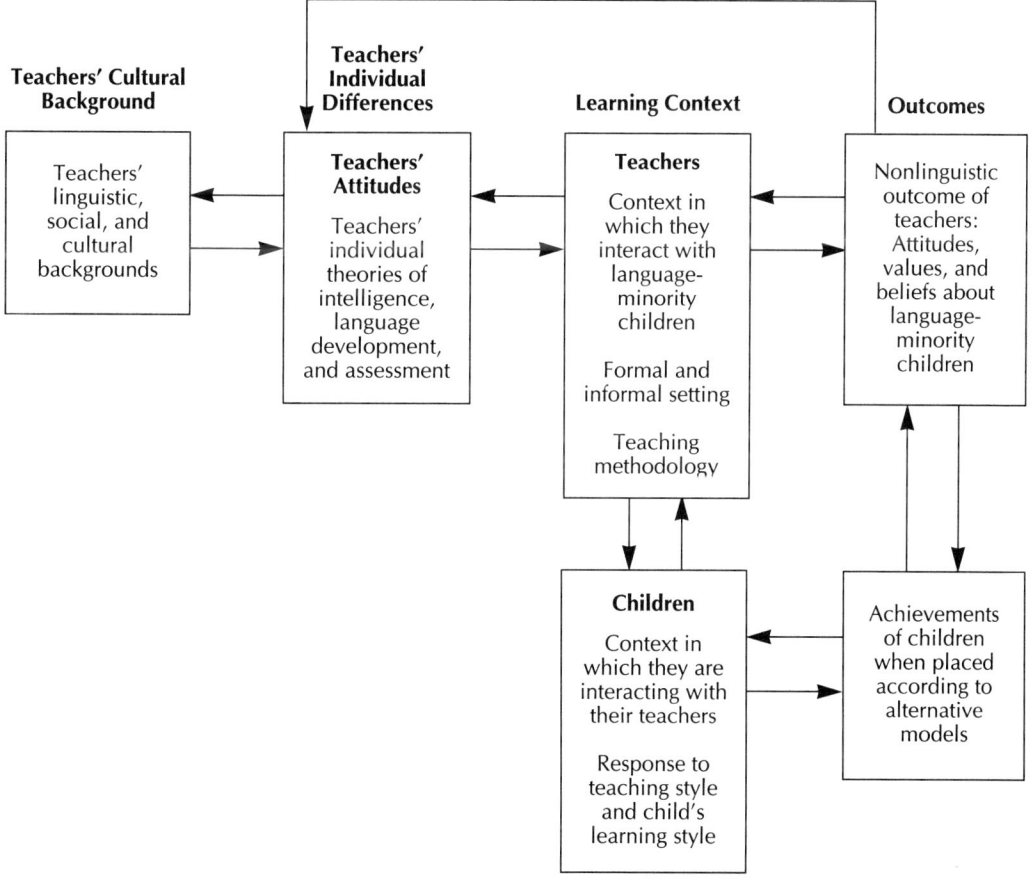

FIGURE 7.1 Modified model: Teachers' cultural background and attitudes, teaching context, methodology, and outcomes of attitudes.

ment. In contrast, the focus of the original model was on the second language learners, such as children.

The original socioeducational model emphasized the formal and informal settings for learning a second language in the third stage. In our adapted version, we hold that because teachers come from different language backgrounds, their instructional use of language in the classroom will also differ. We also believe that the children who are being taught the second language also influence the teacher's behaviors because we conceptualize the teacher-child relationship as a two-way interaction (see Figure 7.1). Thus, the second language instruction situation in the classroom is more than a formal context for learning a second language; it also provides an informal context for a dynamic interaction between the teacher and the children. Relatedly, Baker (1992) pointed out that the socioeducational model recognized the relationship among the multiple factors interacting in a cyclical and dynamic manner, characteristics that we also recognized in our modified version of the model.

Finally, in the fourth stage of the socioeducational model, Gardner and his colleagues (1983) suggested that both linguistic and nonlinguistic outcomes are possible in a second language learning situation. In our modified version, we mainly focus on nonlinguistic outcomes, including teachers' beliefs toward language-minority children (see Figure 7.1). We examined these nonlinguistic outcomes in this study using teacher interviews, classroom observations of teachers' and children's behaviors, teachers' ratings of children's cognitive and linguistic development and placement recommendations, and language assessment scales and an alternative developmental method (QUEST) given to the children.

Factors Affecting Second Language Learning

Regarding how teachers' beliefs toward second language learning can influence how they teach language minority children, Saville-Troike (cited by Plata, 1986) asserted that educators need to be aware that their attitudes have a more important impact than the curriculum content itself. She recommended that educators become knowledgeable about and aware of the cultural and linguistic backgrounds of students. Banks and McGee Banks (1993) emphasized the need for teachers to create in their classrooms positive images of different ethnic groups through the use of books, instructional materials, strategies that are sensitive to racial differences, thereby helping minority children to feel valued and empowered.

Regarding the second factor of intelligence development and its assessment, teachers have historically continued to accept the traditional models of giftedness, which result in an underrepresentation of language-minority children in gifted classrooms. Authors have tried to explain this problem. For example, Melesky (cited by Marquez, 1992) and Shaklee (1992) pointed out that language-minority children are not being identified for gifted programs because of an overreliance on standardized tests, which have major methodological problems. In addition, Shaklee asserted that teachers do not know how to recognize cultural and linguistic giftedness, since most of them are often not fluent in the minority child's first language and are not familiar with the normal process of first and second language acquisition. As a consequence, teachers misinterpret the normal process of second language learning as a language or learning problem, or even as mental retardation. Marquez (1991) and Sternberg (1992) conceptualized this minority underrepresentation problem as narrow theoretical frameworks explaining superior intelligence or giftedness that are transmitted to educators. They pointed to the need to develop pluralistic concepts of giftedness that include the culture of the individual being assessed, a change that could reduce the biases of standardized tests.

Other authors have acknowledged the link between assessment and instruction. For example, Damico (1991) asserted that some assessment problems have traditionally influenced language-minority children's educational outcomes. Gonzalez (1993) claimed that theories specifically designed for language-minority children can help find alternative assessment procedures, not only to make accurate diagnostic decisions but also to design appropriate instruction. Yawkey and Juan (1993) recognized the need to link assessment with instruction and listed five major interrelated instructional strategies that give more accurate information about students' developmental stages and examine teachers' instructional decisions used with language-minority children: (1) conducting observations, (2) determining the children's developmental levels, (3) individualizing instruction, (4) using directed dialogue, and (5) exploring the child's family characteristics, needs, and resources. By implementing these strategies, we can help meet the language-minority child's unique instructional needs.

Regarding the third factor of bilingualism and multicultural education issues, bilingualism has been both criticized and shown to have advantages in the research literature. Reynolds and Kamphaus (1990) stated that criticism of bilingualism appears in the literature with biases and inaccuracies because this process is misunderstood in the literature, for two reasons: (1) applied psychology has not had research interests in bilingualism, depicting it as retarding intelligence and handicapping the acquisition of English, and (2) American society at large has a negative attitude toward bilingualism in relation to racial and political issues regarding immigrant groups. Reynolds and Kamphaus (1990) pointed out some of the advantages of bilingualism, including extensive and varied encoding abilities due to having dual language systems, a vast repertoire of solutions for problem solving, and the production of elaborate and creative ideas.

Regarding multicultural education issues, Cummins and Stedman (cited by French, 1992) stated that in order to provide an environment conducive to learning, school districts must endorse a philosophy of cultural pluralism. Additionally, instruction must reflect an understanding of how students' linguistic and cultural characteristics influence learning. Ogbu and Matute-Bianchi (cited by Trueba, 1991) pointed out that language-minority children face social structural constraints, such as prejudice and poverty, that affect their school success. Banks and McGee Banks (1993) pointed out that the school curriculum used with language-minority children needs to reflect their cultural experiences.

In sum, the socioeducational model developed by Robert Gardner and his colleagues (1983), the modified version of this model as related to this study's objectives and research questions, and the more important factors affecting the second language learning process presented above provide a framework for understanding the methodology and results of this study.

METHOD

Research Design

The research questions, theoretical framework, and the instruments were integrated in the qualitative analysis of data, which used six instruments (see Figure 7.2). The theoretical framework was separated into four areas: (1) teachers' personal backgrounds, (2) teachers' attitudes and individual differences, (3) the learning context of children, and (4) the outcome of teachers and of children. The six instruments were (1) teachers' interview, (2) classroom observation, (3) teachers' ratings of children's first and second language proficiency, (4) bilingual children's cognitive and language development summary, (5) LAS (De Avila & Duncan, 1987), and (6) QUEST (Gonzalez, 1991, 1994, 1995). To analyze the data, the teachers' interview responses (see Appendix 7B) and the teachers' and children's classroom observations (see the section on observations later in this chapter) were separated into different nominal categories. Different clusters of interview questions and classroom observation categories were used to answer different research questions (see Figure 7.2).

Subjects

Teachers. The first group of subjects consisted of 6 first-grade teachers who were selected for this study because the 13 children referred for evaluation with QUEST (Gonzalez, 1991, 1994a, 1995) during kindergarten were placed in their classrooms. These 6 teachers were employed by three different public elementary schools located in a low SES "barrio" in a metropolitan area of the southwest region of the United States. Four of the teachers were Hispanic (1 male and 3 females), and 2 were white (both females). Three of the

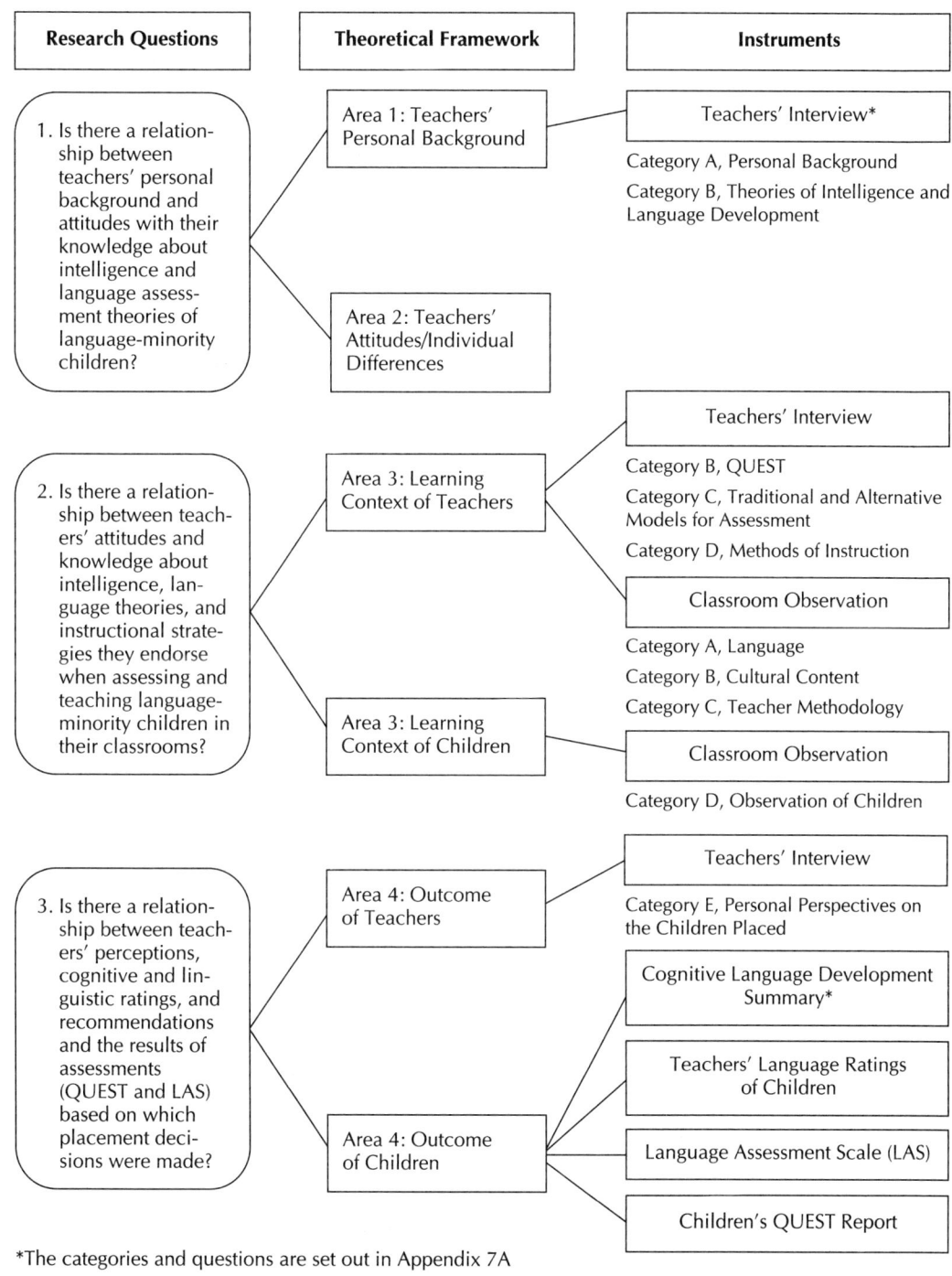

FIGURE 7.2   Integration of research questions, theoretical framework, and instruments.

Hispanic and 1 of the white teachers taught in regular bilingual classrooms, and 1 Hispanic and 1 white teacher taught in gifted bilingual and English monolingual classrooms, respectively.

Children. The second group of subjects consisted of 13 bilingual Hispanic first-graders attending three different elementary public schools. Eleven of these children were males, and 3 were females, and their ages ranged from 7 to 8 years by the time of the study. These 13 children were selected because they were referred for assessment with QUEST (Gonzalez, 1991, 1994a) for possible giftedness by their kindergarten teachers one year prior to the data collection for this study. Based on QUEST results, 7 children (6 males and 1 female) were placed in regular gifted or bilingual gifted first-grade classrooms, and 6 children (5 males and 1 female) were placed in regular bilingual first-grade classrooms. "Language-minority children" is a very broad term used in many ways. In this study, we use it to refer to children who come from a non-English background and have different levels of English and Spanish proficiencies. Particularly we refer to Hispanic children living in homes where either English or Spanish, or both, are spoken.

Instruments

Open-Ended Interview. The open-ended interview developed for this study contained five areas: the teachers' (1) personal cultural and linguistic backgrounds, (2) beliefs on theories of intelligence and second language development, (3) beliefs on standardized and alternative assessments, (4) preferred instructional methods, and (5) decisions on children's placement (see Appendix 7A for a list of questions). This interview consisted of 23 questions; 16 pertained to the first four areas and the last 7 questions pertained to the fifth area.

The interview questions were pilot-tested twice using five graduate students of educational psychology before they were administered to the teachers. In addition, for the purpose of ensuring the reliability of the operational definitions of the nominal categories created for coding the interview questions, two judges independently coded the transcribed responses of two pilot case studies. The two judges were also graduate students of educational psychology. A high reliability ($r = .93$) was obtained between the two judges. These nominal categories were created for exploring the research questions and for the analysis and interpretation of the patterns found (see Appendix 7B for a list of the nominal categories used for coding the interview questions).

Classroom Observations. The teachers and the children were observed during an instructional activity involving two different content areas: reading and math. The observations were coded based on three categories in order to compare the teachers' verbal explanations of their beliefs given in the interviews and their actual behaviors: (1) the language used in the classroom, (2) the cultural atmosphere of the classroom, and (3) the teachers' instructional style and the children's learning style. Two graduate students of educational psychology were used as judges to ensure reliability of data analysis. The students serving as judges independently rated the videotapes. When calculating the reliability coefficient, the ratings were considered in agreement when they coincided in the absence or presence of particular behaviors. A high reliability ($r = .97$) was found between judges.

Bilingual Children's Cognitive and Language Development Summary. The Bilingual Children's Cognitive and Language Development Summary was filled out by the teachers in order to compare their answers with the teachers' interviews and classroom observations and the QUEST and LAS results. This qualitative instrument posed seven open-ended questions about the child's language, problem-solving skills, peer relationships, and play and work behaviors. The teachers were also asked to circle words from a group of 45 adjectives that best described the child.

Teachers' Ratings of Children's Language Proficiency. The teachers were asked to fill out the Teachers' Ratings of Children's Spanish and English Language Proficiency developed by Gonzalez (1991). The instructions required the teachers to rate the child's level of language proficiency in Spanish and English on a 5-point Likert scale (5 = proficient, 4 = superior, 3 = intermediate, 2 = poor, 1 = nonspeaker) on the components of vocabulary, grammar, syntax, and academic and social language at both the comprehension and production levels. In addition, two affirmative-negative questions were asked about code mixing and code switching.

Language Assessment Scale (LAS). For the purpose of this study, the LAS (De Avila & Duncan, 1987) was administered individually to the children in order to obtain the first and second language proficiency level of each child. The LAS is a multiple-item paper-and-pencil standardized test that has two parallel forms in Spanish and English, measuring the child's oral language abilities. The estimated time for administering each language, Spanish or English, individually is 30 minutes. The LAS has been demonstrated to have validity and reliability. Level 1, K through fifth grade, was used. It was scored by a trained staff member from the school district.

Reports of the Qualitative Use of English and Spanish Tasks (QUEST). The QUEST was used to assess the threefold interaction of cognition, culture, and language on verbal and nonverbal conceptual development in language-minority children. The QUEST has five nonverbal and verbal classification tasks that use animal and food objects portraying differences and similarities of the conceptual, symbolic, and linguistic representations of gender in Spanish and English (Gonzalez, 1991; Gonzalez, Bauerle, Felix-Holt, 1994). The three verbal tasks are labeling, defining, and justification of sorting; and the two nonverbal tasks are sorting and category clue (for a complete description of the tasks see Gonzalez, 1991, 1994a, 1995). Whenever possible each child was assessed once in English and once in Spanish. Two evaluators administered QUEST in order to ensure reliability of the diagnoses and recommendations. The QUEST reports contain (1) a summary of behavioral observations, (2) the diagnosis for each language administration, and (3) a placement recommendation.

Procedure

The procedure for collecting the data had six steps:

1. Obtain consent to conduct the study from the University of Arizona, the school district, and the three principals of the elementary schools targeted
2. Obtain consent from the teachers to participate in the study
3. Conduct the teachers' open-ended interviews
4. Conduct teachers' and children's classroom observations
5. Administer the LAS individually to the children
6. Obtain the Teachers' Rating of Children's English and Spanish Language Proficiency and the Bilingual Children's Cognitive and Language Development Summary from each teacher for each child.

For conducting the teachers' interviews, appointments were scheduled outside class time at the teachers' convenience. The teachers were interviewed in their classrooms by the first author for approximately one hour. Interviews were audiotaped to increase the accuracy of data analysis. The interviews were conducted in either Spanish or English or both, depending on the teacher's language preferences. The teachers were interviewed before the first classroom observation was conducted in order to obtain information about the curriculum areas to be taught during the following two weeks. This order of events was planned because the researchers were interested in observing two content areas: reading and math. Only approximate dates for the observations were given to the teachers in order to try to prevent teachers from changing their normal classroom instructional behaviors. The classroom observations were videotaped to ensure reliability in data analysis. Observations lasted for one-half hour to one hour, depending on the length of the content being taught. The children were tested individually in a quiet room with the LAS for approximately 30 minutes. Finally, the teachers were asked to complete within a two-week period the Language Ratings of Children's Spanish and English Language Proficiency, and the Bilingual Children's Cognitive and Language Development Summary.

Methodology of Data Analysis and Explanation

The results of this study will be presented as individual cases because this is an exploratory and descriptive study. This in-depth study is also using multiple sources of evidence, allowing a broader range of research issues to be addressed. Yin (1994) asserted that a multiple-case study design allows researchers to pursue the discovery of patterns in a particular area of interest. This design can help explain why some cases in this study have predictable results and some have contrary results. Yin (1994) described the five steps for doing case study analysis: (1) select a theory to explore issues; (2) select cases and data; (3) use the instruments; (4) develop individual case reports; and (5) apply cross-case analysis to find conclusions, modify the theory, or develop policy implications. These procedures were adapted to this study. Since several theories on attitudinal belief systems, second language learning, giftedness, and bilingualism were explored, data were collected on selected subjects, data collection procedures were specifically created and selected, each case study was written individually, and a cross-case analysis was done.

We assumed that the constructs of teachers' behaviors and beliefs are intimately related. We view the teachers' instructional behaviors in the classroom as the expression of their underlying philosophical and theoretical understandings of the nature of learning and development in children. Several authors have acknowledged this interrelationship of beliefs, knowledge levels, and instructional behaviors in teachers. For instance, Richardson (cited by Gonzalez, 1994b) considered knowledge a subjective psychological process related to beliefs, which in turn were related to their classroom practices (behaviors). Kagan (cited by Gonzalez, 1994b) reported that teachers' content domain and the instructional programs and materials that they used were also related to their belief systems. Relatedly, Gonzalez (1994b) pointed out that sociocultural personal and professional experiences influence teachers' beliefs and teaching practices. Thus, this study had the objective of exploring the relationship between teachers' explicitly articulated beliefs about how to instruct language-minority children and how they developed cognitively and linguistically, and their observed instructional behaviors in the classroom.

RESULTS AND DISCUSSION

The results are presented as case studies using a sequential procedure for data analysis (see Figure 7.2), which is synthesized in a discussion and elaboration of findings across cases for each research question. Each of the six case studies gives descriptive information using specific instruments for answering the research questions related to the socioeducational modified model (Gardner et al., 1983). A summary of the results obtained from the instruments for each research question is shown in the figure for each case. Figures 7.4 through 7.8 in Appendix 7C summarize the findings. (Pseudonyms are used.)

First Research Question

The first research question inquired whether a relationship existed between teachers' personal and educational experiences and their belief systems about intelligence and language development in language-minority children. This question is related to the socioeducational model used as a theoretical framework since it acknowledges that teachers' personal and educational experiences influence their beliefs. The patterns found across the six case studies show that these experiences do influence their attitudes about language-minority children's development.

Personal Experience: Bilingual and Bicultural Identification. The personal experience of the teachers was investigated using the individual interviews (see Figure 7.2). Raymond, Sylvia, Julia, Mildred, and Monica considered themselves bilingual since they spoke Spanish and English fluently. Raymond, Sylvia, Julia, and Monica considered themselves bicultural since they were living in mainstream American and Hispanic cultures. Although Marcy grew up in a Jewish community and Mildred had taught extensively on a Navajo reservation, these two majority teachers did not consider themselves bilingual or bicultural. This can be explained as representing a difference between the constructs of race and culture. Culture is learned due to belonging to an ethnic community or practicing certain traditional behaviors, which Marcy and Mildred did not feel they shared.

Personal and Educational Experience with Language-Minority Children. Based on the interviews (see Figure 7.2), all the teachers reported having had formal training in teaching language-minority children. Marcy, Mildred, and Raymond had training in English as a Second Language. Raymond, Julia, Sylvia, and Monica reported having done their teacher training in bilingual education and having bilingual endorsements. The Hispanic teachers (Raymond, Sylvia, Julia, and Monica) discussed having extensive experience educating language-minority children; however, they did not focus their responses as much on formal but on personal experiences with the Hispanic community as it represented their own culture. Raymond and Sylvia reported living in the same neighborhood as the language-minority children they were teaching. However, Raymond was not Spanish dominant and did not use Spanish in his personal life or in his classroom. Julia reported that her motivation to become a bilingual teacher was to help language-minority children with whom she had grown up. The two majority teachers, Marcy and Mildred, did not discuss culture as part of their personal experience and did not use Spanish as a primary language when teaching.

Theories of Intelligence and Language Development. The data in this area were collected using individual teachers' interviews (see Figure 7.2). Marcy, Raymond, Mildred, and Monica stated the belief that intelligence is innate, but they were referring to the *potential* for developing intelligence, not an actual quotient. All four acknowledged as well the secondary influence of the external environment, by offering stimulation and opportunities to develop intelligence. Marcy and Raymond believed that intelligence and language development were similar for majority and minority children. Raymond and Mildred stated that receiving stimulation during sensitive developmental periods was important for intelligence and language development. Raymond believed that language is developed by being exposed to a particular rhythm and sound system. Mildred recognized the presence of individual differences in the genetic component of intelligence, which affected the rate of language learning in children. Thus, Mildred thought that although children may receive different environmental stimulation, such as being exposed to a monolingual or bilingual context, individual differences in their genetic endowment would result in different rates of language and intelligence development in both majority and minority children. Monica believed that home experiences and prior knowledge also influenced intelligence and language development, and because minority children were exposed to two different languages, their development would be different from monolingual majority children's development.

Sylvia and Julia believed in environmental theories for intelligence development and had close links to the children's culture. They discussed their personal experiences of living in a Hispanic "barrio" and being educated in the same school system as the language-minority children whom they were teaching. They were dominant Spanish speakers and used Spanish in their personal lives and the school setting. They emphasized the importance of their personal experience in influencing their knowledge and perspectives about intelligence development in language-minority children. Sylvia described intelligence and language as developing from experience, and thought that although these experiences would be different for children from the majority or minority cultures, the presence of individual experiences occurred in both groups of children and the learning process would be similar for both groups. Sylvia explained language development as a process that develops from the experience of hearing and speaking a language in a particular cultural environment. Julia claimed that intelligence develops in a nonsequential order and differently for all individuals, yet there were similarities in the potential for intelligence development present in majority and minority children. However, Julia thought that minority children were not given the same educational opportunities as majority children. She believed that language develops naturally and that individuals show different rates of language learning. Julia explained the common oral language delay in minority children as lack of stimulation received at home.

Conclusions for the First Research Question. Based on the summary of the teachers' interview responses, we can conclude that the teachers with Hispanic cultural and language experiences supported the influence of language and culture on intelligence development and endorsed environmental theories of intelligence development more strongly. Teachers who lacked a second language or culture tended to emphasize innate theories of intelligence development more strongly than environmental ones. Regarding language developmental theories, all the teachers, minority and majority, discussed environmental factors (e.g., experiences, opportunities, stimulation). Most tended to believe that the process of language development is similar for majority and minority children. The difference in the positions endorsed by minority and majority teachers was on the role that they gave to individual differences and environmental factors. Teachers with Hispanic language and cultural experiences tended to emphasize differences in the learning environments (e.g., quality of curriculum, learning opportunities at home) that minority and majority children were exposed to. Monolingual and monocultural teachers tended to emphasize innate cognitive individual differences present within majority and minority groups, which would influence the rate of first and second language learning.

Second Research Question

The second research question inquired about the relationship between teachers' beliefs and knowledge about intelligence and language theories, and the assessment and instructional strategies they endorse and use for teaching language-minority children. This question is related to the modified socioeducational model used as a theoretical framework since it also recognizes the formal and informal context in which learning takes place: the reciprocal interaction between teachers' and language-minority children's behaviors.

Alternative Assessment. The teachers' beliefs about alternative assessment were investigated using the individual interviews (see Figure 7.2). Raymond, Sylvia, Marcy, and Julia supported the use of alternative types of assessment for language-minority children. Monica and Mildred believed that the use of both standardized and alternative assessment was needed to assess language-minority children. In addition, all the teachers claimed using their own personal observations for assessing the intelligence development of language-minority children; however, each reported a different focus. Julia and Mildred observed the problem-solving abilities of the children, Marcy observed the progress of children, Raymond compared children of the same chronological age, and

Sylvia used other teachers' observations along with her own to make a more "objective" evaluation.

Teachers' Observations. Behavioral data on the teaching of math and reading contents was compared to the interview data, including teachers' theories of intelligence and language development in language-minority children and teachers' reports on whether they adapted instructional content or language (see Figure 7.2).

A relationship was found between what most of the teachers reported in the interviews and their actual behaviors when teaching language-minority children. Marcy and Mildred reported that they did not adapt the content or language when teaching language-minority children. The use of Spanish was not seen in Marcy's classroom, and the content that she taught was not culturally relevant for language-minority children. This majority teacher's belief in innate theories of intelligence development was linked with her belief and practice that changing the instructional methods of reading and math would not help language-minority children's learning since she considered intelligence development to be the same for both majority and minority children. When asked about her contribution to the education of language-minority children, she did not always perceive her personal cultural experiences as influencing the way she taught these children. She gave other explanations: "I accept everybody" and "I do not belong to the Hispanic culture, so I could not treat the children in the same manner as the Mexican teachers."

Sylvia and Julia claimed in the interview that they supported environmental intelligence theories, which was in agreement with their observed practice of adapting their instruction in content and language to meet children's individual needs. Their instructional strategies and classroom environments were culturally relevant for language-minority children. When Sylvia and Julia were asked how they contributed to teaching language-minority children, they connected closely with the Hispanic culture and viewed their personal backgrounds as significantly influencing the way they taught.

Although Raymond and Monica endorsed innate theories of intelligence development, due to their bilingual education training and their bilingual/bicultural Hispanic background, they could recognize the importance of adapting the cultural content and language of the instructional materials. However, Monica's interview responses and practices coincided; Raymond's did not. It was observed that Monica did adapt content and language to meet the needs of the bilingual children and also encourage them to participate and work independently and creatively in her classroom.

The two exceptions to the close connections between their belief systems articulated in the interview and their instructional behaviors observed were Raymond and Mildred. Raymond reported in the interview that he had no problem adapting instruction for language-minority children; however, he did not use Spanish or include cultural content when observed in his classroom. This practice was different from what he had stated in the interview. Two factors can explain why language and culture content were not present in Raymond's classroom during both observations: he had lost his Spanish language in the military, and it was his first time teaching in a bilingual classroom.

Mildred objected to a classroom observation; therefore, it was not possible to compare her actual instructional behavior to the theoretical beliefs that she articulated in the interview. Her lack of cooperation may be interpreted as some fear or shyness in having a researcher visit her classroom, and probably her perception of possibly being evaluated negatively or criticized may show some insecurity and lack of assertiveness in her professional abilities.

Children's Observations. The children were observed to examine their responses to the teachers' instructional strategies. In Marcy's classroom, Robert and Vicky were attentively participating in a math activity. Robert was using humor when working on a problem with his partner. Vicky was aware and responding to her environment. The learning styles of these two students worked well with Marcy's teaching style. Jimmy, however, was not very attentive. He was having difficulty staying on task and did not show the enthusiasm of the other two children. The behavior the children exhibited during the observation was related to the developmental theories Marcy had claimed she endorsed during the interview. She had stated that she accepted all students, and this belief came across in the democratic way that she was observed treating everybody in her classroom.

The children responded well to Sylvia's teaching styles. Maria was the only child present during the first observation when Sylvia was teaching reading in Spanish. During the first observation, Sylvia taught with culturally relevant materials using a Spanish book. Maria was observed responding well to Sylvia's teaching style.

Felipe, George, and Rudy were in Raymond's English reading classroom the first observation day, since they were considered to be dominant in English. When Felipe and Rudy were observed interacting with Raymond during the reading lesson, they did not appear very attentive. Raymond's teaching style did not seem to work well with these children's learning styles.

Sylvia was observed teaching math to Maria, Felipe, George, and Rudy on the second observation day. Maria, Felipe, and George were attentive; Rudy was not. The four children responded well to Sylvia's use of positive verbal encouragement, and also to her use of both Spanish and English as methods for instruction of math.

Hector was observed twice in Julia's classroom: once during reading and once during math activities. In the first observation, he was paired with another child during a problem-solving activity; in the second observation, he worked independently. Hector seemed to respond well to Julia's teaching style. The beliefs that Julia reported during the interview were evident in her classroom. She used Spanish and had culturally relevant materials available when teaching reading and math. Finally, the children in Monica's classroom were observed to be very involved. The only student who seemed off task was Carlos, showing behaviors that Monica described as typical. All the children seemed to respond well to her teaching style. Monica reported endorsing innate theories of intelligence development during the interview. Her teaching style and methodology were observed to be congruent with her statements during the interview, since she tried to match the children's different individual needs and to stimulate their potential for development.

Conclusions for the Second Research Question. Based on the analysis of the summaries of the teachers' interview responses and the classroom observations, we can conclude that the teachers' cultural and language backgrounds and their beliefs influence how they teach language-minority children. The teachers with little or no Spanish background did not believe that adapting cultural content and language of instructional materials and methodologies was important for providing a quality education for language-minority children. Among the Hispanic teachers, their minority culture and language background seemed to have more of an influence than the developmental theories they endorsed. It is interesting to note that the cultural and linguistic background of teachers is highly influential on what contribution they perceive their personal backgrounds are making on the education of language-minority children. A reasonably close relationship between the theoretical belief systems about intelligence and language development in language-minority children that the teachers reported endorsing in the interviews and their actual practices in their classrooms when teaching language-minority children was also found.

Third Research Question

The third research question refers to the relationship between the teachers' cognitive and linguistic ratings of the children and the LAS results, and the teachers' and QUEST independent evaluators' placement recommendations for the children.

Teacher's Language Ratings of Children. A relative close relationship between the Teachers' Language Ratings and the results of the LAS was found for most of the teachers. Marcy's, Sylvia's, Mildred's, and Monica's ratings of each child's first and second language proficiency coincided with the scores that the children placed in their classrooms had obtained on the LAS. Julia rated Hector's language proficiency in Spanish at the same level as his scores on the LAS, but in English she rated him at a much lower level than the score he had obtained on the LAS. Raymond's ratings of the children's English language proficiency were equivalent to the actual scores they had obtained on the LAS. However, he rated these children's level of language proficiency in Spanish at a higher level in three out of four cases. This lack of coincidence between Raymond's ratings and the LAS scores may be due to the fact that he was not proficient in Spanish.

Teachers' and QUEST Recommendations. A relationship was found between the placement recommendation given by Marcy and the QUEST results for the three children placed in her classroom: Jimmy, Robert, and Vicky. There was a coincidence between Marcy's descriptions of Jimmy and the recommendations reported by QUEST evaluators. Marcy was concerned about Jimmy's behavior since she felt he needed to be put on probation for the second grade. Marcy perceived Jimmy to be at a low cognitive and linguistic developmental level in comparison to his peers. Relatedly, QUEST evaluators reported that Jimmy did not want to follow instructions for completing the tasks and that he quickly tired. The evaluators recommended that Jimmy be given special stimulation to help maintain his attention and enrich his development. Marcy had positive recommendations for the other children, and she felt they were appropriately placed. Marcy described Robert as verbal, social, and creative in the teacher rating form and also in the interview. The QUEST evaluators described Robert as curious, friendly, and having great initiative and sense of humor. In addition, both Marcy and the QUEST evaluators described Vicky as a child with good verbal abilities. Robert and Vicky were highly recommended for the gifted program by both Marcy and the QUEST evaluators.

Raymond felt that all the children in his classroom were placed appropriately, and he made many references to their emotional development when describing them. Raymond described George as having emotional problems. When George was assessed using QUEST, he did not want to work on the tasks, and he finished the assessment process only with great resistance. George was not recommended to be placed in a gifted program. In addition, Raymond felt that the placement recommendation in a regular classroom was appropriate for Dan. The evaluators who used QUEST described Dan as average and noncreative. Raymond also stated that Dan was an average boy and not gifted.

Rudy was an interesting case because of the relationship between his actual placement and what QUEST evaluators recommended. Raymond felt that Rudy could be gifted; however, he did not think he was ready to be in a gifted program because of his emotional problems. Rudy was placed in a first-grade gifted classroom and remained there for only a few weeks before returning to his original regular classroom. There were inconsistencies found when Rudy was assessed with QUEST. The evaluators reported that Rudy had attained a high level of cognitive development in the first language administration, but in the second language administration, he was found to be functioning at a low level. The evaluators recommended that Rudy stay in a regular classroom and that he be tested later for giftedness.

Sylvia was the co-teacher of George, Dan, and Rudy. Although she also described the children using emotional factors, she offered different perspectives than Raymond did. She did not believe that George had emotional problems; however, in her description of the children, she described George as passive-aggressive. She said that he seldom asked questions or smiled and he was not a risk taker; he did not want to be wrong, and he liked to be in control. Sylvia felt that Rudy was appropriately placed in a regular classroom, but added that she was concerned about his social skills because he was unhappy and always arguing with his classmates, behavior that affected his school work. Felipe and Maria were described by Sylvia very positively, and she thought they were appropriately placed in her classroom.

Julia felt that Hector was appropriately placed in her classroom. She described him as lazy, passive-aggressive, a follower, having good spatial perception skills, and doing only the minimum required. She stated that Hector had problems verbalizing his thoughts and communicating his ideas. Mildred, co-teaching with Julia, described Hector somewhat differently: she said he was a sneaky, power hungry, and competitive boy, who was making no effort to learn. Mildred believed that Hector could benefit from being placed in a regular classroom the next year; however, she stated that it needed to be a challenging environment. Although Hector was found to be a quick thinker and tuned into contextual cues by the QUEST evaluators, he was brief with his answers and did only the minimum when working on the tasks. Hector was not recommend for a gifted program but for an enriched environment by QUEST evaluators.

Monica believed that three of the children were appropriately placed in her classroom. She did not think that Carlos was placed appropriately because he did not finish his work, gave up too soon, was clumsy, and was a loner. Monica focused on Carlos's behavioral problems. However, she also reported that Carlos had a lot of prior knowledge that he brought to class, a description that coincided with the QUEST report. The QUEST evaluators did not mention behavioral problems, but they reported that Carlos used prior knowledge he had learned from television about animals.

Conclusions for the Third Research Question. The comparison of the Teacher's Language Proficiency Ratings of English and Spanish with the LAS scores has been helpful for viewing the congruency of the outcomes when placing language-minority children. The findings show that teachers can use alternative instruments to measure the children's language proficiency levels. In addition, there was a close connection between the teachers' and the QUEST evaluators' descriptions and recommendations, indicating external predictive validity for QUEST diagnoses.

Conclusions

Based on the findings of this study, in relation to the first research question, it can be concluded that the personal linguistic and cultural backgrounds of teachers influence their theoretical beliefs systems about how language-minority children develop cognitively and linguistically. Teachers with a minority cultural and linguistic background, similar to the language-minority Hispanic children they were teaching, tended to support environmental intelligence theories more strongly than majority teachers did. The minority teachers acknowledged the influence of culture and language on cognitive development, while the majority teachers endorsed innate intelligence theories. In addition, although both minority and majority teachers supported environmental theories when explaining first and second language development, minority teachers tended to adapt the content and language of instructional materials and curriculum more often in their practice of teaching language-minority children than did majority teachers.

Regarding the second research question, results show a consistent relationship between the beliefs that teachers articulated during the interviews and their actual behaviors, observed in their instructional practices. In addition, two other patterns were found. First, majority and minority teachers with little or no Spanish background were found not to adapt their instructional materials and curriculum to the individual needs of culturally and linguistically diverse children. That is, for most teachers, their Spanish background, and not their ethnic or cultural background, seemed to have more influence on their teaching behaviors than the intelligence and language theories that they endorsed. Second, when asked how they contributed to teaching language-minority children, only the teachers more closely connected with the Hispanic culture perceived their cultural and linguistic personal backgrounds as influencing positively the way they taught.

In relation to the third research question, findings show a coincidence between teachers' recommendations and ratings of children's cognitive and linguistic abilities and the diagnoses obtained with QUEST. These findings reveal that QUEST has predictive external validity for placing language-minority children in either regular or gifted bilingual classrooms. These results also show that the teachers' ratings and the QUEST can be valuable alternative measures for evaluating the academic progress of language-minority children and placing them. In addition, the teachers' ratings of the children's language proficiency were congruent with the children's LAS scores, showing that teachers can use both instruments to measure language-minority children's Spanish and English proficiency levels.

This study did have limitations. The first was that the interview questions were not administered in the exact order as designed to be given, which could affect one content of information conveyed by subjects. The changes were made because the interviewer wanted to follow the interviewee's train of thought. However, in an effort to maintain the same order across subjects, the data obtained from the interviews were reorganized in the data analysis process. This change of order of administration did not affect the accuracy of the information or the content and meaning conveyed by the subjects. A second limitation pertains to the teacher's interview measure. The original purpose of the interview was to obtain specific information about the teachers' theoretical belief systems. However, the interview served as a counseling session for the interviewees, who appeared to be in need of expressing their feelings and thoughts on different psychological aspects of the children they were teaching.

A third limitation of this study involves the coding categories of the teachers' and children's classroom observations. The design for coding the observation categories was operationally defined using only nominal categories—criteria that could not be easily interpreted by other judges. In a future study, these categories need to be redefined using duration, latency, frequency, or degree of occurrences criteria. However, in this study it was possible to use number of occurrences for ensuring reliability between judges, since the study was interested only in whether behaviors were occurring. A fourth limitation of this study involved the number of subjects; the sample was too small to make any generalizations. In a future study, more subjects, teachers and children, will be needed for conducting statistical analyses.

REFERENCES

BACA, L. M., & CERVANTES, H. T. (1989). *The bilingual special education interface*. New York: Merrill.

BAKER, C. (1992). Attitudes and language. In L. M. Malave & G. Duquette (Eds.), *Language, culture, and cognition* (pp. 22–47). Clevedon, England: Multilingual Matters.

BANKS, J. A., & MCGEE BANKS, C. A. (1993). *Multi-cultural education issues and perspectives* (2nd ed.). Needham Heights, MA: Allyn and Bacon.

BIALYSTOK, E. (1990). The competence of processing: Classifying theories of second language acquisition. *TESOL Quarterly, 24*(4), 635–649.

DAMICO, J. S. (1991). Descriptive assessment of communicative ability in limited English proficient students. In E. V. Hamayan & J. S. Damico (Eds.), *Limiting bias in the assessment of bilingual students* (pp. 115–217) Austin, TX: Pro-Ed.

DE AVILA, E. A., & DUNCAN, S. E. (1987). *The Language Assessment Scales*. Monterey, CA: McGraw-Hill.

FRASIER, M. M. (1987). The identification of gifted black students: Developing new perspectives. *Journal of the Education of the Gifted, 10*(3), 155–180.

FRENCH, R. L. (1992). Portfolio assessment and LEP students. In *Proceedings of the Second National Research Symposium on LEP Students Issues: Focus on evaluation and measurement 1* (pp. 249–272). Washington, DC: U.S. Department of Education.

GARDNER, R. C., LALONDE R. N., & PIERSON, R. (1983). The socio-educational model of second language acquisition: An investigation using Lisrel causal model. *Journal of Language and Social Psychology, 2*(1), 1–14.

GONZALEZ, V. (1991). *A model of cognitive, cultural, and linguistic variables affecting bilingual Spanish/English children's development of concepts and language.* Doctoral dissertation, University of Texas at Austin. (ERIC Document Reproduction Service No. ED 345 562)

GONZALEZ, V. (1993). Special voices. *NABE NEWS, 16*(6), 23–26.

GONZALEZ, V. (1994a). The assessment of language-minority students: A critical discussion of models and approaches. *NABE NEWS, 17*(8), 5–6, 38.

GONZALEZ, V. (1994b). *Taking the risk to change schools from within: Educators' cognitive growth through multicultural education.* Paper presented at the American Educational Research Association 1994 Annual Meeting, New Orleans, LA.

GONZALEZ, V. (1995). *Cognition, culture, and language in bilingual children: Conceptual and semantic development.* Bethesda, MD: Austin & Winfield.

GONZALEZ, V., BAUERLE, P., & FELIX-HOLT, M. (1994). A qualitative assessment method for accurately diagnosing bilingual gifted children. *NABE '92–'93 Annual Conference Journal* (pp. 37–52). Washington, DC: NABE.

GONZALEZ, V., BAUERLE, P., & FELIX-HOLT, M. (1996). Theoretical and practical implications of assessing cognitive and language development in bilingual children with qualitative methods. *Bilingual Research Journal, 20*(1), 93–131.

GONZALEZ, V., & YAWKEY, T. D. (1993). The assessment of culturally and linguistically diverse students: Celebrating change. *Educational Horizons, 73*(1), 41–49.

HADAWAY, N., & MAREK-SCHOROER, M. F. (1992). Multidimensional assessment of the gifted minority students. *Roeper Review*, 73–77.

HAMAYAN E. V., & DAMICO, J. S. (1991). Developing and using a second language to explain language theories. In E. V. Hamayan & J. S. Damico (Eds.), *Limiting bias in the assessment of bilingual students* (pp. 39–76). Austin, TX: Pro-Ed.

HAMERS, J. F., & BLANC, M. (1982). Towards a social-psychological model of bilingual development. *Journal of Language and Social Psychology, 1*(1), 29–49.

KAUFMAN, A. S., & KAUFMAN, N. L. (1983). *K-ABC: Kaufman Assessment Battery for Children.* Circle Pines, MN: American Guidance Service.

MARQUEZ, J. A. (1992). Incorporating community perceptions in the identification of gifted and talented Hispanic students. *Journal of Educational Issues of Language-Minority Students, 10*, 117–127.

MOSS, P. A. (1992). Shifting conceptions of validity in education measurement: Implications for performance assessment. *Review of Educational Research, 62*(3), 229–258.

OLLER, J. W. (1991). Language testing research: Lessons applied to LEP students and programs. In *Proceedings of the First Research Symposium of Limited English Proficient Students' Issues: Focus on Evaluation and Measurement.* Washington, DC: U.S. Department of Education

OLLER, J. W., & PERKINS, K. (1978). *Language and education: Testing the test.* Rowley, MA: Newbury House.

PLATA, M. (1986). Factors affecting the assessment of bilingual pupils. *Journal of Instructional Psychology, 13*(3), 122–130.

REYNOLDS, E. C., & KAMPHAUS, R. W. (1990). *Handbook of psychological and educational assessment of children's intelligence and achievement.* Needham Heights, MA: Allyn and Bacon.

SANTOS DE BARONA, M., & BARONA, A. (1991). Assessment of culturally and linguistically different preschoolers. *Early Childhood Research Quarterly, 6*(36), 363–376.

SHAKLEE, B. D. (1992). Identification of young gifted students. *Journal for the Education of the Gifted, 15*(2), 134–144.

SMITH, J., LA ROSA, B., & CLASEN, R. (1991). Underrepresentation of minority students in gifted programs: Yes! It matters! *Gifted Child Quarterly, 35*(2), 81–83.

SNOW, C. E. (1992). Perspectives on second-language development: Implications for bilingual education. *Educational Research, 21*(2), 15–19.

STERNBERG, R. J. (1991). *Metaphors of mind.* Cambridge: Cambridge University Press.

THORNDIKE, R. L., HAGEN, E. P., & SATTLER, J. M. (1986a). *Guide for administering and scoring the Stanford-Binet Intelligence Scale* (4th ed.). Chicago: Riverside.

THORNDIKE, R. L., HAGEN, E. P., & SATTLER, J. M. (1986b). *Technical manual of the Standford-Binet Intelligence Scale* (4th ed.). Chicago: Riverside.

TRUEBA, H. T. (1991). Learning needs of minority children: Contributions of ethnography to educational research. In L. M. Malave & G. Duquettte (Eds.), *Language, cultural and cognition* (pp. 137–158). Clevedon, England: Multilingual Matters.

WECHSLER, D. (1991). *Manual for the Wechsler Intelligence Scale for Children* (3rd ed.). San Antonio, TX: Psychological Corporation.

YAWKEY, T. D., & JUAN, Y. (1993). Linking assessment and instruction: Extending the match. *NABE News, 17*(3), 9, 18, 34.

YIN, R. K. (1994). *Case study research: Design and methods* (2nd ed.). Thousand Oaks, CA: Sage.

APPENDIX 7A: TEACHERS' INTERVIEW QUESTIONS

A. Personal Background

1. Are you bilingual and/or bicultural? (Please explain.)
2. What is your cultural and linguistic background?
3. What is your experience with language-minority children?

B. Theories of Intelligence and Language Development

1. According to your view, how does intelligence develop?
   Follow with: How does intelligence develop in language minority children?
2. According to your view, how does language develop?
   Follow up with: How does language develop in language-minority children?
3a. Please give an example of how you teach reading.
3b. Do you adapt your teaching of reading (instructional model) for language-minority children?
3c. Do you or the children use Spanish in the classroom in the reading class?
4a. How do you teach math?
4b. Do you adapt your teaching of math (instructional model) for language-minority children?
4c. Do you or the children use Spanish in the classroom in the math class?

C. Traditional and Alternative Models for Assessment

1. Based on your experience, what do you think about standardized testing for identifying gifted language-minority children?
2. Based on your experience, what do you think about alternative assessment methods for identifying gifted language-minority children?
3. Do you think that both standardized and alternative methods or just one method should be used?

D. Methods of Instruction

1. What content areas did you teach this year?
2. What are the methods (instructions, tools, tests) you use to assess a child's cognitive and language development?
3. How do you think your personal background or experience has influenced the way you teach language-minority children?
4. When language-minority children have learning problems in the classroom, what do you think the cause is?

E. Personal Perspectives on the Children Placed

1. [Name of child] was placed into your classroom. Do you think that he/she was accurately placed into your classroom? Why do you think this?
2. Can you describe the child's cognitive and linguistic abilities?
3. Based on developmental norms, how do you think this child compares to the other children in the classroom?
4. Any other concerns or differences compared to others in his/her classroom?
5. Can you describe and compare the child's achievement at the beginning of the year compared to the end of the year?
6. What would you recommend for this child for the next academic school year?

Appendix 7B: Categories for Coding Teachers' Responses to Interview Questions

Category A: Personal Background

A. Bilingualism
   1. Teacher considered self bilingual. The teacher speaks two languages fluently.
   2. Teacher does not consider self bilingual.
B. Biculturalism
   1. Teacher considers self bicultural because of own personal background. The teacher had lived in two cultures. The teacher identified self as being part of an ethnic group.
   2. Teacher does not consider self bicultural (e.g., considers self as only white).
C. Experience teaching minority children
   1. The teacher has extensive teaching experience with language-minority children.
   2. No experience or minimal experience teaching language-minority children.
   3. Teacher reports having taken courses for teaching language-minority children (e.g., English as a Second Language and multicultural education).

Category B: Theories of Intelligence and Language Development

A. Perspectives on intelligence development
   1. Environmental factors, external explanations. The teacher described environmental factors and external stimulation as theories of intelligence.
   2. The teacher described innate theories of intelligence using internal factors influencing intelligence.
   3. Both external and internal were used by the teacher for describing the development of intelligence.
B. Similarities and differences in intelligence development
   1. The teacher believes that intelligence develops differently for language-minority children.
   2. The teacher believes that the development of intelligence is similar in language-minority and -majority monolingual children.
   3. The teacher discussed both similarities and differences between language-minority and -majority monolingual children.
C. Perspectives on theories of language development
   1. The teacher described environmental and external stimulation as influencing language development.
   2. The teacher described innate theories of language development (i.e., internal factors, being born with the ability for language).
   3. The teacher described both environmental and innate theories of language (i.e., external and internal factors).
D. Similarities and differences of language development
   1. The teacher believes that language development is different for language-minority children in comparison to majority monolingual children.
   2. The teacher believes that language development is similar for language-minority and -majority monolingual children.
   3. The teacher discussed both similarities and differences between language-minority and -majority monolingual children.

    E. First and second content areas
        1. Teacher presents content in choral activity.
        2. Teacher uses problem-solving strategies.
        3. Teacher uses cognitive approaches.
        4. Teachers uses large group.
        5. Teacher uses small group.
        6. Teacher discusses the relationship between home and school.
        7. The teacher talked about using individualized instruction. The teacher describes self as being flexible for meeting the individual needs of the children.
        8. Teacher is co-teaching.
        9. Teachers uses language arts and whole language for instruction.
        10. Teacher draws on the child's experiences.
        11. Teacher recognizes the interaction of culture, cognition, and language.
    F. Adaptation of instruction
        1. The teachers discussed adapting instructional strategies for language minorities.
        2. The teacher does not discuss adapting instructional strategies for language-minority children.
    G. Use of Spanish in the classroom
        1. The teacher does not discuss the use of Spanish in the classroom.
        2. The teacher discussed using Spanish a large portion of the time.

Category C: Alternative versus Traditional Models for Assessment

   A. Perspectives on standardized tests
        1. The teacher supports standardized tests for assessing cognitive and language development in language-minority children.
        2. The teacher is not in support of standardized tests for assessing cognitive and language development in language-minority children because they are biased or unfair, and not valid and reliable.
   B. Perspectives on alternative assessment
        1. The teacher is in favor of using alternative assessment to assess language-minority children.
        2. The teacher is not in favor of alternative assessment for language-minority children.
   C. Support of both standardized and alternative assessment
        1. The teacher supports both alternative and standardized tests for assessing language-minority children.

Category D: Method of Instruction

   A. Content area taught this year
        1. Focus is on math, reading, and writing.
        2. Focus is on language arts and whole language.
   B. Teacher's assessment strategies of cognitive and language development
        1. The teacher described using personal assessment procedures (e.g., multiple informants, and observing children in problem-solving situations for assessing their skills, talents, and abilities, etc.).
        2. The teacher described using standardized methods for assessing children.
        3. The teacher described using both qualitative and standardized methods for assessing children.

C. Personal background influencing teaching
   1. The teacher felt that her/his personal background has an influence on her/his teaching. The teacher views self as a role model, feels he/she is making a personal contribution. For example, own culture is similar to language-minority children's, knowing children's first language, having personal experience with language-minority children, and growing up in the neighborhood or similar communities.
   2. The teacher does not feel he or she is contributing to teaching language-minority children.
   3. The teacher explained other reasons for her views of how she/he contributed to the education of language-minority children.
D. Learning problems
   1. Teacher discussed internal reasons for learning problems of language-minority children.
   2. Teacher discussed external reasons for learning problems of language-minority children.
   3. The teacher discussed both external and internal reasons for learning problems of language-minority children.

Category E: Teacher's Perceptions, Recommendations, and Placement

A. Accurate placement
   1. Yes.
   2. No.
   3. Has mixed feelings.
B. Child's behavior described by the teacher
   1. Cognitive descriptions. The teacher described the child's talents and abilities through academic descriptions (e.g., above grade average, curious, likes to look at detail, likes to read, strength in math, etc.).
   2. The teacher described the child's talents and abilities through other behaviors (e.g., has strengths in sports, enjoys drawing, has good coordination, etc.). Teacher described intrapersonal abilities (e.g., self-confident, leader, mature, independent, good socialization skills, good attitudes toward learning, etc.).
   3. Behavioral problems described. The teacher described the child's personal and environmental problems (e.g., comes from a single-parent family, parents are not well adjusted, child has no encouragement at home, has attention deficit, has emotional and medical problems, is defiant and spoiled, etc.).
C. Potential compared to others
   1. The teacher views the child as not working at full potential and is doing the minimum.
   2. The teacher views the child as working at full potential, above average in academic or other developmental areas.
   3. Child is at about the level of others in his/her age group.
   4. Child is below other children in his/her age group.
D. School achievement
   1. The teacher described the child as improving academic, language, or social abilities from the beginning of the year. The teacher views the child as above average.

    2. The teacher does not feel the child has made any improvements in any areas since the beginning of the year. The teacher views the child as below average.
  E. Teacher's recommendations and concerns
    1. The teacher is concerned about academic problems. The teacher has made recommendations for remedial instruction in reading stimulation, a different curriculum, other academic help, or a more challenging environment, etc.
  F. Placement recommendation
    1. Regular (English) second grade.
    2. Regular (bilingual) second grade.
    3. Summer program.
    4. Gifted and talented education (GATE) program.
    5. Gifted program (GATE), on probation.
    6. Discontinue gifted program.
    7. Special education program.
    8. Other recommendations.

APPENDIX 7C: SUMMARIES OF FINDINGS FOR DIFFERENT SUBJECTS

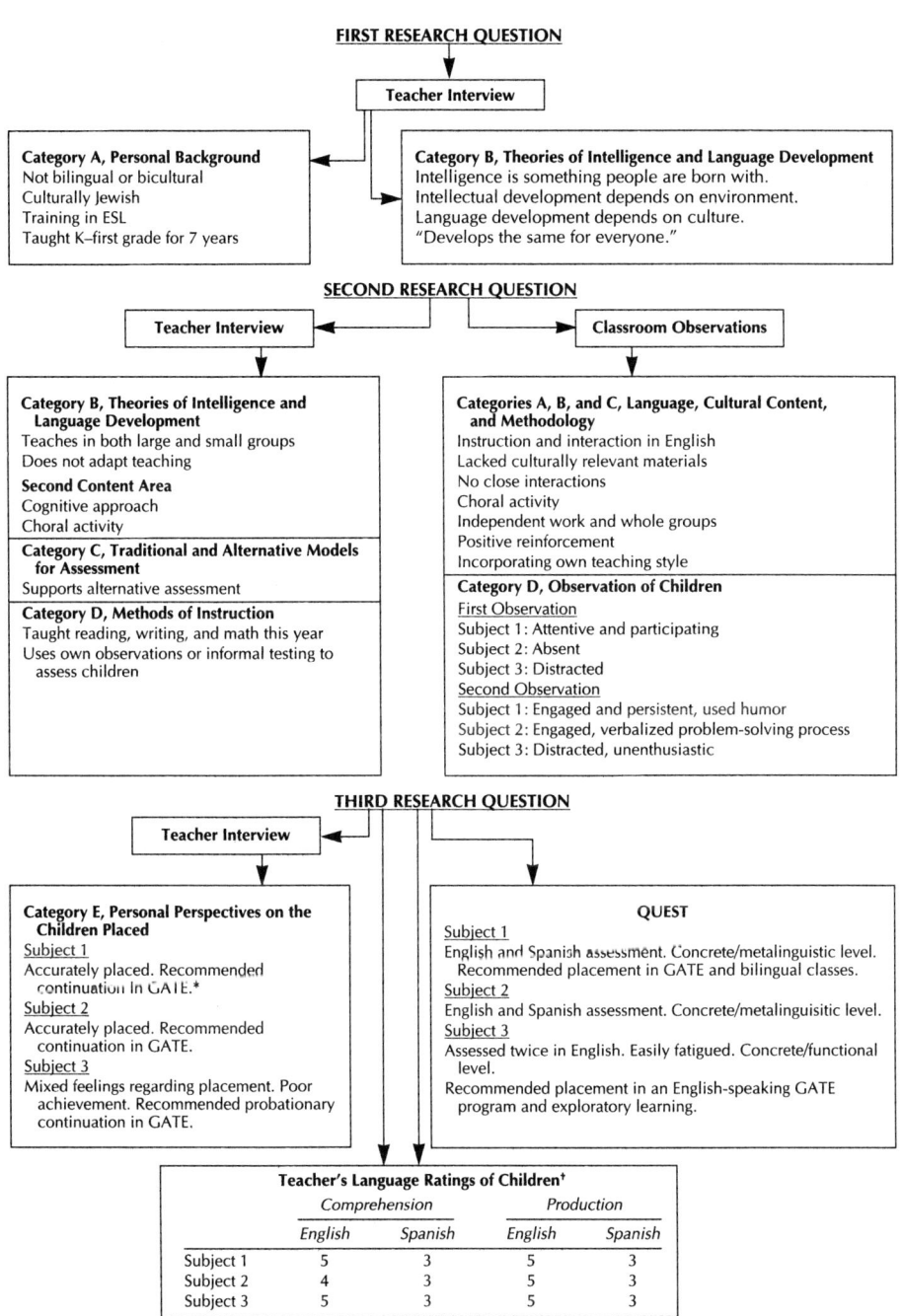

FIGURE 7.3   Summary of findings for Marcy.

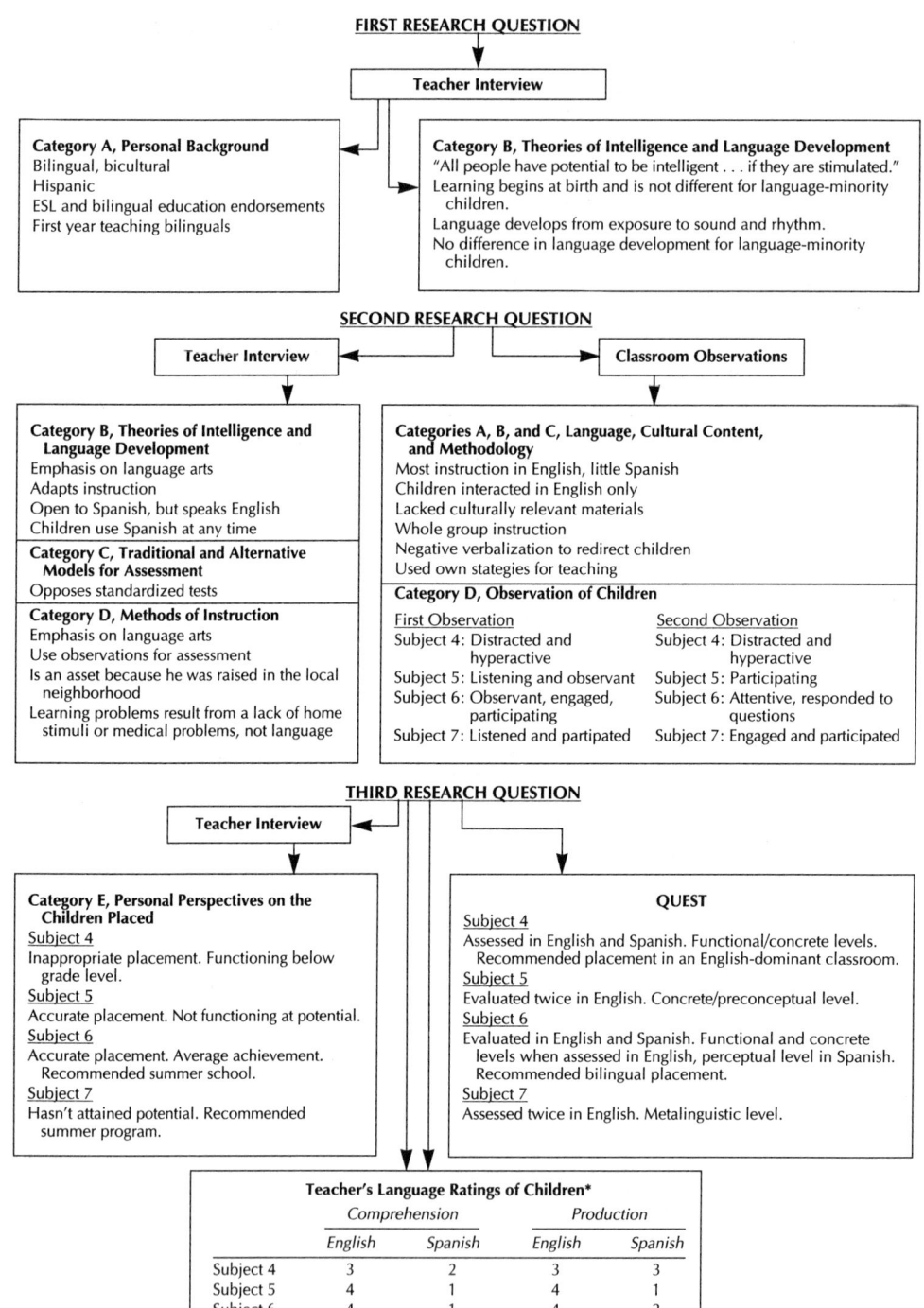

FIGURE 7.4 Summary of findings for Raymond.

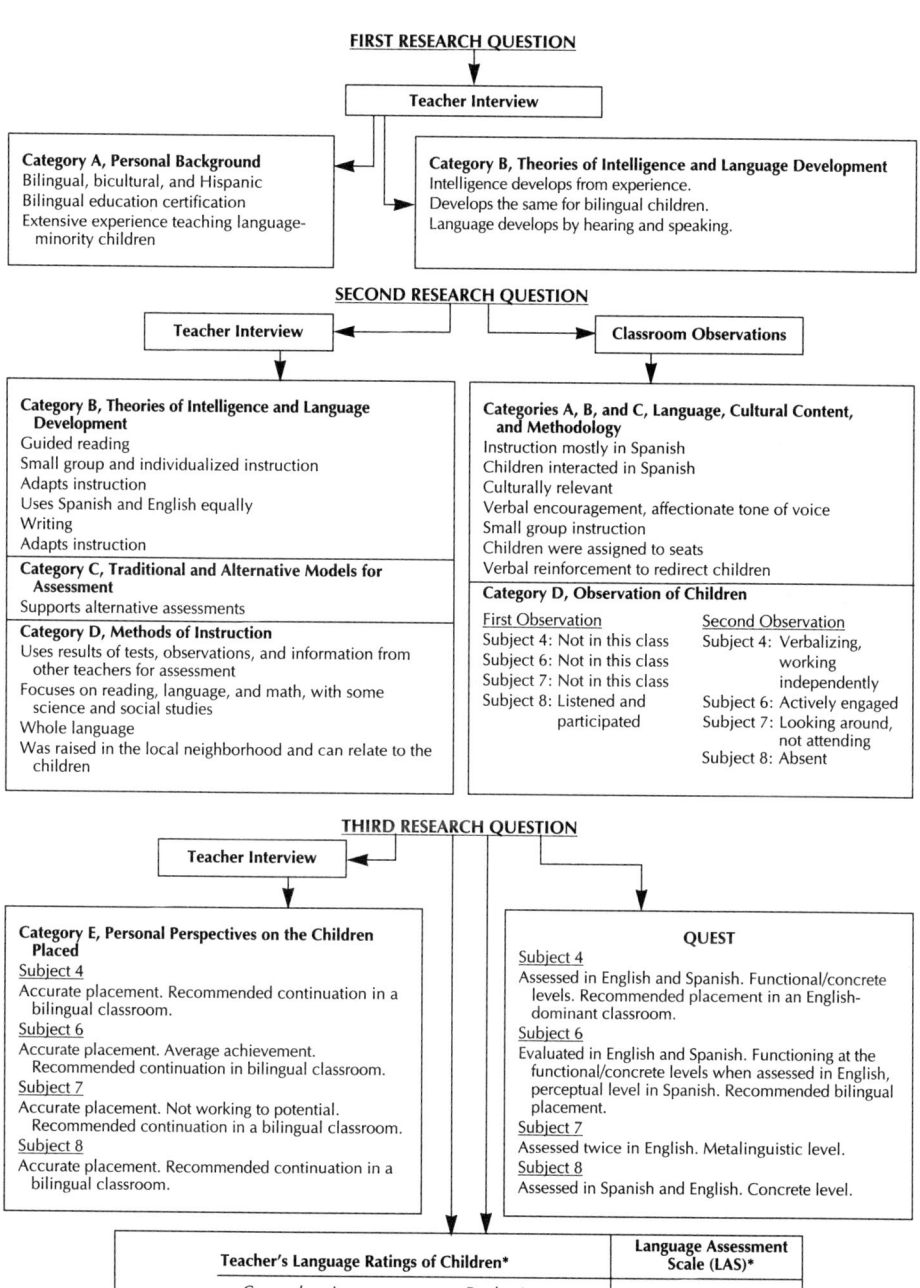

FIGURE 7.5   Summary of findings for Sylvia.

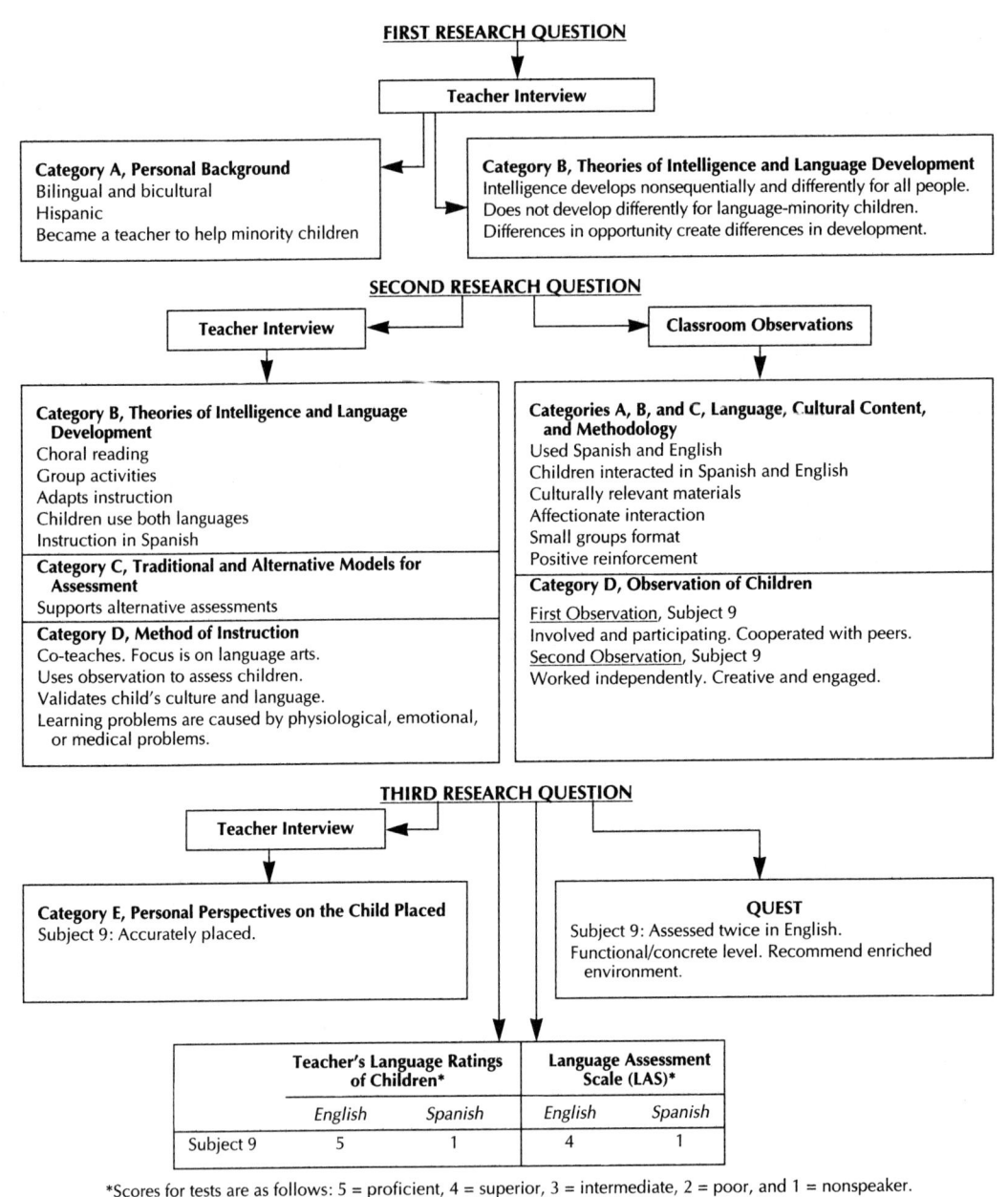

FIGURE 7.6   Summary of findings for Julia.

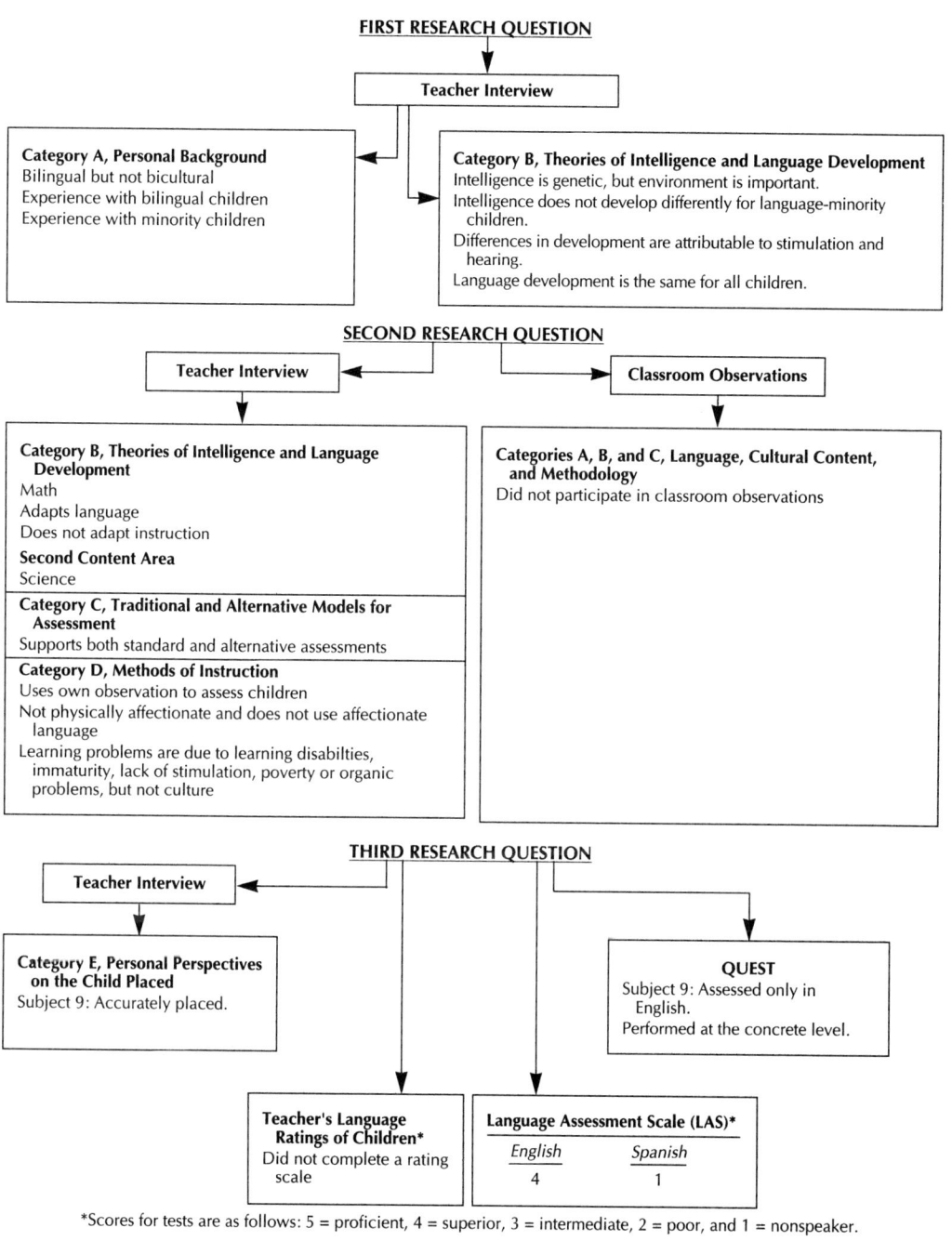

FIGURE 7.7   Summary of findings for Mildred.

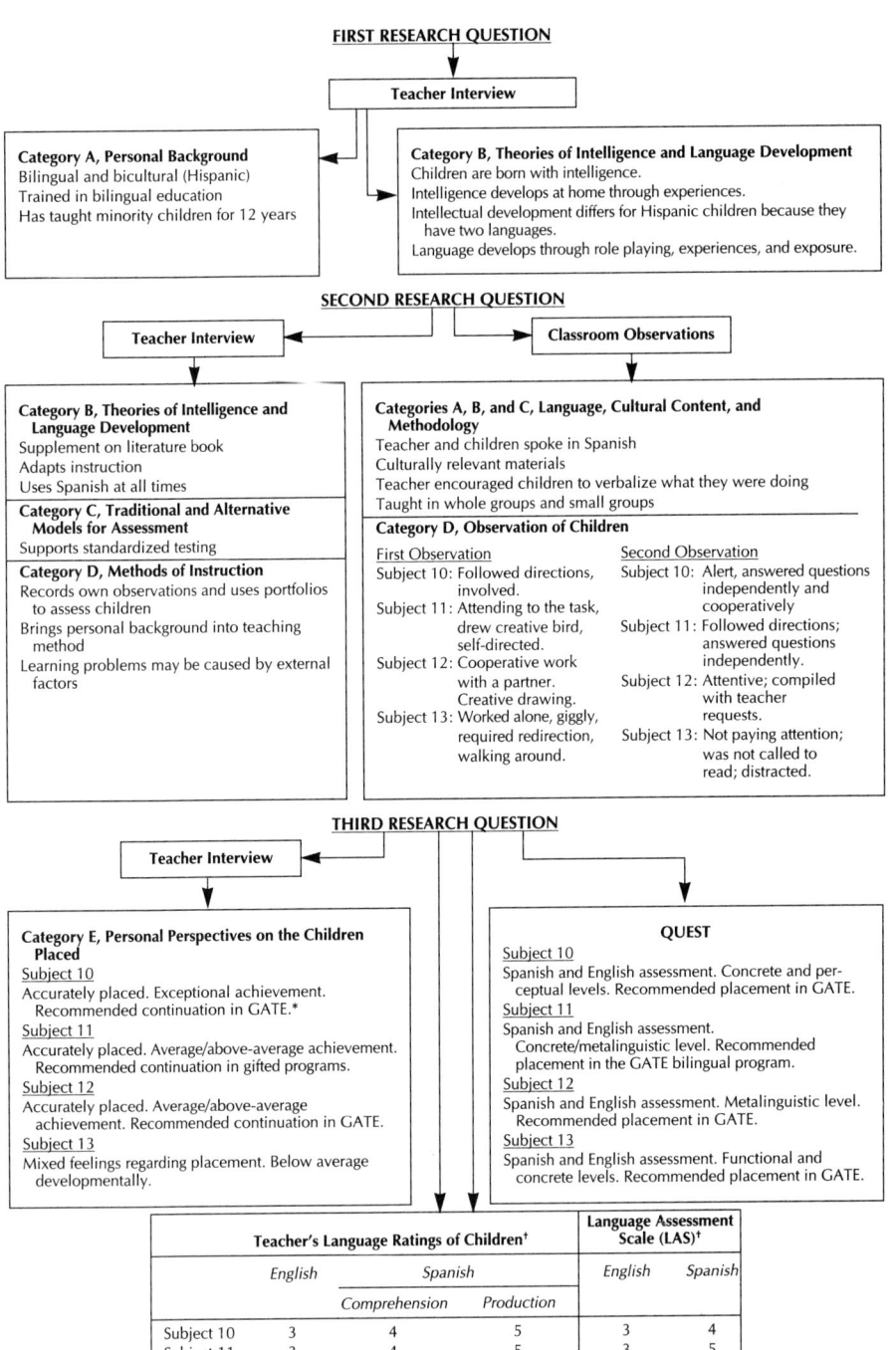

FIGURE 7.8　　Summary of findings for Monica.

CHAPTER 8

Standardized and Alternative Assessments: Diagnosis Accuracy in Minority Children Referred for Special Education Assessment

M. Dynah Oviedo and Virginia Gonzalez

CHAPTER 8 DEALS WITH THE PROBLEMATIC ISSUE OF DIFFERENTIALLY DIagnosing normal second language learning from genuine disabling conditions or disabilities in young minority children. It thus addresses the third and fourth themes of the book: the need to represent the minority perspective in multiple measures of cognition and language in bilinguals. It also addresses the fifth and sixth themes of the book: the need to include in the construct validity of measures of bilinguals the subjectivity and responsibility of evaluators to assume an advocacy role. In addition, the study presented in this chapter highlights the major theme of the book: the sociocultural context for assessment and providing a socioeducational framework to view evaluation.

STUDY OVERVIEW

The purpose of this exploratory study was to examine the concurrent validity of the diagnoses derived for four minority children (two Mexican-Americans and two Native Americans) from standardized measures, such as the Kaufman Assessment Battery for Children (Kaufman & Kaufman, 1983a, b), the Woodcock-Johnson Psycho-Educational Battery–Revised (Woodcock & Johnson, 1989), and the Wechsler Intelligence Scale for Children–Third Edition (WISC, Wechsler, 1991); and alternative measures, including classroom observations, teachers' surveys, and the Qualitative Use of English and Spanish Tasks (QUEST; Gonzalez, 1991, 1994). In addition, the minority children's performance on verbal, nonverbal, and achievement sections of the measures administered was examined. Classroom observations were conducted and developmental histories of the children were reviewed. These children were from low socioeconomic backgrounds and had been referred by their teachers because of difficulties in reading, writing, and math.

The study addressed the following research questions:

1. Are different or similar diagnoses obtained for the same minority child when standardized and alternative measures are administered?
2. What are the patterns of performance among the minority children on the verbal, nonverbal, and achievement sections of the standardized and alternative measures administered?

STATEMENT OF THE PROBLEM

The misdiagnosis and inappropriate placement of a large proportion of minority children in special education classes has resulted in serious consequences for these children, and for the educators serving them as well. Misdiagnosed children have been denied education that would have allowed them an improved chance to succeed in school. In addition, a tremendous demand has been placed on educators and schools to provide a proper education to the children, and resources such as time and money have been improperly used. Shepard and Smith (1983) reported that 50 percent of the funds allocated to learning disabled students in their study were spent on identifying the children.

To avoid these problems, novel practices for assessment must be developed and validated. Additional research pertaining to the advancement of alternative measures and models for accurately assessing and diagnosing minority children is greatly needed. Such research could lead to the development of methods for improving the state of assessment practices for minority children. Harnisch and Mabry (1993) reported that concerns regarding the detrimental effects of testing have focused attention on alternative assessment. In addition, they stated, research investigating alternative assessment has the capability of significantly improving teaching practices and assisting decision makers.

Because of the continued use of standardized tests, some educators have viewed these tests as an acceptable and efficient way to identify exceptional children, but they are wrong. As illustrated by the overrepresentation of minorities in special education programs, standardized tests have not been consistent in correctly identifying learning disabled minority children. Clearly, the demand for new measures that can accurately identify children in need of special education services is pressing. Inadequate assessment measures and practices have led researchers to develop alternative measures designed to distinguish minority children who have real learning disabilities from those who do not, thereby reducing the high number of false-positive diagnoses obtained by using standardized tests. Alternative assessment measures typically acknowledge the interaction of internal and external factors as they influence development (Gonzalez & Yawkey, 1993). An example of an alternative measure that may help to reduce the number of false-positive diagnoses among minority children, is the Qualitative Use of English and Spanish Tasks developed by Virginia Gonzalez (QUEST, 1991, 1994). QUEST takes into account the linguistic, cognitive, and cultural development of minority children. This measure has proved to be effective for providing an accurate differential diagnosis among culturally diverse children who have a genuine learning disability, those who are gifted, and those who are typical second language learners (Gonzalez, Bauerle, & Felix-Holt, 1994a).

The study reported in this chapter has important implications for improved practices and measures that will accurately identify learning disabled minority children. Accurate identification may decrease the amount of time and money improperly spent on minority children who could benefit from regular classroom instruction. Improved practices and measures may also decrease the number of misdiagnosed minority children, thus increasing their chances for success in the mainstream education system.

Assessment Model

The "ethnic researcher" model, the theoretical framework used in this study, postulates that development is the result of the interaction of internal and external factors (Gonzalez & Yawkey, 1993; Gonzalez, Brusca-Vega, & Yawkey, 1997). In this model, assessment is believed to be more appropriate when it is conducted using qualitative measures and knowledgeable evaluators who recognize and honor different cultures. The model accepts the use of standardized tests for fulfilling legal requirements and the accountability needs of school districts but notes that the interpretation of the scores obtained from these tests takes into account the existence of differences between minority and majority children. It also recognizes that the constructs measured by tests of cognitive development are socially constructed (Gonzalez & Yawkey, 1993; Gonzalez, Brusca-Vega, & Yawkey, 1997). Adherents of the ethnic researcher model are aware of differences from the norm; however, these differences are often viewed not as problems but as insights into the learning process of culturally diverse children. This model maintains that the differences between minority and majority children should not be viewed as abnormalities within the minority child.

Literature Review

The American education system has supported the use of standardized measures to assess the cognitive and linguistic abilities of children for countless years. Recently Medina and Neill (1990) noted that standardized testing dominates education in the United States, in spite of the fact that frequently these tests are not appropriate for some children. They noted that standardized tests are often biased, and when they are administered to low-income, female, and minority students, the results rendered are often incorrect and contradictory.

The minority population in the United States is growing. Hodgkinson (1992) analyzed information from the U.S. Census Bureau and reported that by the year 2010, minorities will make up more than half of the nation's population. In fact, not that long ago, in 1988, Anglos were the minority in certain California schools (Mitchell, 1992).

The continued use of standardized tests to identify potentially learning disabled minority school children, compounded by the continued rapid growth of minorities in the United States, will most likely result in an escalation of the proportion of minority children incorrectly placed in special education classes. Witt, Elliott, Kramer, and Gresham (1994) noted that with the increasing number of children from diverse cultures and environments, the task of a purposeful and objective assessment will be a constant challenge for professionals.

The following literature review underscores the need to investigate the measures used for assessing minority children, as well as the disproportionate number of minority children placed in special education classes. It discusses factors that may influence minority children during assessment and the placement decisions made. It begins with a brief history of the overrepresentation of minority children in special education classes, discusses assessing and diagnosing minority children with standardized and alternative measures, examines the examiner's influence on the assessment process, and addresses the role of teachers in the assessment process. The review shows problems with the measures used to assess minority children, and also pinpoints challenges for the evaluators and teachers of minority children.

Demographic Overview of Minority Children in Special Education

The overrepresentation of minority children in special education classes was revealed more than 25 years ago. In 1968, Dunn reported figures from the U.S. Office of Education disclosing that one-third of all special educators in the nation taught in classes for students with mental retardation. Dunn indicated that 60 to 80 percent of the students taught by these special educators were of African-American, Native American, Mexican-American, or Puerto Rican–American descent. Dunn also stated that the educational capability of these children was usually measured by school psychologists who administered a psychometric battery, for the sole purpose of finding out what was wrong with a child.

Literature in the 1970s continued to report a disproportionate number of minority children placed in special education classes. For instance, Mercer

(1973), in a study of children from Riverside, California, Public Schools, reported that the rates of placement in special education classes for African-American and Mexican-American pupils were three and four times greater, respectively, than would be expected from any random sample of the population. Mercer, like Dunn, noted that the higher proportion of minority children in special education classes appeared to result from diagnoses that relied almost exclusively on IQ test scores.

During the 1970s lawsuits were filed on behalf of minority children, directed toward documenting the misuse of standardized tests and improving the assessment process for minority children. For instance, in the case of *Diana v. State Board of Education* (1970) a major charge was that the practice of administering standardized tests in English to Spanish-speaking children was unfair. The decision directed that tests be administered in a child's primary language and that the testing procedures for Mexican-American children must improve (Heller, Holtzman, & Messick, 1982).

In addition to efforts aimed at improving the assessment of minority children, legislation was passed to ensure that special education programs would be available to all who genuinely needed them. In 1975, Public Law 94-142, the Education for All Handicapped Children Act, was signed, guaranteeing the right of a free and appropriate education to all children with disabilities. One stipulation of the law stated that children must be educated in the least restricted environment, and an Individualized Education Program (IEP) must be devised and executed for all children with disabilities (Gollnick & Chinn, 1994).

In spite of the increased awareness of the overrepresentation of minority children enrolled in special education classes and efforts to remedy this problem, research studies in the 1980s continued to report similar findings. For instance, Ortiz and Yates (1983) found that Mexican-American children enrolled in Texas public schools were overrepresented in the category of learning disabled by 315 percent. In an analysis of data from the Office of Civil Rights Surveys covering 1978 to 1984, Chinn and Hughes (1987) reported that minority groups continued to be overrepresented in certain categories. For example, enrollment in classes for the learning disabled continued to be disproportionately high for Native American, Mexican-American, and African-American children. In addition, several researchers reported that minority children were underrepresented in classes for the gifted and talented (Ortiz & Yates, 1983; Chinn & Hughes, 1987).

By the 1990s the overrepresentation of minority children in special education classes was well documented, and legislation for individuals with disabilities expanded. In 1990, Congress revised Public Law 94-142 and named it the Individuals With Disabilities Education Act (IDEA, Gollnick & Chinn, 1994). This law guarantees the same rights as P.L. 94-142 to students with attention deficit disorders, autism, and traumatic brain injury (Gollnick & Chinn, 1994, p. 157).

In the 1990s, a new focus has become alternative assessment. Cizek (1993) asserted that alternative assessments are preferable to standardized tests. Researchers also declared that new assessment instruments, which accurately assess the potential and abilities of minority children, could not be developed until researchers understood the linguistic, cognitive, social, and emotional development of these children (Gonzalez & Yawkey, 1993).

The overrepresentation of minority children in special education classes continues to be a problem. Many researchers are also in disagreement about which measures, standardized or alternative, provide a more accurate view of the cognitive abilities of minority children.

Validity Issues in the Assessment and Diagnosis of Minority Children

The scrutiny surrounding the validity of standardized tests has consistently been an issue among researchers. Traditionally, validity has been separated into three categories: content, construct, and criterion related. The contemporary view, provided by Messick (1995), is that validity is not simply an aspect of the test or assessment but a meaning of the test scores. Furthermore, Messick stated, what must be valid is the interpretations and social consequences of the test scores or any form of assessment, such as observations or portfolios. Messick's view of validity is critical to children referred for special education evaluation because it encompasses the evaluator's interpretations. Gonzalez (1995) found that the evaluator's personality is the most influential factor in the assessment process. Gonzalez and Yawkey (1996) observed that definitions of validity can apply to alternative and qualitative measures because they include the impact of test use and interpretation in real life.

Major criticisms of standardized measures when assessing minority children have centered around inadequate norms, cultural bias, and improper translations of tests originally created in English. For instance, Medina and Neill (1990) reported that the norms of most standardized tests consisted of samples that were frequently comprised of only white, middle-class, mainstream children. These authors also noted that currently used tests have been normed on small populations, which do not represent the national population today.

The cultural bias of items and language used in standardized tests has been widely refuted. Critics of standardized tests have pointed out that many tests consist of competencies and information considered important by the majority culture (Bjorklund, 1995). Moreover, Bjorklund stated, many minority children do not have access to or value the same knowledge that majority children do, making the tests culturally biased. Similarly, Cummins (1991) stated that certain questions, such as, "Who discovered America?" typify mainstream knowledge that minority children may have not been exposed to.

Standardized tests have also been deemed as biased against minority children because of language requirements. For instance, many standardized tests require the use and knowledge of conventional English to render the definition of abstract words, sentence completion, and analogies (Samuda, 1991). Therefore, standardized tests are biased against children who do not speak, or have not yet mastered, the English language. Similarly, on tests that require a verbatim response, children who speak a different dialect are penalized for providing a similar translation but not repeating a sentence exactly (Banks & McGee Banks, 1993).

Consequently, the use of inadequately standardized instruments to assess the cognitive and linguistic abilities of minority children has resulted in their lower scores. Samuda (1991) stated, "As a group non-white students do not score as high as white students on standardized tests" (p. 17). Similarly, Bjorklund (1995) asserted, "Minority children in the U.S. invariably scored lower than white, middle-class children on standardized tests" (p. 374). The lower scores obtained by many minority children has resulted in the misplacement of many into special education programs.

In spite of these disturbing patterns, many authors have viewed standardized tests as useful tools for objectively measuring the cognitive and linguistic abilities of school children in the United States. For instance, Phillips (1982) noted that standardized tests are objective ways to discern whether certain goals and objectives have been accomplished. Phillips and other authors, however, have also warned that most concerns about standardized tests result from the misinterpretation of the test scores. For instance, Reschly (1981) explained that the psychometric properties of standardized tests have been consistently found to be unbiased against minority children, and the possible existing bias may be the result of the ways in which tests are used.

Alternative measures of cognitive and linguistic development have become a new focus in research and an innovative way of assessing minority children referred for special education evaluation. Alternative measures usually provide the evaluator with qualitative information about both the school performance and cognitive development of a child. Those based on the developmental model focus on the strategies and importance of following the thought processes of students (Gonzalez, 1993).

Alternative measures are typically used in conjunction with other measures to render a fuller picture of a child's current level of performance. When alternative measures are used with other measures, an ecological approach to assessment has been followed. Hamayan (1994) claimed that an assumption in ecological assessment is that evaluators learn not only about the child but also about instruction and the larger context in which the child functions.

Standardized and alternative measures of cognitive abilities provide distinct interpretations when used to assess and diagnose the abilities of minority children. Standardized measures provide an estimation of a child's development at a particular point in time. Alternative assessment measures appear to render a more complete estimation of a minority child's development because they are often used in combination with other methods and informants.

Evaluators' Influence on Assessment

The current view of validity highlights the interpretation of scores as the most consequential factor of validity. Considering that the scores obtained from administering assessment measures are interpreted by the evaluator, it is important to discuss some factors that may influence the testing situation and, thus, the interpretation of the scores derived.

Traditionally, standardized tests have been viewed as objective tools unaffected by the person who administered them. The contemporary view realizes that evaluators play an important role in the assessment process. For instance, Roth (cited by Gonzalez & Felix-Holt, 1995) stated that the condition prompted by the evaluation process influences the child's performance, and that the evaluator's values and actions will be related to the measurements selected and interpretations made. The study of evaluators' beliefs presented in Chapter 9 concluded that the cultural and linguistic backgrounds of evaluators influenced their beliefs and consequently the diagnoses and placement decisions made for language-minority children. Gonzalez (1995) asserted that the personality of the evaluator is the most influential factor in the assessment of minority children. The evaluator's values, beliefs, experience, and education will be reflected in the diagnosis and placement decisions regarding minority children referred for special education evaluation. When evaluators assess minority children, they need to be aware of their own characteristics that may influence the assessment process.

The gender of the evaluator has been found to be influential in the assessment process. For instance, Cieutat and Flick (1967) demonstrated that higher IQ scores were obtained when evaluators and students were of the opposite gender. In comparison, Pedersen, Shinedling, and Johnson (1968) stated that female and male children performed better on the Arithmetic subtest of the WISC when tested by female evaluators. Similarly, Quereshi (1968) found that female evaluators, as opposed to male evaluators, evoked more verbal responses and created a more positive testing environment when administering the WISC. Moreover, Back and Dana (1977) observed that young children obtained higher scores on the WISC when assessed by female rather than male evaluators.

The familiarity of the evaluator to the child in relation to test scores has also been examined. Fuchs, Fuchs, Dailey, and Power (1985) reported that disabled preschoolers performed better on IQ tests given by familiar evaluators. In a study of speech- and language-impaired preschoolers, Fuchs, Featherstone, Garwick, and Fuchs (1984) found that the children who were tested by a familiar evaluator performed better on test tasks. Stoneman and Gibson (1978) stated that developmentally disabled preschoolers performed better on motor skills when tested by a familiar evaluator. In a meta-analysis study of familiarity effects, Fuchs and Fuchs (1986) asserted that performance on tests was raised when a familiar evaluator administered them, especially when the tests were difficult and administered to low socioeconomic status (SES) children.

Because of their considerable influence, evaluators must become advocates for minority children. For instance, Damico and Hamayan (1991) have suggested that evaluators have a responsibility to ensure that misidentification does not occur, and they must execute changes to fulfill the needs of minority students referred for evaluation. These authors outlined strategies to develop an advocacy-oriented point of view and thus "decrease bias in the assessment process" (p. 24):

- Evaluators must acquire an advocacy-oriented role and become the main advocate for the student. They should always function with the students' best interest in mind.
- When recommending the use of alternative assessment measures, evaluators must attain endorsements from school administrators, other evaluators, and teachers.
- Evaluators must implement alternative assessment measures.

The research studies reviewed seem only to indicate that the assessment process is greatly influenced in many different ways by the evaluators' beliefs and practices. Evaluators need to be aware that they are the most influential part of the assessment process. They not only decide which measure to use in the assessment process; more important, they interpret the results.

Teachers' Influence on Assessment

A number of researchers have asserted that most referrals for special education evaluation are generated by classroom teachers (Gollnick & Chinn, 1994; Heller, Holtzman & Messick, 1982; Mercer, 1973). Consequently, teachers' backgrounds and classroom practices are instrumental in determining which pupils are in need of special services.

Frequently, teachers are from a culture different form that of their students, and this may often influence their perceptions of their students. Sherritt (1990) reported that many teachers who were trained in states with a low minority population are seeking employment in high-minority-population states. Furthermore, Sherritt reported that most states with a significant minority population do not require multicultural credentials. Therefore, the likelihood of teachers' possessing knowledge about the cognitive and linguistic development of the minority children they teach is slight. As Garcia and Garcia (1989) pointed out, most teachers who are responsible for educating minority children have not been especially trained for this demanding task. The discrepancy between the cultural backgrounds of teachers and students may cause the number of incorrect referrals to spiral, and thus increase the misidentification of minority children as learning disabled. Therefore, it is vital for teachers to understand the cultural background of their students.

Because teachers most often are the providers of referrals, they must realize that the judgments they make about their students greatly determine who will be assessed. They also need to realize that their teaching methods may influence each of their students in a different way; hence, teachers must view their students as individuals.

Teachers' referrals, however, are only the first step in the assessment process. After a child has been referred for special education evaluation, the evaluator's practices and beliefs will determine the outcome of the referral. For instance, the instruments the evaluator decides to use and the interpretation of the scores will rely solely on the knowledge and beliefs of the evaluator. Therefore, the assessment process appears to be an interaction of the teacher's and evaluator's knowledge and beliefs, the type of instrument used, and the child referred.

METHOD

Research Design

The design employed in this study was a multiple case, holistic, and embedded design (Yin, 1994). The data collected were examined in two ways. Individual case studies were used to compare the diagnoses obtained from standardized and alternative measures administered to the same child, and group data were analyzed to look for patterns in the performance of the children.

Several steps were taken to ensure the data quality of the case studies. To increase the reliability of the case study, a database was created and a chain of evidence was maintained (Yin, 1994). In addition, data and investigator triangulations entail using information gathered from multiple sources and assessment methods, which Yin suggested to increase the external and construct validity of the case study. Therefore, multiple case studies were included to increase external validity, and different measures of cognitive ability administered by different evaluators were included to increase construct validity.

Subjects

Four minority children referred for special education evaluation were the participants. The children attended elementary schools located in low socioeconomic neighborhoods in a medium-sized cosmopolitan area in the southwest region of the United States. The children's ages ranged from 7 to 9 years. Two were Native American (one boy and one girl) and two were Mexican-American (one boy and one girl). All children lived in blue-collar, two-parent households.

The criteria for sample selection were determined by a committee comprising educational psychology graduate students enrolled in a graduate seminar on the assessment of minority children at the University of Arizona; the second author, who was the professor of that seminar; and the director of exceptional education for the school district. Initially, 10 English-dominant children who were referred for special education evaluation by their classroom teachers and had parental permission were evaluated using QUEST (Gonzalez, 1991, 1994). They were evaluated by trained graduate students enrolled in the seminar, who also served as committee members. After the administration of QUEST, the committee convened to review and discuss the cases. The committee determined that six participants were in need of further evaluation. The four subjects of this study were selected from these six students on the basis of gender, ethnicity, and family structure in order to include two boys and two girls, and two Native American and two Mexican-American children, who lived in two-parent households.

Consent from the Human Subjects Committee at the University of Arizona and the school district was obtained prior to assessing all the children. In addition, parental permission was granted to review each child's case file. The files, which were compiled by various school district personnel (e.g., school psychologists and diagnosticians), included developmental history reports, social history updates, Individual Educational Programs (IEPs), and reports from previously administered standardized tests of cognitive development and achievement (the Woodcock-Johnson Psycho-Educational Battery–Revised, Woodcock & Johnson, 1989; and the Wechsler Intelligence Scale for Children–Third Edition, Wechsler, 1991). To ensure confidentiality, all irrelevant personal information such as home addresses and telephone numbers were deleted. In addition, pseudonyms were given to all the children to protect their identities.

Instruments

Three standardized measures were used in this study to assess the cognitive abilities of the minority participants: the Kaufman Assessment Battery for Children (K-ABC, Kaufman & Kaufman, 1983a, b), (2) the Wechsler Intelligence Scale for Children–Third Edition (WISC-III, Wechsler, 1991), and (3) the

Woodcock-Johnson Psycho-Educational Battery–Revised (WJ–R, Woodcock & Johnson, 1989). The alternative measures used in this study were QUEST (Gonzalez, 1991, 1994), classroom observations, and teachers' surveys.

Qualitative Use of English and Spanish Tasks (QUEST). QUEST (Gonzalez, 1991, 1994) is an individually administered alternative measure used to assess the cognitive abilities of minority children based on the ethnic researcher model. QUEST consists of plastic figures resembling animal and food objects that are used to demonstrate the verbal and nonverbal dimensions of children's cognitive development. The verbal tasks are labeling, defining, and verbal justification of sorting. The nonverbal tasks are sorting and category clue. Scoring for these five tasks is based on the following developmental stages: no classification, preoperational (perceptual and functional) concrete, and metalinguistic.

The content validity of QUEST was demonstrated by using judges and ensuring that the two forms of the measure were parallel (Gonzalez, 1991, 1994). Evidence of the concurrent validity and reliability of QUEST was demonstrated by using as predictors the IDEA Oral Proficiency Test (Ballard, Tighe, & Dalton, 1979), the Test of Non-Verbal Intelligence (TONI; Brown, Sherbenou, & Dollard, 1982), and the Teacher's Ratings and the Home Language Survey (Gonzalez, 1991, 1994). QUEST has also demonstrated accuracy in identifying culturally diverse children who have a genuine learning disability (Gonzalez et al., 1994a). (A more detailed description of QUEST can be found in Gonzalez, 1991, 1994; see also Chapters 4 and 6 of this book.)

Kaufman Assessment Battery for Children (K-ABC). The K-ABC (Kaufman & Kaufman, 1983a, b) was selected as the standardized measure used to assess the cognitive abilities of the minority children because it is viewed by many researchers as more appropriate for separating learning and cognitive potential. For instance, Valencia (1984), in a study of the concurrent validity of the K-ABC, stated that the measure appeared to be a valid for assessing Mexican-American preschoolers. Davidson (1992), in a study of gifted Native American children, stated that the K-ABC appeared to be culture fair when used to assess the group in her study.

The K-ABC was designed to assess the cognitive development and achievement of children ages $2\frac{1}{2}$ to $12\frac{1}{2}$ years. Kaufman and Kaufman (1983a, b) stated that the K-ABC is appropriate for the clinical assessment and psychoeducational evaluation of learning disabled, minority, and preschool children. The battery consists of 16 subtests, divided to provide five Global Scale scores: (1) Sequential Processing, (2) Simultaneous Processing, (3) Mental Processing Composite, (4) Achievement, and (5) Nonverbal. Depending on age, more or fewer subtests are administered. The Global Scales were designed to allow the examiner to compare the child's ability with the child's achievement. In addition, the Mental Processing Composite Global Scale combines the Sequential Processing and Simultaneous Processing Scales to provide a total estimate of a child's cognitive ability (Kaufman & Kaufman, 1983a, b). The Global Scale scores are based on a standardization of raw scores on subtests, where the average is 100 and the standard deviations are based on 15 points.

Standardization of the K-ABC was based on 2,000 children—100 at every half-year between the ages of 2 years, 6 months, and 12 years, 5 months. The variables of gender, parental education level, race or ethnic group, geographic region, community size, and educational placement were all considered in the sample (Kaufman & Kaufman, 1983a, b). Two variables relevant to this study are cultural background and educational placement. The standardization sample included 157 (7.8 percent) Hispanics and 82 (4.1 percent) termed as "Other," which included Native Americans, Asians, Alaskan Natives, and Pacific Islanders (Kaufman & Kaufman, 1983a, b). The total number of minorities in the standardization sample was 550 (27.5 percent). The K-ABC also included 138 (7 percent) children who participated in special education on either a full- or part-time basis and were placed into one of six categories: speech impaired, learning disabled, mentally retarded, emotionally disturbed, other (including health impaired, orthopedically impaired, multihandicapped, and hard of hearing), and gifted and talented.

The K-ABC is not completely free of biases for the minority and special education population; however, it has been demonstrated that it is the least biased standardized measure of cognitive development available.

Woodcock–Johnson Psycho-Educational Battery–Revised. The Woodcock-Johnson Psycho-Educational Battery–Revised (WJ–R, Woodcock & Johnson, 1989) is an individually administered test of cognitive ability, scholastic aptitude, and achievement. It consists of two parts: the Woodcock-Johnson Tests of Cognitive Ability (WJ–R COG) and the Woodcock-Johnson Tests of Achievement (WJ–R ACH). The WJ–R COG is based on the Horn-Cattell theory of intelligence. The WJ–R COG and the WJ–R ACH each includes a Standard battery and a Supplemental battery. The Standard battery includes 7 tests, and the Supplemental battery contains 15 tests—all designed to measure cognitive ability. The Standard and the Supplemental batteries each include 9 tests designed to measure achievement. The Standard batteries can be used alone or with the Supplemental Battery (Woodcock & Mather, 1989, 1990). The complete WJ–R battery comprises 39 tests. (Not all tests are administered, depending on the age of the subject.) Woodcock and Mather (1989, 1990) stated that the administration of the complete battery is rarely recommended; examiners must discern which tests they need to administer.

The WJ–R was standardized on a nationally representative sample of 6,359 subjects ages 2 to 95 years (Woodcock & Mather, 1989, 1990). The sample did not include any severely disabled students or any subjects who had not been exposed to an English-speaking environment for at least one year. Standard scores are based on a mean of 100 and a standard deviation of 15 points, just as most intelligence test scores are.

Details of the studies pertaining to the concurrent validity of the WJ–R COG and the WJ–R ACH are cited in the Tests of Cognitive Abilities Examiner's Manual (pp. 121–125) and the Tests of Achievement Examiner's Manual (pp. 103–112). Two examples of the independent criterion measures used are the K–ABC Mental Processing Composite and the Achievement Scale.

Wechsler Intelligence Scale for Children–Third Edition. This is an individually administered instrument used to assess the cognitive ability of children ages 6 to 16 years, 11 months (Wechsler, 1991). The WISC–III has maintained many of the fundamental qualities of the previous WISC–R (Wechsler, 1974), but provides updated norms, materials, content, and new administration procedures (Wechsler, 1991). The WISC–III comprises 13 subtests whose scores are used to yield three IQ scores: (1) Full Scale, (2) Verbal Scale, and (3) Performance Scale (Wechsler, 1991). The Full-Scale IQ score comprises the scores obtained from the Verbal and Performance subtests (Wechsler, 1991). Standard scores are based on a mean of 100 and a standard deviation of 15 points, just as most intelligence test scores are.

The standardization sample of the WISC–III was based on information obtained from the 1988 U.S. Census. Variables considered included age, gender, ethnicity, geographic region, and parental education (Wechsler, 1991). The sample contained 2,200 subjects, with 100 females and 100 males in each age group (Wechsler, 1991). Seven percent of the sample were children who had been classified as learning disabled, speech/language impaired, physically impaired, or emotionally disturbed (Wechsler, 1991). A detailed discussion of the studies pertaining to the concurrent validity of the WISC–R is cited in the WISC–III manual (pp. 182–184). In addition, studies that address the equivalence of the WISC–III and other tests of intelligence and achievement are cited in the WISC–III manual (pp. 197–213).

Procedure

Data collection entailed three steps: (1) administering the QUEST to each child, (2) contacting regular classroom teachers and obtaining permission to observe the children for half-hour periods on separate days and conducting half-hour classroom observations with three of the children to establish rapport, and (3) administering the K–ABC, WISC–III, and WJ–R to each child.

The Administration of QUEST. The QUEST (Gonzalez, 1991, 1994) was administered to the subjects by educational psychology graduate students enrolled in a seminar on the assessment of minority children who had received 10 hours of training prior to administration. Graduate students whose schedules coincided were paired. Each pair included one experienced evaluator and one inexperienced evaluator. The evaluators videotaped and completed a report of the child's performance on the QUEST. The reports and videotapes were reviewed by the primary author to verify the categorizations made of the children's responses and to increase the reliability of the children's reported cognitive developmental levels.

Participant Observations in the Regular Classroom. Telephone calls were made and letters were sent to each classroom teacher to gain permission to visit the child. Once permission had been granted, a half-hour observation was made in which the primary author acted as a participant observer. The observations were conducted for the purpose of establishing rapport with the child prior to the administration of the K-ABC, and also to collect some information on the child's classroom behaviors in relation to the teacher's reasons for referral. Events that transpired during the observations were recorded on an observation form. Observations conducted were open-ended and consisted of recording the context, narrative facts of the behavioral observation, and interpretation from the narrative facts. Each observation form was completed immediately after the observation.

Administration of K-ABC. After the observations were completed, the K-ABC (Kaufman & Kaufman, 1983a, b) was administered by the primary author to each child individually. As determined by the ages of the children, 13 of the 16 subtests were appropriately administered to each child. The primary author administered the K-ABC to each child with the exception of one child, Ricardo, who was tested by the primary author and a fellow graduate student. The graduate student served as a recorder and was present to increase rapport. This was considered necessary because Ricardo did not respond verbally to the primary author's attempts to establish rapport during the classroom observation. The K-ABC was administered at the children's school in available rooms, which were comfortable and quiet. Each testing session lasted approximately $1\frac{1}{2}$ to 2 hours, with the first 15 to 20 minutes used to establish rapport with the child. After the testing was concluded, each child was given a small prize.

Research Coding Design

Qualitative data analysis was carried out in three steps. The first step consisted of scoring the K-ABC and QUEST according to the procedures stated in the manuals. The second step consisted of developing coding categories and a file card system to organize and analyze the information included in the database (Bogdan & Biklen, 1992). For the third step, with the purpose of increasing the external and internal validity of the case study analysis, two methods suggested by Yin (1994) were adapted:

1. Developing a general strategy, including "theoretical propositions"
2. Following the analytic technique of pattern matching to be used as part of the general strategy

Developing theoretical propositions involves relying on the model that led to the study to guide the case study analysis, the research questions, and the literature review. Propositions are also useful for determining which data to focus on and which data are irrelevant (Yin, 1994).

Pattern matching consists of comparing a predicted pattern with an empirically based pattern; if the patterns concur, the internal validity of the case study has been increased (Yin, 1994). In addition, if the same predicted pattern is found in other cases, stronger conclusions can be made. This is referred to as theoretical replication across cases (Yin, 1994).

Data Analysis and Design

Qualitative analysis of the case studies entailed adapting a three-step strategy proposed by Yin (1994): (1) stating theoretical propositions, (2) developing a case description, and (3) pattern matching.

In step 1, theoretical propositions were made about the questions and framed according to the ethnic researcher model that guided this study. The theoretical propositions are based on several assumptions of the model:

1. Development is the result of the interaction of internal and external factors.
2. Assessment is more appropriate when qualitative measures are used by evaluators who recognize and honor different cultures.
3. The constructs measured by tests of cognitive development are socially constructed (Gonzalez & Yawkey, 1993; Gonzalez et al., 1997).

In step 2, a descriptive framework for organizing the case studies included a case-by-case analysis and discussion addressing question 1, and a synthesis and discussion of the overall patterns among the cases. In step 3, pattern-matching entailed comparing the case findings to the predicted propositions. The research questions asked and the instruments used to answer the two questions are displayed in Figures 8.1 and 8.2.

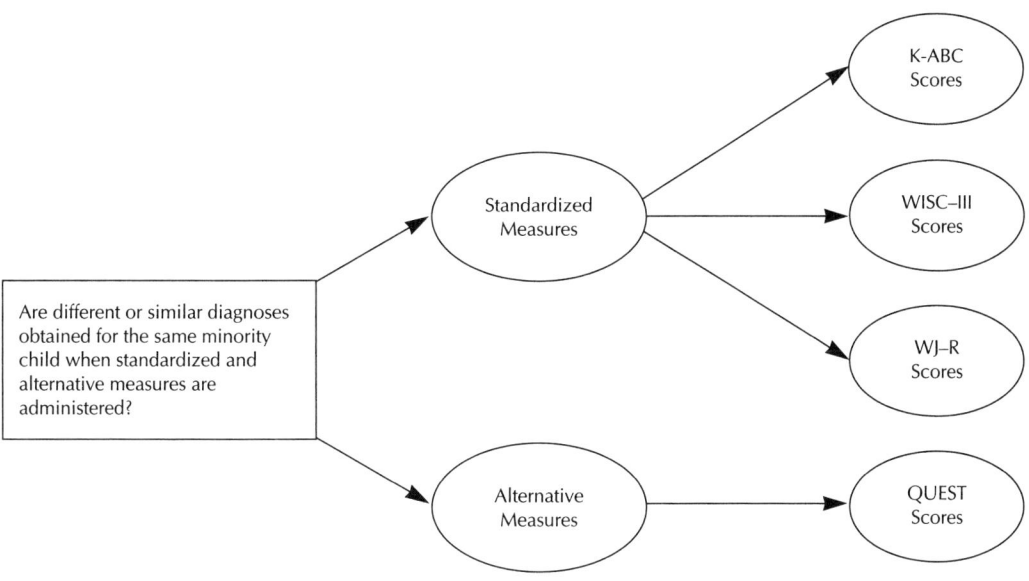

FIGURE 8.1   First research question and instruments used.

CASE STUDIES FOR RESEARCH QUESTION 1

To restate, the first research question was, Are different or similar diagnoses obtained for the same minority child when standardized and alternative measures are administered?

First Case Study: Alejandra

Personal Background. Alejandra is an 8-year-old Mexican-American girl enrolled in a second-grade bilingual (English/Spanish) classroom, where 80 percent of the instruction is given in Spanish. Alejandra's second-grade teacher, however, has reported that most of Alejandra's work needs to be done in English, her dominant language. She was initially referred for special education evaluation in 1993 for speech difficulties, which resulted in a modification of the current curriculum and speech/language services. She did not qualify for services related to a specific learning disability. In 1995, Alejandra was referred once again by her classroom teacher for difficulties in reading and writing.

Alejandra lives with her mother, stepfather, and two younger siblings. As indicated by the social history update included in her file, Alejandra relates

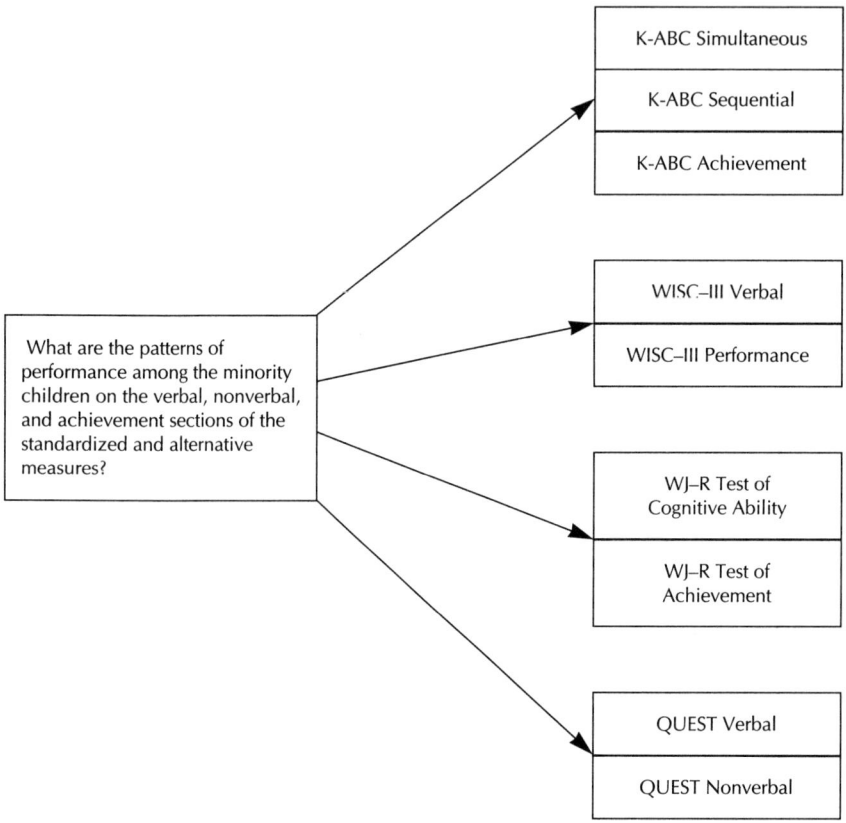

FIGURE 8.2   Second research question and instruments used.

well to her siblings, mother, and stepfather. She also visits her biological father and his family every other week and appears to be adjusted to the visitations. Alejandra does have a mild, but educationally significant, hearing loss in the right ear. No illnesses or other health problems have been reported.

Classroom Observations. During the classroom observations conducted by the primary author, Alejandra appeared quite friendly. She was not shy about asking questions and worked well with the children seated at the table with her. Alejandra displayed a great sense of humor, making witty comments throughout the observation. During a half-hour activity with a partner, Alejandra cooperated well, even though her partner did not. When her partner did not share the materials, Alejandra waited and then completed the work by herself. Alejandra appeared to get along well with her peers at school.

Comparison of Diagnoses Obtained. Alejandra's scores on the WJ–R, WISC–III, K-ABC, and QUEST are shown in Tables 8.1 through 8.4. The diagnoses from these measures shared both similarities and differences.

Similarities. All four measures revealed that Alejandra's performance was average on certain subtests and tasks and below average on others. For instance, Alejandra's overall performance on the WJ–R was reported to be in the low-average range. On the Tests of Achievement, Alejandra's skills were severely deficient in reading and written language and average in mathematics. On the

TABLE 8.1   WJ–R Scores for Alejandra (Case 1)

Tests of Cognitive Ability			Tests of Achievement		
	Standard Score	Percentile		Standard Score	Percentile
Long-Term Retrieval	81	11	Letter-Word Identification	69	2
Memory for Names	76	6	Passage Comprehension	67	1
Visual-Auditory Learning	89	24	Broad Reading	66	1
Short-Term Memory	92	29	Calculation	98	45
Memory for Sentences	85	16	Application Problems	92	31
Memory for Words	100	15	Broad mathematics	94	34
Processing Speed	95	37	Dictation	68	68
Visual Matching	93	33	Writing Samples	65	1
Cross Out	102	55	Broad Written Language	68	2
Auditory Processing	82	12	Science	91	27
Incomplete Words	76	5	Social Studies	88	22
Sound Blending	92	30	Humanities	75	5
Visual Processing	102	56	Broad Knowledge	83	14
Visual Closure	103	59			
Picture Recognition	99	46			
Comprehension Knowledge	78	7			
Picture Vocabulary	67	1			
Oral Vocabulary	90	24			
Fluid Reasoning	104	60			
Analysis-Synthesis	105	64			
Concept Formation	103	59			
Broad Cognitive Ability–Extended Scale	88	21			

TABLE 8.2   WISC–III Scores for Alejandra (Case 1)

Scaled Scores	IQ Scores
Information, 5	Verbal, 83
Similarities, 8	Performance, 96
Arithmetic, 11	Full Scale Verbal Comprehension, 88
Vocabulary, 5	Verbal Comprehension, 79
Comprehension, 6	Perceptual Organization, 96
Digit Span, 10	Freedom from Distractibility, 104
Picture Completion, 12	
Coding, 10	
Picture Arrangement, 10	
Block Design, 10	
Object Assembly, 5	

TABLE 8.3   K-ABC Scores for Alejandra (Case 1)

Mental Processing Subtests	Achievement Subtests	Global Scales
Hand Movements, 15	Faces and Places, 81 ± 11	Sequential Processing, 124 ± 9
Gestalt Closure, 13	Arithmetic, 86 ± 11	Simultaneous Processing, 118 ± 8
Number Recall, 12	Riddles, 83 ± 11	Mental Processing Composite, 124 ± 7
Triangles, 13	Reading/Decoding, 81 ± 8	Achievement, 78 ± 5
Word Order, 14	Reading/Understanding, 73 ± 7	Nonverbal, 121 ± 7
Matrix Analogies, 12		
Spatial Memory, 12		
Photo Series, 13		

Global Scale Comparisons	Significance Level
Sequential Processing = Simultaneous Processing	Not significant
Sequential Processing > Achievement	.01
Simultaneous Processing > Achievement	.01
Mental Processing Composite > Achievement	.01

Note: No strengths or weakness displayed.

TABLE 8.4   Developmental Levels Attained on QUEST for Alejandra (Case 1)

	Verbal General Level	Nonverbal General Level	Verbal Gender Level	Nonverbal Gender Level
Production	Perceptual	Perceptual	No classification	Perceptual
Comprehension	Functional	Perceptual	Perceptual	Concrete

WISC–III, Alejandra's verbal scores fell in the low-average to borderline range, while her scores on the performance scales were in the average range. The K-ABC revealed the widest range of Alejandra's abilities and weaknesses. Her performance on the Achievement Global Scale was in the well-below-average range and on the Mental Processing Composite in the well-above-average range. On QUEST, Alejandra again performed below the expected developmental level on some tasks and average on other tasks. For instance, throughout the assessment, her responses were at the preconceptual level, which is below the expected level for a child of her chronological age. On certain tasks, however, she was able to perform at the expected level. Hence, the overall diagnoses from these measures agreed that Alejandra's cognitive development was average to below average for a child her age.

Other similarities in Alejandra's performances were found on the achievement subtests. For example, the WJ–R and the K-ABC both revealed that Alejandra's reading skills were below average. This finding is consistent with Alejandra's referral for reading difficulties. Another similarity was revealed between the WJ–R and the WISC–III: Alejandra's Arithmetic scores were in the average range.

Consistencies in Alejandra's performances also existed between the subtests and tasks used to assess Alejandra's nonverbal and verbal performance. For instance, the significant differences found on the Global Scale comparisons of the K-ABC revealed that Alejandra's prior acquisition of facts and skills is well below her ability to process information and solve new problems. Therefore, she is able to perform better on problem-solving tasks than on tasks that require more verbal skills. This was consistent with and could explain why Alejandra performed at lower levels on the WJ–R, which demands competent verbal skills to perform well on the Tests of Cognitive Ability and the Tests of Achievement. The WISC–III also requires good verbal skills to perform well on the Verbal scales, and lower verbal skills to perform well on the Performance scales. This could explain why Alejandra scored higher on the Performance scales than on the Verbal scales.

Differences. There were differences as well among Alejandra's performances on the measures administered. For instance, Alejandra's Broad Cognitive Ability–Extended Scale score from the WJ–R classified her performance in the low-average range. Her performance on the K-ABC Mental Processing Composite, however, was in the well-above-average range. Alejandra's higher scores on the K-ABC could possibly reflect the fact that it was administered one year after the WJ–R. A one-year period between the tests may have allowed Alejandra time to improve her problem-solving skills and acquire more knowledge. Furthermore, it is crucial to acknowledge that each of the four measures was administered to Alejandra by different evaluators. This is important because, as Gonzalez et al. (1994b) pointed out, the most consequential tool in the assessment process is the personality of the evaluator. Each evaluator could have interpreted the test results in different ways, potentially producing the slightly different results.

Another difference between the measures was apparent when Alejandra's conceptual development was examined. QUEST provided a fuller picture of her abilities. Examples of the subtests that measure nonverbal and verbal concept formation from the K–ABC include Triangles, Riddles, and Reading/Understanding. The WJ–R subtest Concept Formation measures verbal concept formation, and the subtest Block Design on the WISC–III measures nonverbal concept formation. Alejandra obtained different scores on several of these subtests. For instance, she performed very well on the Triangles subtest, average on the Concept Formation subtest, and below average on the nonverbal and verbal conceptual tasks on QUEST. Her variation in performance can be explained by the slight differences in these measures of conceptual development. The Triangles subtest requires the ability to work under time pressure and provides a model to replicate. Concept Formation is a controlled-learning task that requires giving corrective feedback to the child during the task. Working under time pressure to replicate a model would impede many children's performance. This may have, however, helped Alejandra's performance. This interpretation is logical because Alejandra's teacher reported that she seems to be "unsure of herself academically." The time pressure and exact model could have prompted her to make decisions and take risks she may not have taken in a different situation. Similarly, the corrective feedback given during the Concept Formation task could have provided Alejandra with guidance that may have improved her performance. On QUEST, however, the children are allowed as much time as they need to complete the tasks. They are also required to form their own categories without many restrictions. Alejandra may have had trouble determining exactly what was expected of her. She may have needed the guidelines and time restrictions to help her make her own decisions.

Alejandra's scores on the Concept Formation subtests and tasks also shared some similarities. For instance, on the Reading/Understanding and Riddles subtests, she performed at the below-average level. This performance is consistent with her below-average performance on QUEST and her reported difficulties in reading and writing. The low performance indicates that she may be experiencing difficulties with her prereading skills.

Another important factor is that the subtests on the standardized measures are included as part of a larger battery and cannot be representative of Alejandra's conceptual development. The tasks on QUEST, however, are specifically designed to measure conceptual development and therefore can provide a more accurate estimate. This may also explain some of the differences found in her performances.

The measures administered to Alejandra revealed not only similarities and differences, but also distinctive information. Among the measures, QUEST appeared to provide the most distinctive information. For instance, Alejandra's potential to perform at higher levels, especially when the material presented to her was familiar, was evident on many of the QUEST tasks. In addition, because probing Alejandra's responses is part of QUEST, the evaluators were able to understand the reasoning behind her responses to the familiar items.

QUEST also provided an insight into Alejandra's cultural environment. For example, in the Category Clue task, she sorted the foods according to those she liked. She had trouble deciding where to put the papaya because she had never tasted one before, so she put it in the middle for Mili and Pili to share. (These two names refer to the two visual stimuli—pictures of doll characters—used for one category clue task; for a more specific description of the administration and tasks of QUEST, see Gonzalez, 1991, 1994, 1995b.) Alejandra then changed her mind and moved the papaya to Pili's side along with the other foods she did not like. When she was asked why she moved the papaya, she replied that since she had never tasted a papaya, she was not sure if she would like it, so she gave it to Pili. Alejandra's categorization decisions gave an insightful view to the influences of her daily cultural experiences on her classification skills (i.e., she classified objects based on her likes and dislikes). Another insight into her cultural environment was revealed when she replied that one of the pieces of bread presented to her looked like a microwave because of the dents, and the other flat piece of bread looked as if it had the trace of a shoe on it because it was smashed.

Summary. The four measures administered to Alejandra's shared similarities and differences in the diagnoses they provided. All of the measures revealed that her skills and abilities ranged from below average to average for a child her age. QUEST provided a unique view of the cultural factors influencing Alejandra's thought process. Her potential to perform at higher levels was also clearly demonstrated by QUEST. Demonstrating potential can be consequential to a child referred for a possible learning disability because the referrals are usually based on classroom performance, which is related to school achievement. That a child is experiencing only low achievement in school-related abilities, however, does not mean that he or she has a learning disability. The results of Alejandra's performances clearly demonstrate the limited diagnoses that can be obtained from one measure. Each measure may have resulted in different placement decisions for Alejandra. Thus, the differences in the diagnoses obtained from the four measures signify the importance of using multiple measures when assessing the cognitive development of a minority child, or any other child referred for special education.

Developmental Diagnosis and Recommendations. Results from the standardized tests administered indicated that Alejandra is performing below her expected level on school-related tasks and that her ability to process information and solve new problems is average to above average. Alejandra's memory, auditory and visual processing, and motor and reasoning skills are adequately developed for a child her age.

QUEST revealed that Alejandra's conceptual development is low for a child her age. Her ability to produce and understand the nouns used for naming and defining everyday objects, and the categories and subcategories of these objects, is greatly influenced by her prior knowledge of the objects. Alejandra's ability to classify everyday objects based on their linguistic gender and abstract semantic categories also depends on her prior knowledge of the object. She appears to have good knowledge of the sociocultural meanings of everyday objects.

Based on Alejandra's performances, her difficulties in school-related skills appear to be preventing her from reaching her potential. She appears to have a developmental delay in prereading skills, as evidenced, for example, by her below-average performance on QUEST and her low score on the Vocabulary subtest of the WISC–III. This developmental delay may be due to a lack of stimulation in her classroom environment. Most of Alejandra's classroom instruction is in Spanish, but her dominant language is English. Alejandra may benefit from attending an English-only classroom, where she can be given help to improve her prereading skills. She would also benefit greatly from being given tests designed to assess and confirm her difficulties in reading and writing prior to any modifications. Based on the results of the evaluation conducted in this study, it is noted that Alejandra's placement in a bilingual Spanish/English classroom is not beneficial for her learning and academic performance. She needs to be placed in an English-only classroom in order to learn how to read and write in her dominant language first (i.e., English).

Second Case Study: Ricardo

Personal Background. Ricardo is a 7-year-old Native American boy enrolled in a bilingual (English/Spanish) enrichment first-grade classroom. In 1995, Ricardo was referred by his classroom teacher for "significant" problems in reading, writing, and math. Ricardo was also referred for a vision screening, which revealed that he needed glasses. No health problems were reported in Ricardo's file.

Ricardo lives with his mother, father, and younger sister. His primary language, and the primary language spoken at home, is English.

Classroom Observation. A classroom observation by the primary author revealed that Ricardo is quiet in class. During a small group reading lesson, he read slowly and softly, sounding out each word. When the primary author attempted to talk to Ricardo, he only nodded, never speaking a word. He appeared quite shy. When working on his assignment, Ricardo wandered around the classroom, changing tables every few minutes, finally settling down at a table alone. Ricardo did not talk much to the other children and seemed to prefer to work alone. Ricardo was also quiet while the K-ABC evaluators were attempting to establish rapport, and he remained quiet throughout the assessment.

Comparison of Diagnoses Obtained. Ricardo's scores from the K-ABC and QUEST are shown in Tables 8.5 and 8.6, respectively. The overall diagnoses obtained for Ricardo from these two measures were different. Ricardo's performance on the K-ABC was classified in the well-below-average to below-average range. His performance on QUEST was well above average. The differences in Ricardo's performance could have been influenced by the measures administered. The K-ABC and QUEST measure different facets of cognitive development and have different administration and scoring procedures. For instance, the K-ABC is standardized, and only specific responses are considered valid, whereas QUEST is flexible and does not require specific responses. An advantage of not requiring specific responses is that evaluators are provided with a direct opportunity to understand how the child's personal environment is influencing his or her development. This may have contributed to Ricardo's above-average performance on QUEST. For instance, as the

TABLE 8.5   K-ABC Scores for Ricardo (Case 2)

Mental Processing Subtests	*Achievement Subtests*	*Global Scales*
Hand Movements, 8	Faces and Places, 91 ± 13	Sequential Processing, 78 ± 10
Gestalt Closure, 7	Arithmetic, 72 ± 13	Simultaneous Processing, 82 ± 9
Number Recall, 5	Riddles, 77 ± 11	Mental Processing Composite, 78 ± 8
Triangles, 6	Reading/Decoding, 73 ± 7	Achievement, 75 ± 5
Word Order, 6	Reading/Understanding, 78 ± 7	Nonverbal, 84 ± 8
Matrix Analogies, 8		
Spatial Memory, 11 (S)		
Photo Series, 5		

Global Scale Comparisons	*Significance Level*
Sequential Processing = Simultaneous Processing	Not significant
Sequential Processing = Achievement	Not significant
Simultaneous Processing = Achievement	Not significant
Mental Processing Composite = Achievement	Not significant

Note: S = a strength.

TABLE 8.6   Developmental Levels Attained on QUEST for Ricardo (Case 2)

	Verbal General Level	Nonverbal General Level	Verbal Gender Level	Nonverbal Gender Level
Production	Conceptual/ Metalinguistic	Conceptual/ Metalinguistic	Conceptual/ Metalinguistic	Conceptual/ Concrete
Comprehension	Conceptual/ Metalinguistic	Conceptual/ Metalinguistic	Conceptual/ Metalinguistic	Conceptual/ Concrete

evaluators noted, Ricardo's responses demonstrated a "high cultural influence." QUEST may have provided an opportunity for Ricardo to explain his abilities in his own way. The K-ABC allows only specific responses to be scored correctly. For instance, on the Faces and Places subtest, when Ricardo was presented with the picture of John Wayne, he replied, "That's a cowboy." Although John Wayne was dressed as a cowboy, this general response must be scored as zero.

QUEST also allows the evaluator to probe all responses, which usually results in higher-level responses and additional details about a child's cultural environment. Ricardo's performance on the K-ABC could have been influenced by the fact that it must be administered in an exact manner that does not allow the evaluator to probe responses. Probing appeared to be a critical practice for Ricardo because he responded at the metalinguistic level only after his initial responses were probed. Thus, probing allowed Ricardo to perform at much higher levels on QUEST.

A third factor that may have contributed to the differences in Ricardo's performances is that each test was administered and interpreted by separate evaluators, and the evaluator's personality is a prominent tool in the assessment process (Gonzalez et al., 1994b). Ricardo could have felt more comfortable with one pair of evaluators than the other, or one pair may been more effective at establishing rapport and thus elicited more specific responses.

QUEST appeared to be an invaluable instrument for Ricardo because it allowed him to demonstrate his potential to think at higher levels. The K-ABC produced results that were congruent with his teacher's concerns and reason for referral. The K-ABC revealed that Ricardo was below the expected level in reading, writing, and math. It also showed that no significant differences were found between Ricardo's prior acquisition of facts and skills and his ability to process information and solve new problems. QUEST, however, demonstrated that Ricardo does have the ability to perform at higher levels when probed. He may not be receiving the extra assistance he seems to need at school, which may be one reason that he did not perform at the same level as his age-mates on the K-ABC.

Developmental Diagnosis and Recommendations. Based on Ricardo's performance on the K-ABC, his school aptitude and ability to process information are below the expected level for a child his age. His attention span and concentration were appropriate, which enabled him to demonstrate his excellent short-term memory for visual stimuli on the Spatial Memory subtest. His average score on the Faces and Places subtest indicated that he appears to have a moderate amount of knowledge about the mainstream culture.

QUEST disclosed Ricardo's excellent nonverbal and verbal conceptual development. Ricardo has an exceptional ability to produce and understand the nouns used for naming and defining everyday objects, and the categories and subcategories of these objects. Ricardo also has a superior ability for classifying objects based on linguistic gender, sociocultural meanings, and abstract semantic categories. Thus, Ricardo's nonverbal and verbal conceptual development is superior for his age according to QUEST.

Ricardo's inability to express his emotions, evidenced by his quiet behavior, appears to be interfering with his cognitive potential. This could explain why Ricardo's high cognitive potential was communicated only after his responses were probed. If Ricardo does not receive the special attention he needs to succeed in school, he may continue to experience difficulty and therefore continue to perform below average. Ricardo needs a comfortable classroom environment to help him learn to express his emotions. He would also benefit from teaching strategies that focus on his difficulties as well as his strengths. Ricardo would greatly benefit from another test of cognitive development prior to any modifications in his school curriculum, since the K-ABC and QUEST produced diverse results.

Third Case Study: Lily

Personal Background. Lily is a 9-year-old Native American girl enrolled in a third-grade class. Her primary language and the primary language spoken at home is English. Lily is currently placed in a program for the speech and language impaired. In 1995, she was referred by her classroom teacher for reading and writing difficulties.

Lily lives with her mother, father, older brother, and older sister. No health problems were reported in Lily's file.

Classroom Observation. During the primary author's classroom observation, Lily was talkative. In the class group lesson, Lily replied out loud when questions were asked of the whole class and talked openly to the other children seated at the table with her throughout the entire lesson. The other children also talked a lot and were asked three times by the teacher to settle down. Despite the fact that Lily talked throughout the lesson, she consistently replied appropriately when asked. Her talkative nature during this classroom

TABLE 8.7   K-ABC Scores for Lily (Case 3)

Mental Processing Subtests	Achievement Subtests	Global Scales
Hand Movements, 13	Faces and Places, 83 ± 11	Sequential Processing, 102 ± 10
Gestalt Closure, 6 (W)	Arithmetic, 92 ± 10 (S)	Simultaneous Processing, 95 ± 7
Number Recall, 9	Riddles, 78 ± 11	Mental Processing Composite, 98 ± 7
Triangles, 9	Reading/Decoding, 65 ± 9 (W)	Achievement, 73 ± 5
Word Order, 9	Reading/Understanding, 64 ± 8 (W)	Nonverbal, 105 ± 7
Matrix Analogies, 10		
Spatial Memory, 14 (S)		
Photo Series, 8		

Global Scale Comparisons	Significance Level
Sequential Processing = Simultaneous Processing	Not significant
Sequential Processing > Achievement	.01
Simultaneous Processing > Achievement	.01
Mental Processing Composite > Achievement	.01

Note: S = a strength; W = a weakness.

visit could have been attributed to the fact that a substitute was teaching. This may also have been why so many of the other children were very talkative.

Comparison of Diagnoses Obtained.   Lily's scores from the K-ABC and QUEST are shown in Tables 8.7 and 8.8. The diagnoses obtained from these measures exposed similar ranges in Lily's cognitive abilities. Each test revealed that her cognitive development is below average to average. For instance, on the K-ABC, Lily performed at the average level on the Global Scales, with the exception of the Achievement Scale, on which she performed well below the average in comparison to her age-mates. This scale is designed to provide an estimate of a child's factual knowledge and skills that are usually taught in school or gained from experience. This scale is separate from those

TABLE 8.8   Developmental Levels Attained on QUEST for Lily (Case 3)

	Verbal General Level	Nonverbal General Level	Verbal Gender Level	Nonverbal Gender Level
Production	Functional/Concrete	Functional/Concrete	No classification	No classification
Comprehension	Concrete	Concrete	No classification	No classification

designed to assess problem-solving abilities (Kaufman & Kaufman, 1983a, b). Therefore, Lily's cognitive development can be interpreted as average, while her acquired factual knowledge and skills is well below average. Lily's difficulties on the Reading/Decoding and Reading/Understanding subtests agree with her teacher's concern and reason for referral, which stated that Lily was having difficulties in reading and writing, two skills primarily taught in school and highly associated with school success. Lily's low prior knowledge of facts and skills also explains why the Global Scale comparisons revealed significant differences among all Mental Processing Scales and the Achievement Scale. The significant differences indicated that Lily possesses an exceptional ability to process information and solve new problems that is greater than her prior acquisition of facts and skills.

On QUEST Lily also performed at the expected level for her chronological age on certain tasks and below the expected level on other tasks. For instance, her overall ability was below average for a child her age. For items that she was familiar with, however, her extensive knowledge allowed her to give more elaborate responses and thus perform at higher levels. In contrast, for objects that were not familiar to Lily, she performed at lower levels than expected for her age. Lily's ability to perform better when she has prior knowledge of the material presented to her could explain why her performance on the K-ABC Achievement subtests was low and why she was able to perform at higher levels on QUEST for items that she was familiar with.

QUEST provided Lily the opportunity to exhibit her cognitive potential to perform at higher levels and also provided a glimpse into her cultural environment. Lily told stories about her family during the food tasks. For instance, she replied, "We always eat steak at home.... You cook it on the fireplace, I mean grill.... You buy them at the store; they come in packages.... You eat them with corn and salsa." Lily's stories provided an insightful view of the influence of her cultural daily experiences on her cognitive-conceptual abilities (i.e., definitions using language).

In conclusion, the diagnoses from the K-ABC and QUEST concurred that Lily is at the average level in certain areas of her cognitive development and below average in other areas. Both tests also revealed that Lily performed equally on the nonverbal and verbal sections. In addition, the instruments provided complementary information. For instance, the K-ABC revealed the discrepancies between Lily's achievement in school-acquired facts and skills and her problem-solving abilities. QUEST demonstrated that Lily has the potential to perform at higher levels when she is knowledgeable about the items presented to her and provided a glimpse into the environment in which she is developing.

Developmental Diagnosis and Recommendations. Lily's ability to process information and solve new problems is average for a child her age and superior to her prior acquisition of facts and skills. She is experiencing difficulties in achievement, evidenced by the below-average scores she received on all the Achievement subtests of the K-ABC. Lily's scores were very low on the Reading/Decoding and Reading/Understanding subtests, consistent with her teacher's concerns and reason for referral.

QUEST disclosed that Lily's nonverbal and verbal conceptual development is below average to average. Her ability to produce and understand the nouns used for naming and defining everyday objects and the categories and subcategories of these objects is below average to average, and greatly influenced by her prior experience and knowledge of the items presented to her. Lily's ability to classify objects based on linguistic gender and abstract semantic categories was also below average to average. She appeared to have a good understanding of the sociocultural meanings of many of the objects presented. Thus, her ability to perform at higher developmental levels seems to depend on the extent of her prior knowledge of the objects.

Based on results from the K-ABC and QUEST, Lily's ability to process information, solve new problems, and understand familiar everyday objects is about average. Her performances indicated that her cognitive development is adequate and that she has the potential to think at higher levels. Lily's sufficient cognitive development, ability to listen to and interpret instructions, and ability to remain focused and motivated seem to indicate that a lack of stimulation in Lily's environment is preventing her from reaching her potential. Lily does appear to have difficulties in school-related abilities, such as reading. Therefore, she would benefit from another evaluation using alternative measures designed specifically for reading problems. Lily needs an enriched classroom environment, which can help her improve her school-related skills.

Fourth Case Study: Antonio

Personal Background. Antonio is an 8-year-old Mexican-American boy enrolled in a third-grade classroom. His primary language and the primary language spoken at home is English. Antonio was first referred for speech difficulties in 1994 but did not qualify for services at that time. In 1995, he was referred once again by his classroom teacher, this time for reading and writing difficulties.

Antonio lives with his mother, father, and younger sister. No health concerns were reported in his file.

Comparison of Diagnoses Obtained. Antonio's scores from the K-ABC and QUEST are presented in Tables 8.9 and 8.10. Antonio's range of cognitive abilities based on the diagnoses obtained from these two measures was similar. For example, on the K-ABC, his performances on the Mental Processing subtests were classified at the average to above-average level. Similarly, on

TABLE 8.9 K-ABC Scores for Antonio (Case 4)

Mental Processing Subtests	Achievement Subtests	Global Scales
Hand Movements, 11	Faces and Places, 96 ± 11	Sequential Processing, 115 ± 9
Gestalt Closure, 12	Arithmetic, 111 ± 11 (S)	Simultaneous Processing, 108 ± 8
Number Recall, 14	Riddles, 86 ± 11	Mental Processing Composite, 112 ± 7
Triangles, 11	Reading/Decoding, 76 ± 8 (W)	Achievement, 87 ± 5
Word Order, 12	Reading/Understanding, 77 ± 7 (W)	Nonverbal, 106 ± 7
Matrix Analogies, 11		
Spatial Memory, 10		
Photo Series, 12		

Global Scale Comparisons	Significance Level
Sequential Processing = Simultaneous processing	Not significant
Sequential Processing > Achievement	.01
Simultaneous Processing > Achievement	.01
Mental Processing Composite > Achievement	.01

Note: S = a strength; W = a weakness.

QUEST, Antonio performed average and above average on certain tasks. Antonio's overall diagnoses, however, were not similar. On QUEST, Antonio's performance was below the expected level for a child his age. On the K-ABC Mental Processing Scales, his performance was above average. His performances on the Achievement subtests were below average, with the exception of Arithmetic; on this subtest, his score was above average. The Achievement subtests are designed to assess factual knowledge and skills usually taught in school. Antonio's school-related difficulties could explain why he performed at the above-average level on his ability to process information and solve new problems and below average on the Achievement Global Scale of the K-ABC.

TABLE 8.10 Developmental Levels Attained on QUEST for Antonio (Case 4)

	Verbal General Level	Nonverbal General Level	Verbal Gender Level	Nonverbal Gender Level
Production	Functional	Perceptual	Functional	Perceptual
Comprehension	Perceptual	Perceptual	Concrete	Concrete

On QUEST Antonio's performance was below average, but sometimes average or above average. Antonio appeared to perform at higher levels for objects that were familiar to him, then responding with many details. For instance, when he was presented with elephants in the Defining Production for Animals task, Antonio replied, "They're big and weigh over 6 tons.... They're endangered species.... When they get to be 4 years old, they leave their mother.... Their ears look like birds' wings, except they're bigger.... They throw water out of their trunks, like throwing water from a water hose." Antonio's answers were consistently like this. Even for the very few objects that he could not label, he provided details, though not quite as many. When probed, he could often perform at higher levels. Thus, on QUEST, Antonio's ability to perform at higher levels seems to be dependent on his prior knowledge of the materials presented to him. This could explain why Antonio provided more elaborate responses for the items that were familiar to him and performed below average on the items that were not.

In addition, QUEST provided the evaluators with details about Antonio's cultural environment. For instance, in the Defining Production task, when presented with the chiles, Antonio replied, "You can call them chiles or peppers.... They are something that you eat, and they're very hot ... and you plant them in a garden.... This one looks like a thing from the movie.... When you kill a vampire and get a hammer and go.... Some of them, if you turn them upside down, look like trees. This one looks like a Christmas tree." Antonio made several hand movements when he gave this response, which helped the evaluators understand his explanation. Antonio's nonverbal and verbal communication skills indicated developmental potential, as attested by his flexibility (many categories used for defining objects) and fluency of thinking (a large number of responses for each item), especially when he was culturally familiar with the stimuli.

In conclusion, the K-ABC and QUEST provided unique information on Antonio. The K-ABC, because of the Reading subtests, was able to assess his reading skills. QUEST measured his conceptual development, demonstrated his potential to perform at higher levels, and revealed unique details about his cultural environment. Thus, the K-ABC and QUEST appeared to reveal complementary information pertaining to Antonio's level of cognitive development.

Developmental Diagnosis and Recommendations. Antonio's ability to process information and solve new problems is superior to his prior acquisition of facts and skills. His excellent scores on the Sequential and Simultaneous scales and his good number facility permitted Antonio to perform very well on the Arithmetic subtest of the K-ABC. Antonio's low Achievement scores reflected his difficulties in Reading/Decoding and Reading/Understanding. Furthermore, Antonio's low verbal concept formation appeared to contribute to his difficulties on the Reading/Understanding subtest and to his low performance on verbal conceptual development, as measured by QUEST.

On QUEST, Antonio's nonverbal and verbal conceptual development indicated that his ability to produce and understand the nouns used for naming and defining everyday objects is low and influenced by his prior knowledge of the objects presented. That Antonio seems to be in a transitional stage in conceptual development was reflected in the almost equal number of responses given at the functional and perceptual levels. Antonio's ability to classify items according to their linguistic gender and abstract semantic categories also appears to be in transition. Antonio did display great potential to perform at higher levels. He also appeared to have a good understanding of the sociocultural meanings he provided for many of the objects presented.

Based on the information available, Antonio appears to have an above-average ability to process information and solve new problems. His depressed oral language skills appear to be related to the difficulties he is experiencing in the classroom and his low performance on the Reading/Decoding subtest. Antonio's low socioeconomic status and lack of stimulation could also be contributing to his difficulties. Antonio needs a program to help him develop his oral language skills before any other modifications are made. Antonio also needs to be given an alternative assessment that will accurately assess his reading difficulties. In addition, he would benefit from a classroom environment that focuses on his strengths, such as arithmetic, while providing help with his weakness in oral language skills.

Research Question 1 Conclusion

The first research question, the theoretical proposition, and the findings are presented in Table 8.11. The exploratory analysis of the measures administered to the children in this study indicated that some similarities and differences existed in the diagnoses obtained from each measure. The differences in the diagnoses appear to stem from variations in the instruments. All the instruments used in this study were designed to measure the cognitive development of a child; however, each instrument combines different tests of ability.

TABLE 8.11   First Research Question, Theoretical Proposition, and Findings

Research Question	*Theoretical Proposition*	*Findings*
Are different or similar diagnoses obtained for the same minority child when standardized and alternative measures are administered?	Similar diagnoses will be obtained for the same minority child; however, the alternative measure will be more sensitive, revealing more detailed profiles that include cultural factors.	Diagnoses shared both differences and similarities. QUEST provided a view of the children's cultural environment. QUEST demonstrated the children's potential for learning.

For instance, the K-ABC measures processing style through visual-motor coordination by the Hand Movements subtest and short-term memory by the Spatial Memory subtest, whereas QUEST measures conceptual development by such tasks as labeling and sorting animal and food objects. Although these subtests and tasks both measure cognitive abilities, the approach is different. The variations in the way each test measures cognitive development makes it easy to understand the differences in the diagnoses obtained.

Another important factor contributing to the differences in the diagnoses is that the measures are based on different theories of cognitive development that use different terminology. This fact contributed to the challenge of comparing the diagnoses. Differences were also noted among the classification terms used. For instance, on the WJ–R, a standard score below 69 is classified as "severely deficient." On the K-ABC, a standard score of 69 is considered to be in the lower extreme. Thus, the same standard scores may lead to different diagnostic classifications.

Similarities among the diagnoses appeared to be attributed to the fact that each measure is designed to assess cognitive development. The fact that some similarities existed indicated that each instrument appears to be measuring what it was designed to measure. For Ricardo, whose diagnoses from the K-ABC and QUEST were different, the type of test used to assess his cognitive development seemed to influence his performance. Caution must be used when attributing Ricardo's different performances to the type of test, since many other factors that were not accounted for may have also influenced his performance, such as motivation and quality of rapport established with the evaluators.

The case studies underscore the importance of administering multiple measures that include alternative instruments of cognitive development to assess minority children. Alejandra's different performances on the subtests of the four measures administered exemplified the differences among those measures and the results obtained. Ricardo's performances clearly illustrate the need to use alternative measures of cognitive development. If he had been assessed solely by a standardized measure, a decision to place him in special education might have been made. For Ricardo, the administration of an alternative measure was invaluable and resulted in a fuller assessment of his abilities.

The findings of these case studies emphasize the importance of using multiple measures to assess the cognitive abilities of minority children. Differences between the instruments and diagnoses obtained in these cases could result in an inaccurate estimate of children's cognitive development. An inaccurate estimate may lead to the misidentification of minority children and damaging social and academic consequences. Furthermore, obtaining diagnoses for children requires a comprehensive investigation into the possible causes of the reported difficulties; children need assessors who will act as advocates for them, to ensure that the tests given truly reflect their cognitive abilities.

CHAPTER 8   STANDARDIZED AND ALTERNATIVE ASSESSMENTS

CASE STUDIES FOR RESEARCH QUESTION 2

To restate, the second research question was, What are the patterns of performance among the minority children on the verbal, nonverbal, and achievement sections of the standardized and alternative measures administered?

Patterns of Nonverbal, Verbal, and Achievement Performance

The findings indicated that the children's performance on the nonverbal and verbal subtests and tasks varied. For instance, Alejandra performed better on the nonverbal sections of the WISC–III and QUEST. On the K-ABC, however, she performed better on the Sequential Scale. Alejandra's nonverbal and verbal scores are summarized in Table 8.12. Alejandra's high verbal performance on the K-ABC appeared to be the result of her exceptional ability to solve problems that require her to process information in a serial order.

Ricardo's, Lily's, and Antonio's nonverbal and verbal scores from the K-ABC and QUEST are summarized in Table 8.13. Ricardo performed better on the Simultaneous scale of the K-ABC and better on the verbal sections of QUEST. His higher performance on the Simultaneous Scale may be related to the strength he displayed on the Spatial Memory subtest. Ricardo's higher

TABLE 8.12   Verbal, Nonverbal, and Achievement Performance for Alejandra (Case 1)

Measure	Verbal Scores	Nonverbal Scores	Achievement
WJ–R	Broad Cognitive Ability: 88		Broad Reading: 66 Mathematics: 94 Written Language: 68 Knowledge: 83
WISC–III	Verbal IQ: 83	Performance: 96	
K-ABC	Sequential Scale: 124 ± 9	Simultaneous Scale: 118 ± 8	Achievement Scale: 78 ± 5
QUEST General Level	Production: Perceptual	Production: Perceptual	
	Comprehension: Functional	Comprehension: Perceptual	
Gender Level	Production: No classification	Production: Perceptual	
	Comprehension: Perceptual	Comprehension: Concrete	

TABLE 8.13   Verbal, Nonverbal, and Achievement Performances for Ricardo, Lily, and Antonio

Measure	Verbal Scores	Nonverbal Scores	Achievement
Ricardo			
K-ABC	Sequential Scale: 78 ± 10	Simultaneous Scale: 82 ± 9	Achievement Scale: 75 ± 5
QUEST General Level	Production: Conceptual/Metalinguistic Comprehension: Conceptual/Metalinguistic	Production: Conceptual/Metalinguistic Comprehension: Conceptual/Metalinguistic	N/A
Gender Level	Production: Conceptual/Metalinguistic Comprehension: Conceptual/Metalinguistic	Production: Conceptual/Concrete Comprehension: Conceptual/Concrete	N/A
Lily			
K-ABC	Sequential Scale: 102 ± 10	Simultaneous Scale: 95 ± 7	Achievement Scale: 73 ± 5
QUEST General Level	Production: Functional/Concrete Comprehension: Concrete	Production: Functional/Concrete Comprehension: Concrete	N/A
Gender Level	Production: Comprehension:	Production: Comprehension:	N/A
Antonio			
K-ABC	Sequential Scale: 115 ± 9	Simultaneous Scale: 108 ± 8	Achievement Scale: 87 ± 5
QUEST General Level	Production: Functional Comprehension: Perceptual	Production: Perceptual Comprehension: Perceptual	N/A
Gender Level	Production: Functional Comprehension: Concrete	Production: Perceptual Comprehension: Concrete	N/A

verbal performance on QUEST is understandable since he performed at higher levels only after his responses were probed.

Lily's score on the Sequential Scale of the K-ABC was slightly higher than her score on the Simultaneous Scale; however, both scores were classified in the average range. Lily's performances on the nonverbal and verbal sections of QUEST were exactly the same, an interesting pattern demonstrating that for Lily, the nonverbal and verbal requirements did not make a difference in her performance.

Antonio performed more favorably on the verbal sections of the K-ABC and QUEST, which can be understood by, and is consistent with, his superior performance on the Sequential Scale. His high Sequential score indicated that he is excellent at solving verbal problems that require information to be processed in a serial order.

The children's variations on the nonverbal and verbal sections of the measures indicate that other factors appear to be influencing their performance. For instance, the measures administered are based on different theories of cognitive development and include a variety of tasks, so each child's performances could have been a reflection of their ability to perform the tasks. Another potential factor influencing their performances may have been the quality of rapport established with the evaluator. Since different evaluators administered each of the tests, some of the children may have felt more comfortable with one of the evaluators. For instance, one of the evaluators may have been more patient and understanding with the child, which could have evoked more responses from the child.

That a pattern of low achievement was observed in every case can be explained by the children's reasons for referral: all for difficulties in reading, writing, and math. These are school-related abilities, so the children's low scores on a measure designed to assess school-related abilities would be expected. But there may be other factors that could have contributed to the children's low scores on the Achievement Scale. For instance, Valencia (1984), in a study of Mexican-American preschool children, reported that they scored significantly lower on the K-ABC Achievement Scale. Similarly, Whitworth and Chrisman (1987) reported that the Mexican-American children in their study displayed a large deficiency on the K-ABC Achievement Scale. They also noted that lower scores for minorities on the Achievement Scale are consistently reported in the literature. This work suggests that in this study, the Achievement Scale of the K-ABC may have also contributed to the subjects' low performance.

Research Question 2 Conclusion

The second research question, the theoretical proposition stated, and the patterns found are presented in Table 8.14. The pattern predicted for the sub-

TABLE 8.14 Second Research Question, Theoretical Proposition, and Findings

Research Question	*Theoretical Proposition*	*Findings*
What are the patterns of performance among the minority children on the nonverbal, verbal, and achievement sections of the standardized and alternative measures?	The Native American and Mexican-American children will perform better on the nonverbal sections, and low on the achievement scales, of the standardized and alternative measures.	The children's performances on the nonverbal and verbal sections of the standardized and alternative measures varied. All of the children scored low on the achievement scales.

jects' nonverbal performance was not observed. As indicated by the children's varied scores, other factors were influencing their performances. The variations in their performances can be partly attributed to the differences in tests. The pattern expected for the children's performance on the achievement scales was observed. The children did score low on the achievement scales of all the tests administered, not a surprising finding because all had been referred for difficulties in school-related abilities such as reading and writing.

The subjects' performances on the verbal, nonverbal, and achievement sections were measured to describe any possible patterns. Many other factors, such as motivation, prior knowledge of the test material, and quality of rapport established, may have influenced the children's performance.

Conclusions

This study used four case studies to explore the differences and similarities in the diagnoses obtained from standardized and alternative measures of cognitive development. This small sample size limits the findings of this study to the individual children, so generalizations from the results of these cases may not be made to any other children's performances on standardized and alternative tests of cognitive ability. Yin (1994) differentiated between "statistical generalization" and "analytic generalization." He stated that analytic generalization is a goal in experiments and multiple-case study research and aims to advance and generalize theories. Although the findings of this study may not be generalized to a large population, they may help advance the ethnic researcher model.

Another limitation of this study was that extensive referrals of the children's difficulties from their classroom teachers were not obtained. Extensive referrals that specifically describe the children's difficulties are beneficial to making an accurate diagnosis. They may also disclose pertinent information about the children's abilities or difficulties that can be resolved prior to assessment. The resolution of problems prior to testing may circumvent the assessment process and thus decrease the possibility of misidentification. Furthermore, knowing who referred the child and understanding the reasons for the referral are consequential to the assessment process. For instance, as noted in the literature review, most referrals for special education are generated by classroom teachers. Some teachers may not understand the cultural background of their students and may confuse normal development with a possible learning disability. An extensive referral may be able to detect this kind of confusion.

A third drawback of this study was that additional information on the child's home environment was not collected. This information would have been extremely helpful in understanding the child's difficulties and making recommendations.

Future studies are needed that include a larger sample size and statistical procedures to confirm the similarities and differences of the instruments observed in this study. A larger, systematic study that compares the diagnoses obtained from alternative measures such as QUEST and standardized measures like the K-ABC is crucial to researchers, educators, and children. In addition, future studies that investigate the home environment of a child referred for special education evaluation may help in providing recommendations to the child's parents and teacher. Studies that aid in determining the most accurate and appropriate way to assess minority children referred for special education assessment must continue.

REFERENCES

BACK, R., & DANA, R. H. (1977). Examiner sex bias and Wechsler Intelligence Scale for Children scores. *Journal of Consulting and Clinical Psychology, 45*, 500.

BALLARD, W. S., TIGHE, P. L., & DALTON, E. F. (1979). *IDEA Oral Language Proficiency Test.* Whittier, CA: Ballard & Tighe.

BANKS, J. A., & McGEE BANKS, C. A. (1993). *Multicultural education: Issues and perspectives* (2nd ed.). Needham Heights, MA: Allyn and Bacon.

BJORKLUND, D. F. (1995). *Children's thinking: Developmental function and individual differences* (2nd ed.). Pacific Grove, CA: Brooks/Cole.

BOGDAN, R. C., & BIKLEN, S. K. (1992). *Qualitative research for education: An introduction to theory and methods* (2nd ed.). Needham Heights, MA: Allyn and Bacon.

BROWN, L., SHERBENOU, R. J., & DOLLARD, S. J. (1982). *Test of Nonverbal Intelligence (TONI).* Austin, TX: Pro-Ed.

CHINN, P. C., & HUGHES, S. (1987). Representation of minority students in special education classes. *Remedial and Special Education, 8*(4), 41–46.

CIEUTAT, V. J., & FLICK, G. L. (1967). Examiner differences among Stanford-Binet items. *Psychological Reports, 21*, 613–622.

CIZEK, G. J. (1993). Alternative assessments: Yes, but why? *Educational Horizons* 72(1), 36–40.

CUMMINS, J. (1991). Institutionalized racism and the assessment of minority children: A comparison of policies and programs in the United States and Canada. In R. J. Samuda, S. L. Kong, J. Cummins, J. Pascual-Leone, & J. Lewis (Eds.), *Assessment and placement of minority students* (pp. 95–108). Toronto, Ontario, Canada: C. J. Hogrefe.

DAMICO, J. S., & HAMAYAN, E. V. (1991). Implementing assessment in the real world. In E. V. Hamayan & J. S., Damico (Eds.), *Limiting bias in the assessment of bilingual students* (pp. 303–316). Austin, TX: Pro-Ed.

DAVIDSON, K. L. (1992). A comparison of Native American and white students' cognitive strengths as measured by the Kaufman Assessment Battery for Children. *Roeper Review* 14(3), 111–115.

DUNN, L. M. (1968). Special education for the mildly retarded—Is much of it justifiable? *Exceptional Children, 7*, 5–22.

FUCHS, D., FEATHERSTONE, N. L., GARWICK, D. R., & FUCHS, L. S. (1984). Effects of examiner familiarity and task characteristics on speech- and language-impaired children's test performance. *Measurement and Evaluation in Guidance, 16,* 198–204.

FUCHS, D., & FUCHS, L. S. (1986). Test procedure bias: A meta-analysis of examiner familiarity effects. *Review of Educational Research, 36*(2), 243–262.

FUCHS, D., FUCHS, L. S., POWER, M. H., & DAILEY, A. M. (1985). Bias in the assessment of handicapped children. *American Educational Research Journal, 22,* 185–198.

GARCIA, I., & GARCIA, P. A. (1989). Testing for failure: Why children fail in school and life. *Teacher Education Quarterly, 16*(4), 85–91.

GOLLNICK, D. M., & CHINN, P. C. (1994). *Multicultural education in a pluralistic society* (4th ed.). New York: Macmillan.

GONZALEZ, V. (1991). *A model of cognitive, cultural, and linguistic variables affecting bilingual Spanish/English children's development of concepts and language.* Doctoral dissertation, University of Texas at Austin. (ERIC Document Reproduction Service No. ED 345 562)

GONZALEZ, V. (1993). Assessment of language minority students: An awakening experience. *NABE News, 17*(2), 9–10, 26.

GONZALEZ, V. (1994). A model of cognitive, cultural, and linguistic variables affecting bilingual Spanish/English children's development of concepts and language. *Hispanic Journal of Behavioral Sciences, 16*(4) 396–421.

GONZALEZ, V. (1995a). The relationship between identity, culture, and language. *NABE News, 18*(5), 41–42, 46.

GONZALEZ, V. (1995b). *Cognition, culture, and language in bilingual children: Conceptual and semantic development.* Bethesda, MD: Austin & Windfield.

GONZALEZ, V. (1996). Do you believe in intelligence? Sociocultural dimensions in the assessment of intelligence in majority and minority students. *Educational Horizons, 75*(1), 45–52.

GONZALEZ, V., BAUERLE, P., & FELIX-HOLT, M. (1994a). A qualitative assessment method for accurately diagnosing bilingual gifted children. *NABE Annual Conference Journal 1992–1993* (pp. 37–52). Washington, DC: NABE.

GONZALEZ, V., BAUERLE, P., & FELIX-HOLT, M. (1994b). Deriving educational implications from using qualitative methods. *NABE News, 17*(7), 13–14, 30.

GONZALEZ, V., BRUSCA-VEGA, R., and YAWKEY, T. D. (1997). *Assessment and instruction in culturally and linguistically diverse students with or at-risk of learning problems: From research to practice.* Needham Heights, MA: Allyn and Bacon.

GONZALEZ, V., & FELIX-HOLT, M. (1995). Influence of evaluators' prior academic knowledge and beliefs on the diagnosis of cognitive and language development in bilingual Hispanic kindergartners. *New York State Association of Bilingual Education Journal, 10,* 34–45.

GONZALEZ, V., & YAWKEY, T. D. (1993). The assessment of culturally and linguistically different students: Celebrating change. *Educational Horizons, 73*(1), 41–49.

HAMAYAN, E. V. (1994). Moving to a more ecological view of assessment. *NABE News, 18*(1), 29–30.

HARNISCH, D. L., & MABRY, L. (1993). Issues in the development and evaluation of alternative assessments. *Journal of Curriculum Studies, 25*(2), 179–187.

HELLER, K. A., HOLTZMAN, W. H., & MESSICK, S. (1982). *Placing children in special education: A strategy for equity.* Washington, DC: National Academy Press.

HODGKINSON, H. L. (1992). *A demographic look at tomorrow.* Washington, DC: Institute for Educational Leadership, Center for Demographic Policy.

KAUFMAN, A. S., & KAUFMAN, N. L. (1983a). *The Kaufman Assessment Battery for Children: Administration and scoring manual.* Circle Pines, MN: American Guidance Service.

KAUFMAN, A. S., & KAUFMAN, N. L. (1983b). *The Kaufman Assessment Battery for Children: Interpretive manual.* Circle Pines, MN: American Guidance Service.

MEDINA, N., & NEILL, D. M. (1990). *Fallout from the testing explosion: How 100 million standardized exams undermine equity and excellence in America's public schools* (3rd ed.). Cambridge, MA: National Center for Fair and Open Testing.

MERCER, J. R. (1973). *Labeling the mentally retarded.* Berkeley, CA: University of California Press.

MESSICK, S. (1995). Validity of psychological assessment: Validation of inferences from persons' responses and performances as scientific inquiry into score meaning. *American Psychologist, 50*(9), 741–749.

MITCHELL, R. (1992). *Testing for Learning.* New York: Maxwell Macmillan International.

ORTIZ, A. A., & YATES, J. R. (1983). Incidence of exceptionality among Hispanics: Implications for manpower planning. *NABE, 7,* 41–53.

PEDERSEN, D. M., SHINEDLING, M. M., & JOHNSON, D. L. (1968). Effects of sex of examiner and subject on children's quantitative test performance. *Journal of Personality and Social Psychology, 10,* 251–254.

PHILLIPS, J. E. (1982). The complications of accountability: Do standardized tests treat minorities fairly? *NASSP Bulletin, 66*(457), 28–30.

QUERESHI, M. Y. (1968). Intelligence test scores as a function of sex of experimenter and sex of subject. *Journal of Psychology, 69,* 277–284.

RESCHLY, D. J. (1981). Psychological testing in educational classification and placement. *American Psychologist, 36*(10), 1094–1102.

SAMUDA, R. J. (1991). The new challenge of student assessment and placement. In R. J. Samuda, S. L. Kong, J. Cummins, J. Pascual-Leone, & J. Lewis (Eds.), *Assessment and placement of minority students* (pp. 15–24). Toronto, Ontario, Canada: C. J. Hogrefe.

SHEPARD, L. A., & SMITH, M. L. (1983). An evaluation of the identification of learning disabled students in Colorado. *Learning Disability Quarterly, 6*(2), 115–127.

SHERRITT, C. (1990). Multicultural teacher preparation: A study of teacher migration patterns and certification requirements. *Teacher Educator, 25*(4), 16–21.

STONEMAN, Z., & GIBSON, S. (1978). Situational influences on assessment performance. *Exceptional Children, 46,* 166–169.

VALENCIA, R. R. (1984). Concurrent validity of the Kaufman Assessment Battery for Children in a sample of Mexican-American children. *Educational and Psychological Measurement, 44,* 365–372.

WECHSLER, D. (1991). *Wechsler Intelligence Scale for Children–Third Edition: Manual.* New York: Psychological Corporation.

WHITWORTH, R. H., & CHRISMAN, S. M. (1987). Validation of the Kaufman Assessment Battery for Children comparing Anglo and Mexican-American preschoolers. *Educational and Psychological Measurement, 47,* 695–702.

WITT, J. C., ELLIOTT, S. N., KRAMER, J. J., & GRESHAM, F. M. (1994). *Assessment of children: Fundamental methods and practices.* Madison, WI: Brown and Benchmark.

Woodcock, R. W., & Johnson, M. (1989). *Woodcock-Johnson Psycho-Educational Battery—Revised.* Hingham, MA: Teaching Resources Corporation.

Woodcock, R. W., & Mather, N. (1989). *WJ–R Tests of Achievement: Examiner's Manual.* In R. W. Woodcock & M. B. Johnson, *Woodcock-Johnson Psycho-Educational Battery–Revised.* Allen, TX: DLM Teaching Resources.

Woodcock, R. W., & Mather, N. (1989). *WJ–R Tests of Cognitive Ability—Standard and Supplemental Batteries: Examiner's Manual.* In R. W. Woodcock & M. B. Johnson, *Woodcock-Johnson Psycho-Educational Battery–Revised.* Allen, TX: DLM Teaching Resources.

Yin, R. K. (1994). *Case study research: Designs and methods* (2nd ed.). Thousand Oaks, CA: Sage.

CHAPTER 9

Influence of Evaluators' Beliefs and Personal Backgrounds on Their Diagnostic and Placement Decisions*

VIRGINIA GONZALEZ, PATRICIA BAUERLE, WENDY BLACK, AND MARIA FELIX-HOLT

CHAPTER 9 HIGHLIGHTS THE MAJOR THEME OF THE BOOK, THE SOCIOcultural context for assessment, by providing a socioeducational framework to view evaluation. Within this sociocultural-socioeducational perspective, materials and tests need to be analyzed because they are used subjectively by evaluators. The study presented in this chapter provides a holistic view to the assessment of language-minority children, since informants' and evaluators' cultural and linguistic backgrounds, perspectives, knowledge level, and attitudes are important to the assessment process. The third and fourth themes of the book are also represented in this chapter, which refer to the need to depict a minority perspective in multiple measures of cognition and language in bilinguals. This chapter also represents the fifth and sixth themes of the book, which refer to the need to include in the construct validity of measures of bilinguals the subjectivity and responsibility of evaluators to assume an advocacy role.

The purpose of this study was to reconstruct the process of how evaluators' beliefs and cultural-linguistic backgrounds influence their diagnostic and

---

*The authors thank the 10 graduate students majoring in educational psychology who took the Testing of Minorities course during the fall 1992 semester taught by Virginia Gonzalez and who volunteered to participate in this study. The first author is grateful to the College of Education at the University of Arizona for providing funding for making this project possible through a Small Grant and and an Incentive Grant.

placement decisions for language-minority children. Our objective was to investigate the effect of the subjectivity present in evaluators' personality factors on the assessment of these children. Our argument is that reaching diagnostic and placement decisions requires evaluators to go through a subjective interpretation process that is based primarily on deriving inferences and elaborations from assessment data. This subjectivity is especially present when evaluating language-minority children because qualitative and standardized assessments yield contradictory evidence. More specifically, in this study, 10 graduate students majoring in educational psychology and taking a course in testing of minorities were interviewed about their beliefs on intelligence and first and second language development, their cultural and linguistic backgrounds, and their diagnostic and placement decisions for bilingual Hispanic kindergartners they had assessed, as well as a vignette case study portraying contradictory results stemming from standardized and qualitative measures.

The critical literature review that follows presents five personal characteristics of evaluators that affect their diagnostic and placement decisions: their attitudes, knowledge levels, familiarity with examinees, gender, and the rapport they establish with examinees. The literature review discusses the interaction of all these factors. Following the literature review is a description of the methodology used in this study, the qualitative analysis of patterns found across subjects, and discussion and conclusions.

LITERATURE REVIEW

Effect of Evaluators' Personalities

We start this literature review by referring to the resulting metaprocess in this research study. That is, the same effect that evaluators' personalities had on their examinees that we were studying also influenced our interviewers and research data. We refer to the idiosyncratic variables, such as the interviewers' personality styles and ethnic backgrounds, that influenced the amount of probing that they were inclined to do with the subjects' responses to the interview questions. Although we tried to be objective in our data collection procedures and instruments, we could not control the most important tool for assessment: the personality of evaluators. With this metaprocess present in our data, we want to illustrate the process that most evaluators are not even aware of: the extent to which their personalities influence their diagnostic and placement decisions, especially when they are working with language-minority children.

Research has documented the presence of evaluators' biases when studying the language proficiency of adolescent and adult second and foreign language learners (e.g., Cummin, 1990; LeVine & Haus, 1987; Wigglesworth, 1993). Some studies have investigated the effect of evaluators' personality factors, such as their gender and ethnicity, on the test performance of majority adult examinees. For instance, Franco and LeVine (1985) studied the effects of evaluators' variables on the self-disclosure of college sophomores. They found that "gross examiner variables such as gender and ethnicity as well as more subtle variables such as verbal style of administration can significantly affect personality test results" (p. 195). However, there is a paucity of research examining which characteristics of evaluators or which interaction patterns influence the test performance of language-minority children (Fuchs & Fuchs, 1989). Clearly, more research is needed on this important area (Fuchs, Fuchs, Power, & Dailey, 1985).

Effect of Evaluators' Beliefs. Evaluators' beliefs affect the performance of examinees. As Holland (1980) stated, "Each professional, as well as the student and his or her parents, interprets the vast amounts of varied information through previous experiences, biases, beliefs, and perspectives" (p. 553). In fact, biases, beliefs, and perspectives are related to evaluators' attitudes. There are different definitions of attitudes, but for the purposes of this study, we use Baker's (1992) definition: that attitudes involve cognitive components (thoughts and beliefs), affective components (feelings toward an object or subject), and behavioral components (a readiness for action). Attitudes, says Baker, can be measured by using self-reports and observation of behaviors.

In this study self-reports in the form of interviews with open-ended questions were used to tap cognitive components of attitudes referring to subjects' thoughts and beliefs about intelligence and first and second language development. The subjects' actual diagnosis and placement decisions for bilingual Hispanic kindergartners from their own assessments and a vignette case study were used for exploring the relationship between cognitive and behavioral components of attitudes. Thus, the cognitive component of attitudes in the form of beliefs relates to the knowledge evaluators have acquired through professional training. That is, the particular assessment models and philosophies they endorse are related to their beliefs about how language-minority children develop cognitively and linguistically. Knowledge and beliefs are related to experiences, such as professional training and cultural-linguistic backgrounds, which in turn are expressed through behaviors.

Effect of Evaluators' Professional Training. The graduate students participating as evaluators in this study engaged in professional training endorsing the ethnic researcher assessment model, which emphasizes culture and language as developmental factors portraying the interaction among internal and external factors, with idiosyncratic factors affecting development, and also measuring potential for learning instead of just the children's verbal cultural knowledge. (For a more thorough explanation of this model, see Gonzalez & Yawkey, 1993.) The graduate students were stimulated to discuss and compare both the traditional medical model, which endorses a deficit-oriented paradigm, and the ethnic researcher model, which endorses a developmental perspective. In addition, research on intelligence and first and second language theories conducted during the past 30 years, with an emphasis on the past 5 years, was discussed critically to provide students with the opportunity to review their attitudes, beliefs, and thoughts while acquiring new knowledge. Moreover, this study provided them an opportunity to accumulate actual experience on the assessment of language-minority students. Their practical experience using standardized and qualitative assessments for identifying gifted Hispanic bilingual kindergartners and their interviews about their assessments gave to this study a measure of the behavioral components of attitudes.

A study conducted by Carpenter (1992) showed the effect of professional training on the cognitive and behavioral components of attitudes held by evaluators. According to Carpenter, training and experience in specific domains may influence those trained in the deficit paradigm to shift their thinking to a different paradigm. For instance, evaluators with low- and middle-level knowledge were found to base their decisions purely on the children's performance in English and consequently relied on the deficit model. In contrast, evaluators with training and experience in theories and best practices with language-minority children took into account linguistic and cultural backgrounds and shifted from deficit to difference paradigms in clinical assessments. Thus, evaluators with an increase in their knowledge base tended to decrease their attributions given to internal disorders in minority children and increase their attributions given to the second language learning status of language-minority children. According to Carpenter, "Less knowledgeable clinicians diagnosed children as disordered, recommended English speech-language therapy, and attributed performance to language disorder more frequently than subjects with higher knowledge base scores" (p. 151).

The presence of biases in evaluators' ratings of second language learning proficiency has also been recognized. Douglas (1994) noted that raters of the performance of second language learners are biased for specific features of the discourse due to their different ability levels for interpreting the examinee's responses. Douglas suggested that we need "more 'think-aloud' studies of rating processes" (p. 135) in order to understand the process that evaluators go through for rating the examinees' language performance. Including more information on the evaluators' individual characteristics (their knowledge level and previous professional training) will increase the validity of the interpretation of the second language learners' assessment. Douglas stated, "Validity is a concept related to the interpretation of test performance. Unless we can understand the bases of evaluators' judgments, our interpretations based on those judgments are likely to be flawed" (p. 136).

Offering professional training to teachers on the assessment of language-minority students is highly important. Teachers have been found to overrate the oral language proficiency of their students, especially those who receive high grades in their classes (LeVine & Haus, 1987). This issue is particularly important because Ysseldyke and Thurlow (1984) found that once teachers had referred high school students for evaluation, the probability of these students' being placed in special education was very high. They wrote, "Once a student is referred, 92 percent are evaluated, and 73 percent of the students who are evaluated are actually placed in special education" (p. 59). They attributed this high probability of placement in special education to psychometrically inadequate tests and problems in the diagnostic system, such as the medical model assumption that the diagnostic team needs to find the student's internal problem.

Finally, training evaluators to increase their cultural and linguistic knowledge is important for communicating with parents of language-minority children. For example, Koocher (1994) reported that discussants who examined a vignette case study of an immigrant child who became the focus of a cultural conflict between parental values and school values argued that school psychologists can educate parents as to the different choices, but parents should make the final decision as to what educational interventions or placements are best for the child. Psychologists can also search for objectives common to both the home and school culture. These two objectives can be accomplished by evaluators only if they have been properly trained in the cultural and linguistic factors affecting minority families.

Effect of Evaluators' Familiarity with Examinees. Some studies have documented the effect of familiar and unfamiliar evaluators on the test performance of young children on intelligence standardized tests. For instance, Sacks (1952) found that 3-year-old children received significantly higher IQ scores when tested by a familiar evaluator than when tested by an unfamiliar one. Kinnie and Sternlof (1971) found that the IQ scores of both middle- and lower-class children could be significantly improved by providing them with some familiarity with examiners and verbal and nonverbal stimuli before the test.

Other studies have found that preschool and school-age, moderately to profoundly language-impaired children obtained significantly higher scores on the Clinical Evaluation of Language Functions (CELF) comprehensive language test when assessed by familiar examiners. The CELF comprises an auditory comprehension and an oral verbal expression scale. In one study, children were tested by a familiar and an unfamiliar examiner in a crossover design, with each examiner testing both language-impaired and non-language-impaired students (Fuchs et al., 1985). The time of the testing was controlled, and familiarity consisted of home visits and a 20–30-minute one-to-one play session prior to testing. In a second study Fuchs, Fuchs, and Power (1987) found that children with learning disabilities performed significantly higher with evaluators who spent one hour playing with them prior to the testing. In addition, black and Hispanic children have been found to perform significantly higher with familiar than with unfamiliar evaluators (Fuchs & Fuchs, 1989).

Effect of Evaluators' Gender. Studies have found that the gender of the evaluator interacts with the gender and age of the examinee, especially because developmental factors of young children influence their test performance. Quereshi (1968) found a significant interaction between the evaluator's and examinee's gender and interpreted these differences as due to four possible factors:

1. Female evaluators tend to be more liberal when scoring tests than male examiners.
2. Female evaluators do more inquiring than male evaluators.
3. The rapport established by female evaluators led to a more positive psychological atmosphere than the one established by male evaluators.
4. Female evaluators elicited more verbal responses from examinees than male evaluators.

Significant differences in IQ scores have also been found to be affected by the gender of the examiner, with female evaluators obtaining higher scores of children than male evaluators do, especially when assessing young children (Back & Dana, 1977). This difference seems to be unrelated to the evaluator's amount of experience. However, when males have been instructed on how to build rapport more effectively and have spent 15 minutes with the child on the day prior to testing, no significant differences were found for the full scale sores (Back & Dana, 1980). Nevertheless, significant differences were found for subtest scores of the Wechsler Intelligence Scale, with male evaluators obtaining higher scores on the Arithmetic and Vocabulary subtests and female evaluators obtaining higher scores on the Object Assembly subtest (Back & Dana, 1980). Yet in testing-the-limits procedures used with the Picture Arrangement and Block Design subtests of the Wechsler Intelligence Scale, evaluators have been found to provide different numbers of clues that have not affected young children's performance significantly (Sattler, 1969). Thus, it seems that professional training can make a difference in the effect that evaluators' gender can have on the test performance of young children. Additionally, the administration of tests is influenced by the socialization process through which the evaluators and the young children have developed their gender identity.

Effect of Rapport Established Between Evaluator and Examinee. The quality of rapport between the examiner and the child to be evaluated has a significant effect on test scores. For instance, Sacks (1952) and Sattler and Theye (1967) showed that the rapport established between the evaluators and young children made a significant difference in examinees' IQ scores. The type of feedback provided by evaluators, such as approval or disapproval, has also been reported to affect children's performance on verbal learning tasks (Katz, Henchy, & Allen, 1968). However, the influence of feedback has also been shown to be related to the individual needs of the children being tested. Thus, both evaluators' and children's personality characteristics affect the quality of rapport established in a testing situation because a different chemistry results from the interaction of both personalities within a particular context.

Interaction of Evaluators' Personalities and Their Diagnostic and Placement Decisions

The literature has shown different personality characteristics of evaluators interacting with the idiosyncratic factors brought by examinees to the testing situation. Some of these characteristics relate to the prior experiences that evaluators and examinees have had within a particular sociocultural environment. For evaluators, one of these prior experiences refers to their professional training. Evaluators' beliefs and knowledge acquired in professional training are always contextualized within a particular philosophical perspective. In addition, no two evaluators will respond similarly to the same professional training because their idiosyncratic personality characteristics, such as their cultural-linguistic backgrounds and their gender and ethnic identities. Thus, studying the effect of the subjectivity brought to the testing situation by evaluators on their diagnostic and placement decisions can potentially improve practices in evaluating language-minority children.

RESEARCH QUESTIONS

We asked five research questions for exploring evaluators' beliefs, cultural-linguistic backgrounds, and their level of awareness of the effect of their personalities on the assessment of language-minority children:

1. What are the beliefs held by evaluators on cognitive and language development and qualitative and standardized measures for language-minority children?
2. Are evaluators' cultural-linguistic backgrounds related to their beliefs?
3. Are evaluators' behaviors related to their beliefs and cultural-linguistic backgrounds?
4. Are evaluators' beliefs related to their diagnostic and placement decisions for actual and control case studies?
5. Are evaluators aware of the effect of their personalities on the diagnosis and placement of language-minority children?

METHOD

Research Design

Given that the first purpose of the study was to investigate what aspects of evaluators' beliefs and cultural-linguistic backgrounds influence the assessment of language-minority children, a combination of the exploratory-interpretative and the analytical-nomological methodological approaches was adopted. We sought to gain an understanding of the assessment of language-minority children, using established replicable procedures.

In accordance with the exploratory-interpretative methodological approach, this study was primarily concerned with ensuring validity (Grotjahn, 1987). To ensure validity in this approach, openness, characterized by avoidance of framing the data to a specific theory, is required until the data are structured by the informants. Thus, subjects are considered to be knowledgeable informants who collaborate with the researchers for the construction of a theoretical model that can explain the data (Grotjahn, 1987). Grothjahn pointed out that the informants' "subjective theories are of central importance for the process of theory construction" (p. 65). Thus, through this approach, the subjects' verbalizations were used to guide the process of theory construction.

Following the exploratory-interpretative paradigm and in order to ensure validity, a triangulation of data, theory, and methodology was used. For each subject, triangulation of data consisted of the following:

- Protocols of the children assessed by the subjects
- Explicit verbalizations during a semistructured interview of each subject
- Comparison of subjects' verbalizations to those of their partners
- Subjects' diagnostic and placement decisions of a real and control case studies

Triangulation of the theories employed consisted of those explicit or implicit beliefs that the subjects related during the course of the interview in reference to theories of intelligence and first and second language development. Triangulation of the methodology employed consisted of a semistructured interview with open-ended questions, including the presentation of a vignette case study. In addition, the subjects' responses were treated as qualitative data, which, due to the amount of probing done by interviewers, can be considered think-aloud protocols.

In accordance with the analytical-nomological paradigm, objectivity, reproducibility, reliability, standardization, validity, and representativity were employed as criteria. Objectivity consisted of tape recording and transcribing the interviews given to all subjects and assigning each subject within a pair of evaluators, whenever possible, to two different interviewers. Random assignment of evaluators to interviewers was not used because schedule convenience was the most important factor taken into consideration for assigning subjects. Reliability consisted of calculating the number of agreements and disagreements for the transcriptions across four coders (the four authors of this chapter, two of whom had also served as interviewers). In addition, the measures employed to ensure objectivity and reliability contributed to the replicability of the study. Validity measures consisted of subjects' diagnostic and placement decisions for an actual case and a vignette case study. Construct validity was established by conducting a pilot test of the interview questions with a subject who had similar characteristics to the sample of this study. The representativity of this study includes graduate students majoring in educational psychology who may become evaluators. It can be questioned whether a similar study may be needed among practicing professionals.

Subjects

Fifteen graduate students majoring in educational psychology at a major state university in the southwest area of the United States, who took a course on the assessment of minorities, were invited to volunteer to participate in an interview exploring their beliefs and cultural-linguistic backgrounds. These students had evaluated Hispanic bilingual kindergartners of low socioeconomic status using the Qualitative Use of English and Spanish Tests (QUEST, Gonzalez, 1991, 1994, 1995) as part of their course requirements. Their instructor was the first author of this chapter. From those 16 graduate students, 2 (the second and fourth authors) became the interviewers, and 12 volunteered to participate in the study. (One moved out of town before the interviews began.)

Of the remaining 11 volunteered subjects, 3 were males and 8 were females; their ages ranged between 22 and 55 years old (1 was between ages 22 and 25, 5 were between ages 26 and 35, 3 were between ages 36 and 45, and 2 were between ages 46 and 55. They were 1 Asian-American, 2 Middle Eastern–Americans, 3 African-Americans, 4 European-Americans, and 1 South Asian international student. However, 1 of these 11 volunteered subjects was invited to participate in the pilot study, leaving a final sample of 10 subjects. The subject participating in the pilot study was a female European-American between 26 and 35 years of age. (This subject is described in Gonzalez & Felix-Holt, 1995.) Five of the 10 subjects in the final sample administered QUEST to two different children, and the other 5 subjects administered QUEST to one child. All assessed kindergartners were from a Hispanic bilingual background and attended the same public school in a low socioeconomic status "barrio" in a metropolitan city of the southwest region of the United States.

Instruments

Interviews. A semistructured open-ended interview was developed with 18 open-ended questions in three areas:

1. Beliefs about cognitive-linguistic development and alternative and standardized measures (9 questions)
2. Evaluators' cultural-linguistic backgrounds (3 questions)
3. Diagnostic and placement decisions about a child assessed by each subject using QUEST (Gonzalez, 1991, 1994), the second language administration of QUEST to the same child assessed by a different pair of evaluators, and a vignette case study presenting contradictory results in standardized and alternative assessments (6 questions)

Appendix 9A contains the interview questions. According to Carpenter (1992), when presenting ambiguous cases, this ill-structured content would allow opportunity to explore the influence of individual characteristics on the evaluators' diagnostic and placement decisions. For the purposes of this study, and following Carpenter's recommendations, contradictory assessments' results were presented to the subjects in the vignette case study of a language-minority child.

QUEST. Gonzalez (1991, 1994, 1995) developed a model that explains the concept formation process in bilingual children and identified two knowledge representational systems dependent on the particular cognitive, linguistic, and cultural characteristics of the content learned. The first conceptual representational system is abstract, universal, and nonverbal; the second is semantic, verbal, and culturally and linguistically bound. Cognitive factors were considered abstract knowledge representations instantiated in cultural symbolic conventions and in linguistic structures and markers. Cultural and linguistic factors were selected because Spanish assigns linguistic gender to both animate and inanimate abstract conceptual categories, corresponding to culturally important symbolic distinctions, expressed through linguistic rules and markers. In contrast, English assigns linguistic gender to only some animate conceptual abstract categories. The model from which the classification tasks were derived was based partially on Piagetian theory (Piaget, 1967) and on the constraint model (Markman, 1984, Waxman, 1990). This model was found to have construct validity as shown by parametric and nonparametric tests (Gonzalez, 1991, 1994, 1995).

The five derived verbal and nonverbal classification tasks were designed to assess bilingual children's general and linguistic gender conceptual processes for two different abstract, symbolic, and linguistic semantic categories represented by animals (animate) and food (inanimate) objects. Stimuli used for the five classification tasks were plastic full-color objects representing 14 groupings reflecting the interaction of cognitive, cultural, and linguistic factors. Stimuli groupings were validated using judges for ensuring construct validity and three pilot tests for ensuring content validity (Gonzalez, 1991, 1994, 1995). Three of these five classification tasks are verbal (labeling, defining, and verbal justification of sorting) and two are nonverbal (sorting and category clue).

Labeling is operationalized as a verbal production task that measures language development at two levels: the object level, reflecting word knowledge, and the gender level, indicating knowledge of the linguistic structures and markers for gender assignment. Defining is operationalized as a verbal production and comprehension task that measures verbal conceptual development as it gives information of the child's ability to produce and understand basic and nonbasic semantic categories. For the labeling task, the child is presented plastic objects and asked to name them ("What do you call this?"), while giving her one item at a time, followed by the defining task at the production level in which the child is asked four probes to elicit a description of the object(s) ("What is a _____?" "What is a _____ like?" "Tell me something about a _____," and "What does a _____ look like?"). Next, for tapping the comprehension level of the defining task, the child is given a definition that points to verbal and nonverbal clues for class inclusion categories of objects (taxonomic categories: superordinate, intermediate, and subcategories). This definition is repeated three times, and then the child is asked to define three different kinds of items.

The sorting and verbal justification of sorting tasks measure nonverbal and verbal concept formation at the production level based on the interface of linguistic gender assignments, sociocultural symbolic meanings, and abstract semantic categories. For the sorting task, the child is asked to group the objects by linguistic gender, followed by the verbal justification of sorting task in which the child is asked to explain the order imposed on the objects and is presented with metalinguistic counterexamples that change groupings and labels. Category clue is a nonverbal comprehension level task that measures the child's ability to understand metalinguistic hints given by linguistic gender assignment and to construct links of metalinguistic clues, symbolic meanings, and semantic categories. For the category clue task, the child is provided with a model of how to group objects by linguistic gender using two pictures of identical dolls; then she is asked to sort the objects following the model provided, to explain her groupings, and to answer metalinguistic counterexamples that change groupings and labels.

The scoring system is divided into five-point assignment areas: language development, verbal and nonverbal general, and verbal and nonverbal gender areas. Based on their scores, children are diagnosed on conceptual development (for an extended description of scoring, see Gonzalez, 1991, 1995). General areas include any valid criteria that the child uses for classification (e.g., color, functions, subcategories). Gender areas include classification criteria based on physical gender for animates, linguistic gender assignment for inanimates, or functional use for both animates and inanimates. Thus, children's responses to the five tasks administered in both languages were scored twice, assigning points for both general and gender areas. The language development area was categorized into three levels: low (0–2 points), moderate (3–5 points), and high (6–8 points), according to the number of labels produced by the child. For the other four areas, children's responses were categorized into five stages based partially on Piaget's theory (1965): (1) no classification (affective responses, juxtaposed groupings, and graphic collections), (2) preconceptual: perceptual (extralinguistic features—color, size, shape, parts of objects), (3) preconceptual: functional (thematic relations), (4) symbolic representation (symbolic play, acting out, onomatopeic sounds), (5) analogical reasoning (comparisons), (6) concrete (taxonomic categories showing class inclusion), (7) creativity (uniqueness of responses, and fluency and flexibility of thinking), and (8) metalinguistic (taxonomic semantic categories). Some of these developmental levels (1, 2, 3, 6, and 8) have been shown to be valid and reliable in previous data-driven studies (Gonzalez, 1991, 1994, 1995; Gonzalez, Bauerle, & Felix-Holt, 1994, 1995). Other developmental levels (4, 5, and 7) are being pilot-tested in more recent data-driven studies (Gonzalez, Riojas-Clark, & Bauerle, 1996; Gonzalez, Riojas-Clark, Bauerle, & Black, 1996).

Vignette Case Study

David (a pseudonym) was 5 years, 10 months old at the time of the assessment. He was a third-generation Mexican-American child, who was a passive bilingual, with English as a first language and some understanding of Spanish. David's parents' ratings of the child's language proficiency indicated an above-average level for English and "not quite adequate in comparison with peers" for Spanish. David was classified by the Language Assessment Scales (LAS; De Avila & Duncan, 1986) as a non-Spanish speaker and a fluent English speaker.

On the parents' survey, David's parents reported that he made new friends easily, and everybody seemed to like him. He liked to ask questions and make people laugh with his anecdotes. When playing with other children, David liked to be in charge and to organize games; when by himself, David liked to draw and do homework. He was described as friendly, observant, curious, talkative, energetic, independent, outgoing, cooperative, imaginative, and creative. David's classroom teacher was a monolingual English speaker of Anglo ethnicity. The teacher's survey described him as a highly verbal child who asked many questions and told many anecdotes related to academic activities. His teacher reported his greatest abilities to be in math; he performed at higher levels than his peers in logical operations (seriation, conservation of number, and classification). David's teacher also reported that he liked to draw, especially in his journal, in which he worked intently, taking a lot of time to make complete illustrations. David was described as enthusiastic regarding all aspects of school, as an actively involved child who persevered in academic activities, and as a risk taker who used trial and error. He was admired by his peers because he was competitive in a positive way, and he liked to cooperate with others while taking the leadership role. In sum, David was described by his teacher as active, creative, observant, and curious.

When administered the QUEST (Gonzalez, 1991, 1994, 1995), David was diagnosed as performing at concrete and metalinguistic levels for the production and comprehension tasks when forming verbal and nonverbal concepts in English and Spanish. On the Raven's Coloured Progressive Matrices (Raven, 1976), David scored at the seventy-ninth percentile and seventh stanine. The district required as the standard criterion for placement in the gifted education program a score in the ninety-seventh percentile or above on a standardized intelligence test. The Raven's Coloured Progressive Matrices is a standardized test measuring spatiotemporal relationships considered to be a nonverbal intelligence "g" (general) factor.

However, in spite of the low score on the Raven's Coloured Progressive Matrices, the information given by David's parents and classroom teacher and by QUEST was used as the primary criteria by the multidisciplinary assessment committee. It was recommended that David be placed in a bilingual gifted first-grade classroom the following school year, because he had shown an ability to form verbal concepts, a command of the English language above age-appropriate levels, and a good understanding of the Spanish language in the QUEST administration. This recommendation was based on the belief that David could develop his strengths and use the great amount of creativity, imagination, verbal and social skills, and intrinsic motivation demonstrated through QUEST in a bilingual gifted classroom. (See Gonzalez et al.,1994, for a complete description of this case study.)

Procedure

Students taking the selected graduate course in testing of minorities assessed bilingual Hispanic kindergartners and were invited to be interviewed about their beliefs and cultural-linguistic backgrounds. Sessions for the interviews were scheduled at the convenience of the participants and lasted approximately 45 minutes. Interviews were collected between 4 to 10 months after the subjects finished the course. They were conducted on a one-to-one basis and were audiotaped and later transcribed to ensure reliability in the data analysis.

The second and fourth authors of this chapter functioned as interviewers and had also taken the same graduate class on the testing of minorities with the subjects for this study. At the time of data collection, these two interviewers were also graduate students of the same educational psychology department that the subjects were in, and they had been involved in the administration of QUEST in Spanish and English to the same pool of bilingual children whom the subjects had assessed. One of the interviewers was of Mexican-American ethnic background, and the other was of European-American background. Both interviewers were females between 26 and 35 years of age.

Data Analysis Design

With the purpose of conducting a systematic analysis and synthesis of data, interpretation will follow the three types of focus suggested by Bogdan and Biklen (1982):

1. Thesis or propositions related to the paradigm proposed in this study
2. Themes that encompass theoretical formulations emerging from data analysis in the form of patterns or abstract conceptual categories
3. Topics that include descriptions of specific findings.

Thus, the qualitative analysis of evaluators' interview responses will yield to common thesis, themes, and topics that will help synthesize findings into conclusions.

A qualitative coding scheme was developed on the basis of the three theses that emerged on the transcripts. Three nominal categories were developed based on the content found in the interviews (see Appendix 9B for a complete list of nominal categories and subcategories) corresponding to the three theses found in this study:

1. Evaluators' beliefs about cognitive and first and second language development and measures
2. Evaluators' cultural-linguistic backgrounds
3. Evaluators' diagnostic and placement decisions.

This coding scheme was pilot-tested in three of the transcripts by the four authors working independently, and an interrater agreement of .89 and .85 was obtained correspondingly between each of the two pairs of raters.

RESULTS

First Thesis: Evaluators' Beliefs About Cognitive and Language Development and Measures

The first thesis refers to the evaluators' beliefs about cognitive and first and second language development and measures; it corresponds to the first research question of this study. The summary of group data will be discussed in relation to the nominal categories presented in Appendix 9B.

The first theme of this first thesis refers to beliefs about personal definitions of psychological constructs, including intelligence, language, culture, and similarities and differences between majority and minority students. On beliefs about intelligence, most subjects endorsed that both nature and nurture influence intelligence development. Most defined intelligence as transferring thinking processes and knowledge to new situations and making symbolic or abstract conceptual relationships. For instance, one subject stated, "Intelligence is how to transfer abstract knowledge to different situations according to what you see as similar to a prior situation." When asked about their beliefs on language development, most subjects also endorsed the nature and nurture interactionist view. Most believed that the presence of a human capacity for learning languages interacted with the cultural environment, which included attitudinal belief systems and role models. Language and intelligence development were also related. Most subjects viewed language as a tool for learning because verbal intelligence was considered an important area in most tests, and also because language could lead to higher abstract cognitive processes, such as metacognition and metalinguistic awareness. One subject explained, "Language influences intelligence because it is a tool for metacognition, as you can use language to understand concepts." Subjects also mentioned that learning from the first language could be transferred to the second language, or vice versa, and that language helped cognitive development. Another respondent purported: "If intelligence is social application of knowledge, then individuals from minority cultures develop intelligence quicker because they can transfer concepts between two cognitive sets at an early age."

Next, the role of culture was related to intelligence development. Most subjects stated that cultural views are passed on through language, and they endorsed the view that differences occur among definitions of intelligence because of cultural values and needs present in different societies. These subjects also mentioned that intelligence tests reflected these cultural values held in a particular society and made intelligence culturally bound. Representative of others, one subject stated, "The intelligence potential is present in everyone; what is different is the cultural environment." Thus, the most common view of these subjects was that the sociocultural environment powerfully affects the development of intelligence.

Finally, the fifth topic discussed was similarities and differences between majority and minority students in intelligence development. Most subjects held the view that intelligence development is the same for all, because language is a tool for learning for both monolinguals and bilinguals. Some subjects also explained differences between monolingual and bilingual students, such as:

- These are individual differences among particular children.
- Different contextual factors affect children (e.g., family, socioeconomic status).

- Developmental time for language learning is longer for bilinguals in comparison to monolinguals due to the presence of two linguistic systems and the need to develop social and academic language proficiency.
- The process of second language learning is easier for younger children.
- The different linguistic structures and semantic characteristics of the two languages learned affect the thinking process positively.

Thus, most respondents believed that teaching methodologies for monolingual and bilingual students should reflect cultural and linguistic differences.

The second theme established in this first thesis refers to beliefs about measurement: norms; attitudes of researchers, test developers, and evaluators reflected in tests; multiple measurements; validity and reliability; ameliorating problems in assessing language-minority students; and qualitative and quantitative instruments.

The first topic of this second theme referred to the belief held by most subjects that bilingual children need to be tested in both languages and with culturally appropriate materials. One subject said, "Language-minority children should be tested in their own language, and standards from one culture should not be used for measuring abilities of children who belong to another culture. The results are meaningless if evaluators do that." The second topic emphasized the need for evaluators to be familiar with the cultural and linguistic backgrounds of language-minority children when testing them. As one subject stated, "Evaluators should not consciously or unconsciously impose their own mainstream cultural values when testing language-minority children, but should know what language is spoken at the children's home and their cultural background information." The third topic that emerged from the interviews stressed the need for evaluators to make language-minority children comfortable in the testing situation. "Evaluators need to take care of language-minority children tested by making them feel comfortable, because assessment is mostly a matter of attitudes, and language-minority children should not be put at a disadvantage," noted one subject.

When asked about their views on standardized and qualitative assessments, subjects offered cautionary thoughts and recommendations. The need for a complete and holistic battery of different types of assessments, including alternative ones, was related. One individual cautioned, "Evaluators should be aware of the limitations of standardized tests when used for different purposes than the ones that they were developed and normed for." Most subjects also saw the need for evaluators to value individual differences in language-minority children, to avoid stereotypical attitudes, and to assess language-minority children with nonbiased instruments in order to help them get needed services. Many interviews referred to limitations found in standardized tests, such as inappropriate norms for language-minority children, the need to interpret scores with caution, and the effect of evaluators' personal characteristics on even tests considered to be more objective, such as standardized tests. For instance, a subject commented, "Language-minority children should be assessed with instruments that are not biased, and evaluators should be aware of the influence of their attitudes on the objectives for which the instruments are used." Next, subjects' beliefs about qualitative assessments referred to advantages, such as emphasis on developmental processes and superiority to standardized tests, as well as some disadvantages, such as the need to be developed further, and the fact that it is impossible to develop general instruments for different cultures. One subject commented, "Qualitative instruments help us to understand development better as their administration is individualized."

The last topic sought to investigate the influence of the use of QUEST on the beliefs of subjects. Most subjects stated that they had become:

- More sensitive to the limitations of standardized tests when assessing language-minority children, such as the emphasis on verbal abilities
- Aware of the importance of emphasizing nonverbal performances
- Aware of the need to assess in the first language of the children
- Aware of the need to make children comfortable and avoid anxiety-producing testing situations
- Aware of the need for alternative assessments
- More aware of the important role that evaluators' attitudes play when assessing language-minority children

Illustrating the limitations of tests that rely on highly verbal abilities, one subject stated, "I have realized that some language-minority children may know the meaning of some concepts but may not be able to express it." Another subject revealed a compelling scenario: "I have become more aware of the language problem when testing language-minority children and my not being able to speak Spanish. So I thought at first that something was wrong with the children, but then I realized that they did not understand English. So I have become more aware of my limitations." Another subject stated that she "was able to realize that language-minority children are able to see different sides of things through the different languages that they have." As shown by this topic and as stated by Douglas (1994), the professional training evaluators receive is important for reducing the bias effect of their knowledge levels on their diagnostic decisions for language-minority children.

Second Thesis: Evaluators' Cultural-Linguistic Backgrounds

Regarding the second thesis, referring to the evaluators' cultural-linguistic backgrounds, and the second research question referring to whether evaluators' backgrounds were related to their beliefs, four topics were found. The first topic referred to the positive influence of traveling and living in another culture on the values and beliefs held by subjects toward the assessment of language-minority children. One subject, who had spent three months in Asia and about three and a half months in Europe, said that her traveling helped her "to become aware that our views of reality are dictated by our culture, and that is just one version of reality, and that many people of different cultures can interpret reality differently based upon their values and meanings they give to life. The task of minority assessment just points out that you have to be sensitive to those differences and not place judgment."

The second topic emerged from the interviews as subjects stated that the experience of assessing language-minority children had a positive influence on the beliefs they held. They had realized the importance of external factors on development, the presence of individual differences, and the subsequent need to use different assessment strategies to match these individual needs of examinees. For instance, one subject noted that her assessment experience helped her "to be more sensitive to other factors that are not just strictly in the classroom environment. You look at the interrelationships with parents, siblings, the socioeconomic status, and language ability. You cannot just look at one single isolated area of the life of the child and then make an assessment based on that." They also realized the need to learn theory of second language learning and the need to use testing-the-limits techniques. Interviewees additionally referred to the positive influence of the research literature they had read about the assessment of language-minority children on their beliefs and attitudes. Fourth, subjects revealed that their personal multicultural and multilingual background and professional training were related to their level of awareness of bicultural issues. One subject commented, "I think that my abilities to speak another language besides English has helped me tremendously to assess better the language-minority child, because I was more empathetic."

Third Thesis: Relationship of Evaluators' Personal Backgrounds, Beliefs, and Assessment Behaviors

Regarding the third thesis, referring to diagnostic and placement decisions, and the third research question, referring to whether evaluators' backgrounds and beliefs were related to their assessment behaviors, 10 topics emerged. The first topic referred to the influence of traveling and living in another culture on the sensitivity to differences held by the subjects. For instance, one subject remarked, "I've done a lot of traveling, a lot of looking into other ways of life. I have a definite interest in other ways of doing things. I am very sensitive, I think, to cultural diversity and alternative ways of receiving and expressing your created version of reality." A second emerging topic was the sensitivity to biases when assessing language-minority students that was related to the personal and professional experiences of subjects. A subject observed, "Being monolingual probably hindered me in my recognition of giftedness in a bilingual child; probably I wasn't as sensitive as I could have been if I had been bilingual." A third topic developed as some related the fact that their lack of testing experience left questions about the accuracy of their behaviors when assessing language-minority children. One subject explained, "I needed a lot of more practice in assessment. I did not have a lot of experience at that time. I didn't feel comfortable because I was still fumbling, and that just made it worse for the child." For others, having had past testing experience positively influenced their views on the behaviors of evaluators. A subject said that experience working with children helped "for establishing very fast rapport with children and know where they are at."

Relating personal characteristics to their assessment behaviors, subjects who had a minority background reported feeling more empathic regarding language-minority children's performance. One subject said, "I think being a minority has helped me in assessing language-minority children because, as they say, 'It takes one to know one,' and I understand how minority children feel living in a country that is different from theirs. So I feel sympathy because I've been down that road. I was a minority child, and I went to grade school here [in America] too, so I had to struggle to learn the new language too." Another topic referred to the influence of personality traits (being sensitive, being highly attentive to details, personal biases such as moods, stressing fairness, establishing good rapport, being open-minded and patient) on assessment behaviors. One subject realized that "my biases, my personal characteristics—if I'm frowning or smiling at the child, if I'm in a bad mood—is a large portion of how my behaviors can influence the assessment of the child." For nearly all subjects, varied experiences led to the belief that establishing a good rapport is the most important aspect of assessing young children, encapsulated in this comment: "What I am concerned with in a testing situation is establishing rapport with the child. Whatever is my and the child's culture and language—this is what I'm supposed to do."

Subjects who did not speak Spanish yet assessed children whose first language was Spanish had many unanswered questions about the accuracy of their assessment. Most reported a willingness to learn Spanish and noted the usefulness of it for their future professional lives. One interviewee revealed, "I felt that when the child started to speak in Spanish, I could not communicate any longer with him and that I needed to learn Spanish. It was not the child's problem, but it was my problem that I could not speak Spanish." Most subjects recognized that not only the lack of Spanish, but also the lack of knowledge in linguistic and language development, can hinder their ability as evaluators to make accurate decisions when assessing language-minority children. One subject discovered she needed "more information about language to assess minority children, like the levels of language and conceptual ability, like metalinguistic abilities. I have never heard of that, and it could hinder my decisions." Thus, as pointed out by Carpenter (1992), evaluators with training in theories and best practices for assessing language-minority children take into account external variables affecting test performance, such as the extent of their knowledge about cultural-linguistic differences. The last topic within this third thesis came forth as subjects acknowledged their awareness that the assessment of language-minority children was a course assignment, and that could have affected their assessment behaviors and placement decisions.

Fourth Thesis: Effect of Evaluators' Beliefs on Diagnostic and Placement Decisions

Regarding the fourth thesis, referring to the fourth research question about the effect of evaluators' beliefs on their diagnostic and placement decisions, four topics arose. The first topic demonstrated that subjects used their beliefs about bilingual and gifted education as well as the validity and reliability of measures as rationales for explaining their placement decisions. One subject stated, "This child performed at very high levels nonverbally, and I think that he showed above-normal verbal conceptual abilities too, so I would place him in a gifted classroom." Second, most referred to the use of personal observations as rationales for explaining placement decisions. For instance, a subject concluded, "I think that it is still too early for placing this child, because she is only in kindergarten, and I need to see how she does in a normal classroom."

Some subjects felt they were unable to make a recommendation, stating the need for more information for making placement decisions, such as observations across contexts. One subject commented, "I cannot make a placement decision for this child because I need to see how he does in the classroom, and also include parents and teachers as informants." In fact, there was a strong overall belief among these subjects of the need for a complete battery of assessments examining multiple developmental areas in order to make accurate diagnostic and placement decisions. "I need to assess the child's performance also in math and his social skills, because it seems that he does very well nonverbally in the QUEST, but I need to use other instruments as well," a respondent remarked.

Finally, regarding the fifth thesis, some subjects made explicit statements about the relationship of their personal backgrounds, beliefs, and diagnostic and placement behaviors. One subject stated, "I feel as if my knowledge of Spanish helped me to understand how language affects intelligence and also for being fairer when I evaluated a bilingual child."

DISCUSSION

Our findings support the fact that the evaluators' cognitive components of attitudes such as their beliefs do influence their theoretical conceptualizations and beliefs and, ultimately, their diagnostic and placement decisions made for language-minority children. In relation to the internal validity of QUEST and based on the findings, it seems that when assessing language-minority children, this qualitative measurement identifies additional and useful information that is overlooked by standardized testing. This additional information refers to the "subjectivity" brought by evaluators' cultural and linguistic backgrounds and their beliefs about constructs assessed when making diagnostic and placement decisions for language-minority children. This additional information can be helpful for educators and evaluators in developing Individualized Educational Programs (IEPs).

It is also important to highlight that the idiosyncratic variables present in the interviewers (the second and fourth authors of this chapter), such as their personality style and ethnic backgrounds, had an influence on the amount of probing that they were inclined to do with the subjects' responses. For example, due to the amount of probing, one of the interviewers always stimulated subjects to produce longer responses. Thus, there was a metaprocess effect on the data; the same personalities of evaluators that we were trying to study had an effect on our interviewers, subjects, and research data.

Major implications derived from the findings of this study relate to assessment practices with language-minority children, as well as with the training of evaluators who work with this population. Four theses, corresponding to the first four research questions, with several emergent topics for each research question, were found in the data. Figure 9.1 presents a paradigm for the analysis of evaluators' awareness of how their personality factors influence their diagnostic and placement decisions with language-minority children. This paradigm will be explained in relation to the fifth research question.

Regarding the first research question, referring to the evaluators' beliefs about cognitive and first and second language development and measures, most subjects had a holistic view in which both internal and external factors interacted in development. Most understood the positive influence of cultural and linguistic factors on cognitive development. In general, there was not much variation in the theories of intelligence and first and second language learning endorsed by most subjects, which may be due to the effect of the lectures included in the class and their prior knowledge accumulated in different classes. When comparing language-minority and -majority children, most subjects perceived more similarities than differences (e.g., language is a tool for learning for all children, need for a battery of assessments, individual differences are present in all children), but also recognized the cultural-linguistic differences that need to be taken into account when assessing language-minority children (e.g., testing in both the first and second languages, familiarity with cultural-linguistic background of examinee, limitations of standardized tests). Subjects' beliefs about standardized and qualitative assessments were shown to be dynamic; the actual assessment experience with language-minority children led these subjects to some changes in their attitudinal belief systems. For most of these graduate students in educational psychology, the one-to-one interaction within an assess-

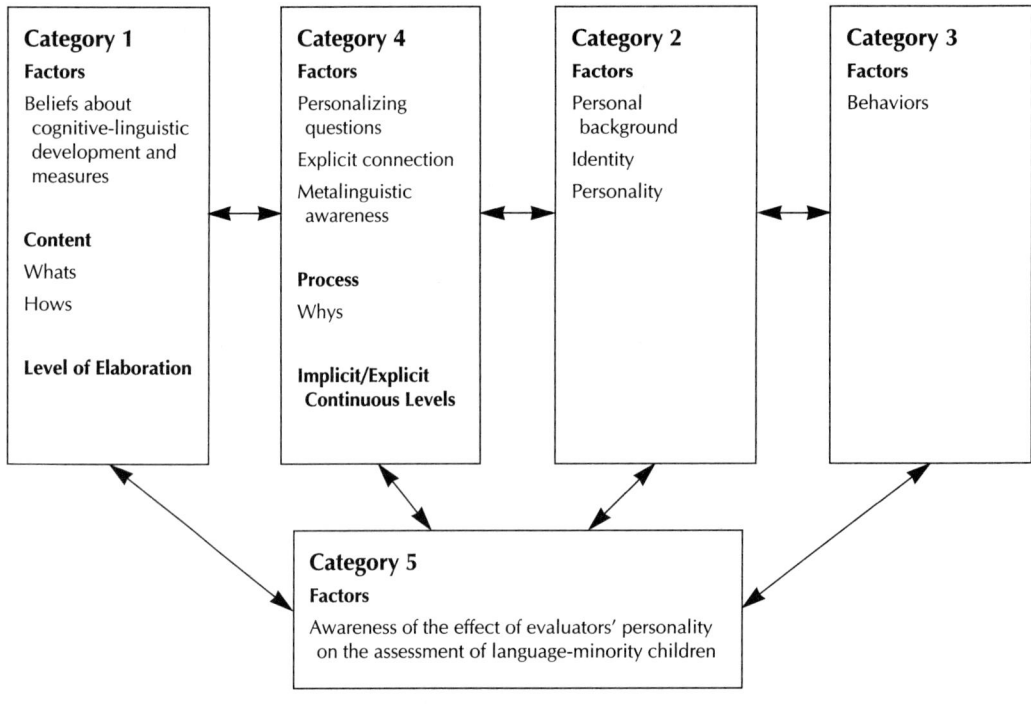

FIGURE 9.1 Paradigm for the analysis of evaluators' awareness of the effect of personality factors on diagnostic and placement decisions.

ment situation stimulated them to think about their limitations as evaluators stemming from their knowledge or lack of prior experience with culturally and linguistically diverse children, and on other external factors affecting the performance of the child (e.g., family situation, socioeconomic status).

Regarding the second research question, findings revealed the presence of an effect of the cultural-linguistic backgrounds of evaluators on their beliefs, such as exposure to other linguistic and cultural realities and ways of living and the presence or absence of experience and training, prior to the course of testing minorities, on assessing language-minority children. Regarding the third research question, findings pointed to the presence of a relationship between evaluators' backgrounds and beliefs and their assessment behaviors. Most subjects were aware of the influence of their backgrounds and beliefs on their assessment behaviors with language-minority children. That is, they felt that the fact that they were of a minority or majority background had affected their beliefs and behaviors when assessing language-minority children. Thus, who the evaluators are—their identities and values—does influence the evaluation situation. Subjects were also aware of the effect of their personality characteristics and traits on how they behave when assessing language-minority children. The presence or absence of relevant prior knowledge was also recognized as part of their personal backgrounds and was also seen as having an effect on their assessment behaviors with language-minority children. Subjects were willing to recognize their own limitations that hinder their assessment behaviors and the performance of the language-minority child in the testing situation (e.g., lack of knowledge of constructs assessed or of the first language of the minority child assessed). Thus, subjects could recognize the effect of external factors on the assessment process, such as their own personality and knowledge levels.

Regarding the fourth research question, findings revealed that evaluators' beliefs were related to their diagnostic and placement decisions with language-minority children. Beliefs used as rationales for justifying diagnostic and placement decisions reached by subjects referred to both constructs being measured and the characteristics of measures used. Most subjects held a holistic view of assessment, endorsing the use of batteries of both alternative and standardized measures, as well as multiple informants across contexts and developmental areas.

Regarding the fifth research question posed, findings revealed that some subjects could make an explicit connection among their experiences, beliefs, and placement decisions. The paradigm presented in Figure 9.1 provides a framework for understanding the synthesis of findings in this study. In this paradigm, evaluators' beliefs are considered to be related to content knowledge of the "whats" and the "hows" of assessing language-minority children. In addition, this paradigm proposes that assessment behaviors of evaluators, including their diagnostic and placement decisions, are affected by their beliefs and personal backgrounds. Finally, this paradigm proposes that evaluators' personal backgrounds (their personality and identity) can help them to gain awareness of and explicitly articulate their beliefs, showing metalinguistic awareness and resulting in personalizing the interview questions posed to them.

The findings in this study revealed that some subjects who had a minority or multicultural background were explicitly aware of the influence of their own personalities on the assessment process when working with language-minority children. They felt genuinely empathic because they knew firsthand what being a minority meant and could see the advantages of using their own subjectivity for building a better rapport and having an insightful view when assessing language-minority children. However, subjects who were of a majority monolingual background could also develop sensitivity, and some change of their attitudes occurred in developing a more open-minded vision when exposed to the complex and challenging task of assessing language-minority children. Thus, this study points out the importance of professional training for evaluators; both minority and majority background graduate students needed to acquire the necessary knowledge and to develop empathic attitudinal belief systems that could lead them to become advocates of language-minority children.

One limitation of the study may be that the presentation of the typewritten vignette case study may not be generalizable to other formats, such as videos or audiotapes (Cook & St. Lawrence, 1990) or to actual assessments of cases. A second possible limitation is that more probes were made for the interview questions related to placement for both the actual and vignette case studies than for other content included in the interview. However, more reasons for explaining diagnostic and placement decisions were given by subjects because of their experience in assessment and some personality traits such as assertiveness. A third possible limitation may have been the need to define more fully terms used in the interview questions or to use simpler terminology. For instance, some subjects asked for a definition of the term "language-minority children." However, due to the methodology used in this study, we considered it critical to allow subjects to develop their own definitions, beliefs, and attitudes about concepts and readings discussed in class. In addition, some of the subjects were not familiar with the criteria for placement in a gifted program or for labeling a child as gifted. This lack of knowledge may have influenced the placement decisions that respondents were asked to make during the interview.

Another limitation of the study related to its sample. More than half of the subjects were from a minority background themselves, which may have influenced their responses; they stated that their cultural-linguistic backgrounds had influenced their assessment behaviors. For instance, most subjects expressed the need to have empathy and consider the language-minority child's personal background in the testing situation (e.g., they were aware of their demeanor with the child, tried to be fair, and tried to make the child feel comfortable in the testing situation). Other limitations refer to the methodology used in the study; for example, the subjects were not assigned randomly to interviewers, and the interviews took place a long time after subjects took the graduate seminar on minority assessment (4 to 10 months).

CONCLUSIONS

There is a theoretical and professional need in the fields of bilingual education and school psychology for developing alternative assessments based on scholarly and data-driven research for language-minority children. This need is reflected in the adoption of new alternative assessments for these children by school districts across the nation. This study contributes relevant knowledge to both areas to improve models for training professionals involved in diagnosing language-minority children. At the same time, this study also contributes to both bilingual education and school psychology by its implications for improving assessment practices with language-minority children.

REFERENCES

BACK, R. D., & DANA, R. H. (1977). Examiner sex bias and Wechsler Intelligence Scale for Children scores. *Journal of Consulting and Clinical Psychology, 45,* 500.

BACK, R. D., & DANA, R. H. (1980). Self-help for male WISC examiners by pretest exposure to children. *Perceptual and Motor Skills, 51,* 838.

BAKER, C. (1992). *Attitudes and language.* Clevedon, England: Multilingual Matters.

CARPENTER, L. J. (1992). The influence of examiner knowledge base on diagnostic decision making with language minority children. *Journal of Educational Issues of Language Minority Students, 11,* 139–160.

COOK, D. J., & ST. LAWRENCE, J. S. (1990). Variations in presentation format: Effect on interpersonal evaluations of assertive and unassertive behavior. *Behavior Modification, 14,* 21–36.

CUMMING, A. (1990). Expertise in evaluating second language compositions. *Language Testing, 7,* 31–51.

DE AVILA, E. A., & DUNCAN, S. E. (1986). *The Language Assessment Scales.* Monterey, CA: CTB/McGraw-Hill.

DOUGLAS, D. (1994). Quantity and quality in speaking test performance. *Language International, 6,* 125–144.

FRANCO, J. N., & LEVINE, E. (1985). Effects of examiner variables on reported self-disclosure: Implications for group personality testing. *Hispanic Journal of Behavioral Sciences, 7,* 187–197.

FUCHS, D., & FUCHS, L. S. (1986). Test procedure bias: A meta-analysis of examiner familiarity effects. *Review of Educational Research, 56,* 243–262.

FUCHS, D., & FUCHS, L. S. (1989). Effects of examiner familiarity on black, Caucasian, and Hispanic children: A meta-analysis. *Exceptional Children, 55,* 303–308.

FUCHS, D., FUCHS, L. S., & POWER, M. H. (1987). Effects of examiner familiarity on LD and MR students' language performance. *RASE: Remedial and Special Education, 8,* 47–52.

FUCHS, D., FUCHS, L. S., POWER, M. H., & DAILEY, A. M. (1985). Bias in the assessment of handicapped children. *American Educational Research Journal, 22,* 185–198.

GONZALEZ, V. (1991). *A model of cognitive, cultural, and linguistic variables affecting bilingual Spanish/English children's development of concepts and language.* Doctoral dissertation, University of Texas at Austin. (ERIC Document Reproduction Service No. ED 345 562)

GONZALEZ, V. (1994). A model of cognitive, cultural and linguistic variables affecting bilingual Hispanic children's development of concepts and language. *Hispanic Journal of Behavioral Sciences, 16*(4), 396–421.

GONZALEZ, V. (1995). *Cognition, culture, and language in bilingual children: Conceptual and semantic development.* Bethesda, MD: Austin & Windfield.

GONZALEZ, V., BAUERLE, P., & FELIX-HOLT, M. (1994). A qualitative assessment method for accurately diagnosing bilingual gifted children. *NABE '92–'93 Annual Conference Journal* (pp. 37–52). Washington, DC: NABE.

GONZALEZ, V., BAUERLE, P., & FELIX-HOLT, M. (1996). Theoretical and practical implications of assessing cognitive and language development in bilingual children with qualitative methods. *Bilingual Research Journal 20*(1), 93–131.

GONZALEZ, V., & FELIX-HOLT, M. (1995). Influence of evaluators' prior academic knowledge on the diagnosis of cognitive and language development in bilingual

Hispanic kindergartners. *New York State Association for Bilingual Education Journal, 10*(1), 34–45.

GONZALEZ, V., RIOJAS-CLARK, E., & BAUERLE, P. (1996). *Identifying gifted bilingual Hispanic kindergartners with alternative sociocultural dual language assessments.* Paper presented at the Annual meeting of the New York American Educational Research Association, New York.

GONZALEZ, V., RIOJAS-CLARK, E., BAUERLE, P., & BLACK, W. (1996). *Cultural and linguistic giftedness in Hispanic kindergartners: Analyzing the validity of verbal and nonverbal standardized and alternative assessments of cognitive and Spanish/English language proficiency.* Unpublished manuscript. Tucson, AZ: The University of Arizona.

GONZALEZ, V., & YAWKEY, T. D. (1993). The assessment of culturally and linguistically diverse students: Celebrating change. *Educational Horizons, 72*(1), 41–49.

GROTJAHN, R. (1987). On the methodological basis of introspective methods. In C. Færch & G. Kasper (Eds.), *Introspection in second language research* (pp. 54–81). Philadelphia: Multilingual Matters.

HOLLAND, R. P. (1980). An analysis of the decision making processes in special education. *Exceptional Children, 46,* 551–553.

KATZ, I., HENCHY, T., & ALLEN, H. (1968). Effects of race of tester, approval-disapproval, and need on Negro children's learning. *Journal of Personality and Social Psychology, 8,* 38–42.

KINNIE, E. J., & STERNLOF, R. E. (1971). The influence of nonintellective factors on the IQ scores of middle- and lower-class children. *Child Development, 42,* 1989–1995.

KOOCHER, G. (1994). Culture and sex role expectations. *Ethics and Behavior, 4,* 75–83.

LEVINE, M. G., & HAUS, G. (1987). The accuracy of teacher judgment of the oral proficiency of high school foreign language students. *Foreign Language Annals, 27,* 505–521.

MARKMAN, E. M. (1984). The acquisition of hierarchical organization of categories by children. In C. Sophian (Ed.), *Origin in cognitive skills.* The 18th Annual Carnegie Symposium on Cognition (pp. 376–406). Hillsdale, NJ: Lawrence Erlbaum Associates.

PIAGET, J. (1967). *Mental imagery in the child, a study of the development of imaginal representation.* New York: Oxford University Press.

QUERESHI, M. Y. (1968). Intelligence test scores as a function of sex of experimenter and sex of subject. *Journal of Psychology, 69,* 277–284.

RAVEN, J. C. (1976). *Coloured progressive matrices.* London: H. K. Lewis.

SACKS, E. L. (1952). Intelligence scores as a function of experimentally established social relationships between child and examiner. *Journal of Abnormal and Social Psychology, 33,* 716–721.

SATTLER, J. M. (1969). Effects of clues and examiner influence on two Wechsler subtests. *Journal of Consulting and Clinical Psychology, 33,* 716–721.

SATTLER, J. M., & THEYE, F. (1967). Procedural, situational, and interpersonal variables in individual intelligence testing. *Psychological Bulletin, 68,* 347–360.

WAXMAN, S. R. (1990). Linking language and conceptual development: Linguistic cues and the construction of conceptual hierarchies. *The Genetic Epistemologist 17,* 13–20.

WIGGLESWORTH, G. (1993). Exploring bias analysis as a tool for improving rater consistency in assessing oral interaction. *Language Testing, 10,* 305–335.

YSSELDYKE, J. E., & THURLOW, M. L. (1984). Assessment practices in special education: Adequacy and appropriateness. *Educational Psychologist, 9,* 123–136.

Appendix 9A: Interview Questions

Beliefs About Cognitive-Linguistic Development and Measures

1. According to your knowledge, how does intelligence develop in culturally and linguistically diverse (CLD) children?
2. According to your knowledge, how does language develop in CLD children?
3. According to your view, what is the role that culture plays in the development of intelligence?
4. Is language development similar or different in majority and CLD children?
5. Is the development of intelligence similar or different in majority and CLD children?
6. What are your views about assessing CLD children?
7. What are your views about standardized assessments?
8. What are your views about qualitative assessments?
9. In what ways did your experience of administering QUEST influence your views about the assessment of CLD children?

Evaluators' Cultural-Linguistic Background

10. Are you bilingual and/or bicultural?
11. How do you think your personal background influenced your assessment?
12. What past experience(s) have you had in assessing CLD children?

Diagnostic and Placement Decisions

13. What changes in the observations section would you have made?
14. What changes in the diagnostic section would you have made?
15. Would you have recommended this child to be placed in a gifted program?
16. In what ways does reading the report of the additional evaluation of the same child affect your views about the assessment procedure itself?
17. In what ways does reading the report of the additional evaluation of the same child affect your recommendation for placing this child?
18. What placement would you recommend for this child (control case) for next year?

APPENDIX 9B: CATEGORIES FOR ANALYZING EVALUATOR'S RESPONSES TO THE INTERVIEW

Beliefs About Cognitive-Linguistic Development and Measures

I. Development
   1. Personal definitions of psychological constructs
       a. Intelligence and culture
       b. Interaction between cognition and language
       c. Similarities and differences between minority and majority students
II. Measurements
   1. Norms
   2. Test reflect attitudes of researchers, test developers, and evaluators
   3. Multiple measurements
   4. Validity and reliability
   5. Ameliorating problems in assessing language-minority students
   6. Qualitative and quantitative instruments

Evaluator's Cultural-Linguistic Background

1. Knowledge of another language
    a. Monolingual
    b. Intermediate
    c. Bilingual
2. Contact with another culture
    a. Extended
    b. Brief (traveling)
    c. None
3. Experience in assessing majority students
4. Experience in assessing minority students
5. Experience in assessing special education students
6. Academic coursework related to assessment and multiculturalism
7. Ethnic/cultural identification

Diagnostic and Placement Decisions

1. Objective and subjective processes used for evaluation
2. Verbal and nonverbal behaviors
3. Dual language performance
4. Qualitative and quantitative data used for evaluation
5. Placement of case evaluated
    a. Regular gifted
    b. Bilingual gifted
    c. Regular mainstream
    d. Other

6. Placement after reading other language evaluation of case assessed
    a. Regular gifted
    b. Bilingual gifted
    c. Regular mainstream
    d. Other
7. Placement of control case
    a. Regular gifted
    b. Bilingual gifted
    c. Regular mainstream
    d. Other

CHAPTER 10

The Impact of Paradigmatic Shifts on Second Language Research
Patterns and Conclusions

VIRGINIA GONZALEZ

THE RESEARCH STUDIES PRESENTED IN THIS BOOK FOCUS ON HOW COGNItive and linguistic processes develop in children and adults who are learning a second language, and on the development of alternative assessments for bilingual children. These two clusters of studies within second language research have evolved dynamically since the late 1970s, reflecting a change of paradigms stemming from cognitive psychology. This shift in the theoretical perspectives used to study second language learning has influenced the training and ideas that all of us—my collaborators and myself—have been exposed to during our graduate studies.

    The intergenerational and intragenerational collaboration portrayed throughout this book—the exchange of novel ideas between mentors and mentees, and ultimately among colleagues—also represents the dynamic renewal of the area. Engaging in collaborative research with peers and students gives researchers the opportunity to open new research questions and explore them creatively. Working as a team also influences our intrinsic motivation to pursue the discovery of new knowledge since we can engage in a productive dialogue that stimulates our critical thinking processes. In fact, the conclusions in this chapter represent the product of many brainstorming sessions that I have engaged in with my students in graduate seminars on second language learning, cognitive development, and assessment. By playing the role of the instructor, I also enjoyed with my graduate students the luxury of having time to think and discuss ideas, to become a scholar, and ultimately to see patterns in the field of second language research.

Regarding the first cluster of studies on the development of cognitive and second language learning processes in children and adults, the first conclusion refers to the change of paradigms from unidimensional to multidimensional theories. During the late 1960s and early 1970s, most theories started to consider the relationship of language and cognition, which led to the realization that learning a second language affects the construction of new verbal concepts that positively influence intelligence development (as discussed in Chapter 2). Since the mid-1980s, most second language research studies presented a multidimensional view that includes cultural, social, and other external factors in the triple interaction with cognitive and linguistic factors. Thus, there has been a shift from unidimensional theories, focused on the study of cognitive structures such as perception and memory, to multidimensional theories, focused on higher-level mental processes, such as concept formation and creativity or giftedness. Moreover, multidimensional approaches also consider the different kinds of intelligences besides the traditionally measured logico-mathematical and verbal skills, which in the past were studied as special talents and abilities not directly related to intelligence.

We have come to the understanding within multidimensional approaches that cognitive processes, such as the effect of first and second languages, have to be explained as the result of the interaction between internal and external factors (as discussed in Chapter 2). Most contemporary theories now hold that intelligence is influenced by culture and by content knowledge, as well as first and second language processes, all of them external sociocultural factors. For instance, children and adults who are second language learners present different knowledge levels and learning strategies depending on the content area studied, such as abstract nouns, or a specific linguistic structure, such as linguistic gender or the verb "to be" (as exemplified in Chapters 5 and 6). That is, children and adult second language learners present different developmental levels if the first and second language linguistic structures are common or unique.

A second related conclusion refers to the understanding of the difference between knowledge acquired, such as first and second language learning, and potential or capacity for learning (as exemplified in the case studies presented in Chapters 7 and 8). According to contemporary developmental theories, knowledge acquisition is a cognitive process influenced by external sociocultural factors. I view the potential for learning as a range of innate capacities that need to be stimulated within a nurturing environment. In addition, both internal and external factors interact in the development of internal potential, and within this interaction both factors become indissoluble. Capacities can be universal; they are general content-free potentials that need to be developed within a sociocultural environment, resulting in culturally loaded cognitive and linguistic abilities in children and adults. However, there is a gap between contemporary knowledge in cognitive psychology and second language learning theory and the measures used to assess cognitive and linguistic processes in children and adults who are learning a second language.

The third conclusion refers to individual differences considered to be present in second language learning and in cognitive and intelligence development. We cannot stereotype the needs of minority and majority children and adults learning second languages (see Chapters 7, 8, and 9). Instead we need to take into account their idiosyncratic characteristics when we instruct and assess them. Every child or adult learning a second language has individual abilities, aptitudes, rates of language acquisition, strengths, and weaknesses. Researchers and educators need to adapt to these individual needs in order to improve their instructional and assessment methodologies (as findings in Chapters 3 and 4 show). Overgeneralizations stemming from research findings are dangerous, especially when they are done across populations not represented in the sample. Thus, the idiosyncrasies present in every person need to be respected and celebrated when doing research. That is the reason why many of the studies presented in this book include subjects as researchers and collaborators, through the use of thinking-aloud protocols for exploring subjects' insights to their internal mental processes. In addition, respect for idiosyncratic characteristics needs to be present when researchers conduct qualitative studies, including case studies, that focus on a deep analysis of multiple individual variables.

The fourth conclusion refers to the consideration that second language learning is a lifetime process that changes due to the influence of external factors (e.g., the amount and kind of contact with the target language, the exposure to cultural experiences linked with the native use of the target language, and the specific contextual use of the target language in work or personal situations). This dynamic process of evolution of proficiency is also influenced by internal factors (e.g., attitudes, beliefs, values, motivation, and in general the willingness to acquire a second language that is linked with a new cultural representational system). Many second language learners, especially adults, have the misconception that learning a language means only acquiring a new "abstract" and neutral code for communicating "objective" information. Instead, in the studies presented in this book, second language learning is viewed primarily as an immersion process in a new way of using verbal symbols to represent new external realities, the ones conceptualized by native speakers. True or genuine second language learning in both children and adults involves new concept formation, or accommodation of internal representations, which will affect their cognitive (e.g., intelligence) and affective (e.g., personality, identity, self-concept, and self-esteem) processes. Thus, becoming bilingual also means a change of internal representations of cultural reality for the learner. Moreover, since conceptual learning of a second language also encompasses becoming bicognitive and bicultural, a bilingual goes through a shift of cultural paradigms and personal identity.

The fifth conclusion refers to the presence of a developmental continuity in the cognitive and affective processes children and adults experience when becoming bilingual, bicognitive, and bicultural. Traditionally, laypeople have thought that children are better second language learners than adults because they are going through a "sensitive period" for language development. In fact, evidence accumulated from research studies conducted during the past 20 to 30 years shows that children outperform adults in second language learning tasks only in the area of phonological development or pronunciation of new sounds in the target language. This phenomenon occurs because of maturational factors; young children have a plastic development of their motoric points and modes of articulation, which typically ends during early adolescence. Only in rare cases do adults retain this plasticity for pronunciation of new sounds, which will then become a special talent in comparison to the majority of adults. In fact, adults outperform young children in all other developmental areas when learning a second language, such as cognitive processes (i.e., verbal and nonverbal concept formation, memory, perception), metacognitive processes (i.e., learning strategies such as elaboration and integration; metamemory, or thinking about memory; metalearning, or self-improvement in learning; and metalinguistic awareness, or thinking about the symbolic meanings of language), and linguistic processes (i.e., vocabulary learning, grammar, syntax, listening comprehension, reading, and writing). Adults have already formed the cognitive and linguistic processes they will use as tools for acquiring a new language, while children have to engage in a double and simultaneous process of language learning and the development of their cognitive, metacognitive, and linguistic processes.

In relation to the second cluster of studies presented in this book—alternative assessment of bilingual children—there are three related conclusions. First, common to the first cluster of studies, we can see in alternative assessments the representation of multidimensional cognitive, cultural, and linguistic processes to be measured. The area of second language assessment still has the problematic presence of the wide use of discrete standardized tests of intelligence and language proficiency, constructed using unidimensional approaches. Standardized tests measure constructs at the performance level only. They provide not an index of innate capacities and learning potential but of the amount of cultural and linguistic content knowledge learned. In fact, standardized tests measure products, and not processes such as learning and mental capacity. To help solve this problem, an increasing number of alternative or qualitative assessments are being developed with improved psychometric characteristics, such as construct validity and reliability (discussed in Chapters 7, 8, and 9). Alternative assessments can measure core developmental processes that focus on problem-solving abilities. These qualitative measures can also evaluate the potential required to perform tasks because they provide adequate criterion and construct validity to use in selecting a suitable normative sample. With alternative assessments, we have come to understand that the potential for learning or mental capacity cannot be measured independent of cultural and linguistic factors due to the indissoluble nature of the interaction of internal and external factors on cognition. We cannot pretend to measure potential as an innate ability, but we can measure learning capacity within specific cultural and linguistic environments. Thus, alternative assessments constructed using developmental theory provide evaluators a dynamic tool to infer and interpret a range of developmental continuous processes that are content driven.

The second conclusion, common to the first cluster of studies, refers to the advantage that alternative assessments provide by allowing the individualization of evaluation. Individualizing assessment is extremely important in second language learning because each child or adult will develop his or her own learning strategies, problem-solving strategies, verbal and nonverbal concepts, and forms and levels of knowledge (as discussed throughout most chapters in this book). Following the specific train of thought of the individual will help evaluators understand the unique interaction among cognitive, cultural, and linguistic factors occurring in second language learners.

A third related conclusion refers to the fact that alternative assessments can also differentiate between potential or capacity for learning and acquired knowledge in children and adults. Alternative measures allow researchers and educators to link assessment with instruction by understanding the difference between the measurement of potential for learning and the amount of information or knowledge acquired. Relatedly, assigning a fixed number to capacities or potentials for learning, especially in young children, is inappropriate because they are dynamic and their actual values will change across the life span. Even for adults who are still in the process of second language learning, measuring their second language proficiency with fixed values is inappropriate because of the rapid developmental changes they are experiencing, which in many instances resemble the ones that children also go through. Moreover, capacities for learning are present in both children and adults, which when measured are also influenced by external factors such as the evaluator's attitudes, knowledge levels, and personal background (discussed in Chapter 9).

In summary, the chapters in this book have explored the paradigmatic shift that has occurred in second language research during the past two decades. The most important patterns found across the two clusters of studies in this book refer to cognitive and linguistic processes in children and adults and alternative assessment of bilingual children. In the chapter conclusions, we have emphasized the theoretical and practical implications that researchers and educators can use when studying, instructing, and assessing children and adults who are learning second languages.

Take care and good luck in your professional activities.

Index

Abstract
  categories, 35, 36, 48, 122, 128, 259
  concepts, 40, 48, 105, 114, 140
  thinking, 21
Accommodation process, 36, 114
Achievement test, 1, 7, 8, 11, 13, 82, 85, 239
Ackerman, B. L., 57
Alegria, J., 89
Alexander, P. A., 22, 45, 82
Aliohi, N., 21
Allen, H., 275
Anderson, J. R., 23, 25–26, 32
Anderson, R. C., 22, 43, 82
Anglin, J., 26
Asher, S. R., 83, 85
Assessment, 8–9, 14–15, 22, 37, 48, 56–57, 61, 80–85, 94, 191–193, 195, 197, 202, 206, 227, 232–237, 241–242, 247, 260, 269, 272, 298
  alternative, 1, 3, 13–15, 47, 80–82, 84–86, 190, 192–193, 197, 200, 206, 227–229, 232–233, 235–236, 238, 243, 260, 263, 285, 298
  alternative models, 8, 190, 229
  dynamic, 14
  ecological, 14
  evaluators' influence on, 234–235
  qualitative, 13, 37–38, 40, 48, 83, 85, 272
  standardized, 8, 15, 21–22, 37, 39, 82–84, 190, 192–193, 197, 200, 206, 227–234, 236–237, 243, 248, 260, 263, 270, 272, 285
  teachers' influence on, 235
Assimilation process, 36, 69, 114

Asymmetric models, 97–99
Au, T. K., 43
Avoidance, 91–93

Baca, L. M., 191
Back, R., 234, 274
Baker, C., 192–194, 196
Balkan, L., 10
Ballard, W., 238
Banks, J., 196, 198, 233
Barik, H., 10
Barke, E., 21
Barona, A., 13, 191–192
Bates, E., 24, 26
Bauerle, P., 40, 48, 191, 193, 202, 229, 280
Bayes-Braem, P., 26, 30–31, 42–43
Bennet, D., 192
Ben-Zeev, S., 21
Bernal, E., 6, 12, 81–82
Bertelson, A., 89
Bialystock, E., 106–110, 122, 126, 162, 170, 173, 192
Bicultural
  adults, 19, 119
  children, 19, 119
  identification, 204
Biklen, S., 115, 127, 166, 174, 242
Bilingual, 21, 37, 39–41, 47–48, 104, 118, 156
  adults, 19, 33, 47, 56, 80, 207
  children, 1–2, 9–10, 13, 19–22, 25, 32–35, 37, 39, 42, 47, 48, 56–58, 61–62, 71–74, 76–78, 80–87, 89, 91–92, 96–97, 99–100, 114, 191, 198, 201–202, 207, 298–301

303

Bilingual (*cont.*):
    education, 19–20, 22, 37–40, 46–48, 80–81, 86, 116, 120, 204, 281–292
    Hispanic children, 1, 42, 84, 114, 271
    identification, 204
Bilingualism, 2, 9–12, 20–22, 38–40, 45, 47, 80–81, 83, 89–93, 95–100, 193, 197, 203
Bilinguals, 21–26, 32–33, 38–41, 44–48, 57, 81, 84, 89, 94–95, 190, 227, 269
Biliteracy, 10
Bishop, D., 88
Bjorklund, D. F., 233
Black, W., 280
Blanc, M., 26, 194
Bloom, L., 26, 28
Bodgan, R., 115, 127, 166, 174, 242
Bowen, J., 22
Bowerman, M., 26, 29, 35, 41, 43
Bowey, J., 88
Bowman, L., 31, 43
Bradley, L., 88
Brison, S., 23
Brown, A., 26, 29–30, 43, 45, 84, 94, 110
Brown, L., 238
Bruner, J. S., 21, 26, 28, 43
Brusca-Vega, R., 37, 229
Bryan, J., 8
Bryan, T., 8
Bryant, P., 88–89
Burt, M., 159
Butterworth, A., 88

Callanan, M., 26, 42
Carlson, H., 21
Carpenter, L. J., 272, 277, 287
Carringer, D., 10
Cary, L., 89
Casson, R., 4, 5
Category formation, 31, 38, 43
Cervantes, H., 191
Chamot, J., 106–108, 110, 124–126, 172–173
Chappel, C. R., 57
Chinn, P., 231, 235
Chomsky, N., 26
Cicala, J. A., 6
Cieutat, U., 234
Cizek, G., 232

Clark, E., 12, 23–24, 26, 29–30, 41–42
Clasen, R., 192
Classification tasks, 38, 41–42
Cluster reduction, 60
Cognition, 2, 4, 10, 19, 22–23, 26–29, 33, 37–40, 46, 48, 56, 80, 83, 113–114, 126, 156, 163, 173, 190, 201, 227, 269
    bilingual, 40, 227
Cognitive
    ability, 38, 84, 87, 233, 238–240, 247, 260
    development, 9–11, 14, 19–22, 26–27, 30, 33, 37, 40, 45, 47–48, 56, 68, 80, 82, 84, 114, 161, 191–193, 196–198, 212, 229–232, 236–239, 241–242, 253–260, 263–264, 275, 278, 282–285, 298
    factors, 38–39, 45, 57, 82–83, 87, 104–107, 113–115, 128, 140, 142, 149, 170–171, 302
    flexibility, 10, 21
    and language development, summary, 201–202
    performance, 20, 47, 81
    reorganizational process, 44
    representation, 35, 41
    strategies, 148, 172–173
    variables, 33, 41–42, 56, 80, 82–83, 86, 89, 111, 127
Cohen, A., 140, 146
Collins, A., 119–120
Compton, A., 60
Concept
    construction, 37, 40, 48, 108, 112, 114, 118, 150
    development, 32
    formation, 5, 21, 25, 39, 44, 104–105, 107–108, 112–113, 115, 122, 141, 147, 157, 161–163, 165, 167, 170, 180, 248, 279
    mediation hypothesis, 23
Conceptual
    development, 19, 26, 32, 34–35, 37–39, 42–43, 45, 47–48, 82, 114, 201, 248, 250, 253, 256, 258–260, 279
    factors, 34–36, 112
    learning, 36, 104, 115, 151

Constraint
  approach, 26, 31–32, 42–43
  model, 42, 44
Cook, D. J., 292
Cromer, R., 26, 29
Crosby, C., 23, 40
Cultural
  environment, 249, 259
  factors, 34–36, 38–40, 45, 47, 56,
    82–84, 104–105, 107, 112, 114,
    127–128, 131, 137, 140–142, 149,
    151, 170, 249, 273, 302
  variables, 33, 41, 56, 82, 89, 104, 111,
    127
Culture, 2, 4–11, 14–15, 19–20, 25–26,
  28, 31–37, 39–40, 43–45, 48, 56, 80,
  83, 104, 108, 113, 115–117, 126,
  164, 173, 192, 194, 201, 204, 206,
  212, 238, 242, 253, 299
Cummins, J., 3, 9–10, 21–22, 56, 81, 85,
  197, 232, 270

Dailey, M., 234, 271
Dallas, M., 25
Dalton, E., 238
Damico, J. S., 14–15, 192, 197, 235
Dana, R., 234, 274
D'Anglejan, A., 24
Darcy, E., 21
Davidson, K., 238
De Avila, E., 12, 57, 81–82, 94, 198, 201
Dechert, H., 146
Deletion and cluster reduction, 60–61, 169
De Mello, G., 157–159, 163, 181
Desrochers, A., 23, 25, 40
Developmental phases, 109, 115, 124–
  126, 130–133, 135–145, 147–150,
  167, 170–172, 174, 177, 181
Diagnosis, 9, 22, 37–38, 40, 57, 72, 76–
  78, 80–81, 83–86, 89, 100, 191–192,
  202, 211, 227–229, 231–236, 243,
  249, 253–254, 257–260, 264–265,
  269–270, 273–275, 288
Diaz, R., 10
Ding, B., 69, 89
Distinctive features model, 57–58, 60,
  62, 69
Dollar, S. J., 84, 94, 238
Dorwick, T., 169

Douglas, D., 272
Dual-code model, 23–24, 40–41
Dulay, H., 159
Duncan, S., 94, 198, 201
Dundes, A., 4
Dunn, L. M., 63–64, 230–231
Duran, L., 84
Durgunoglu, A., 25

Elder, L., 89
Elliott, S. N., 230
English as a second language, 56–57, 63,
  67, 70, 77, 82, 85, 167, 204
Erickson, J. G., 56, 81–82, 85
Ervin-Tripp, S., 45
Evaluators, 3, 14–15, 83–85, 227, 232,
  234–236, 242, 247–251, 260, 263,
  269–292
  behavior, 286–288
  beliefs, 282–288
  cultural-linguistic background,
    285–286
  familiarity, 273–274
  gender, 274
  personality, 275
  rapport, 274–275
Exploratory-interpretive paradigm, 111
Extralinguistic
  cultural factors, 149, 151, 170–171
  knowledge, 108, 115, 119–120,
    122–124, 126–128, 162

Færch, C., 111–112
Fathman, A., 24
Featherstone, N. L., 234
Feldman, C., 21
Felix-Holt, M., 40, 48, 191, 193, 202,
  229, 234, 277, 280
Ferguson, C., 60–61, 87
Finnemann, M., 157, 161
Fishman, J., 22, 81
Flavell, J., 26, 35, 43
Flick, G., 234
Flowers, L., 146
Folklore, 1–8, 14
Forms of knowledge, 108, 112, 115,
  123–124, 126, 133, 141–144, 147,
  149, 157, 167, 171–172, 174–175,
  177–178, 182

Francis, J., 88
Franco, F., 157–158, 163, 165, 181, 271
Frasier, M., 191
Freizer, D., 60–61, 87
French, R. L., 192, 197
Frost, J., 88
Fuchs, D., 234–235, 271, 273
Fuchs, L., 234–235, 271, 273
Furth, H., 26, 29

Garcia, I., 236
Garcia, P., 236
Gardner, R., 193–194, 196, 198, 203
   socioeducational model of, 193–194
Garreton, M., 157, 160–162, 165, 175
Garwick, D. R., 235
Gelman, S., 26, 42
Gender, 12, 34–36, 105–106, 114–115,
   119, 121–122, 126, 128, 130–132,
   134, 136–137, 139–141, 144–148,
   153–155, 166, 170, 201, 234, 239,
   253, 259, 279–280
   evaluators, 270–271, 274
Genesee, F., 25
Getzels, J., 9, 11
Gibson, S., 235
Giftedness, 1–12, 14–15, 38, 81, 83, 86,
   100, 196–197, 200, 203, 211
   folkloric view, 1–7, 14–15
   historical view, 1, 2, 14–15
Glusman, M., 43
Gollnick, D. M., 231, 235
Gonzalez, V., 3, 5, 8–9, 12, 14, 22, 24, 32–
   33, 35–37, 40–42, 48, 56, 78, 83–85,
   87–88, 94, 106–107, 112, 114, 118,
   140, 166, 190, 191–193, 197–198,
   200–203, 224–227, 232, 234, 238,
   240, 242, 247, 249, 252, 271,
   277–280, 281
Gopnik, A., 26
Gowan, J., 9, 12
Gray, W., 26, 30–31, 42–43
Gresham, F., 230
Grotjahn, R., 111, 276
Guilford, L. P., 12
Gulutsan, M., 10
Guntermann, G., 157, 159–161,
   165–166

Hadaway, N., 192
Hagen, E., 192
Hakuta, K., 24, 45, 56
Halle, M., 87
Hamayan, E., 14–15, 192, 233, 235
Hamers, J., 194
Hare, V. C., 22, 45, 82
Harley, B., 24
Harnisch, P., 228
Haugen, E., 21
Haus, G., 270, 273
Havassy, B., 12, 57, 81–82
Havelka, J., 23, 40
Hayes, J., 146
Healey, W. C., 57
Heller, K. A., 235
Henchy, T., 275
Henderson, N., 21
Higgs, T., 157–158, 163–165, 178, 181
Holland, R. P., 271
Holtzman, W., 235
Homonymy, 60–61, 69, 87, 91–93
Hughes, S., 231
Hutchinson, J., 26, 31–32

Ianco-Worrall, A., 21
Iglesias, A., 56, 81–82
Ijaz, H., 13–14, 26, 30, 42
Imagery, 23, 125, 143–144, 150
Incongruent generalization, 91–93
Individual differences, 149
Ingram, D., 60–61, 87
Inhelder, B., 26, 28, 41–42
Instruction, 80, 190–193, 197
Intelligence, 9–10, 14, 20–22, 27, 37, 39,
   48, 82–85, 94, 191–195, 197,
   199–200, 204–207, 209, 212, 240,
   270–272, 299
Interview process, 148
Intralinguistic knowledge, 108, 115, 120,
   122, 124, 126–128, 151, 162
Inversion, 60–61, 69, 87, 91–93
IQ tests, 1, 7–11, 13, 84, 231, 234, 240,
   273–275

Jackson, P., 9, 11
Jacoby, L., 25
Jain, M., 23

Johnson, D., 26, 30–31, 42–43
Johnson, M., 227, 234, 238–239
Jakobson, R., 57–60, 62, 64, 67, 69–71, 77, 87
Jones, S., 21
Jorm, A., 88
Juan, K., 197

Kagan, J., 203
Kamin, L., 81–82
Kamphaus, R., 197
Kang, K., 24
Karmiloff-Smith, A., 26, 29, 44, 106–110, 124, 126, 140, 172–173
Kasper, G., 111–112
Katz, I., 275
Kaufman, A., 11, 192, 227, 237, 239, 241, 253
Kaufman Assessment Battery for Children (K-ABC), 192, 227, 237–238, 241, 243–248, 251–263, 265
Kaufman, N., 11, 192, 227, 237, 239, 241, 253
Kellerman, E., 24
King, M., 23
Kinnie, E., 273
Kirsner, K., 23
Kirtley, C., 88
Knorre, M., 169
Knowledge representation, 25, 33, 46
Kolers, P., 23
Koocher, G., 273
Kramer, J., 230
Krashen, S., 159

Lalonde, R., 193
Lambert, A., 10, 21, 23, 40
Landry, R., 9, 21
Language 4–5, 19–32, 34–45, 47–48, 56, 58–59, 62, 69–72, 77, 80, 83–87, 90–99, 104, 108–132, 134–150, 153, 156, 158, 160–164, 172–173, 190, 192–194, 197, 201, 206–207, 212, 227, 245, 269
  Assessment Scale, 94, 190, 196, 198–199, 210–202, 209–210, 212, 280
  development, 9, 19–30, 33, 37–39, 43, 47–48, 56, 68, 72–73, 80, 114, 191, 193, 195, 198–199, 202, 204–207, 209, 212, 270–271, 275, 282–285
  first, 35–38, 47–48, 57, 62, 66, 70–71, 73, 77, 80–81, 83, 85–87, 94, 97, 99–100, 105, 113–114, 125, 140, 156, 159–163, 165, 197, 201
  learning, 22, 40, 47, 108–112, 114–116, 120–122, 124–128, 134, 139–140, 142–150, 206
  learning strategies, 110, 123–124, 127–128, 134, 139, 141–147, 149, 161, 170, 174
  minority children, 1–4, 6, 8–15, 22, 48, 56, 190–201, 203–204, 207, 209, 212, 234, 269–273, 275–276, 282–285, 292
  proficiency, 9–10, 21–22, 28, 81, 82, 85, 87, 89, 91, 94, 97, 99–100, 113, 164, 201, 209–210, 273, 301
  second, 1, 9, 10, 35–38, 47–48, 62, 66, 70–72, 77, 80–81, 83–87, 94, 97, 99–100, 104–120, 122, 124–126, 140, 145–151, 156, 161, 164, 170–171, 173, 182, 185, 193–198, 201–203, 206, 298
  theories, 272
La Rosa, B., 192
Larsen-Freeman, D., 159
Leopold, W., 21
Le Vine, E., 270–271, 273
Lewis, J., 13
Lightbrown, P., 45
Lindsay, R., 25, 43
Linguistic
  content 139, 141
  development, 40, 82, 192, 196, 210, 232, 235, 278
  factors, 34–36, 38–41, 45–47, 57, 82, 84, 104, 106–107, 112–114, 127, 140, 142, 273
  representation, 35
  structures, 34, 36–37, 40, 48, 105, 115
  transfer, 60, 62, 69, 74
  variables, 33, 41, 56, 80, 82–83, 89, 104, 118
Lockhart, R., 23
Lundberg, I., 88

Mabry, L., 228
MacLean, M., 88
Macnamara, J., 26, 28
Madler, G., 25
Maestas, J., 84
Maldonado-Colon, E., 22, 84
Mann, V., 89
Mapping process, 19–20, 26, 38–39, 42–45
Marchetti, R., 159
Marek-Schoroer, M., 192
Markman, E., 26, 31–32, 42–43, 278
Marquez, J., 6, 196–197
Mather, N., 227–239
Matsuyama, V., 26, 33
Matute-Bianchi, M., 198
McCarthy Cognitive Scales, 63–68
McCarthy, D., 63–64
McGee Banks, C., 196, 198, 233
McWhinney, B., 24, 26
Mediation theory of semantics, 40
Medina, N., 229–232
Medley, F., 157, 160–162, 165
Melesky, A., 196
Menn, L., 60, 69, 88
Mercer, J. R., 10–11, 81–82, 230–231, 235
Merriman, W., 31, 43
Mervis, C., 26, 30–31, 42–43
Messick, S., 3, 8, 23, 232, 235
Metacognitive strategies, 148–150, 172–173
Metalinguistic
 awareness, 10–12, 21, 23, 32, 39, 115, 164, 301
 knowledge, 32
Mettzoff, A., 26
Miller, K., 26, 32, 43
Minority children, 1, 8–9, 11, 13–14, 22, 84, 192, 227–238, 241, 244, 249, 259, 261, 263
 gifted, 1–2, 6, 8, 9, 11–13, 15
Mitchell, R., 230
Molina, S., 64, 94
Morais, J., 89
Moss, P., 3, 191
Multidimensional model, 1, 112
Mykelbust, H. R., 63–64

Natural phonology theory, 57, 60, 62, 64, 87
Neill, D., 229, 232
Nelson, K., 26, 29–30, 41–43
Nie, H., 69, 89
Norman, D. A., 43

Ogbu, J., 198
Oller, J. W., 22, 29, 44, 56, 59, 81–82, 85–86, 191
Olver, R., 26, 28, 43
O'Malley, J. M., 106–108, 110, 124–126, 172–173
Ortiz, A. A., 22, 81, 84–86, 231

Paivio, A., 22–25, 40–41
Palermo, D., 26, 32, 43
Palij, M., 40
Palinscar, A., 110
Paradigmatic shifts, 298–301
Pascual-Leone, J., 13–14
Payne, K. T., 81–82
Peal, E., 10, 21
Pearson, P. D., 22, 43, 82
Pederson, D., 234
Peirce, C. S., 29
Perkins, K., 81
Perrin, K. L., 57
Peterson, D., 88
Phillips, J., 233
Phonological
 development, 56–58, 60–61, 66–67, 71–73, 75, 77–78, 81, 86–89, 99
 strategies, 60–61, 64–65, 69–74, 76, 80, 87–100
Phonological Development Test, 56–58, 60, 65, 68–70, 75–78, 94
Piaget, J., 21, 26–28, 30, 41–43, 56, 161, 278, 280
Pierson, R., 193
Plata, M., 192–196
Potter, M., 25
Pountain, C., 157–158, 163, 178
Power, M., 234, 271, 273
Priestly, T., 60, 87

Quereshi, M., 274
QUEST, 37, 40, 48, 190–191, 196, 198–201, 209–212, 227, 237–238, 240–241, 243–245, 247–265, 277–278, 280–281, 289

Ragosta, P., 192
Ramirez, M., 6
Raven, J. C., 281
Rawen, R., 45
Read, C., 89
Reading readiness, 56–57, 80–82, 87–94, 97–100
Reduplication, 60–61, 69, 87, 91–93
Reid, C., 68
Renzulli, J. S., 6
Representation
  of knowledge, 22, 24, 41, 43, 142
  of meaning, 38
Representational
  abstract systems, 37, 109, 114, 140
  processes, 25, 38, 41–44, 88, 140, 145
  semantic systems, 37, 114, 140
  systems, 22–25, 32, 34–41, 43–44, 47, 48, 81, 109, 114, 140
Reschly, D., 233
Rescorla, L., 43
Rey, M., 45
Reynolds, E. C., 197
Rice, M., 26, 28
Richardson, V., 203
Riojas-Clark, E., 1, 280
Robinett, B., 110, 125, 173
Roediger, H. L., 25
Roldán, M., 165
Role-playing task, 134, 148
Rosch, E., 26, 30–31, 42–43
Roth, 234
Ruggeri, M., 157–158, 163, 181
Russo, R., 106–108, 110, 124–126, 172–173

Sacks, E. L., 273
Saer, D., 20
Samuda, R., 11, 15, 233
Santos de Barona, M., 13, 191–192

Sattler, J., 192, 274
Saville-Troike, M., 196
Schachter, J., 24, 110, 125, 173
Schallert, D. L., 22, 45, 82
Schlesinger, I., 26
Schwenflugel, P., 45
Second language learners, 45, 112, 120, 124, 149–151, 156–163, 165–166, 172, 175, 178–179, 181–182, 184–185, 196, 229
Selinger, H., 146
Semantic
  categories, 26, 30–36, 38–47, 108, 113, 115, 118, 122, 126–132, 134–137, 140–141, 148, 153, 157, 163–164, 167, 173, 250, 279
  concepts, 24, 30–32, 48, 140, 166
  content, 139
  development, 19, 26, 32, 34, 38–39, 43, 45, 47
  features hypothesis, 26, 29–30
  functional hypothesis, 26, 29
  knowledge, 30
  prototype hypothesis, 26, 30
Ser and *estar*, 156–160, 162–188
Sera, M., 156–157, 163–164, 175
Seymour, P. K., 89
Shaklee, B., 196–197
Shankweiler, D., 88
Share, D. L., 88
Shen, M., 21
Shepard, L., 228
Sherberou, R. J., 84, 94, 238
Sherritt, C., 235–236
Shinedling, M. M., 234
Shipley, E., 26
Sinclair-de-Zwart, H., 26–28, 41
Skutnabb-Kangas, T., 21, 85
Slobin, D., 26, 28
Smith, M., 23, 88, 192, 228
Snodgrass, J., 25
Snow, C., 10, 191
Snowling, M., 88
So, K. F., 25
Sociocultural
  content of knowledge model, 26, 32
  factors, 11, 13–14, 22, 25, 29, 32, 38, 41–42, 44–45

Spanish
- native speakers, 156–157, 162–164, 166–168, 175, 183, 185
- as a second language, 24, 116–117, 156, 160, 165–167, 170

Special education, 11, 22, 81, 84–85, 168, 191–192, 227–228, 230–239, 249–260, 264–265, 273
Srihdar, K., 56, 81–82
Stampe, D., 57, 60, 64, 69, 86
Stern, S., 6
Sternberg, R., 197
Sternlof, R. E., 273
Stevens, A., 119–120
Stewner-Manzaneres, G., 106–108, 110, 124–126, 172–173
Stigler, J., 26, 32, 43
St. Lawrence, J. S., 292
Stoneman, Z., 235
Stormer, J., 57
Strong cognition hypothesis, 26–27, 30, 41
Substitution, 60, 62, 69, 87, 91–93
Swain, M., 10, 72
Symbolic
- meaning, 34, 36–37, 105, 113–115, 118, 122–123, 128, 130–131, 134, 151, 153
- representation, 23, 25, 35, 44, 56–57, 114

Symmetric models, 94–99

Taylor, O., 26, 42, 81–82
Teacher
- attitudes, 190, 193, 195
- behaviors, 203
- beliefs, 191–193, 195–196, 203–204, 206, 209, 212
- language ratings, 209
- perceptions, 1

Terman, L. M., 8
Testing, 83
Test of Non-verbal Intelligence (TONI), 84, 94, 238
Theye, F., 274
Thorndike, R. L., 192
Thurlow, R., 273
Tighe, P. L., 238
Torrance, E., 12

Torrance, J. P., 12
Toukamaa, P., 21, 85
Treiman, R., 88
Triple interactional model, 33–37, 39–41, 44, 47–48, 104, 166
Trueba, H., 11, 198
Tucker, G., 21–22, 24

Valencia, R., 238, 263
Validity, 232, 234, 236, 238, 242, 272, 277, 279
- construct, 3, 8, 56–57, 64–65, 82, 190–192, 232

VanPatten, B., 156–157, 160, 169
Vihman, M., 60, 62, 87
Villareal, H., 169
Von Eckhardt, B., 25
Vygotsky, L., 14, 21, 33

Wagner, A., 81
Watchel, G., 31
Waxman, S., 26, 31, 42–43, 278
Weak cognition hypothesis, 26, 28–29, 41–42
Wechsler, D., 192, 227, 237, 240
Wechsler Intelligence Scale for Children (WISC), 10, 192, 227, 234, 237, 240, 243–248, 250, 261, 274
Weeks, T., 60–61, 87
Wells, G., 26
Wepman, J., 64
White, P., 146
Whorf, B., 26, 31
Wigglesworth, G., 270
Wilkin, D. A., 11
Witt, J. C., 230
Woodcock-Johnson Psycho-Educational Battery, 227, 237–239, 243–248, 260
Woodcock, R., 227–239

Yates, J., 22, 84, 231
Yawkey, T. D., 9, 37, 85, 192–193, 197, 229, 232, 242, 271
Yin, R., 203, 236, 242, 264
Yoshioka, J., 20
Ysseldyke, J. E., 273

Zhang, Y., 68, 89
Zirkel, P., 81, 85